£14.99

CONTRACT LAW & TORT

CHRIS TURNER

Hodder & Stoughton
A MEMBER OF THE HODDER HEADLINE GROUP

Orders: please contact Bookpoint Ltd, 78 Milton Park, Abingdon, Oxon OX14 4TD. Telephone: (44) 012354 827720, Fax: (44) 01235 400454. Lines are open from 9.00–6.00, Monday to Saturday, with a 24 hour message answering service. Email address: orders@bookpoint.co.uk

A catalogue record for this title is available from The British Library

ISBN 0 340 749342

First published 2000
Impression number   10 9 8 7 6 5 4 3 2 1
Year   2005 2004 2003 2002 2001 2000

Typeset by Wearset, Boldon, Tyne & Wear
Printed in Great Britain for Hodder & Stoughton Educational, a division of Hodder Headline Plc, 338 Euston Road, London NW1 3BH by J. W. Arrowsmith Ltd, Bristol.

CONTENTS

CHAPTER 3 THE OBLIGATIONS UNDER A CONTRACT OR CONTENTS OF A CONTRACT

CHAPTER 4 VITIATING FACTORS

CHAPTER 9 VICARIOUS LIABILITY

CHAPTER 10 GENERAL DEFENCES

PART 3 REMEDIES IN CONTRACT AND TORT

CHAPTER 11 REMEDIES IN CONTRACT AND TORT

LIST OF FIGURES

LIST OF ABBREVIATIONS

B	Baron of the Exchequer Court	LC	Lord Chancellor
CA	Court of Appeal	LJ	Lord Justice (plural LJJ)
CJ	Chief Justice	MR	Master of the Rolls
HL	House of Lords	PC	Privy Council
J	Judge (plural JJ)	V-C	Vice-Chancellor

ACKNOWLEDGEMENTS

The author wishes to thank a number of people for their support, advice or encouragement during the production of this text. I would firstly like to thank the editorial staff at Hodder, in particular Clare Smith for allowing me to proceed with the title and Melanie Hall for her support throughout. I owe particular thanks to Jacqueline Martin who has remained a good friend and a major source of inspiration throughout our association. I would also like to thank my colleagues at Bournville and in OCR for all their encouragement. Finally, I would like to thank Karen, James and Sally for the time that I should have spent with them and the understanding they constantly show in allowing me to continue with this and other projects.

The author would also like to acknowledge the following academic works:
Cheshire, Fifoot & Furmston's *Law of Contract* Butterworths; Richards *The Law of Contract*, Pitman; T. Anthony Downes *Textbook on Contract*, Blackstones; W.T. Major & Christine Taylor *Law of Contract*, Pitman; Robert Upex *Davies on Contract*, Sweet & Maxwell; Richard Stone *Principles of Contract Law*, Cavendish; Treitl *The Law of Contract*, Butterworths; Beale, Bishop, Furmston *Contract Cases and Materials*, Butterworths; Smith and Thomas *A Casebook on Contract*, Sweet & Maxwell; Michael A. Jones *Textbook on Torts*, Blackstones; John Cooke *Law of Tort*, Pitman; Vivienne Harpwood *Principles of Tort Law*, Cavendish; Margaret Brazier & John Murphy *Street on Torts*, Butterworths; Alan Pannett *Law of Tort*, Pitman; D. Baker *Tort*, Sweet & Maxwell; W.V.H. Rogers *Winfield & Jolowicz on Tort*, Sweet & Maxwell; W.V.H. Rogers *The Law of Tort*, Sweet & Maxwell; Richard Kidner *Casebook on Torts*, Blackstones; Tony Weir *A Casebook on Tort*, Sweet & Maxwell; Hepple and Matthews *Tort – Cases and Materials*, Butterworths; Donald Harris *Remedies in Contract and Tort*, Butterworths.

Every effort has been made to trace copyright holders but this has not been possible in all cases; any omissions brought to our attention will be corrected in future printings.

PREFACE

This book is primarily aimed at students on A Level Law courses, of whatever examining board, but there is no reason why it should not be used by any first-time student of contract law or tort.

The book is a companion to the very successful textbooks on *The English Legal System* by Jacqueline Martin and on *Criminal Law* by Diana Roe. The Resources Workbooks in the same series, *The English Legal System* by Jacqueline Martin and *Substantive Law* by myself, also supplement these three texts.

Incorporating contract and tort in the same text, although not commonplace, is not merely about being able to save money by buying one book to cover both areas of law, although this in itself is perfectly justifiable. Putting both areas in the same volume is logical and justifiable as they fit together as civil law areas in comparison to the criminal law. Contract law and tort are both mostly common law subjects and have much in common. In any case litigants very often have the choice of suing in either or both. Moreover, on many degree courses the subject of 'obligations' is taught which in essence incorporates elements of both contract law and tort.

Another benefit of producing a single book covering both contract and tort is in being able to use certain sections of the book for comparative purposes. While contract and tort are both areas of the civil law they serve very different purposes, and for that reason, as well as the historic intervention of equity, available remedies operate in very different ways.

With both subjects being common law areas a large part of the book is devoted to cases and case notes, and these are separated out in the text for easy reference. I make no apology for the amount of space devoted to the cases since it has always been my experience that students are able to follow and understand principles of law best when they are able to relate them to actual situations and for too long they have had to buy case books as well as texts to achieve this end.

Since the book is also intended to be a practical learning resource rather than a mere text each section of the book contains 'Self assessment questions'. Some of these questions are mere comprehension, while others are designed to be more thought provoking. In some cases there are other activities of various types based on the content that can be undertaken by the reader.

Each section of the book also contains a 'Key facts chart' which summarises the important points contained in the section, and which can also act as a revision aid. Besides this many sections of the book also contain a section entitled 'Points for discussion'. These occur where there are controversial points that are often the subject of essay titles in examinations. Finally, there is also a brief explanation of how to attempt a problem question on contract, in Chapter 1 in the section on offer and acceptance, and on how to attempt an essay question in tort, in Chapter 6 in the section on nervous shock.

I hope that you will gain as much enjoyment in reading on contract and tort, and answering the various questions as I have had in writing this book, and above all that you gain much enjoyment and interest from your study of the law.

TABLE OF ACTS OF PARLIAMENT AND OTHER INSTRUMENTS

TABLE OF CASES

INTRODUCTION

THE ORIGINS OF CONTRACT LAW

Much of the modern law of contract law developed in the nineteenth century and derives from the *laissez-faire* principles of economics that were the hallmark of the industrial revolution. Nevertheless the origins of contract law are much more ancient than that and are to be found in the early common law of the Middle Ages. Society at that time was preoccupied with land ownership and interests in land. As a result the law of that time was also mainly concerned with property rights.

The distinction that the law drew in terms of identifying the enforceability of rights was between formal agreements and informal ones. A formal agreement was one made in writing and which was authenticated by the practice of 'sealing'. This is the origin of the deed which was the method accepted for transfer of land and interests in land up to 1989, when the requirement to complete the document by the process of sealing was relaxed in favour of the already common practice of witnessing the document.

Two principal types of formal agreement, required to be under seal to be enforceable, developed during the twelfth century:

- A covenant – such an agreement was usually to do something, for example an agreement to build a house. The available remedy that developed in relation to such agreements was specific performance.

- A formal debt – this was again an agreement under seal, but to pay a sum of money. This agreement was actionable as an 'obligation' and the available remedy was the payment of the debt.

Informal agreements also gradually gained the recognition of the law. These became known as 'parol' agreements following the simple meaning of the word at the time: 'by word of honour'. The clear problem with informal agreements was the availability of proof of their actual existence in order to be able to enforce their provisions. Two particular actions developed for informal agreements:

- An action for debt – this was usually in respect of an oral agreement for the sale of the goods, and the remedy sought was usually the price of the goods.

- Detinue – this was a claim in respect of a chattel due to the person bringing the action, for instance for delivery of a horse or other livestock.

The more modern law of contract begins with the law of 'assumpsit' in the fourteenth century. This had its origins in the tort of trespass, and was an action in respect of the breach of an informal promise. The assumpsit was the undertaking to carry out the promise.

Moving even further forward in time, one of the most essential requirements of modern contract law, the doctrine of consideration, was also established. The consideration was the reason for the promise being given, and was based on the assumption that nobody does anything for nothing.

THE CHARACTER OF MODERN CONTRACTS

It is common for non-lawyers to assume that a contract is an official agreement of some kind that is written down, and probably prepared by a lawyer. This, of course, is not the case. We all make many contracts every day, even though we rarely put them in writing or contemplate the consequences of making them.

For instance, this morning I had to go to Oxford. I parked my car in the multi-storey car park at Wolverhampton station, taking the ticket from the machine at the entrance. Inside the station I bought a newspaper. On the train I bought a cup of coffee and a slice of cake.

There is nothing exceptional about any of these events. I gave no thought to contract law in relation to any one of them, but I was making a contract in every case.

What then if on opening the newspaper I found that only the cover pages were printed on? How about if I bit into my cake to find a piece of finger inside it? Finally, how would I feel on returning from Oxford if I found my car stolen or crashed into? In all these instances I would want at least my money back, and probably some other form of remedy. At that point I would be very eager to know about the contractual nature of the arrangements I had made.

What distinguishes a modern-day contract then is not whether it is in writing or not (as may have been absolutely critical in former times) but that it is an agreement made between two parties, by which they are both bound, and which if necessary can be enforced in the courts.

It can be in written form, but most often it will be made orally, and can even be made by conduct, as is often the case in auctions. Such contracts are called simple contracts.

Some contracts because of their nature have to be in writing or evidenced in writing. These contracts we call speciality contracts, and the most common is a contract for the transfer of land, but these are beyond the scope of this book.

A contract is essentially a commercial agreement, an agreement between two parties which is enforceable in law. It is based on the promises that two parties make to each other. However, while the law rightly protects many of the promises that we make to one another, not all promises are contractual. For instance, a beneficiary under a will has in effect been promised that inheritance and has a legal right to receive it. The will is not, however, covered by contract law. The heir has promised nothing in return for the inheritance.

A contract can alternatively be called a bargain. One party makes a promise in return for the promise of the other and the promises are mutually enforceable because of the price that one party has paid for the promise of the other.

Many of the rules of contract law came about in the nineteenth century. At that time people believed very much in the idea that there was freedom of contract. This is a nice idea – that we are all free to make whatever contracts we want, on whatever terms we want.

It does not, of course, bear much relationship with reality. Commonly the two parties to a contract have unequal bargaining strength. A prospective employee at interview is rarely telling the prospective employer what conditions (s)he is prepared to work for, but is trying to impress to get the job. Consumers too, even though they may have the choice where to buy from, will rarely negotiate the terms of the transaction they are making. More often than not in the present day contracts with businesses will be done on the latter's 'standard forms'.

As a result of this, Parliament in the twentieth century has produced many laws inserting, or implying, terms into contracts which the parties themselves have not chosen but by which they both are bound.

So the notion of freedom of contract is not as straightforward as it seems, and a party to a contract has to be aware of the numerous contractual obligations by which (s)he will be bound other than those which (s)he has personally negotiated.

WHY WE ENFORCE CONTRACTS

As we have seen, then, a contract is an enforceable agreement between two parties. The rules regarding enforceability of agreements obviously grew out of the need for certainty in relationships, whether between businesses or between private individuals. We can none of us safely conduct ourselves without knowing that we are able to rely on arrangements that we have made.

The enforceability of contracts is based on three significant factors:

● An agreement made between two parties creates legitimate expectations in both that the terms of the arrangement will be carried out and that they will receive whatever benefit is expected from the agreement.

● Parties will commonly risk expenditure or do work in reliance on a promise that a particular agreement will be carried out.

● It is simply unfair that if one party is ready to perform, or indeed has performed, their part of the bargain the other party should escape or avoid his or her obligations without some means of redress for the injured party.

THE ORIGINS OF LIABILITY IN TORT

The law of torts, as with the law of contract, has its origins in the early common law of the Middle Ages. It is similarly based on obligations.

The word 'tort' comes from the French word meaning wrong. So a tort is a wrong, and, since we are concerned in tort with remedying wrongs rather than punishing them, it is a civil wrong. In the modern law the emphasis in tort has developed very much towards a law of interrelated duties. As a result of that the law of negligence has achieved increasing importance, and has developed numerous individual aspects.

However, the historical background was very different. The law of torts developed initially, through the early writ system, as a response to specific circumstances, and as a means of providing remedies for the damage done in commonly recurring situations. Where a person had suffered loss or damage of a particular kind the early courts would design a new writ, an original writ, to suit the circumstances. This helps explain the very disparate range of interests to which the law of torts applies. It also helps to explain why it is correct really to refer to the 'law of torts' rather than 'tort law', and why there is no single, coherent pattern of liability for all interests covered by the law of torts.

The early law, then, developed remedies of two main types:

● An action for trespass – this was a means of providing a remedy for direct interferences, the common examples being interferences with land, with property, and with the person himself or herself.

● An action on the case – this being originally a means of remedying indirect interferences.

As a result individual torts gradually developed with different ingredients required to prove liability. Sometimes these overlapped but more often, together with the shortcomings of the writ system itself, they could mean that a potential claimant was left without a remedy because his factual circumstances did not fit the specific requirements of a tort.

THE FUNCTIONS AND PURPOSE OF THE LAW OF TORTS

Winfield, the leading textbook on tort, has said that

'Tortious liability arises from the breach of a duty primarily fixed by law; such duty is towards persons generally and its breach is redressed by an action for unliquidated damages.'

The standard model for liability in tort in the modern day would be that the defendant's act (or omission) has through the defendant's fault caused damage to the claimant of a type which is recognised as attracting liability.

There are two precise aims of the law of torts which also, to a degree, point towards the main two remedies available, damages and injunctions:

- Compensation – the main outcome of a successful tort action is to compensate the victim of the wrong to the extent of the damage suffered.

- Deterrence – the most satisfactory way of dealing with any wrong is to ensure that it does not happen again, or even better, to prevent it occurring at all.

A third possibility that exists in other jurisdictions but not to any great extent in England and Wales is to punish. The most usual way of doing this is through the awarding of 'exemplary' or punitive damages. In America, for instance, a jury in a personal injury action can award punitive damages reflecting their dissatisfaction with the wrong.

COMPENSATION

As will be seen in Chapter 11, the purpose of tort damages is, as far as is possible for money to do so, to put the injured party in the position (s)he would have been in had the tort not happened.

The simple question here is whether the system does in fact adequately compensate the victims of the wrongs. A number of points must be considered in this respect:

- For a start only those who can show fault are able to bring a successful action.

- The tort system is incredibly expensive to run. The Pearson Committee in 1978 identified that the cost of operating the system amounted to 85 per cent of the money paid out to successful claimants. This is why right up to the present Woolf reforms there have been moves to try and reduce the costs of civil justice.

- Claiming through the tort system is also subject to delays. Again the Pearson Committee found that an average time for resolution of personal injury claims was three and a half years. This was one of the reasons originally for changing the jurisdiction of the High Court and County Court in the Courts and Legal Services Act 1990.

- Very often a claimant will be forced to settle for less than (s)he actually claimed for and therefore is not fully compensated for the wrong suffered.

- Worst of all is the maxim 'never sue a man of straw'. In other words a claimant can go without compensation at all where the tortfeasor is of insufficient means to justify suing in the first place.

DETERRENCE

Within the tort system most deterrent effects will operate generally on a market level rather than specifically against individuals. In many instances it is corporations or other large bodies that are responsible for committing torts, but even where torts are committed by private individuals damages awarded will usually be paid from a claim for insurance.

The obvious example of this is where a person's negligence causes a car crash. The 'third party' element of their motor insurance will be claimed against to pay for the damage to the other car and also to compensate any injuries caused to other parties to the accident. The driver at fault will lose his or her 'no claims bonus', the insurance premiums will increase in amount, and this then is the deterrent effect: in order to avoid high insurance premiums the driver must drive safely and carefully and avoid causing accidents. The same principle operates at a higher level with a company's public liability or employers' liability insurance.

Of course, deterrence can operate on other levels. Where professionals are sued successfully not only are their insurance premiums at risk of increasing but their reputations can be damaged, sometimes irreparably. High awards of damages in defamation actions may not harm the publishers of the defamation as much as the reputation it can give them for inaccuracy and falsehood.

Overall, then, the principle of deterrence in tort is based on the aims of reducing both the frequency and costs of wrongdoing.

COMPARISONS WITH OTHER METHODS OF COMPENSATION

Many of the problems associated with seeking compensation through the tort system identified above were considered in detail by the Pearson Commission in 1978 which was set up following the 'thalidomide scandal'. Children were born with severe deformity to limbs after their mothers were prescribed a drug during pregnancy. The children had no proper action available to them since at the time the drug had its disastrous effect on them they were not yet born.

The Commission was required to assess the appropriate means of compensating death and personal injury:

- in the course of employment

- in road traffic accidents

- through the manufacture, supply or use of goods or services

- on premises belonging to or occupied by another

- otherwise caused by the act or omission of another where compensation is recoverable only on proof of fault or under the rules of strict liability.

The Commission did not recommend the abolition of the tort system in the case of personal injury and fatal accident. It did nevertheless accept all of the criticisms referred to above and did recommend the introduction of a partial system of 'no-fault' liability through a strengthening of the social security system in the case of road traffic accidents and industrial injuries, as well as some extension of strict liability in the case of product liability.

There is a precedent for a no-fault scheme of compensating personal injuries. Such a scheme was set up in New Zealand in 1972. Under this comprehensive scheme claimants suffering a personal injury would make their claim through a state body, the Accident Compensation Commission. Benefits are payable on a weekly basis with up to 80 per cent of earnings and lump sum payments in the case of some permanent disabilities, although these are inevitably lower than could be gained through the tort system. The principal opposition to introducing this type of compensation in the UK seems to be the cost to public funds and it is unlikely that the UK would introduce such a scheme in the future.

There are of course some alternatives to the tort system already in place.

SOCIAL WELFARE AND SOCIAL SECURITY

Public responsibility for the victims of personal injury is demonstrated in a number of ways through contributory and non-contributory benefits, and through health and welfare support. Medical treatment is available through the National Health Service without having to make immediate payment. A wide range of benefits is available for those suffering personal injury and permanent disability, although in all cases benefit rates are set only at subsistence levels. The victim of a tort has the option still to use the tort system to gain higher levels of compensation.

PRIVATE INSURANCE

Many victims of torts have private insurance that they are able to claim on. This may be standard life insurance in the case of fatal accidents. There are also accident insurance policies now available as well as insurance for permanent disabilities making it impossible for the person affected to continue employment.

CRIMINAL INJURIES COMPENSATION BOARD

Where the act causing the injury has also been prosecuted as a crime then it is also possible to make a claim from this publicly-funded scheme. Awards under the scheme are generally set at very low levels, however.

OCCUPATIONAL SCHEMES

Many people enjoy extended wages during sickness and absence through injury in their contracts of employment. In the case of injuries sustained at work there are often compensatory payments available from employers. Occupational pension schemes often allow for early retirement on health grounds. Finally, many workers who are members of trade unions receive payments from benevolent funds during periods of absence from work through illness and injury.

DISTINGUISHING BETWEEN CONTRACT LAW AND THE LAW OF TORTS

Sometimes both the law of contract and the law of torts are seen as a general law of 'obligations'. Certainly both branches of the law compensate victims for the harm done to them. Both branches of the law are also ultimately based on duties owed by one party to another.

The traditional distinction between the two is the character of the duty owed. In the case of tort specific duties are imposed by law and apply to everyone. In contract law the duties are imposed by the parties themselves and only operate to the extent agreed upon before the contract was formed. Similarly, in the case of tort the duty is usually owed generally to all persons likely to be affected by the tort. In contract law, on the other hand, the duty is only to the other party to the contract.

Nevertheless, the distinction is not always so clear and there are many complications and overlaps. In the law of contract many duties are now imposed on parties by statute and as a result of European law irrespective of the actual wishes of the parties to the contract. This has been particularly the case in the area of consumer contracts. In the law of torts in those situations where the law does allow recovery for a pure economic loss the distinction between the two again is blurred somewhat.

There can be overlap, too, in areas such as product liability where there can be a claim for negligence and also for breach of implied statutory conditions under the contract. In such circumstances a choice is sometimes made whether to sue a manufacturer in tort or a supplier under contract law.

Similar complications have arisen in the field of medicine. Normally we would expect legal actions to be brought in medical negligence in tort. However, where a patient has taken advantage of private medicine the rules of contract law can be invoked if they may have a more satisfactory answer, if for instance the contractual duty is higher than the duty in tort.

Difficulties can also arise because of the doctrine of privity in contract law and the exceptions to it, although legislation has removed some of the hardships here, though the absence of a contractual relationship again may not prevent an action being bought for a breach of a duty in tort if such a duty exists.

PART 1 THE LAW OF CONTRACT

CHAPTER 1

PRINCIPLES OF FORMATION

1.1 OFFER AND ACCEPTANCE

1.1.1 THE NATURE OF AGREEMENT

We know from our introduction to the law of contract that the law concerns 'bargains' that are made between parties. The major significance of the word bargain is that it involves an agreement that is binding on both parties. In contract law, then, it is insufficient merely that an agreement exists between two parties but rather that it involves that specific type of agreement which is enforceable by both parties.

A contract will be completed when both sides honour an agreement by carrying out their particular side of the bargain. It is said to be a breach of contract when a party fails to do so. However, because of the special nature of contractual agreements, we cannot identify a breach of contract where we may feel that we have not got what we paid for or 'bargained' for, without first showing that the agreement was indeed a contract.

So our first objective in a contract case may be to prove that there is actually a contract in existence. We can tell if it is a contract because to be

so it must have been formed according to certain standard rules. It will only be a contract where there is:

- An agreement – which is based on mutuality

- consideration – which means that both sides are bound to give something to each other

- intention – to be legally bound by the terms of the agreement.

These elements are considered in these next three sections.

A contractual agreement is said to exist when a valid offer is followed by a valid acceptance. This seems straightforward enough, and where one person offers to sell something to another party who accepts the price and agrees to buy then there is no difficulty.

In practice though we know that negotiations can be much more complex than this and, on the other hand, that agreements can be identified which appear to have none of these formal negotiating steps: purchasing goods from a vending machine is a classic example of that.

In *Butler Machine Tool Co. v Ex-Cell-O Corpora-*

tion (1979) Lord Denning Master of the Rolls suggested that judges should decide whether a contract existed by examining the evidence in its totality rather than trying to apply a strict test of offer and acceptance. Even if other judges sympathised with the logic of this they would not publicly admit it, so we still have to return to the traditional test of offer and acceptance.

1.1.2 THE NATURE OF AN OFFER

A person who makes an offer is called an offeror. The person to whom the offer is made, and who is therefore able to accept it, is called the offeree.

The offer is a statement of intent by the offeror to be legally bound by the terms of the offer if it is accepted, and the contract exists once acceptance has taken place. Where the offer is plainly stated, e.g. 'Would you like to buy my car for £8,000?', then there is no problem. The question is easily identified as an offer, and you only have to say 'Yes, I will buy your car for £8,000' for there to be an easily identifiable acceptance too.

It is not always the case, however, that the first stage in negotiations is an offer. Often the first step is an entirely passive state and is not therefore open to acceptance, e.g. a tin of beans sitting on a supermarket shelf. This is not an offer and is called an invitation to treat, in other words an invitation to the other party to make an offer, usually an offer to buy. The contract is then formed by the agreement to sell which is the acceptance in this case. Figure 1.1 illustrates this in diagram form.

Examples of invitation to treat

Goods displayed on shelves in a self-service shop

These are not an offer that is then accepted when the customer picks the goods from the shelves. They are an invitation to treat, an invitation to the buyer to make an offer to buy. This is done by the customer taking them to the cash desk where the contract is formed when the sale is agreed.

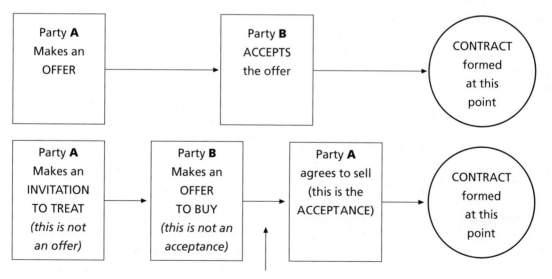

FIGURE 1.1 *The point at which a contract is made in a standard offer and acceptance, and where there is firstly an invitation to treat*

PHARMACEUTICAL SOCIETY OF GB V BOOTS CASH CHEMISTS LTD (1953)

Boots altered one of their shops to self-service. Under s.18 of the Pharmacy and Poisons Act 1933 a registered pharmacist was required to be present at the sale of certain drugs and poisons. It was important to know where the contract was formed. CA held that the contract was formed when goods were presented at the cash desk where a pharmacist was present, not when taken from the shelf.

The rule preserves the freedom of contract of the shopkeeper and sensibly allows the shopkeeper to accept or refuse a sale. This might be particularly important where a child selects alcohol from shelves in an off-licence and tries to buy it.

Goods on display in a shop window

Again there is no offer, only a display of the goods that the customer might go into the shop and offer to buy.

FISHER V BELL (1961)

A prosecution under the Offensive Weapons Act 1959 failed due to bad drafting of the Act. The offence was to offer for sale prohibited weapons. The shopkeeper displaying a flick knife in the window was not offering it for sale. It was a mere invitation to treat.

Goods or services advertised in a newspaper or magazine

Here a contract will not be formed until the person seeing the advertisement has made an offer to buy, which has then been accepted.

PARTRIDGE V CRITTENDEN (1968)

A prosecution for 'offering for sale' a wild bird under the Protection of Birds Act 1954 failed. The advertisement 'Bramblefinch cocks, bramblefinch hens, 25s each' was not an offer but an invitation to treat.

An invitation to council tenants to buy their property

GIBSON V MANCHESTER CITY COUNCIL (1979)

Gibson returned his completed application form when receiving an invitation to buy his house from the council. When there was a change of policy by the council Gibson's action for breach of contract failed. His completed application was an offer to buy, not an acceptance of any offer by the council.

A mere statement of price

The mere fact that a party has indicated a price which (s)he would find acceptable does not make it an offer.

HARVEY V FACEY (1893)

Harvey wanted to buy Facey's farm and sent a telegram 'Will you sell me Bumper Hall Penn? Telegraph lowest price'. Facey's telegram replied 'Lowest price acceptable £900'. Harvey tried to accept this but could not. It was merely a statement of price not an offer.

Lots at an auction

The rule in fact derives from auctions. The lot is the invitation to make a bid. Bidding is an offer to buy, and the acceptance is the fall of the auctioneer's hammer at which point the contract is formed.

BRITISH CAR AUCTIONS V WRIGHT (1972)

A prosecution for offering to sell an unroadworthy vehicle failed. At the auction there was no offer to sell, only an invitation to bid.

Situations which are not invitation to treat

Sometimes in situations that we would normally associate with invitation to treat, the circumstances involved or the nature of the words used mean that there has in fact been an offer rather than an invitation to treat. These include:

Advertisements involving a unilateral offer

If the advertisement indicates a course of action in return for which the advertiser makes a promise to pay, then (s)he is bound by this promise.

CARLILL V THE CARBOLIC SMOKE BALL CO. LTD (1893)

The company advertised a patent medicine, the smoke ball, with the promise that if a purchaser used it correctly and still got flu, then the company would pay them £100. Mrs Carlill did get flu after using the smoke ball in the correct fashion. The court enforced her claim for the £100. The promise was an offer that could be accepted by anyone who used the smoke ball correctly and still got flu.

A statement of price where an offer is also intended

A mere statement of price is not binding, but if other factors indicate that an offer is included in the statement then it will be binding if it is accepted.

BIGG V BOYD GIBBINS (1971)

In response to the offer of a lower price the claimant wrote 'For a quick sale I will accept £26,000'. The defendant replied 'I accept your offer'. The claimant then wrote "I thank you for accepting my price of £26,000. My wife and I are both pleased that you are purchasing the property'. His first letter was an offer that the defendant had accepted.

Competitive tendering

Normally an invitation to tender for the supply of goods or services is no more than an invitation to treat. For instance, a company want their office painted. They invite tenders and various decorators will respond with different prices for the work. The company is free to choose any of the decorators, not necessarily the cheapest. If, however, the company has in its advertisement

activity

QUICK QUIZ

Explain whether the following involve offers or mere invitations to treat:

1 A sign in a shop window reading:

> **SPECIAL OFFER**
> **BAKED BEANS**
> **ONLY 6p PER TIN**

2 My friend has an old sports car that I particularly like. When I ask him how much he would sell it for he replies: 'You could not buy a car like that for less than £20,000 these days.'

3 An advertisement in a local newspaper which reads:

> YOU MUST NOT MISS
> SUPERSTORES
> SPECIAL OPENING BONANZA
> MICROWAVE OVENS RRP £199
> ONLY 99P
> TO OUR FIRST 10 CUSTOMERS

agreed that the work will go to the tender with the lowest price, then it is bound to give the work to the bidder with the lowest price.

HARVELA INVESTMENTS LTD v ROYAL TRUST CO. OF CANADA LTD (1986)

The Trust company had invited tenders from two interested parties for the purchase of some land. The sale would go to the party making the highest bid. The party making the lowest bid had tendered a price of $2,100,000 or $101,000 in excess of any other offer. When it was accepted and Harvela, the party making the higher bid, found out they sued successfully. The wording of the invitation to tender made it an offer that could only be accepted by the highest bidder.

There may also be an obligation on the party inviting tenders to consider all tenders regardless of whether a tender is accepted.

BLACKPOOL AND FYLDE AERO CLUB LTD v BLACKPOOL BOROUGH COUNCIL (1990)

The club had held the concession to run pleasure flights from the council's airport for many years. When the concession was due for renewal the council put it out to competitive tender, and invited tenders from other parties. All tenders were to be submitted in unmarked envelopes in a particular box by 12 noon on a specific date. The council stated that it would not be bound to accept any bid. The club placed its bid in the box at 11.00 a.m. but by accident the box was not emptied after this time and its bid was not therefore considered. The concession was given to another group, R.R. Helicopters. When the council later discovered its mistake they at first decided to repeat the exercise but were threatened with legal action by R.R. Helicopters. The club claimed breach of a contract to consider all tenders delivered by the due time. Their claim was upheld. The court felt that there was an implied undertaking to operate by the rules that they had set, even though the invitation to tender for the concession was only an invitation to treat.

1.1.3 THE RULES OF OFFER

Once we know whether a party is making an offer, and is then intending to contract, we must be satisfied that the offer conforms to the rules to show whether it is a valid offer or not.

The offer must be communicated to the offeree

It is impossible to accept something of which you have no knowledge.

TAYLOR v LAIRD (1856)

Taylor gave up the captaincy of a ship and then worked his passage back to Britain as an ordinary crewmember. His claim for wages failed. The ship owner had received no communication of Taylor's offer to work in that capacity.

An offer can be made to one person but it can also be made to the whole world

Anyone can then accept the offer who has had notice of it.

CARLILL v THE CARBOLIC SMOKE BALL CO. (1893)

The company's claim that they had no contract with Mrs Carlill failed. They had made their offer generally and she had accepted by buying the smoke ball, using it and still getting flu.

The terms of the offer must be certain

If the words of the offer are too vague then the parties might not really know what they are contracting for and should not then be bound.

GUTHING v LYNN (1831)

When a horse was purchased a promise to pay £5 more 'if the horse is lucky …' could not be an offer. It was too vague.

It is possible to withdraw the offer, and this can be done any time before the offer is accepted

ROUTLEDGE v GRANT (1828)

Grant had offered his house for sale on the understanding that the offer would remain open for six weeks. When he took it off the market within the six weeks that was legitimate because there had been no acceptance.

If, however the offeree paid money to the offeror to keep the offer open, then (s)he would be bound to do so.

The offeror must communicate the withdrawal of the offer to the offeree

BYRNE V VAN TIENHOVEN (1880)

On 1 October Van Tienhoven wrote to Byrne offering to sell certain goods. On 8 October he changed his mind and sent a letter withdrawing the offer. On 11 October Byrne accepted the offer in a telegram. On 15 October he confirmed this in writing. On 20 October Byrne received Van Tienhoven's letter withdrawing the offer. It was invalid because it had not been received until after Byrne's acceptance.

This shows how important it is to keep a track of dates as well as other information during contractual negotiations.

The withdrawal need not be communicated personally by the offeror

It can be done by a third party, provided that the party is a reliable source of information for the offeree.

DICKINSON V DODDS (1876)

Dodds had offered to sell houses to Dickinson. When Berry notified Dickinson that Dodds had withdrawn the offer this was acceptable. Berry was shown to be a mutual acquaintance on whom both could rely.

It is not possible to withdraw a unilateral offer if the other party is in the act of performing his or her part

In a unilateral contract the offeree actually accepts by performing his or her side of the bargain (as in *Carlill*). It would clearly be unfair to prevent this once the other party had begun.

ERRINGTON V ERRINGTON AND WOODS (1952)

A father bought a house and mortgaged it in his own name. He promised his son and daughter-in-law that it would become theirs when they had paid off the mortgage. When the father died and other members of the family wanted possession of the house their action failed. The father's promise could not be withdrawn so long as the couple kept up the mortgage repayments, after which the house would be theirs.

Termination of offer

An offer can be terminated in a number of ways:

- It can be accepted, in which case there is a contract (or indeed it could be refused or met with a counter-offer in which case there is no contract).

- It can be properly withdrawn, as we have seen above.

- The time for acceptance can lapse.

- A reasonable time can have lapsed. (It would be rare that an offer could stay open indefinitely)

RAMSGATE VICTORIA HOTEL CO. LTD V MONTEFIORE (1866)

Montefiore had offered to buy shares in June but the company only issued the shares in November. It was held that his offer to buy had lapsed.

- When one of the parties dies. Generally this may operate in different ways depending on which party dies. If the offeree dies then this will cause the offer to lapse and his or her representatives will be unable to accept on his or her behalf. If an offeror dies, however, (s)he may still be bound by an acceptance that is made in ignorance of the offeror's death.

1.1.4 THE RULES ON ACCEPTANCE

The acceptance must be communicated to the offeror

Just the same as for the offer, communication is required. Otherwise the unscrupulous might hold people to offers of which they were unaware. It goes without saying then that the acceptance must be a positive act, and that acceptance cannot be taken from silence.

FELTHOUSE V BINDLEY (1863)

An uncle and nephew had negotiated over the sale of the nephew's horse. The uncle had said 'If I hear no more from you I shall consider the horse mine at £30 15s'. On sale of the nephew's stock, the auctioneer failed to withdraw the horse from the sale as instructed by the nephew. The uncle tried to sue the auctioneer in tort but failed. He could not prove the horse was his. The nephew had not actually accepted his offer to buy.

The acceptance can be in any form, in writing, by words, or conduct

Of course, if the offeror requires it to be in a specific form then it must be in that form or it will be invalid.

YATES V PULLEYN (1975)

An option to purchase land was required to be exercised by notice in writing '… sent by registered or recorded delivery post'. When the option was sent by ordinary post only it was invalid.

The postal rule

Where use of the ordinary postal system is the normal, anticipated or agreed means of accepting then the contract is formed at the time the letter of acceptance is posted, not when it is received (the postal rule).

ADAMS V LINDSELL (1818)

The rule began with this case where wool was offered for sale, an acceptance by post was requested and sent, but not received until long after the wool had been sold. The rule developed then from the possible injustices caused by delays in the postal system in its early days.

The rule applies even where the letter is never received, rather than merely delayed.

HOUSEHOLD FIRE INSURANCE V GRANT (1879)

Grant made a written offer to purchase shares. Notification of acceptance was posted but never received. When the company went into liquidation, Grant's claim that he was not a shareholder and should not be liable for the value of the shares failed. He had become a shareholder even though unaware of it.

It is possible to avoid the effects of the postal rule by stating in the offer that there will be no contract until the acceptance is actually received, in which case the contract is only complete on communication of the acceptance.

HOLWELL SECURITIES V HUGHES (1974)

An attempt to use the postal rule failed where the acceptance was required to be 'by notice in writing'. The fact that actual notice was required meant that the postal rule did not apply.

In the case of more modern methods of communication the picture is not so clear. The important factor seems to be how instantaneous the method is.

BRINKIBON LTD V STAHAG STAHL (1983)

Previous case law had stated that an acceptance by telex, like telephone, was immediate enough communication to be effective straightaway. This case, however, concerned a telex received out of office hours. HL held that this could only be effective once the office was reopened.

Faxes and e-mail are even more modern forms of communication and the same problems and the same principles are likely to apply.

The acceptance must be unconditional

This is the so-called 'mirror image rule'. The acceptance must conform exactly with the terms of the offer or it is invalid and no contract will have been formed. It follows that any attempt to vary the terms of the offer is a counter-offer, terminating the original offer which cannot then be accepted.

HYDE V WRENCH (1840)

Wrench offered to sell his farm to Hyde for £1,000. Hyde rejected this and offered to pay £950, which Wrench rejected. When Hyde then tried to accept the original price and Wrench would not sell Hyde's action failed. The original offer was no longer open for him to accept.

A mere enquiry about the terms of the offer, however, is not a rejection of it. This means that the offer is still open to acceptance by the offeree.

STEVENSON V MCLEAN (1880)

In a response to an offer to sell iron the price and quantity were accepted but the offeree wished to know whether delivery could be staggered. Hearing nothing further the claimant sent a letter of acceptance. He sued on discovering that the iron had been sold to a third party. The defendant's claim that there had been a counter-offer failed. It was not a rejection of the offer, merely an enquiry about it, and the offer was still open to acceptance.

activity

LEGAL PROBLEM SOLVING

Consider the following situation:

On 11 May Andy wrote to his friend Brian offering to sell Brian his Cup Final ticket for £150.

Brian posted a letter on 12 May which said:

Dear Andy,
About the Cup Final tickets. £150 seems a bit on the steep side. I don't mind paying a bit over the odds but I'd be happier paying £100. Or could I pay you £100 now, and the other £50 when I'm paid again at the end of the month?

Yours Brian

Later in the day Brian wrote again to Andy:

Dear Andy,
I've thought again about that ticket. I really want to go and it's cutting it a bit fine to get one from anywhere else. I'll pay you the £150.
Yours Brian

He posted the letter the same night.

Andy received Brian's first letter on the morning of 13 May and sold the ticket to another friend Chris at work that day. When Andy returned home that evening Brian's second letter had been delivered in the later post.

Brian missed the Cup Final and now seeks your advice.

Answering the question:

There are four essential ingredients to answering problem questions:

- Firstly, you must be able to identify the important facts in the problem, the ones on which the answer may depend.

- Secondly, you will need to know and understand the law which is likely to apply in the situation.

- Thirdly, you will need to be able to apply the law to the facts.

- Fourthly, you will need to be able to draw conclusions from that process. This is particularly so where the problem asks you to advise. If you are advising then your client is depending on you to say what to do in the circumstances.

The facts:

Unlike in real life, it is common when a tutor or an examiner makes up a problem for nearly all of the facts to be relevant in some way. Even so they may still need to be put into some logical order to connect them to the law you need to use. Here the key facts seem to be:

1 Andy made an offer to Brian on 11 May of a Cup Final ticket for £150.

2 On 12 May Brian replied that he would prefer to pay £100 to £150, and alternatively asked if he might pay £150 in two instalments.

3 Later on 12 May Brian sent a straightforward letter of acceptance.

4 Andy sold the ticket to Chris on 13 May after receiving Brian's first letter.

5 Andy received the second letter later the same day.

6 All of these communications were carried out by post.

The law:

We know because the problem is all about whether Andy is obliged to sell the tickets to Brian or not that it concerns formation, and particularly offer and acceptance; indeed the word offer is used in the situation. From this and other facts we can deduce what particular rules are important to solving the problem. The appropriate law would appear to be:

- A contract can only be formed if there is an agreement, which is a valid offer followed by a valid acceptance.

- An offer can be withdrawn any time before acceptance – *Routledge* v *Grant* (1828).

- An offer must be communicated – *Taylor* v *Laird* (1856).

- But this must be communicated to the offeree – *Byrne* v *Van Tienhoven* (1880).

- A contract is formed once the offer is accepted.

- The acceptance must be communicated to the offeror – *Felthouse* v *Bindley* (1863).

- Where the post is the normal, anticipated method of accepting then the contract is formed when the letter is posted not when it is received – *Adams* v *Lindsell* (1818).

- A counter-offer is a rejection of the offer that is no longer open to acceptance – *Hyde* v *Wrench* (1840).

- But a mere enquiry has no such effect – *Stevenson* v *McLean*(1880).

Applying law to fact:

It is tempting to look at Brian's first letter and see it as a counter-offer. Of course, if we do that there is nothing left to answer about. This should be a pointer in itself, but really in any problem where a particular act can be seen as one thing or the other we need to look at both or all possibilities.

On the other hand, if we do not see it as a counter-offer it means Brian's second letter could be an acceptance ('I'll pay the £150'). We need to examine the first letter then to decide whether we think the first part is a definite rejection of the offer, and if not whether the second part is only an enquiry.

If we accept that it is then our next real concern is that Andy has sold the ticket. Can he do this? Well if there was a counter-offer he can with no thought to Brian. If not then he needs to tell Brian before he sells it.

The final part of the problem is whether the postal rule applies or not. Andy has not sold the ticket until after he receives Brian's first letter. If the letter has no contractual significance then Brian has in effect withdrawn the offer without informing Andy. Brian on the other hand has accepted in his second letter. If the postal rule applies, (which appears possible here because all the communications are by letter) then the acceptance takes place when the letter is posted, not when Andy receives it after he has sold the ticket. The contract is formed at the time the letter is posted and Andy would be in breach of contract by selling the ticket to Chris.

Conclusions:

It just remains now to make a judgement based on our analysis above whether to advise Brian to sue Andy or not. Just as in real life there might not be a definite or straightforward answer, the point is to reach a logical conclusion by using the law correctly.

Now using the above as a guide make your own attempt at the problem.

POINTS FOR DISCUSSION

PROBLEMS ASSOCIATED WITH OFFER AND ACCEPTANCE

Many contracts in a modern commercial context are not formed as the result of one party straight-forwardly accepting the simple offer of the other. This would be too restrictive and rigid. Businesses contract in a variety of ways and may be subject to disagreements, rejections, compromises and even threats before ever an agreement is reached. Sometimes people, too, will negotiate to try to get something different than what is first offered. We have already seen the effect that a counter-offer can have on the parties. When does a mere enquiry end and a counter-offer begin? That is a question that judges will often be called on to answer.

A further complication is the common use of 'standard forms' by businesses. These are used so that the business can be sure of always dealing on terms advantageous to it. This may not cause any problems in a consumer sale. When two businesses are contracting, however, it can prove a nightmare. This is the so-called 'battle of the forms'. One business makes an offer on its standard forms. The customer accepts on its. The two forms may be entirely contradictory. The question is which terms are taken as being the contractual ones in the case of a conflict between the two businesses.

The general rule in the modern day is to take the last counter-offer as having been accepted, and give effect to its terms in the contract.

DAVIES & CO. LTD V WILLIAM OLD (1969)

Shopfitters, following their successful tender, contracted with the architects in a building contract to sub-contract to the builders. The builders under instruction from the architects issued an order for work to the shopfitters. They did this on their own standard form that included a clause that they would not pay for work until they themselves had been paid. When the shopfitters later sued for some work that had not been paid for their action failed. The builders' standard form was a counter-offer that the shopfitters had accepted by carrying on with the work.

The problem is further compounded because often the services or goods are provided before any settled agreement is reached. In a later conflict the courts may find a contract does exist provided there has been no major disagreement between the parties. Sometimes, however, this is impossible.

BRITISH STEEL CORPORATION V CLEVELAND BRIDGE AND ENGINEERING CO. (1984)

Cleveland Bridge were sub-contracted to build the steel framework of a bank in Saudi Arabia. The work required four steel nodes that they asked BSC to manufacture. BSC wanted a disclaimer of liability for any loss caused by late delivery. The parties were never able to agree on this and so no written agreement was ever made. BSC, however, did make and deliver three of the nodes, but the last was delayed because of a strike. Cleveland Bridge refused to pay for the three nodes and claimed that BSC was in breach of contract for late delivery of the fourth. Because there was a total disagreement over a major term, the judge in the case found it impossible to recognise that a contract existed. He did order that BSC be paid for what they had supplied.

1.2 CONSIDERATION

1.2.1 THE NATURE AND PURPOSE OF CONSIDERATION

As we have said before, the law of contract deals with bargains. The rules of contract seek to differentiate between agreements where there is something to be gained by both parties, as is the case in a contract, and agreements which are purely gratuitous, as are gifts.

The giving of 'consideration' by both sides was the traditional method of ensuring that the agreement was contractual, and if no consideration could be found then the agreement could not be enforced. The exception to this would be an agreement made by deed.

A simple, early way of defining consideration came in *Currie* v *Misa* (1875) where it was described in terms of benefit and detriment. If I contract with you over my contract law textbook for £15 I am

activity

SELF ASSESSMENT QUESTIONS

1 What is an offer?

2 What is the major difference between an offer and an invitation to treat?

3 What would happen if a customer in a supermarket took tins of beans from a shelf but changed her mind and discarded them before reaching the cash desk?

4 What would happen if I ordered goods advertised in a magazine and the seller wrote back to say that supplies were exhausted?

5 What makes a unilateral offer different to an invitation to treat?

6 Can there be more than one offeree to an offer?

7 Why is it important to notify an offeree before withdrawing the offer?

8 In what way is it better for an offeree that negotiations prior to a contract are all carried out by letter?

9 If I fax my acceptance of an offer to a company out of office hours when is the contract formed?

10 If you find my lost dog and return it to me and later see an advertisement in the newspaper offering a reward for return of the dog can you claim it?

KEY
FACTS

- A contract is made where there is an agreement between two parties
- An agreement is a valid offer followed by a valid acceptance
- Offer must be distinguished from an 'invitation to treat' – *Pharmaceutical Society of GB* v *Boots Cash Chemists Ltd* (1953), and from a mere statement of price – *Harvey* v *Facey* (1893)
- Competitive tendering is different – *Harvela Investments Ltd* v *Royal Trust Co. of Canada Ltd* (1988)
- An offer must be communicated – *Taylor* v *Laird* (1856)
- An offer can be made to the whole world – *Carlill* v *The Carbolic Smoke Ball Co. Ltd* (1893)
- The terms of the offer must be certain – *Guthing* v *Lynn* (1831)
- An offer can be withdrawn any time up to acceptance – *Routledge* v *Grant* (1828)
- The withdrawal must be communicated to the offeree – *Byrne* v *Van Tienhoven* (1880)
- This can be by a reliable third party – *Dickinson* v *Dodds* (1876)
- Unilateral offers do not require acceptance, only performance – *Errington* v *Errington and Woods* (1952)
- An offer ends – on acceptance, on proper withdrawal, on lapse of time, on death of one of the parties
- Acceptance must be communicated – *Felthouse* v *Bindley* (1863)
- If use of the post is the normal, anticipated method of acceptance the contract is formed on posting (the postal rule) – *Adams* v *Lindsell* (1818)
- Even if the acceptance is never received – *Household Fire Insurance* v *Grant* (1879)
- Acceptance must be unconditional – *Hyde* v *Wrench* (1840)
- But mere enquiries are not rejections of the offer – *Stevenson* v *McLean* (1880)

FIGURE 1.2 *Key fact chart for offer and acceptance*

gaining the benefit of the £15 but have the detriment of giving up the book. For you it is the other way round. A more sophisticated definition was provided in *Dunlop* v *Selfridge* (1915) where the House of Lords approved Sir Frederick Pollock's definition (*Pollock on Contracts*) that

'an act of forbearance of one party, or the promise thereof, is the price for which the promise of the other is bought, and the promise thus given for value is enforceable'

In fact, although the judges are saying that they will not in contract law enforce a promise which has not been paid for in some way, in modern cases they have been shown to be willing to see almost any promise made in a commercial context as contractual. Therefore consideration can be surprisingly little, and it can seem difficult to fit the theory to real situations.

1.2.2 EXECUTORY AND EXECUTED CONSIDERATION

Contract law would have no meaning unless it enforced promises as well as actual acts. Executory consideration is simply the exchange of promises to carry out acts or pass property at a later stage. If one party breaks their promise and fails to do what they are supposed to do under it, then they are in breach of contract and may be sued.

In unilateral contracts, however, the party making the unilateral offer is under no obligations until the other party performs (executes) their side of the bargain. This is called executed consideration, and a common example is a reward. We have already seen this principle in operation in Mrs *Carlill*'s case.

1.2.3 THE RULES OF CONSIDERATION

Consideration need not be adequate but it must be sufficient

This sounds like complete nonsense because adequacy and sufficiency appear to be the same thing.

In fact lawyers are using adequacy in its everyday

form, i.e. whether the parties are promising things of fairly equal value. Adequacy will be decided by the parties themselves. The courts are not interested in whether there has been a good or a bad bargain made, only that a bargain exists.

THOMAS V THOMAS (1842)

A man before his death expressed the wish that his wife be allowed to remain in the house although this was not in his will. The executors carried out this wish and charged the widow a nominal ground rent of £1 per year. When they later tried to dispossess her they failed. The moral obligation to carry out the man's wishes was not consideration but the payment of ground rent, however small and apparently inadequate, was.

On the contrary, sufficiency is used here as a legal term, and it means that what is promised must be real, tangible and have some actual value.

WHITE V BLUETT (1853)

A son owed his father money on a promissory note. When the father died and his executors were trying to recover the money the son tried to claim that he was not bound to pay. He claimed an agreement with his father that the debt would be forgotten in return for the son's promise not to complain about the distribution of the father's assets in his will. The son failed. The promise was too intangible to be consideration for the father's promise to forego the debt.

What is real, tangible and of value is not always easily distinguishable.

WARD V BYHAM (1956)

A father of an illegitimate child promised the mother money towards its upkeep if she would keep the child 'well looked after and happy'. The mother would be doing nothing more than she was already bound by law to do in looking after the child. The court were prepared to enforce the agreement, however, since there is no obligation in law to keep a child happy, and the promise to do so was seen as good consideration.

In fact, even things of no apparent worth have been classed as consideration.

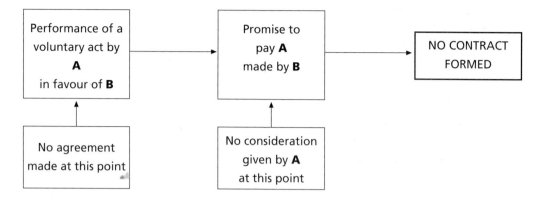

FIGURE 1.3 *Past consideration in operation*

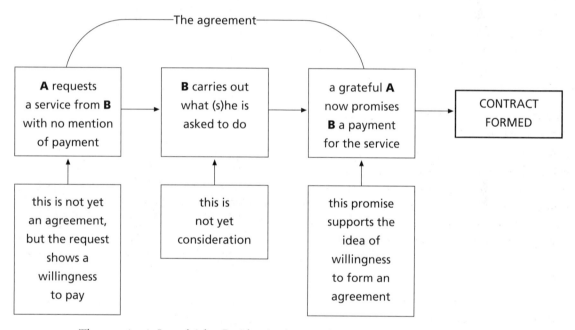

FIGURE 1.4 *The exception in* Lampleigh *v* Braithwaite *in operation*

CHAPPELL V NESTLÉ CO. (1960)

Nestlé had offered a record, normally retailing at 6s 8d (not quite 34p), for 1s 6d (7.5p) plus three chocolate bar wrappers to promote their chocolate. On receipt the wrappers were thrown away. They were still held to be good consideration when the holders of the copyright of the record sued to prevent the promotion because they would receive substantially fewer royalties from it.

The accusation that if a court wishes to enforce a promise in a commercial context it will always find something to act as consideration seems to be proved when set against the reasoning in some cases (see later: *Williams* v *Roffey Bros. & Nicholls Contractors Ltd* (1990)).

Past consideration is no consideration

This is another strange sounding rule. It simply means that any consideration given cannot come

QUICK QUIZ

....

Consider the following events and decide whether a contract has been formed or whether consideration is past:

1 While I was away on holiday it was very hot at home too. My neighbour Joe noticed that some of my flowers were dying and so he watered them every day, saving them. I was very pleased when I returned and I told him that I would give him £20 for all his trouble. I have not given Joe the money and he wonders if he is actually entitled to it.

2 Last month I had to go to a meeting in Coventry. My car would not start so I asked one of my students Daniel who has a car if he would take me there. He readily agreed and gave me a lift there and waited to give me a lift back also. On our return I gave Daniel money for the petrol and promised him that I would also buy him a new text book costing £22.50 that he was saving for. I have since told Daniel that I will not buy the book.

....

before the agreement but must follow it. It is a sensible rule in that it can prevent the unscrupulous from forcing people into contracts on the basis of providing goods or services which they have not ordered. Quite simply, in any case it is a promise that has not been agreed to by both parties in their contract.

The basic rule

It will usually occur where one party has done a voluntary act and is trying to enforce the other party's later promise to pay.

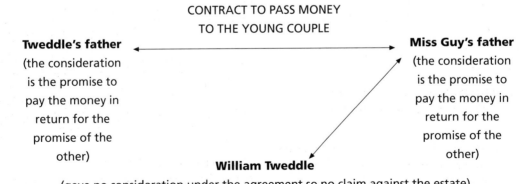

FIGURE 1.5 *The rule of consideration in* Tweddle *v* Atkinson

RE McARDLE (1951)

A son and his wife lived in his mother's house that on her death would be inherited by her son and three other children. The son's wife paid for substantial repairs and improvements to the property. The mother then made her four children sign an agreement to reimburse the daughter-in-law out of her estate. When she died and the children refused to keep this promise the daughter-in-law sued unsuccessfully. Her consideration for their promise was past, it came before they signed the agreement to repay her.

The exception to the rule

The rule will not always work justly, as the above case shows. In certain circumstances the rule will not apply. Where one of the parties has requested a service, the law sensibly concludes that (s)he is prepared to pay for it. Even though that service is then carried out without any mention as to payment, or any apparent contractual agreement, a promise to pay coming after the service is performed will be enforced by the courts. This is known as the rule in *Lampleigh v Braithwaite* from the case of that name.

LAMPLEIGH v BRAITHWAITE (1615)

Braithwaite was accused of killing a man and asked Lampleigh to get him a King's pardon. This Lampleigh achieved at considerable expense to himself, and Braithwaite, in gratitude, promised to pay him £100, which he in fact never did. Lampleigh's claim that there was a contract succeeded. Because the service was requested, even though no price was mentioned at the time, it was clear that both parties would have contemplated a payment. The later promise to pay was clear evidence of this.

Figures 1.3 and 1.4 show in diagrammatic form how this works.

The consideration must move from the promisee (the person to whom the promise is made)

Again the rule sounds complex but simply means a person cannot sue or indeed be sued under a contract unless (s)he has provided consideration.

TWEDDLE v ATKINSON (1861)

Fathers of a young couple who intended to marry agreed in writing to each settle a sum of money on the couple. The young woman's father died before giving over the money and the young man then sued the executors to the estate when they refused to hand over the money. Even though he was named in the agreement he failed because he had given no consideration for the agreement himself.

Figure 1.5 expresses the situation in diagrammatic form.

Performing an existing duty cannot be the consideration for a new promise

The basic rule

Merely doing something that you are already bound to do can never be sufficient to amount to consideration. This applies firstly where the duty is a public one created by law.

COLLINS v GODEFROY (1831)

A police officer was under a court order to attend and give evidence at a trial. It was important to the defendant that the officer attended so he promised to pay him a sum of money to ensure that he did so. The promise to pay was not contractual and unenforceable. There was no consideration for it.

It also applies where the duty has arisen under an existing contract.

STILK v MYRICK (1809)

Two members of a ship's crew deserted. The captain promised the remaining crew that they could share these two men's wages if they got the ship safely home. The promise was held not to be binding on the ship's owner. Sailors were bound by their contract to cope with the normal contingencies of the voyage, which could include these desertions, so there was no consideration for the captain's promise.

The exceptions to the rule

It will be consideration where what is given is more than could be expected from the duty. The extra element is the consideration for the new promise. Again this will apply where a public duty is exceeded.

GLASSBROOK BROS. V GLAMORGAN COUNTY COUNCIL (1925)

During a strike a pit owner asked for extra protection from the police and promised a payment in return. When the strike was over the pit owner refused to pay claiming that the police were in any case bound to protect his pit. His argument failed. The police had provided more men than they would normally have done so there was consideration for the promise.

Again it also applies where the existing duty is a contractual one and a party has given more than was identified as necessary in the contract.

HARTLEY V PONSONBY(1857)

Involved similar facts to *Stilk* v *Myrick* but here only 19 members of a crew of 36 remained. A similar promise to pay more money to the remaining crew was enforceable because the reduction in numbers made the voyage much more dangerous. In agreeing to continue in these circumstances they had provided good consideration for the promise to pay them extra money.

It has also been accepted, albeit by the Privy Council, that a promise to perform an existing obligation made to a third party can be valid consideration for a fresh agreement.

PAO ON V LAU YIU LONG (1980)

Both parties owned companies. The major asset in Pao's company was a building that Lau wished to purchase. An agreement was made whereby Lau's company would buy Pao's company in return for a large number of shares in Lau's company. To avoid the damage that sudden trading in this number of shares might cause Lau inserted a clause in the contract that Pao should retain 60 per cent of the shares for at least one year. (We could call this agreement 1.) Pao wanting a guarantee that the shares would not fall in value and a subsidiary agreement was made at the same time by which Lau would buy back 60 per cent of the shares at $2.50 each. Pao later realised that this might benefit Lau more if the shares rose in value and therefore refused to carry out the contract unless

---

the subsidiary arrangement was scrapped and replaced with a straightforward indemnity by Lau against a fall in the value of the shares. Lau could have sued at this point for breach of contract but, fearing a loss of public confidence in his company as a result, agreed to the new terms. (We could call this agreement 2). When the value of the shares did then fall Lau refused to honour the agreement and Pao then sought to enforce the indemnity. Lao offered two defences. Firstly, that the second agreement, the agreement to indemnify Pao, was past consideration. Secondly, that Pao had given no consideration for the second agreement since it only involved doing what he was bound to do under the first agreement, pass the company in return for the shares. In response to Lau's first defence PC applied the rule in *Lampleigh* v *Braithwaite*. Lau's demand that Pao should not sell 60 per cent of the shares for one year was a request for a service that carried with it an implied promise to pay. This implied promise was later supported by the actual promise to indemnify Pao. The second of Lau's defences also failed. There was consideration. Pao, by continuing with the contract, was protecting the credibility and financial standing of Lau's company and the price payable in return for this was the indemnity.

The same reasoning can be used to find consideration by third parties to a contract where an agency relationship can be identified and where the agreement protects the commercial credibility of the contract.

NEW ZEALAND SHIPPING CO. LTD V A.M. SATTERTHWAITE & CO. LTD (1975) (THE EURYMEDON)

This is a complex case demonstrating how far the courts are prepared to strain the simple meaning of consideration in order to enforce an agreement that they believe must be enforced. Carriers contracted with the consignors of goods to ship drilling equipment. The carriers hired stevedores to unload the equipment, and these stevedores by their negligence caused substantial damage to it. The carriers' contract with the consignors contained a clause limiting their liability in the event of breach. The clause also identified that the protection offered by the limitation would extend to any servant or agent of the carriers. There were two questions for the court. Firstly the court had to decide whether there was a contractual relationship between the stevedores and the consignors. If so the court was then required to determine whether the stevedores had provided any consideration for the promise by the consignors to be bound by the limitation clause. This was clearly questionable because the stevedores were doing nothing more than they were contractually bound to the carriers to do, unload the ship. PC accepted that there was a contractual relationship based on agency and that the promise made to the carriers by the stevedores could provide consideration in return for the promise made by the consignors to be bound by the limitation clause.

A very recent exception to the basic rule occurs where, the party making the promise to pay extra receives an extra benefit from the other party's agreement to complete what (s)he was already bound to do under an existing arrangement.

WILLIAMS V ROFFEY BROS. & NICHOLLS CONTRACTORS LTD (1990)

Roffey Bros., builders, sub-contracted the carpentry on a number of flats they were building to Williams for £20,000. Williams had under-quoted for the work and ran into financial difficulties. Because there was a delay clause in Roffey's contract meaning they would have to pay money to the client if the flats were not built on time, they promised to pay Williams another £10,300 if he would complete the carpentry on time. When Williams completed the work and Roffey's failed to pay extra his claim to the money succeeded. Even though Williams was only doing what he was already contractually bound to do Roffey's were gaining the extra benefit of not having to pay the money for delay to the client. Williams was providing consideration for their promise to pay him more for the work merely by completing his existing obligations on time.

One point to remember: there was no attempt on Williams's part to extract the extra money by threats or coercion. The rules of economic duress would in any case have prevented him from succeeding. What is clear from the case is that the courts do not want promises made in a business context to be broken. To prevent this they will find consideration even though we may find it hard to find anything real or tangible about it.

A promise to accept part of an existing debt in place of the whole debt cannot be enforced

This is because there is no consideration for such a promise.

The basic rule:

This was first stated in *Pinnel's Case* (1602) which held that payment of a smaller sum than the debt itself on the due date can never relieve the liability of the debtor to pay the whole debt, so the creditor can always sue for the balance of the debt which is unpaid.

The rule can operate fairly where the creditor is giving in to pressure by the debtor to accept less.

D.C. BUILDERS V REES (1965)

Builders were owed £482 for the balance of work they had completed. After several months waiting for payment, and at a point where they were in danger of going out of business, they reluctantly accepted an offer by the Rees's to pay £300 in full satisfaction of the debt. When the builders then sued for the balance they were successful. They were not prevented by the agreement to accept less, which in any case was extracted from them under pressure.

It can also sometimes seem to operate unfairly where the debtor genuinely relies on the promise of the creditor.

FOAKES V BEER (1884)

Dr Foakes owed Mrs Beer £2,090 after a court judged against him. The two reached an agreement for Foakes to pay in instalments, with Mrs Beer agreeing that no further action would be taken if the debt was paid off by the agreed date. Later Mrs Beer demanded interest, which is always payable on a judgement debt, and sued when Foakes refused to pay. She was successful as a result of *Pinnel's* rule.

There are two basic exceptions where the agreement to pay less than the full debt can be enforced: accord and satisfaction and promissory estoppel.

Accord and satisfaction

In other words, there is an agreement to accept something other than the money from the existing debt. This might take a number of forms:
An agreement to accept an earlier payment of a smaller sum than the whole debt. (This was what actually happened in *Pinnel's Case*.)

Say I owe you £100 that I am due to pay on 1 March. You then agree to accept a payment of £80 made on 1 February. You will be unable to sue for the remaining £20.

- An agreement to accept something other than money instead of the debt.
  Say I owe you £1,000 and you accept instead my stereo hi fi, worth about £800. You have the opportunity to place whatever value you wish on the goods. If you accept them in place of the money the full debt is satisfied.

- An agreement to accept a part payment together with something else, not to the value of the balance of the debt.
  Say I owe you £100 and you agree to accept £50 together with a law book worth £21.99. In cash value you have only received £71.99 but again the debt has been paid.

The doctrine of promissory estoppel

The doctrine acts as a defence to a claim by a creditor for the remainder of the debt where part payment has been accepted. The essential elements of the doctrine require that:

- There must be an existing contractual relationship between the claimant and the defendant.

- The claimant must have agreed to waive (give up) some of his or her rights under that contract (the amount of the debt that has been unpaid).

- The claimant has waived these rights knowing that the defendant would rely on the promise in determining his or her future conduct.

- The defendant has in fact acted in reliance on the promise to forego some of the debt.

The effect of the doctrine if these points are shown is to prevent (estop) the claimant from going back on the promise because it would be unfair and inequitable to do so.

Lord Denning developed the doctrine from the older doctrine of waiver.

CENTRAL LONDON PROPERTY TRUST LTD v HIGH TREES HOUSE LTD (1947)

From 1937 the defendants leased a block of flats in Wimbledon from the claimants to sublet to tenants. When war started it was impossible to find tenants and so the defendants were unable to pay the rent. The claimants agreed to accept half rent, which the defendants continued to pay. By 1945 the flats were all let and the claimants wanted the rent returned to its former level and sued for the higher rent for the last two quarters. They succeeded but Lord Denning stated *in obiter* (a statement made by the way rather than as a binding principle) that had they tried to sue for the extra rent for the whole period of the war they would have failed. Estoppel would prevent them from going back on the promise on which the defendants had relied so long as the circumstances persisted.

activity

MULTIPLE CHOICE QUESTIONS

In the following situations select the appropriate statement from the choices which follow:

1 Mary, a student, asks Donald her teacher if he will give her good tuition for which she will pay him £100.

A There is a contract. Mary will have to pay the £100 to Donald.

B Mary will be able to sue Donald if his tuition is not good.

C Donald cannot demand the £100 from Mary. He is only doing his duty.

D Donald can sue for the £100 if Mary does not pay it.

2 Sid, the manager of a firm, promises Danny, a packer, £100 on top of his wages if he will stop at work late one evening to get out a rush order.

A There is no contract. Danny is only doing his job.

B Danny is entitled to the £100. He is doing extra to his normal job.

C Danny can only be paid the £100 if he does £100 worth of extra work.

D Sid can sue Danny if he refuses to stay late.

3 Dave, a builder, owes his supplier £50,000 for materials. Dave has been unable to sell the house he has recently built at a profit due to a slump in the property market, and has only £45,000. The supplier agrees to accept the £45,000 to prevent Dave from going out of business. Six months later the supplier has learnt that Dave has just gained a building contract worth £5 million.

A Dave will have to pay the remaining £5,000 to the supplier immediately.

B Dave can use the supplier's promise as a defence to a claim for the money.

C The supplier can recover the materials used by Dave.

D Dave can sue the supplier.

activity

SELF ASSESSMENT QUESTIONS

1 What is consideration?

2 Why is it unimportant whether the consideration is adequate or not?

3 What is the difference between something that is sufficient and something that is adequate?

4 Why is it impossible to form a contract with consideration that is past?

5 In what ways could the rule that consideration must move from the promisee be said to be unfair?

6 Why is it difficult to see the distinction between the principles in *Stilk* v *Myrick* (1809) and *Williams* v *Roffey Bros. & Nicholls* (1990)?

7 Is there any relevance to promissory estoppel in the modern day?

8 Do the exceptions to Pinnel's rule always cover every possible problem?

1.3 INTENTION TO CREATE LEGAL RELATIONS

1.3.1 THE TWO PRESUMPTIONS
We all regularly make arrangements with each other, and we may even be doing things in return for something, and this seems as though there is consideration too.

However, we do not always intend that if we fail to keep to an agreement the other party should be able to sue us. Nor would it be sensible for the courts to be filled with actions on all of the broken promises that are ever made. My children may expect their pocket money regularly but would you want them to be able to sue if I forget to give it to them one week?

The law makes a sensible compromise by assuming that in certain situations we would usually not intend the agreement to be legally binding, while in others we usually would. The first covers social or domestic arrangements where it is presumed there is no intention to be legally bound. The second concerns commercial or business agreements where an intention to be legally bound is presumed. In either case the facts can show that the presumption should not apply. So intention is very much decided on the facts in individual cases.

1.3.2 SOCIAL AND DOMESTIC AGREEMENTS

Arrangements between family members are usually left to them to sort out themselves and are not legally binding.

BALFOUR V BALFOUR (1919)

A husband worked abroad without his wife who had to stay in England due to illness, and promised her an income of £30 per month. When the wife later petitioned for divorce her claim to this income failed. It had been made at an amicable point in their relationship, not in contemplation of divorce. It was a purely domestic arrangement beyond the scope of the court.

Where husband and wife are estranged an agreement between them may be taken as intended to be legally binding.

MERRITT V MERRITT (1970)

Here the husband had deserted his wife for another woman. An agreement that he would pay his wife an income if she paid the outstanding mortgage was held by the court to be intended to create legally-binding obligations.

Sometimes, of course, families make arrangements that appear to be business arrangements because of their character. In such cases the court will need to examine what the real purpose of the arrangement was.

JONES V PADAVATTON (1969)

A mother provided an allowance for her daughter under an agreement for the daughter to give up her high-paid job in New York, study for the bar in England and then return to practice in Trinidad where the mother lived. When the daughter was finding it difficult to manage on the allowance the mother then bought a house for her to live in, part of which the daughter could let to supplement her income. They later quarrelled and the mother sought repossession of the house. The daughter's argument that the second agreement was contractual failed. The court could find no intent.

If money has passed hands then it will not matter that the arrangement is made socially. It will be held as intended to be legally binding.

SIMPKINS V PAYS (1955)

A lodger and two members of the household entered competitions in the lodger's name but paying equal shares of the entry money and on the understanding that they would share any winnings.

If parties put their financial security at risk for an agreement, then it must have been intended that the agreement should be legally binding.

PARKER V CLARKE (1960)

A young couple were persuaded by an older couple to sell their house to move in with them, with the promise also that they would inherit property on the death of the old couple. When the two couples eventually fell out and the young couple was asked to leave their action for damages succeeded. Giving up their security was an indication that the arrangement was intended to be legally binding

1.3.3 COMMERCIAL AND BUSINESS AGREEMENTS

An arrangement made within a business context is presumed to be intended to be legally binding unless evidence can show a different intent.

KEY FACTS

- Consideration is 'the price for which the promise of the other is bought' – *Dunlop* v *Selfridge* (1915)
- Executory consideration is where the consideration is yet to change hands, executed consideration is consideration that has already passed.
- Consideration need not be adequate – *Thomas* v *Thomas* (1842)
- But it must be sufficient, that is it must be real, tangible and have value – *Chappel* v *Nestlé Co.* (1960)
- Consideration must not be past – *Re McArdle* (1951)
- Except where it is a service that has been requested – *Lampleigh* v *Braithwaite* (1615)
- A person seeking to sue on a contract must have given consideration under it – *Tweddle* v *Atkinson* (1861)
- Carrying out an existing contractual obligation cannot be consideration for a new promise – *Stilk* v *Myrick* (1809)
  - Unless something extra is added to the contract – *Hartley* v *Ponsonby* (1857)
  - Or a third party's interests are involved – *Pao On* v *Lau Yiu Long* (1980)
  - Or an extra benefit is to be gained – *Willams* v *Roffey Bros. & Nicholls Contractors Ltd* (1990)
- Part payment of a debt can never satisfy the debt as a whole – *Pinnel's Case* (1602)
- Although there are exceptions to the rule including accord and satisfaction (where the debt is paid in a different form), and estoppel (where a party waiving rights is prevented from going back on the promise because of reliance by the other party) – *Central London Properties Trust* v *High Trees House Ltd* (1947)

FIGURE 1.6 *Key fact chart for consideration*

EDWARDS V SKYWAYS LTD (1969)

An attempt to avoid making an agreed ex gratia payment in a redundancy failed. Although ex gratia indicates no pre-existing liability to make the payment, the agreement to pay it once made was binding.

The offer of free gifts where this is to promote the business can still be held to be legally binding.

ESSO PETROLEUM CO. LTD V COMMISSIONERS OF CUSTOMS AND EXCISE (1976)

Esso gave free World Cup coins with every four gallons of petrol purchased. The Customs and Excise wanted to claim purchase tax from the transaction. Since Esso were clearly trying to gain more business from the promotion there was held to be intention to be bound by the arrangement.

However, it is possible for the agreement to contain no intention to be legally binding where that is specifically stated in the agreement itself.

JONES V VERNONS' POOLS LTD (1938)

The Pools company inserted a clause on all coupons stating that 'the transaction should not give rise to any legal relationship ... but be binding in honour only ...'. When a punter claimed that the company had lost his winning coupon and sought payment he failed. The clause prevented any legal claim.

The same type of principle applies with so-called comfort letters. Although such letters are worded so that they appear almost to amount to a guarantee, they do not and will not give rise to legal obligations.

KLEINWORT BENSON LTD V MALAYSIAN MINING CORPORATION (1989)

Kleinwort lent £10 million to Metals Ltd, a subsidiary of MMC. The parent company would not guarantee this loan but issued a comfort letter stating their intention to ensure Metals had sufficient funds for repayment. When Metals went out

KEY FACTS

- There are two rebuttable presumptions – that in social and domestic arrangements there is no intention to be legally bound, and in commercial and business dealings there is

- An arrangement between husband and wife will not normally be legally binding – *Balfour* v *Balfour* (1919)

- Unless the couple is estranged – *Merritt* v *Merritt* (1970)

- An agreement will be binding where the parties have spent money on it – *Simpkin* v *Pays* (1955)

- And also where they have acted to their detriment – *Parker* v *Clarke* (1960)

- An agreement made in a business context is usually binding – *Edwards* v *Skyways Ltd* (1969)

- Even where free gifts are promised to promote sales – *Esso* v *Commissioners of Custom and Excise* (1976)

- Some agreements are binding in honour only – *Jones* v *Vernons Pools Ltd* (1938)

- Comfort letters create no legal obligations – *Kleinwort Benson* v *Malaysia Mining Corporation* (1989)

- Sometimes the judges take a pragmatic view of an agreement – *Julian* v *Furby* (1982)

FIGURE 1.7 *Key facts chart for intention to create legal relations*

of business without repaying Kleinwort the latter's action based on the comfort letter failed. If they had wanted a guarantee they should have insisted on one.

Sometimes judges will find that parts of an agreement are intended to be legally binding, and other parts are not.

JULIAN v FURBY (1982)

An experienced plasterer helped his daughter and son-in-law to alter and furnish their house. When the couple split up he sued the son-in-law for the price of the materials he had bought and also for his labour. The court agreed that there should be payment for the materials but not for the man's labour which was felt to be no more than any father would do for his daughter.

activity

SELF ASSESSMENT QUESTIONS

1 How do courts decide if an agreement is intended to be legally binding?

2 Why should an agreement within a family not be legally binding?

3 How will businesses try to get round the rules on intention?

4 When might a husband be bound by an agreement with his wife?

5 Consider whether there is an intention to be legally bound in the following situations:

A Alan agrees that he will buy his son a book in return for mowing the lawns.

B James agrees to take his secretary Dawn out for a meal for getting an urgent job finished quickly at very short notice.

C I ask my daughter to give up her part-time job for a week to proof read a draft of a textbook and promise to pay her.

D Skinny Co. usually give their employees a £50 Christmas box but this year they have decided against it.

CHAPTER 2

OTHER FACTORS AFFECTING FORMATION

2.1 FORM

Form is not an aspect of contract law that most A Level syllabuses now concern themselves with. However, it can in some instances be an important issue, and it is therefore worth knowing at least the basic rules. It is not, however, likely to be a major part of any A Level Contract exam.

2.1.1 THE GENERAL CHARACTER OF CONTRACTS

It is generally fair to say that with the majority of contracts the form in which they are made is not an issue. We make contracts every day, and probably all day long, without ever contemplating their legal significance and certainly without worrying about the specific form in which we have created them.

We can distinguish between 'simple contracts' and 'speciality' contracts.

In the case of simple contracts these can be made orally, in writing, or possibly even be implied by conduct. An example is where an auctioneer completes a contract at an auction by the fall of his hammer (although this might also be accompanied by words such as 'sold to the lady in the red dress').

● With contracts made in this way there is no requirement for there to be any particular form.

● Evidence of compliance with the basic rules of

formation will be sufficient to make such contracts enforceable in law.

However, speciality contracts are required to have been created in a specific form to gain their validity.

● The 'form' in question will be to do with being written or evidenced in writing.

● This formal requirement indicates that a higher level of proof of the existence of the contract is required.

● Speciality contracts are concerned with more significant property such as land or other transferable interests.

Speciality contracts come in one of three types:

● agreements which must be created in the form of a deed

● agreements which must be made in writing

● agreements which need only to be evidenced in writing e.g. in a memorandum

2.1.2 AGREEMENTS WHICH MUST BE CREATED IN THE FORM OF A DEED TO BE VALID

Traditionally any transaction that involved the conveyance of land or an interest in land had to be in a deed in order to be valid.

A deed was a document which was drafted on parchment, signed by the parties to the agreement, an impression was made in sealing wax on the document, which was then delivered up by hand. In this way it was signed, sealed and delivered.

Under the Law of Property (Miscellaneous Provisions) Act 1989 s.1(1), the requirement that the document be 'sealed' has been abolished. Now the document will be valid if it is made clear on the face of it that it is intended to act as a deed, and is validly executed. A new requirement is for the document to be formally witnessed, but this is no more than was already standard practice anyway.

A deed is also the standard means used for transferring gifts that are unsupported by consideration. The classic example here is charitable gifts.

2.1.3 CONTRACTS THAT MUST BE IN WRITING TO BE VALID

A number of these exist. They are usually identified in a statute that will also outline the requirements.

They include cheques and other negotiable instruments. They also include credit agreements that must be in the prescribed form and conform to the requirements of the Consumer Credit Act 1974.

Finally they include sale or disposition of other interests in land. Section 40 Law of Property Act 1925 and the doctrine of part performance formerly governed these. Now, however, such contracts come under s.2(1) Law of Property (Miscellaneous Provisions) Act 1989 which provides that

'a contract for the sale or other disposition of an interest in land can only be made in writing and only by incorporating all the terms which the parties have expressly agreed in one document or, where contracts are exchanged, in each'

The potential problem created by the repeal of the doctrine of part performance is that it makes it less easy for equity to intervene where there is a dispute over form.

2.1.4 AGREEMENTS NEEDING ONLY EVIDENCE IN WRITING TO BE VALID

These are those contracts that are governed by the Statute of Frauds 1677.

Following the repeal of s.40 Law of Property Act the only contract requiring evidence in writing is a contract of guarantee. This is a promise made by one party to a second party to meet the debts of a third party in the event of the third party defaulting on the debt.

The basic rule is under s.4 Statute of Frauds that requires the agreement to be evidenced in a written note or memorandum. This memorandum must:

● be signed by the guarantor (or his/her agent);

● clearly be a signed admission of the existence of a contract; and

● contain all the material terms of the agreement, including the identities of all the parties involved and the precise subject matter of the contract.

The guarantee is enforceable provided it is evidenced in writing in this way.

2.2 PRIVITY OF CONTRACT

2.2.1 THE BASIC RULE AND ITS EFFECTS

This is possibly the most contentious of all the rules of contract. Simply stated it is that any person who is not a party to the contract can neither sue nor be sued under it.

This is very similar to the proposition in consideration, that a person who has not given consideration under the contract cannot sue or be sued. We have already seen this in operation in *Tweddle v Atkinson* (1861). Here even though the claimant was named in a written agreement he was unable to claim an enforceable third party right.

The rule is an old one.

SELF ASSESSMENT QUESTIONS

1 In what circumstances will form be an issue in determining the contractual validity of an agreement?

2 What is the common thread that runs between agreements requiring specific form?

3 What is a deed? In what ways has the required form of a deed changed in recent years?

4 What is the common characteristic of contracts that must be created in written form?

5 What exactly is a guarantee?

KEY FACTS

- Simple contracts can be made orally, in writing or by conduct
- Speciality contracts will need to be created by the appropriate form or method
- They mostly have to do with land or interests in land
- Under the Law Reform (Miscellaneous Provisions) Act 1989 transfers of land must be in the form of a deed, having been signed and witnessed
- Cheques and other negotiable instruments will need to be in writing
- Guarantees need to be evidenced in writing

FIGURE 2.1 *Key fact chart for form*

PRICE V EASTON (1833)

Here Easton had agreed with a third party that if that third party did specified work for him he would pay £19 to Price. While the work was completed by the third party Easton failed to pay Price who then sued. Price's claim was unsuccessful. He had given no consideration for the arrangement and was not therefore a party to the contract.

The modern statement of the rule is found in Lord Haldane's judgement in:

DUNLOP PNEUMATIC TYRE CO. LTD V SELFRIDGE & CO. LTD (1915)

In the contract Dew & Co., wholesalers, agreed to buy tyres from Dunlop. They did so on the express undertaking that they would not sell below certain fixed prices. They also undertook to obtain the same price fixing agreements from their clients. Dew sold tyres on to Selfridge on these terms but Selfridge broke the agreement and sold tyres at discount prices. Dunlop sought an injunction. They failed for lack of privity. In HL Lord Haldane said, 'only a person who is a party to a contract can sue on it. Our law knows nothing of a *jus quaesitum tertio* arising by way of contract. Such a right may be conferred by way of property, as, for example, under a trust, but it cannot be conferred on a stranger to a contract as a right to enforce the contract *in personam* …'.

The rule has a number of consequences:

- A person receiving goods as a gift may be unable to sue personally where the goods are defective.

- In such a case it may prove embarrassing to try to enlist the help of the actual purchaser of the goods.

- Even if the purchaser does sue (s)he may be able to recover only for their own loss, not necessarily the loss suffered by the donee of the gift.

- The rule may well prevent enforcement of services that have already been paid for. This was the case in *Price* v *Easton* (1833).

- The rule may also mean that a benefactor's express wishes are denied, as was the case in *Tweddle* v *Atkinson* (1861).

- More dramatically still, in commercial contracts, as Lord Dunedin said in *Dunlop* v *Selfridge* (1915) 'the effect … is to make it possible for a person to snap his fingers at a bargain definitely made, a bargain not unfair in itself, and which the person seeking to enforce it has a legitimate interest to enforce…'.

2.2.2 EXCEPTIONS TO THE STRICT APPLICATION OF THE DOCTRINE

Not surprisingly, the rule is unpopular and many attempts have been made to avoid the harsh effects of the rule on enforcing third party rights in a contract. This is done using a variety of means, none of which has affected the basic rule. This remains intact.

Statutory exceptions

Parliament is not bound by the strict rules of contract in enacting new provisions, and so there are a number of statutory inroads into the rule.

Section 148 (7) of the Road Traffic Act 1988 obliges a motorist to take out third party liability insurance. Another motorist who is involved in an accident with this motorist can then rely upon it. The insurance is enforceable despite the fact that the other motorist lacks any privity in the insurance contract.

By the Married Woman's Property Act 1882 a husband can take out insurance in his own name but for the benefit of his wife and children. They can enforce the terms of the insurance although they are not parties to the contract.

However, the courts will not allow an Act to be used for an incorrect purpose.

BESWICK V BESWICK (1968)

Here a widow was trying to enforce an agreement between her husband and her nephew for the latter to provide her with a weekly annuity on the death of the former. The agreement was a condition in the sale of her husband's business to the nephew. The widow clearly lacked privity to the agreement and had provided no consideration for it. Her attempt to use a provision in s.56 of the Law of Property Act 1925 that referred to 'other property' failed. The reasoning was that the Act referred only to real property (land or interests in land) and could not be applied to purely personal property.

Trust law

Despite lacking privity a party identifying third party rights under a contract may be able to show that a trust of the rights is created in his or her favour.

GREGORY & PARKER V WILLIAMS (1817)

Parker owed money to both Gregory and Williams. Since he could see no way of organising settlement himself he assigned all of his property to Williams on the understanding that Williams would then pay off the debt to Gregory. Williams failed to pay over the money to Gregory who, because he was not a party to the agreement, was unable to sue on it in contract law. The court was nevertheless prepared to accept that a trust of the money had been created in Gregory's favour, which was then enforceable against Williams.

However, the court will not accept that a trust is created unless the claimant can show an express intention that he should receive the benefit.

LES AFFRETEURS REUNIS S.A. V WALFORD (1919) (WALFORD'S CASE)

Walford was a broker who negotiated an agreement between a charter party and the owner of a vessel, but was obviously not a party to the agreement. The agreement contained a stipulation that Walford should receive a 3 per cent commission from the shipowners. They failed to pay. The court was prepared to accept that a trust was created only because he was named.

The courts will not in any case accept that a trust is created unless the interest claimed conforms to the general character of a trust.

GREEN V RUSSELL (1959)

Here an employer had insurance in his own name that also covered certain employees including Green. There was, however, no such requirement in the contract of employment. When both were killed in a fire CA concluded that there was no trust in favour of Green since the employer could have surrendered the policy at any time.

In this way the cases in which a claimant might claim that a trust is created are probably quite limited.

Restrictive covenants

This is another device created by equity by which a party selling land retains certain rights over the use of the land. The restriction thus created must be a negative one, for example preventing use of the land for business purposes.

The covenant is said to run with the land. So, if properly created, it will bind subsequent purchasers of the land even though there is no privity between them and the original seller. This will apply even if the land retained by the original seller has also been sold on.

TULK V MOXHAY (1848)

Tulk owned land in London that he sold with an express undertaking that it would never be used to build property on. The land was then re-sold on numerous occasions, each time subject to the same undertaking. Moxhay bought it knowing of the limitation but nevertheless intended to build on it. Tulk successfully sought an injunction. The court accepted that it would be against conscience for Moxhay to buy knowing of the restriction.

The device, though, operates only in respect of land. The courts have resisted attempts to extend the principle to cover other property. So it will not be available merely as a method of controlling pricing of goods.

TADDY V STERIOUS (1904)

Tobacco manufacturers sold tobacco to wholesalers with an express clause in the contract requiring that retailers should not sell below fixed prices. When this agreement was breached the manufacturer tried to argue that *Tulk* v *Moxhay* (1848) applied. The court rejected this argument out of hand.

The rule in **Dunlop *v* Lambert** *(1939)*

This common law rule states that a remedy can be granted notwithstanding the absence of privity of contract 'where no other would be available to a person sustaining loss which under a rational legal system ought to be compensated by the person who caused it...'.

The rule has recently been both approved and applied.

DARLINGTON B.C. V WILTSHIER NORTHERN LTD (1995)

The council wanted a new recreation centre. In order to avoid certain financial restraints it was under it hired Morgan Grenfell who in turn hired the builders of the new centre. A collateral agreement provided for Morgan Grenfell to pay the builders, Wiltshier Northern Ltd, and for the council to reimburse Morgan Grenfell and for Morgan Grenfell to assign all rights they might have against Wiltshier to the council. When £2 million worth of defects was discovered in the building the council obviously wished to sue. Morgan Grenfell would be unable to recover in tort having no proprietary interest in the building. The council would normally be prevented from suing because of their lack of privity in the building contract. However, Lord Diplock applied the principle in *Dunlop* v *Lambert* (1839) and allowed the action. The justification was that Morgan Grenfell was the fiduciary of the council and had assigned their rights in the building contract over to the council.

Privity of estate in leases

Where an owner of land creates a lease in favour of another person the terms of the lease are in effect contractual obligations. These terms are more usually known as the 'covenants' of the lease and are enforceable by both parties because there is privity between them.

The principle of 'privity of estate' means that the landowner will be able to enforce the covenants also against anybody to whom the holder of the lease assigns their lease. By ss.141 and 142 Law of Property Act 1925 a tenant will also be able to enforce covenants of the lease against a new owner of the freehold, as will that new landlord be able to enforce them against the tenant.

Procedural rules

In very rare instances rules of procedure have been used to get round the effects of the doctrine of privity. Such a course has only succeeded because to do so has corresponded to the actual promise made, and because all of the parties are present in the court.

SNELLING V JOHN G. SNELLING LTD (1973)

Three brothers were all directors of their own company, John G. Snelling Ltd, which was financed by loans from the three brothers. When the company borrowed money from a finance company the three brothers entered an agreement with one another that until such time as the finance company loan was repaid if any of them resigned their directorship in the company they would forfeit the amount of their own loan to the company. The company was not a party to this agreement. One brother later did leave the company and sued the company for his loan. The remaining two brothers applied to join the company as defendants and counterclaimed on the basis of the agreement reached between the three brothers. The court upheld their argument. Even though the company was not a party to the agreement the brothers and the company were in many ways the same. A stay of execution of the brother's claim was the appropriate order.

The so-called 'holiday cases'

We will discuss the issue of recovery for mental distress and the 'holiday cases' at a later stage under damages. However, significant development was made in these cases in respect of third party rights.

JACKSON V HORIZON HOLIDAYS (1975)

Mr Jackson had booked a 'family holiday' which fell far short of the contract description. He sued the holiday company not only on his own behalf but for his family also. The company, while accepting liability, disputed that they should pay damages in respect of the family. HL held that the loss of enjoyment suffered by the family was in effect a loss to the contracting party himself. He had paid for a 'family holiday' but not received it. Damages were awarded on this basis. This would appear to be straining the law a long way, albeit in order to achieve a just result.

The courts, though, have indicated that this method of getting round the doctrine of precedent is confined to 'holiday contracts'. See later *Woodar Investment Development Ltd* v *Wimpey Construction (UK) Ltd* (1980) where the House of Lords, while not expressly overruling the *Jackson* case, held that there was no general principle allowing a party to a contract to sue on behalf of third parties injured by a breach of the contract. Lord Wilberforce's view was that *Jackson* fell into a specialist group of contracts involving families where it was intended that the benefit of the contract be shared between the members of the family.

Protecting third parties in exclusion clauses

A party to a contract can include an exclusion clause or a limitation clause in a contract. Traditionally, however, a sub-contractor would be unable to claim the benefit of the exclusion clause, even if named under it.

SCRUTTONS LTD V MIDLAND SILICONES LTD (1962)

A shipping company was carrying a drum of chemicals for the claimants under a contract containing a clause limiting damages in the event of breach to $500. Stevedores sub-contracted to the shipping company did $1800 worth of damage, sought to rely on the limitation clause and failed owing to lack of privity. However, Lord Reid did feel that there could be 'success in agency if the bill of lading makes it clear that the stevedore is intended to be protected by the provisions...'.

Despite this there have been situations in which such a third party has been able to claim cover under an exclusion clause despite lacking privity.

> ### NEW ZEALAND SHIPPING CO. LTD V A. M. SATTERTHWAITE & CO. LTD (1975) (THE EURYMEDON)
>
> In this PC case the stevedores were able to succeed and rely on an exclusion clause in a similar action. The reasoning given by Lord Wilberforce was that the stevedores were identified as agents in the contract.

Collateral contracts

This is a mechanism that might succeed when a claimant complains that a contract has been formed through reliance on a collateral promise made by a third party who is not a party to the contract.

> ### SHANKLIN PIER V DETEL PRODUCTS LTD (1951)
>
> Owners of a pier were assured by Detel's representatives that their paint was suitable to paint the pier and would last a minimum of seven years. Relying on this assurance the pier owners instructed their painting contractors to paint the pier with Detel's paint. The paint was in fact unsuitable and peeled. The court held that Detel was liable on the promise despite an apparent lack of privity in the painting contract.

Agency, assignment and negotiable instruments

All of the exceptions we have so far considered are enforceable either because of principles contained in individual cases or because they rely on areas of law other than contract, such as trust law.

There are, however, three major exceptions to the doctrine which are outside the A Level syllabuses. A detailed analysis is therefore not necessary, but they are worth knowing. They are the rules of agency, the process of assignment, and the rules regarding negotiable instruments.

- Where one party acts as an agent for another (known as the principal), the agent can make and carry out contracts with a third party on the principal's behalf. The significance of this is that the agent can make agreements by which the principal is bound despite the apparent lack of privity. Where all of the appropriate rules are complied with then the principal and the third party are able to sue and be sued by each other under the contract made by the agent.

- Assignment is a specific system devised for the transfer of property rights. This may be appropriate for instance with debts. If the assignment of the debt conforms to the proper rules of assignment then the party to whom the debt is assigned can sue the debtor despite the apparent lack of privity between them.

- Negotiable instruments were originally a device of merchant traders. The rules devised by the merchants were eventually given statutory force in the Bills of Exchange Act 1882. Possibly the most common form of negotiable instrument with which we are familiar in modern times is the cheque. By various processes it is then possible to transfer ownership of the property identified in the instrument, in the case of a cheque a sum of money.

POINTS FOR DISCUSSION

REFORM AND RIGHTS OF THIRD PARTIES IN CONTRACTS

We have already seen at the beginning of this section some of the harsh effects that the doctrine of privity can have in preventing third parties from enforcing rights which appear to have been granted them in contracts.

The fact that judges have been prepared to allow

so many exceptions to the basic rule is a fair indication of a general dissatisfaction with the operation of the doctrine. In many cases indeed judges have themselves called for legislative reform, particularly because of the complexities that are caused by there being so many different exceptions.

This is not a new feeling and as early as 1937 the Law Revision Committee was recommending reforms. In simple terms they suggested that third parties should be able to enforce provisions in a contract which 'by its express terms purports to confer a benefit on a third party...'.

More recently the Law Commission in its *Consultation Paper No. 121* argued that there should be a 'third party rule' in privity. Nevertheless, it rejected various proposed courses of action:

● Extending the number of exceptions – rejected because there were already too many.

● Leaving enforcement of third party rights to promisees under the contract – rejected as too onerous a burden and no guarantee it would happen.

● Introducing a general rule preventing privity from denying any third party rights – rejected as too vague, and might 'open the floodgates' to claims.

So the Law Commission favoured a more precise rule whereby third parties would only be able to enforce rights identified in the terms of the contract as intending to confer a legally enforceable benefit on the third party.

Even here the Law Commission felt that parties to the contract should be able to vary such terms where the contract specifically allowed for such variation.

The Law Commission has subsequently prepared a draft bill in a further report *No. 242*. Its major provision is contained in s.1(1) by which:

'*a person who is not a party to a contract (in this Act referred to as a third party) may in his own right enforce the contract if: (a) the contract contains an express term to that effect; or (b) subject to subsection (2) the contract purports to confer a benefit on the third party.*'

The first ground under subsection (a) is self-explanatory. The second ground is subject to subsection (2). It states that ground (b) will be unavailable to a third party where 'on the proper construction of the contract it appears that the parties did not intend the contract to be enforceable by a third party...'. In consequence it seems only those rights actually conferred by the contract can be enforced.

One final recommendation of the Law Commission here is the abolition of the rule that consideration must move from the promisee that would otherwise defeat the reform.

These reforms are now in the Contract (Rights of Third Parties) Act 1999. The Act contains some amendments from the Law Commission's draft bill. Certain types of contract are excluded, notably those contracts where other legislation already applies. Another inclusion is a rule preventing a third party from suing an employee who is in breach of his contract of employment. This is to protect workers where they take legitimate industrial action. Another exception is the 'statutory contract' under s.14 of the Companies Act 1985, which gives shareholders the right to sue officers of the company on issues arising from the memorandum and articles of association.

2.3 CAPACITY

2.3.1 INTRODUCTION

It would probably make more sense to refer in this section to incapacity rather than capacity since it involves limitations to the general assumption that all parties to a contract have the power to enter into it.

The law ultimately is concerned with promoting freedom of contract. In this way the logic of rules

activity

SELF ASSESSMENT QUESTIONS

1 What are the major justifications for the rule on privity of contract?

2 What is the connection between the doctrine of privity and the requirement of consideration in a contract?

3 In what ways is the doctrine of privity unfair?

4 Why is it not possible to argue that whenever a third party right is identified in a contract it automatically creates a trust?

5 Other than where Parliament grants enforceable third party rights by statute, what are the most effective exceptions to the basic rule on privity?

6 To what extent are the Law Commission's suggested reforms likely to address the problems of all third parties affected by the doctrine of privity?

KEY FACTS

- The basic doctrine of privity is that nobody can sue or be sued under a contract who is not a party to the contract – *Dunlop* v *Selfridge* (1915)

- Put another way, nobody can enforce a contract who has not provided consideration under the contract – *Tweddle* v *Atkinson* (1861)

- Since the rule unfairly prevents third parties identified as gaining rights under a contract from enforcing those rights a number of exceptions to the strict rule have developed:

  – Statutory exceptions as with third party insurance under the Road Traffic Act 1988

  – Stating that a trust is created in favour of the third party – *Gregory & Parker* v *Williams* (1817) – but only so long as the interest conforms to the character of a trust – *Green* v *Russell* (1959)

  – Restrictive covenants – *Tulk* v *Moxhay* (1848) – but only in relation to land, not other interests – *Taddy* v *Sterious* (1904)

  – The rule in *Dunlop* v *Lambert* (1939) – *Darlington B.C.* v *Wiltshier Northern Ltd* (1995)

  – Privity of estate in leases

  – Procedural rules – *Snelling* v *John G. Snelling Ltd* (1973)

  – The 'holiday cases' – *Jackson* v *Horizon Holidays* (1975)

  – Protection given to third parties in exclusion clauses – *New Zealand Shipping Co.* v *Satterthwaite & Co. Ltd* (1975)

  – Collateral contracts – *Shanklin Pier* v *Detel Products Ltd* (1951)

  – Agency, assignment and negotiable instruments

  – Now parliament has legislated to enable third parties to enforce rights that they are given under a contract

FIGURE 2.2 *Key fact chart for privity of contract*

on capacity is aimed at protecting certain types of person who may enter a contract, either for their own protection or for the protection of the party who contracts with them. It will do so to avoid an unfair advantage being taken by a party in a superior position. The law does not necessarily prevent such people from entering contracts, but the consequences both for the party who lacks full capacity and the party with whom they deal may be different.

The law sensibly distinguishes between natural persons and artificial persons, the latter being corporations of whatever type.

In the case of natural persons there are three classes that may be affected by capacity: people who are drunk, mental patients, and minors. The last group is probably the most important.

2.3.2 MINORS' CONTRACTS

The Family Law Reform Act 1969 made some significant changes to the law on minority. Firstly, prior to the Act this group of people was referred to as 'infants' rather than 'minors'. Secondly, the group comprised all those under the age of 21 whereas now it comprises those under 18.

One effect of the Act may have been to temporarily reduce the significance of the rules relating to minors since they now applied to a much smaller group of young people. However, since 1969 time has moved on again. Young people are more mobile and many more are probably now living away from their parents. So minors' contracts may be important once more.

Minors' contracts are divided into three categories representing the consequences for the parties to the contract in each case. They are:

● Contracts which are valid and therefore enforceable against the minor.

● Contracts which the minor may enter but can also back out of if required and which are therefore voidable.

● Contracts that are unenforceable against the minor and which in practical terms therefore may be difficult for him or her to make.

The nature of these categories means that they can and should serve as much as a guide for the adults who contract with minors as for the protection of the minors themselves.

Valid or enforceable contracts

Those contracts that a party may feel secure in making with a minor themselves divide into two further categories:

Contracts for necessaries

The common law traditionally accepted that minors should pay for those goods and services actually supplied to them that are necessaries according to their station in life.

CHAPPLE V COOPER (1844)

A minor whose husband had recently died contracted with undertakers for his funeral. She later refused to pay the cost of the funeral claiming her incapacity to contract. The court held her liable to pay the bill. The funeral was for her private benefit and was a necessary as she had an obvious obligation to bury her dead husband.

The purpose and effect of such a rule is clear. It is to allow minors to enter into contracts beneficial to them, but at the same time to prevent unscrupulous businesses from taking advantage of their youth and inexperience.

Necessary does not have to mean the same as necessity. As Baron Alderson said in *Chapple* v *Cooper*, 'the proper cultivation of the mind is as expedient as the support of the body…'. So it can be more than just food and clothing. As a result what is a necessary may differ according to the particular minor.

The courts have established a two-part test for determining what is a necessary and therefore what will be enforceable in the individual case:

● The goods or services must be necessary

according to the 'station in life' of the particular minor.

- The goods or services must also suit the actual requirements of the minor at the time of the contract.

NASH V INMAN (1908)

A Cambridge undergraduate, the son of an architect, was supplied with clothes to the value of £122, including 11 'fancy waistcoats' priced at 2 guineas each (£2.10) by a Savile Row tailor. While the supply of such clothing could be appropriate to the station in life of the undergraduate, the contract was not enforceable because facts showed that the minor was already adequately supplied with clothes. Therefore those that the tailor supplied could not be classed as necessaries.

Clearly then what is a necessary varies according to the minor's background. Thus, what is a 'necessary' for the son or daughter of the managing director of a large public company may not be a 'necessary' for the son or daughter of the car park attendant in the same company.

But of course the supplier will not only have to demonstrate that the goods supplied are necessaries in relation to the particular minor, but that the minor also has need of them at the time of the contract.

Under s.3 Sale of Goods Act 1979, 'Where necessaries are sold and delivered to a minor, or to a person who by reason of mental incapacity or drunkenness is incompetent to contract, he must pay a reasonable price therefor.'

This then leads on to two further points concerning necessaries:

- The minor is only liable to pay for goods that are actually supplied. This may mean that executory contracts are unenforceable.

- The minor is even then only obliged to pay 'a reasonable price'. Therefore even though the supplier is able to enforce the contract (s)he may be unable to recover the actual contract price.

One final point concerns contracts containing harsh or onerous terms. Even though a minor has been supplied with necessaries according to the established tests the contract may still be unenforceable if the terms of the contract are prejudicial to the minor's interests.

FAWCETT V SMETHURST (1914)

The minor hired a car in order to transport luggage. This, on the face of it, was a necessary. Nevertheless, under a term in the contract the minor was to be held absolutely liable for any damage to the car regardless of how it was caused, on which basis the court felt the contract to be too onerous and therefore unenforceable against the minor.

Beneficial contracts of service

The common law again sensibly concludes that the minor may need to support himself or herself financially, and therefore must have the capacity to enter contracts of employment. School leaving age is 16 and this is two years below the age of majority.

Such a contract would be prima facie valid and therefore enforceable. However, from an early time it was accepted that the contract would only be binding on the minor if on balance the terms of the contract were substantially to the benefit of the minor. The court would have to look at the whole contract. The fact that some of the terms act to the minor's detriment will not automatically invalidate the contract of service providing that it still operates mostly for the minor's benefit.

CLEMENTS V LONDON AND NORTH WESTERN RAILWAY COMPANY (1894)

The minor had taken up employment as a porter with the railway company. He agreed to join the company's insurance scheme as a result of which he would relinquish any rights he might have under the Employer's Liability Act 1880. In the event of an accident the statutory scheme would be of greater benefit to the minor since it covered a wider range of accidents for which compensation could be claimed, although the levels of compensation were lower. When the minor tried to claim that he was not bound by the employer's scheme he failed. Viewing the whole contract on balance it was generally to his benefit.

By comparison, where the contract is made up of terms, which are predominantly detrimental to the minor, then the court will have no choice but to invalidate the contract as a whole.

DE FRANCESCO V BARNUM (1890)

Here a 14-year-old girl entered into a seven-year apprenticeship with De Francesco to be taught stage dancing. By the apprenticeship deed the girl agreed that she would be at De Francesco's total disposal during the seven years, and that she would accept no professional engagements except with his express approval. He was under no obligation to maintain her or to employ her. In the event that he did employ her the scales of pay were set extremely low. She was also obliged not to marry except with his permission. Finally De Francesco was able to terminate their arrangement without notice whenever he wished. When the girl was set to accept other work De Francesco's action to prevent it failed. The provisions of the apprenticeship deed were held to be unfair and unenforceable against her. They were not substantially for her benefit.

As can be seen from the last case, the principle has not been limited in its application to contracts of service only but has been extended in its application to cover contracts of apprenticeship, education and training, since it is to the general advantage of a minor that (s)he should secure the means of acquiring a livelihood. During this century the courts have taken an even more progressive view of those circumstances which can be classed as a beneficial contract of service.

DOYLE V WHITE CITY STADIUM LTD (1935)

Here the principle was extended to cover a contract between a minor who was a professional boxer and the British Boxing Board of Control. By the agreement the minor would lose his 'purse' (payment for the fight) if he were disqualified. The agreement was held to be binding on the minor since it was not only to encourage clean fighting but also proficiency in boxing, and was therefore for the benefit of the minor.

CHAPLIN V LESLIE FREWIN (PUBLISHERS) LTD (1966)

In this case the principle was extended to a contract to write an autobiography.
This was held to be similar to a contract for services and was beneficial to the minor, and so was binding on him.

It follows that, since contracts for necessaries and beneficial contracts of service are enforceable against the minor, if the goods or service are not necessaries or if the contract of service is not beneficial then these contracts are voidable by the minor.

Voidable contracts

This category of contracts made by minors refers to those contracts which, though the minor might enter with perfect validity, he or she may nevertheless avoid by repudiating his or her obligations under the contract while still a minor or within a reasonable time after reaching the age of 18.

The common feature of such contracts is that they involve subject matter of some permanency. So they are otherwise known as contracts of continuous or recurring obligations. They involve long-term interests and the law sensibly considers that, while a minor should be able to enter such contracts, (s)he should also be in a position to repudiate all obligations and avoid further liability if so desired, providing the repudiation occurs sufficiently early.

There are four principal classes of contracts falling within this category. They are:

● contracts to lease property

● contracts to purchase shares in a company

● contracts to enter a partnership

● contracts of marriage settlement

It is clearly the case that such contracts are voidable by the minor because of their potentially onerous nature. Nevertheless, if the minor chooses not to repudiate the contract then (s)he will obviously be bound by all of the obligations falling under the contract, e.g. a minor will be bound by the usual covenants in a lease, and will be bound also by outstanding amounts owed on shares.

Whether the minor has repudiated in sufficient time to avoid the contract is a question of fact in each case.

EDWARDS V CARTER (1893)

Here a minor sought to repudiate an agreement under a marriage settlement by which he agreed to transfer the money he would inherit from his father's will to the trustees under the settlement. He tried to repudiate more than a year after his father's death and four and a half years after reaching the age of majority. His argument that he was incapable of repudiating until he knew the full extent of his interest under his father's estate failed. His repudiation was too late in time to be reasonable.

Where the minor repudiates the contract before any obligations under it have arisen, then there are no problems, the contract is simply at an end. The minor cannot be sued on any obligation that would have arisen after this point.

However, where obligations have already arisen before this point then the position is not so clear-cut. Academic opinion seems to favour the view that the minor is bound by debts arising from the contract prior to the date of repudiation.

Where the minor has transferred money under the contract then it would appear that this is not recoverable unless there is a complete failure of consideration.

STEINBERG V SCALA (LEEDS) LTD (1923)

A minor was allotted company shares for which she had made the payment due for the allotment and for the first call. Since she was unable to meet the payments for the further calls she sought to repudiate the contract and also to recover the money which she had already paid over to the company. The court was happy to accept the repudiation. This meant that her name could be removed from the register of shareholders and she would bear no further liability for the company. However, the court was not prepared to grant return of her money. There was no failure of consideration. Even though she had received no dividends or attended any meetings of shareholders, she had received everything she was bound to under the contract. She had been registered as a shareholder.

In contrast the minor may succeed in recovering money paid over if (s)he can prove that (s)he has not received what was promised under the contract.

CORPE V OVERTON (1833)

Here the minor reached an agreement to enter a partnership in three months' time, and to pay £1,000 on signing the partnership deed. The minor paid a deposit of £100. When he repudiated the agreement on reaching majority he was able to recover the deposit since he had received no benefits under the agreement. There was a failure of consideration.

Void or unenforceable contracts

At one time much of the law governing minors' contracts was contained in the Infant's Relief Act 1874. After much call for change in what was a very complex piece of legislation its provisions were eventually repealed in the Minors' Contracts Act 1987. This Act took the unusual step of restoring the common law as it was before the prior Act, with some modification. As a result the law is not without its complexities.

The basic position is that, with the exception of those classes of contracts we have already discussed, a contract made by a minor will not bind him or her and is therefore unenforceable against him or her. To the sensible party contemplating entering into a contract with a minor what this means is that the range of contracts open to a minor is necessarily more limited than that available to an adult. There are therefore situations where it is prudent not to contract with a minor.

What it does not mean is that in the case of contracts other than those already considered they are devoid of legal consequences. For example:

- Even though the minor is not bound by the contract the other party still will be if such a contract is entered.

- If the minor has paid over money under the contract (s)he may be able to recover that money if there is a total failure of consideration.

- If the minor ratifies such a contract on reaching the age of 18 then the ratification will bind the minor. It is not necessary for the contract to be expressly ratified, continuing with the contract may be sufficient for ratification to be implied.

Section 1 of the Infant's Relief Act listed the classes of contract that would be void and unenforceable against the minor. These were:

- contracts for the repayment of money lent or to be lent

- contracts for goods supplied or to be supplied other than necessaries

- accounts stated, i.e. IOUs.

The law has now been somewhat modified by the Minors' Contracts Act 1987. Clearly in modern circumstances many minors might wish to take advantage of the credit and loan facilities now freely available. Such contracts would have been formerly unenforceable against the minor. Furthermore, by the Infant's Relief Act even a guarantee for a loan given by an adult close to the minor would have been unenforceable since a guarantor is said to 'stand in the shoes of the principal debtor'. So it is understandable that there would be a reluctance to offer loans or contract to supply things other than necessaries to minors. In consequence their capacity to contract was restricted.

Now under s.2 of the Minors' Contracts Act a guarantee can be enforced and minors therefore have perhaps gained greater access to credit facilities.

Minors' contracts and the role of equity

We have seen that the aims of the law governing minor's contracts is not so much to restrict or limit the ability of a minor to enter contracts but rather to protect the minor from those who might exploit him or her and take advantage of his or her youth and inexperience.

Logic dictates that the other party to the contract might in certain circumstances require protection from an unscrupulous minor who tries to take full advantage of the minor's contractual incapacity.

Traditionally, while the common law would fail such a party where the contract was unenforceable against the minor, equity could intervene with the remedy of restitution to prevent the minor's 'unjust enrichment'.

R LESLIE LTD V SHEILL (1914)

Here a minor fraudulently misrepresented his age in order to get a loan from the claimant. At common law the claimant could not recover the amount of the loan since this would have the effect of enforcing an unenforceable contract. However, had the contract involved goods then the minor would have been obliged in equity to return them. Restitution would not apply in the same way to the money lent unless the very coins or notes lent were still identifiable in the hands of the minor.

So the doctrine of restitution would still have limited application in preventing the minor's unjust enrichment.

Now the role of equity has been superseded by s.3 of the Minors' Contracts Act 1987. Under this provision:

'(1) Where –

(a) a person ('the claimant') has after the commencement of this Act entered into a contract with another ('the defendant'), and

(b) *the contract is unenforceable against the defendant (or he repudiates it) because he was a minor when the contract was made, the court may, if it is just and equitable to do so, require the defendant to transfer to the claimant any property acquired by the defendant under the contract, or any property representing it.*'

This provision means that it will no longer be vital to prove fraud against the minor to be able to recover from him or her provided there is an unjust enrichment and it is equitable for property to be recovered.

2.3.3 CAPACITY AND MENTALLY DISORDERED PERSONS

Mental patient and mental disorder has become the subject of widespread definition in modern times, and the administration of the property of mental patients subject to numerous rules. However, the contractual capacity of such people is still predominantly the subject of common law rules as with minors.

In considering the capacity of such a party to contract the first question for the court to determine is whether at the time of contracting that party was suffering from a mental disability to the extent that (s)he was incapable of understanding the nature of their act.

If this is the case then the contract will be voidable by the party with the mental disorder rather than void provided also that the other party to the agreement was aware of the disability – *Imperial Loan Co.* v *Stone* (1892).

A contract made in a period of lucidity however is binding upon the mentally incapacitated person even if they lapse back into mental illness.

Where necessaries are supplied to the person suffering a mental illness s.3 of the Sale of Goods Act 1979 applies once again and (s)he will be obliged to pay a reasonable price for the goods and it will not matter whether the other party is aware of the disability or not.

MULTIPLE CHOICE QUESTIONS

1 From the following choices select the statement which most accurately describes a contract which is enforceable against a minor:

A Brian agrees to lend Sam, aged 17, £5,000 with which Sam is to buy a car.

B James, an unemployed 17-year-old, has agreed to buy an ocean-going yacht, price £20,000.

C Terry aged 17 is hoping to become a chef. He has agreed to sign up for a catering course at his local college that will cost him £300 a term.

D Sally who is 17 has signed an agreement to lease a flat from George.

2 From the following choices select the statement which most accurately describes a contract which is void and unenforceable against a minor:

A Tim who is aged 17 has ordered a suit from Best Man Tailors. His new job in a Sales Department requires that he should wear suit and tie.

B Helen has agreed to become a partner in a business run by her friends Sarah and Melanie.

C Vanessa is 17 and she got married to Tom when she was only 16. Tom recently died in a car crash and Vanessa has contracted with Boxem, a local funeral directors, for Tom's funeral arrangements.

D Simon, aged 16, recently took out a mortgage for a flat. He did so by stating his age as 19 on the application forms.

Under Part VII of the Mental Health Act 1983 the property of a mental patient now falls under the control and jurisdiction of the courts to determine what contracts will bind the individual concerned.

2.3.4 CAPACITY AND DRUNKENNESS

When a party who is also drunk enters into a contract then, provided that they do not know the quality of their actions at the time that the contract is formed, and provided also that their drunkenness is evident to the other party to the contract, the contract is voidable by the drunken person on their return to a sober state – *Gore* v *Gibson* (1845).

However, the party making it may later ratify such a contract – *Matthews* v *Baxter* (1873).

It follows that a contract made with a party who is so drunk as not to know the quality of their act will almost always be voidable since it seems very unlikely that this would then be unknown by the other party.

The same provision concerning necessaries under the Sale of Goods Act 1979 s.3 that applies to both minors' contracts and to mental patients applies also to those who are incapacitated through drunkenness.

2.3.5 THE CAPACITY OF CORPORATIONS

A corporation is a body which is accepted in law as having its own separate legal personality. In this way a corporation can form contracts and sue or be sued in its own name.

A corporation inevitably is made up of a variety of people, whether employees or officers. But, while it is these individuals who run the business of the corporation and make contracts on behalf of the corporation, they can neither sue or be sued. An obvious example of a corporation would be a company registered under the Companies Acts. This should be contrasted with something like a local darts club. The club might represent the interests of the members and act on their behalf, but it would be an unincorporated association. Any legal liability would be on the members themselves. They would be held accountable on any contracts, and the club could not as such sue or be sued.

Incorporation inevitably creates only an artificial legal personality. A company is not a person and therefore will have more limited capacity than would an actual person. So the capacity of a corporation will depend on the way in which it has been formed.

A corporation can be formed in one of three ways:

- By Royal Charter – These charters were commonly given to the original trading companies such as the East India Company. The capacity was determined by the terms of the charter, though it was usually wide.

- By statute – Many of the old nationalised industries and bodies such as the BBC gained their status by Act of Parliament. Their capacity was obviously identified in the statute itself or in regulations made under the statute.

- By registration as a company under the Companies Acts – This would be the most common form of incorporation. Each company on formation has to register certain documents for public inspection. One of these is the memorandum of association that includes one important part called the objects clause. This is, in effect, the constitution of the company and the company may then do anything legal in furtherance of these objects or anything reasonably incidental to them provided it has granted itself the appropriate power. Going beyond the objects is known as *ultra vires* and such actions will be illegal.

SELF ASSESSMENT QUESTIONS

1 Why does the law apply different rules to contracts made by minors?

2 What exactly is a 'necessary', and how does that differ from a necessity?

3 What is the common feature between necessaries and contracts of service or of apprenticeship, education or training?

4 Why does the law allow a minor to 'avoid' the effects of a contract of continuing or recurrent obligations?

5 Why were there different results in *Steinberg* v *Scala (Leeds) Ltd* 1923 and in *Corpe* v *Overton* 1833?

6 Where a contract has been declared unenforceable against a minor, are there any consequences of the contract having been made at all?

7 In what circumstances will equity act against a minor? How different is the provision under s.3 of the Minors' Contracts Act 1987?

8 Why are there special rules on capacity when dealing with people who are drunk or who are mental patients?

9 How does the capacity of a company differ from the capacity of an individual?

KEY FACTS

- Nobody can enter a contract that does not have the capacity to do so

- Contracts made with minors are of three types: those that are enforceable against the minor; those that are voidable by the minor; those that are unenforceable against the minor.

- Contracts enforceable against the minor include those for necessaries – which are measured against the minor's station in life and current needs – *Nash* v *Inman* (1908)

- By s.3 Sale of Goods Act 1979 the minor is only obliged to pay a 'reasonable price' for goods actually delivered

- Enforceable contracts also include contracts of employment, training and apprenticeship, but only if they are substantially to the minor's benefit – *De Francesco* v *Barnum* (1890)

- Voidable contracts are long-term arrangements and include leases, purchase of shares, agreements to enter partnerships etc.

- Any money paid over is only recoverable if there is a total failure of consideration – *Steinberg* v *Scala (Leeds) Ltd* (1923)

- Unenforceable contracts include loans and goods other than necessaries

- Section 2 Minors' Contracts Act 1987 allows that guarantees of such contracts can be enforced

- Section 3 allows the other party to recover goods handed over to the minor in an unenforceable contract if it is just and equitable to do so

- Rules on incapacity also apply in the case of drunkards and mental patients and contracts made during periods of such incapacity will be unenforceable

- Corporations are also limited in the type of contracts that they can make – their limitation will depend on the type of corporation

FIGURE 2.3 *Key fact chart for capacity*

CHAPTER 3

THE OBLIGATIONS UNDER A CONTRACT OR CONTENTS OF A CONTRACT

3.1 PRE-CONTRACTUAL REPRESENTATIONS AND STATEMENTS

3.1.1 INTRODUCTION

We have so far looked at the methods of creating a contract between two parties and some other factors that may have a bearing on the making of a contract or the ability of the parties to enter into such an arrangement.

The terms of a contract are otherwise known as the contents of the contract and they represent what the parties have agreed to do or to give under the contract, in other words their obligations to each other.

Under a contract both sides will have to carry out their side of the agreement for the contract to be completed. It is commonly a failure to honour a contractual obligation, and therefore a breach of a term of the contract, that leads to a dispute.

The terms of a contract can be what the parties have expressly agreed upon, but they can also be what the law has said should be included in the contract and therefore is implied into the contract.

3.1.2 THE PROCESS OF DEFINING AND DISTINGUISHING THE EXPRESS TERMS

Terms that have been expressly agreed upon by the parties will inevitably arise from the negotiations that have taken place prior to the contract being formed and the statements that each party makes to the other at that time. Such pre-contractual statements are generally known as 'representations'.

A pre-contractual statement may be made orally or in writing or indeed may be implied by conduct, as when a contract is formed on the fall of an auctioneer's hammer. The impact that a pre-contractual statement will have on the contract will depend very much on the character of the statement and the context in which it is made.

In this way certain statements made by the parties will have no significance at all in law, while some will actually form the obligations of the contract as terms, and will therefore be enforceable or their breach will lead to remedies. The significance of certain other pre-contractual statements may depend on whether they have been falsely stated or not in which case they may be actionable.

Thus, in negotiations for the sale of my car I might make the following comments:

● It is a 1978 MGB GT.

● It is British Racing Green with gold stripes (in fact the stripe on one side is missing).

● The price is only £7,000.

● It has only had two owners, including myself.

● The previous owner only used it to go shopping (in fact the previous owner was a commercial traveller).

● It has done only 65,000 miles (in fact the true mileage is 165,000).

● It is mechanically perfect.

● It has leather upholstery.

● It has been serviced 'quite often'.

● The petrol consumption is 'reasonable'.

● It is an ace little car.

Even a non-lawyer would see the point that the weight attached to these statements varies, as will also then the contractual significance. The fact that a car is mechanically perfect may be of critical importance to the buyer, but what exactly is an 'ace little car'?

Basically any statement made at the time of the contract or in the period leading up to the contract is a representation. The effect of the statement is to represent that the information contained in the statement is true. One further aspect of the statement at this point is to represent the stated intention of the party making it.

The law rightly has to distinguish between different statements according to the relative significance they will have in law. Where a contract is reduced to writing then the terms are easily identified in the contract itself. Otherwise the following distinctions can be drawn:

● A statement made by a contracting party which may be intended to induce the other party to enter the contract, but was not intended to form part of the contract, is a representation. It may have legal consequences if certain criteria are met. It is not a term since it is not incorporated into the contract.

● A statement made by a contracting party by which (s)he intends to be bound will be incorporated and form part of the contract and is therefore a term. It will have legal consequences, though these may differ according to what type of term it is.

In all cases the court will determine what the intention of the parties was by use of an objective test – what would a reasonable person consider to be the significance of the statement?

There are also some statements made at the time the contract was formed or in the negotiations leading up to it that will attach no liability and have no legal significance. They will be treated as such because the courts can find no reliance placed upon them, or indeed because no sensible person would believe that they would induce a party to enter a contract.

They are of three different types:

Trade puffs

Puffs are the boasts or unsubstantiated claims made by, amongst others, advertisers of products or services to highlight the product they are selling. 'Carlsberg, probably the best lager in the world' is an obvious example of such a boast. It is an exaggerated claim made to boost the saleability of the product. The law will allow the producers some licence to make such statements since it is felt that nobody would be taken in by them, *simplex commendatio non obligat* (literally, a simple recommendation creates no obligation).

Where a different legal view is taken is when the statement, rather than being identifiable as a mere boast, has included a specific promise or what amounts to an assertion of fact.

CARLILL V THE CARBOLIC SMOKE BALL CO. LTD (1893)

Here the Smoke Ball company argued that the claim in the advertisement that the product would do as they suggested was a mere advertising gimmick designed to sell more of the product. Their argument failed because of the promise they made to give £100 to anybody contracting one of the prescribed illnesses after using the Smoke Ball correctly. The fact that they had stated in their advertisement that a sum of money was deposited in a bank to cover such claims was even greater proof of their intention to be bound by their promise.

Opinions

Some statements made by a party to a contract attach little legal significance because they lack any weight. An example of this is a mere opinion. An opinion does not carry any liability for the party making it because it is not based on fact.

BISSET V WILKINSON (1927)

Here a vendor was selling two blocks of land in New Zealand. The purchaser was intending to use the land for sheep farming, where it had not previously been used for that purpose, although sheep had formerly been kept on a small part of the land. The vendor told the purchaser that in his judgement the land could carry 2,000 sheep. In fact it could support nowhere near that number. The purchaser argued that the statement was an actionable misrepresentation. PC held that, owing to the inexperience on which it was based, it was nothing more than an honest opinion, and not actionable therefore.

Obviously if the statement of opinion is known to be untrue by the party expressing it then it can be actionable as a misrepresentation.

Similarly a party will be able to sue on the basis of a false opinion which has been stated by a party with specialist expertise in that field, and therefore who is in a better bargaining position than the party to whom it is addressed.

ESSO PETROLEUM CO. LTD V MARDEN (1976)

Esso acquired a site on which to build a petrol station. On the basis of professional estimates they represented to Marden, a prospective purchaser, that the filling station would have a throughput of 200,000 gallons per year. In fact the local authority refused planning permission for the proposed layout so that pumps would be at the back of the site, and access only from side roads at the rear rather than from the main road at the front of the site. Marden queried the throughput figure but Esso assured him it would be possible. Despite Marden's best efforts sales only ever reached 78,000 gallons, he lost money and was unable to pay back a loan from Esso. Esso sued for repossession and Marden counter-claimed. One of Esso's arguments was that the statement as to the likely throughput of petrol was a mere opinion. This argument failed because of their extensive expertise in the area.

activity

QUICK QUIZ

Which of the following situations do you think is likely to contain a term?

1. Jasvinder is a greengrocer. He puts a poster in his window 'The tastiest apples around'.

2. Andrew is selling his caravan. He describes it as a 'family caravan'. It has one double bed and two couches on which it would be possible for other people to sleep.

3. Annie has been given a computer for a present that she cannot use so she is selling it to Raj. Raj asks if it has a large memory and Annie says that she thinks it has.

4. Sid is selling his motorbike to Colin. He tells Colin that the bike is 'mechanically perfect'. In fact the bike breaks down as Colin is leaving Sid's house.

Type of statement	Contractual significance	Reasoning
Terms	Attach liability (and a range of remedies when they are breached)	Because they are actually incorporated into the contract, and so they become the obligations under the contract
Mere representations	Attach no liability	Because, while they may induce a party to enter into the contract, they are not incorporated into the contract and are not intended to create binding obligations
Misrepresentations	Attach liability (and a range of remedies depending on how deliberately the falsehood was made)	Because even though they are not part of the contract, being false they may have wrongly induced the other party to enter the contract thus vitiating his or her free will
Mere opinions	Attach no liability	Because the other party's opinion is no more valid than our own, and we cannot be said to rely on it
Expert opinions	Attach liability (possibly as terms if they are important enough to have been incorporated in the contract. If not they may still amount to innocent misrepresentations)	Because we do rely, and should be entitled to rely, on the opinion of experts
Trade puffs	Attach no liability	Because the law credits us with more intelligence than to take advertiser's boasts too seriously
Puffs with a specific promise attached	Attach liability *Carlill* v *Carbolic Smoke Ball Co.* (1893)	Because the promise is quite specific and so we can rely on it rather than the puff, since it creates a separate contractual relationship

FIGURE 3.1 *The differing significance attached to various types of pre-contractual statements*

Mere representations

Where a party to a contract has made a representation as to fact, which is intended to induce the other party to enter the contract but which is not intended to form part of the contract, and it is in fact true, there can be no

further contractual significance. The representation has achieved what it was supposed to do but it is accurate so it has also been complied with.

Figure 3.1 expresses the differing significance attached to various types of pre-contractual statements.

KEY
FACTS

- The express terms of a contract represent what the parties have agreed upon – these are often identified in the pre-contractual statements

- Pre-contractual statements are known as 'representations'

- The law distinguishes between:

  – statements which are sufficiently significant to be incorporated into the contract as terms

  – statements which, while not incorporated into the contract, nevertheless were intended to induce the other party to enter the contract – these are mere representations, but if they are false statements they will be misrepresentations

  – statements intended to have no contractual significance at all – these can include trade puffs and mere opinions

- A trade puff has no effect on the contract because it is a mere boast which is not taken seriously, unless some other promise is attached – *Carlill* v *The Carbolic Smoke Ball Co.* (1893)

- An opinion carries no weight unless it is made by an expert – *Bisset* v *Wilkinson* (1927)

FIGURE 3.2 *Key fact chart for pre-contractual representations and statements*

3.2 INCORPORATING EXPRESS TERMS INTO THE CONTRACT

3.2.1 FACTORS RELEVANT TO INCORPORATING TERMS

Clearly the dividing lines between some of the above categories of statements are not always obvious. Where a contract is in writing then generally the terms are as stated in the written contract. Where negotiations leading up to the contract are oral the courts have developed guidelines to determine whether a particular statement is a term of the contract or not.

In order to be a term of the contract the statement must be incorporated and form part of the contract. Whether or not a statement is incorporated as a term can depend on a number of different factors:

The importance attached to the representation
The more importance that is attached to the statement by either party then the more likely it is that it is a term. The logic of this is clear. Where a party relied on a statement to the extent

that without its inclusion as a term in the contract that party would not have entered the contract, then it must be incorporated as a term.

BIRCH V PARAMOUNT ESTATES (LIVERPOOL) LTD (1956)

Here a couple bought a new house from developers on the basis of a promise that the house would be 'as good as the show house'. In fact the house was not as good as the show house and CA concluded that the statement was so central to the agreement that it had been incorporated into the contract as a term.

In this way the effect of the statement being so important may make it a warranty of the contract rather than a misrepresentation as it might otherwise have been.

COUCHMAN V HILL (1947)

In a written agreement for the sale of a heifer (a young female cow, usually one that has not yet had a calf) the conditions of sale included a clause that lots were sold 'with all faults, imperfections and errors of description'. The sale catalogue actually described the heifer as 'unserved' (meaning not yet having been used for breeding). Prior to the making of the contract the buyer asked both the auctioneer and the seller to confirm that the heifer was unserved, and they both assured him that it was. As a result he bought the heifer. However, not long afterwards he discovered that the heifer was having a calf, and in fact it died as a result of having a calf at too young an age. CA concluded that, despite the written terms in the contract, the representation was so crucial to the buyer in making the contract that it was incorporated as a term.

Special knowledge or skill affecting the equality of bargaining strength

Thus where the statement is made without any particular expertise or specialist knowledge to back it up it is less likely to be construed as a term.

OSCAR CHESS LTD V WILLIAMS (1957)

The defendants sold a car to motor dealers for £290 describing it as a 1948 Morris 10. They honestly believed that was the correct age of the car since that was the age given in the registration documents. When the car was later discovered to be a 1939 model the motor dealers sued for breach of warranty. Their action failed. The defendants had no expertise or specialist skill, were reliant on the registration documents and their statement was no more than an innocent misrepresentation.

However, a statement may well amount to a term where the person making it possesses specialist knowledge or expertise and the person to whom it is made is relying on that expertise in deciding to contract.

DICK BENTLEY PRODUCTIONS LTD V HAROLD SMITH (MOTORS) LTD (1965)

The claimant asked the defendants, who were car dealers, to find him a 'well vetted' Bentley car. In other words, one in good condition. The defendants found a car they falsely stated had only done 20,000 miles since being fitted with a new engine and gearbox. In fact it had done 100,000 miles. The claimant later found the car to be unsuitable as well as discovering that the statement about the mileage was untrue and sued for a breach of warranty. CA upheld the claim since the claimant relied on the specialist expertise of the car dealers in stating the mileage.

The time between making the statement and formation of the contract

Sometimes the court may assess that the time lapse between the statement made in the negotiations and the creation of the contract itself is too great to support a claim that the statement is incorporated in the contract as a term.

ROUTLEDGE V MCKAY (1954)

A motor cycle had actually first been registered in 1939 but on a new registration book being issued it was wrongly stated as 1941. In 1949 the current owner, who was unaware of this inaccuracy, was selling the motor cycle and in response to an enquiry as to the age by a prospective buyer gave the age in the registration documents. The prospective buyer then bought the motor cycle a week later in a written contract that made no mention of the age. When he discovered the true age and tried to sue for a breach of a term he failed. The delay of a week was held to be too long to create a binding relationship based on the statement.

Reducing the agreement, including the statement, to writing

Where a contract is made in a written document and a statement made orally between the parties is not included in the written document then the court will generally infer that it was not intended to form part of the contract but is a mere representation.

ROUTLEDGE V MCKAY (1954)

Here since the written agreement made no mention of the age of the motor cycle the court held that it had not been considered important enough to be a term.

Furthermore, where a written agreement is signed this will generally make the contents of the agreement binding irrespective of whether they have been read by the party signing. (A clear warning that we should never sign anything without reading it first.)

L'ESTRANGE V GRAUCOB (1934)

The claimant bought a vending machine from the defendants on a written contract which in small print contained the clause 'any express or implied condition, statement or warranty, statutory or otherwise not stated herein is hereby excluded'. The machine turned out to be unsatisfactory and the claimant claimed for breach of an implied term as to fitness for purpose under the Sale of Goods Act 1893. (Exclusions of liability for the implied terms were possible under the 1893 Act.) She also argued that she had not read the clause and had no knowledge of what it contained. Judgement was initially given to the claimant but on appeal she failed. As Scrutton LJ put it 'When a document containing contractual terms is signed, then, in the absence of fraud, or, I will add, misrepresentation, the party signing it is bound, and it is wholly immaterial whether he has read the document or not.'

(Of course judgements like the above would now be subject to the Unfair Contract Terms Act 1977 and Unfair Terms in Consumer Contracts Regulations 1994.)

It is important to remember that since the passing of the Misrepresentation Act 1967 many of the above claimants would not necessarily have to try to prove that the statement made to them amounted to a term of the contract. The Act allows a claimant an action even in respect of an innocent misrepresentation such as that relating to age of a vehicle found in the registration documents of a vehicle. Prior to this Act there were very limited circumstances in which a claim for misrepresentation could be made. So it was vital for a claimant to prove a statement was a term otherwise (s)he may have had no remedy at all.

3.2.2 THE 'PAROL EVIDENCE' RULE

Traditionally where a party to a written agreement was trying to show that the written document did not fully reflect the actual agreement (s)he would come up against the 'parol evidence' rule. By this rule oral or other evidence that the party was trying to introduce would not be admissible if it was to be used to add to, vary or contradict the terms contained in the written contract.

The rule can easily be justified. Firstly, if the contract had been reduced to writing then it was only logical to suppose that things omitted from the written document actually formed no part of the agreement. Secondly, the danger is that adding terms in after the written agreement leads to uncertainty.

However, many contracts are partly written and partly oral, and over time a number of exceptions to the strict rule have emerged rendering the rule unworkable:

Custom or trade usage

Terms can invariably be implied into a contract by trade custom (see later Section 3.3.2 under Implied terms).

Rectification

Where it can be shown that a written contract inaccurately represents the actual agreement reached by the two parties then equity will allow rectification of the written document. Parol evidence can be introduced to show what the real agreement was. The inaccuracies are removed and replaced if necessary with the substance of the real agreement.

WEBSTER V CECIL (1861)

Webster was trying to enforce his purchase of land where the written document identified the price as £1,250. Cecil was able to show that he had already refused an offer of £2,000, so that the accurate price was £2,250. The price was amended accordingly.

Invalidation by misrepresentation, mistake etc.

Where a claimant is seeking to avoid the consequences of a contract, having discovered that the contract has been made as the result of a mistake or a misrepresentation or other invalidating factor, (s)he is clearly entitled to introduce evidence to that effect (see Chapter 4 on vitiating factors).

Where the written agreement only represents part of a larger agreement

Clearly in some circumstances, as we have already seen, the court is prepared to accept that oral representations, because of their significance, are intended to be as much a part of the agreement as those included in the written document.

J. EVANS & SON (PORTSMOUTH) LTD V ANDREA MERZARIO LTD (1976)

The claimant regularly used the defendants as carriers to ship machinery from Italy and they did so on the defendants' standard forms. Originally the machines, which were liable to rust if left on deck, were always carried below decks. When the defendants started using containers, which would generally be kept on deck, the claimants expressed concern about rusting and were given an oral assurance that their machinery would still be stored below decks. One machine being carried for the claimants was put in a container and by error stored on deck. The container was not properly fastened and subsequently fell overboard. CA allowed the claimant to introduce evidence of the oral assurance, the standard forms did not represent the actual agreement, and the defendants were liable.

Where the contract depends on fulfilment of a specified event

Obviously where the parties have a written agreement but have also agreed that the contract will only come into effect on fulfilment of some other condition, then evidence can be introduced to that effect. There is no attempt to vary the terms of the contract. The evidence of the oral agreement is introduced only to show that operation of the contract has been suspended until fulfilment of the condition.

PYM V CAMPBELL (1856)

Here there was a written agreement to buy a share of the patent of an invention. The claimant sued for a breach of this agreement. In fact there was an oral agreement between the parties that the contract would not come into effect until the patent had been examined and verified by a third party. The defendant was allowed to introduce parol evidence of this.

Collateral contracts

We have already seen how the collateral contract is an exception to the basic rules on privity of contract, allowing a party to sue the maker of a promise on which they have relied even though that party is not a party to the actual contract. A collateral agreement can also be relevant as an exception to the parol evidence rule in certain circumstances. For instance, where a promise is made which is dependent on the making of another contract, the promise is collateral, the making of the other contract is the consideration. Though the promise may only rank as a representation in the major contract it can be raised as evidence of the second or collateral contract.

CITY AND WESTMINSTER PROPERTIES (1934) LTD V MUDD (1958)

The defendant rented a shop for six years, together with a small room in which he slept, and which was known by the claimant landlords. When the lease was up for renewal the landlords inserted a clause restricting use of the premises to the 'showrooms, workrooms and offices only', the effect of which would be to prevent the defendant from sleeping on the premises. He then gained an oral assurance that he could still sleep in the room, on which basis he signed the new lease. The landlords then brought an action for forfeiture of the lease for the defendant's breach of the new clause. It was held that he had broken the terms of the lease, but the landlords were unable to enforce its terms against him because of the collateral contract.

3.3 IMPLIED TERMS

3.3.1 GENERAL

Generally the parties to a contract will be deemed to have included all of the various obligations by which they intend to be bound as express terms of the contract.

There are, however, occasions when terms will be implied into a contract, even though they do not

KEY
FACTS

- To form part of the contract express terms must be incorporated into the contract

- If the contract is written then this presents no problem since the terms are in written form

- Where the contract is oral a number of factors can be taken into account in determining whether or not representations have been incorporated:

  – The importance attached to them by the parties – *Birch* v *Paramount Estates (Liverpool) Ltd (1956)*

  – The relative bargaining strength of the parties – *Oscar Chess* v *Williams (1957)*

  – The extent to which one party relied on the expertise of the other – *Dick Bentley Productions* v *Harold Smith (Motors)* (1965)

  – Whether the representation was put in writing – *Routledge* v *McKay (1954)*

- A party is generally bound by anything that (s)he has signed, whether or not (s)he has read it – *L'Estrange* v *Graucob* (1934)

- Originally the 'parol evidence' rule would prevent a party from introducing evidence of oral agreements not actually in the written agreement – but there are now many exceptions to this rule

FIGURE 3.3 *Key fact chart for incorporating express terms into the contract*

appear in a written agreement or in the oral negotiations that have taken place leading up to the contract.

Terms will be implied into a contract for one of two reasons:

- Because a court in a later dispute is trying to give effect to a presumed intention of the parties, even though these intentions have not been expressed (these are terms implied by fact)

- Because the law demands that certain obligations are to be included in a contract irrespective of whether the parties have agreed on them or would naturally include them (these are terms implied by law – usually this will be as the result of some statutory provision aimed at redressing an imbalance in bargaining strength or seeking to protect a particular group – but it can be by operation of the common law)

3.3.2 TERMS IMPLIED BY FACT

Where terms are implied by fact this is usually as a result of decisions in individual court cases.

The courts have implied terms by fact in a variety of different circumstances:

Terms implied by custom or habit

There is an old maxim that 'custom hardens into right'. For instance, customary rights gained by long use, otherwise known as prescription, are common features in relation to the use of land. Bridle paths and public rights of way are examples of this.

HUTTON V WARREN (1836)

Local custom meant that on termination of an agricultural lease the tenant was entitled to an allowance for seed and labour on the land. The court held that the lease made by the two parties must be viewed in the light of this custom. As Parke B in the Court of Exchequer said 'It has long been settled that in commercial transactions extrinsic evidence of custom and usage is admissible to annex incidents to written contracts, in matters with respect to which they are silent'.

Terms implied by trade or professional custom

The parties to a contract might be bound by an implied trade custom when it is accepted as their deemed intention even though there are no express terms on the matter.

In marine insurance for instance it has long been a custom that there is an implied undertaking on the part of the broker that he will pay the premium to the insurer even where the party insured defaults on the payment.

The custom, however, should operate to give effect to the contract by supporting the general purpose, not to contradict the express terms, and therefore defeat the general purpose.

LES AFFRETEURS REUNIS SA V WALFORD (1919) (WALFORD'S CASE)

In this case that we have already seen in privity of contract, Walford was suing for a commission of 3 per cent that he felt he was owed for negotiating a charter party between Lubricating and Fuel Oils Co. Ltd and the owners of the SS *Flore*. One argument of the defendants was that there was a custom that commission was payable only when the ship had actually been hired. In this instance the French government had requisitioned the ship before the charter party had actually occurred. If the custom was accepted then it would conflict with the clause in the contract requiring payment as soon as the hire agreement was signed, so it was held not to have been implied into the contract.

Terms implied to give sense and meaning to the agreement

Sometimes a contract would be rendered meaningless or inoperable without the inclusion of a particular term, which will be implied to give effect and sense to the agreement.

SCHAWEL V READE (1913)

The claimant wanted to buy a stallion for stud purposes. At the defendant's stables he was examining a horse advertised for sale when the defendant remarked 'You need not look for anything: the horse is perfectly sound. If there was anything the matter with the horse I would tell you'. On this recommendation the claimant halted his inspection and later bought the horse. In fact it turned out that the horse was unfit for stud purposes. Lord Moulton held that, even though the defendant's assurances did not amount to an express warranty as to the horse's fitness for stud, nevertheless they were an implied warranty to that effect.

Terms implied to give business efficacy to a commercial contract

Exactly the same point applies in respect of business contracts. Parties would not enter a contract freely that had no benefit for them or indeed that might harm them or cause them some loss. So the courts will imply terms into a contract that lacks them in express form in order to sustain the agreement as a businesslike arrangement.

THE MOORCOCK (1889)

The defendants owned a wharf with a jetty on the Thames. They made an agreement with the claimant for him to dock his ship and unload cargoes at the wharf. Both parties were aware at the time of contracting that this could involve the vessel being at the jetty at low tide. The ship became grounded at the jetty and broke up on a ridge of rock. The defendants argued that they had given no undertaking as to the safety of the ship. The court held that there was an implied undertaking that the ship would not be damaged. Bowen LJ explained that 'In business transactions such as this, what the law desires to effect by the implication is to give such business efficacy ... as must have been intended at all events by both parties who are businessmen ...'.

This basic principle has been supported in subsequent cases.

Terms implied because of the prior conduct of the contracting parties

Quite simply, where the parties to a contract have a prior history of dealing on particular terms, if those terms are not included in a later contract they may be implied into it if the parties are dealing in otherwise essentially similar terms.

HILLAS & CO. LTD V ARCOS LTD (1932)

In a 1931 contract between the two parties for the supply of standard sized lengths of timber there was included an option clause allowing the claimants to buy a further 100,000 during 1932. The agreement was otherwise quite vague as to the type of timber, the terms of shipment and other features. Despite this the contract was completed and the timber supplied. In 1932 the claimants then wanted the further 100,000 lengths of timber but the defendants refused to deliver them. Their argument was that since the 1931 agreement was vague in many major aspects it was therefore no more than a basis for further negotiations. HL held that, while the option clause lacked specific detail, nevertheless it was in the same terms as the contract of sale that had been completed. It was therefore implicit in the original contract that the option be carried out in the same terms if the claimant wished to exercise it.

The classic test for identifying whether or not a term will be implied into a contract by fact is that laid down in the judgment of Lord Justice MacKinnon in *Shirlaw* v *Southern Foundries Ltd* (1939).

'Prima facie that which in any contract is left to be implied and need not be expressed is something so obvious that it goes without saying; so that if, while the parties were making their bargain, an officious bystander were to suggest some express provision for it in their agreement, they would testily suppress him with a common "Oh of course!"'

This is commonly known as the 'officious bystander test'. It is still in use, and on the face of it is an adequate way of showing that what the court is doing is giving effect to the presumed intention of the parties. However, it imposes a very strict standard and possibly an unrealistic one. While one party will usually be all too willing to accept that the implied term at issue was what (s)he actually intended to be part of the contract, the other party almost inevitably will be arguing the exact reverse, or there would be no dispute. In consequence there will be circumstances in which the 'officious bystander rule' cannot apply.

One example is where one party to the contract is totally unaware of the term that it is being suggested should be implied into the agreement. In this case it could never have been his or her intention that it be included, so the test fails.

If it is uncertain that both parties would have agreed to the term even if it had been included in the agreement, then it is difficult to demonstrate

SPRING V NATIONAL AMALGAMATED STEVEDORES AND DOCKERS SOCIETY (1956)

There was an agreement between various trade unions, including the defendant union, known as the 'Bridlington Agreement', from the meeting of the TUC at which it was reached. The agreement concerned transfer between unions. The claimant joined the defendant union in breach of this rule on transfer but totally unaware of the existence of the agreement. This breach was reported to the TUC Disputes Committee. It then demanded of the defendants that they expel him. When they tried to do so the claimant sued for breach of contract. The defendant union asked that a term should be implied into their agreement with Spring that it should follow the Bridlington Agreement. MacKinnon's 'officious bystander test' was referred to and rejected. If told about the Bridlington Agreement by an officious bystander Spring would have no idea what it was.

that it was their presumed intention and include it by implication, in which case the test fails yet again.

SHELL (UK) LTD V LOSTOCK GARAGE LTD (1977)

By an agreement between the two parties Shell was to supply petrol and oil to Lostock who in return agreed to buy these products only from Shell. In a later 'price war' Shell supplied petrol to other garages at lower prices forcing Lostock to sell at a loss. Lostock wanted inclusion of an implied term in the contract to the effect that Shell would not 'abnormally discriminate' against them. CA refused since Shell would never have agreed to it.

Lord Denning took a more relaxed view of the process of implying terms by fact into a contract. He suggested that the process of implication need not be anything more than to include terms that are reasonable as between the parties in the circumstances of the case. The House of Lords rejected his approach.

LIVERPOOL CITY COUNCIL V IRWIN (1976)

Here the council let flats in a 15-floor tower block. There was no proper tenancy agreement though there was a list of tenants' obligations signed by tenants. There were no express undertakings in the agreement on the part of the landlord. The council failed to maintain the common areas such as the stairs, lifts, corridors and rubbish chutes. These became badly vandalised over time with no lighting and the lifts and rubbish chutes not working. The claimants were tenants in the tower block who withheld the rent in protest. The council sued for repossession. The claimants counter-claimed and argued a breach of an implied term that the council should maintain the common areas. In CA Lord Denning felt that such a term could be implied because it was reasonable in the circumstances. HL though rejected this approach. Lord Wilberforce said that to do this is to 'extend a long, and undesirable, way beyond sound authority'. Lord Cross stated that 'it is not enough for the court to say that the suggested term is a reasonable one the presence of which would make the contract a better or fairer one...' and identified that the 'officious bystander test is the appropriate method for a term to be implied into a contract'. In the event HL were not prepared to accept that the council had an absolute obligation to maintain the common areas, though they did accept that there was an implied term to take reasonable care to maintain the common areas, which they did not feel had been breached here by the council.

3.3.3 TERMS IMPLIED BY LAW – BY THE COURTS

Terms implied into the contract are justified on the basis that they represent the presumed but unexpressed intentions of the parties. Had the parties thought of the particular term they would have naturally included it.

Where a term is being implied into a contract by process of law it is being inserted into the contract irrespective of the wishes of the parties. The justification here is that the law, whether the courts or Parliament itself, wishes to regulate such agreements.

The courts might imply a term by law because it is felt that it is the type of term that should naturally be incorporated in a contract of that type. Once the term has been implied the case will then stand as a precedent for future cases involving the same type of agreement.

LIVERPOOL CITY COUNCIL v IRWIN (1976)

Here HL could not imply a term as a matter of fact that the landlord was responsible for the common areas because it failed the 'officious bystander' test. However, they did accept that there should be a general obligation on a landlord in tenancy agreements to take reasonable care to maintain the common areas.

3.3.4 TERMS IMPLIED BY LAW – BY STATUTE

In the nineteenth century the law of contract was most commonly governed by the maxim caveat emptor (let the buyer beware). The law was very much concerned with the process of contracting and little attention was paid to the fact that in many circumstances one party to the contract was in a significantly inferior bargaining position to the other party. Early statutes such as the Sale of Goods Act 1893 did attempt to redress this imbalance. In the latter half of the twentieth century there has been much more awareness of the needs of consumers, employees and others in contractual relationships. The old maxim has been found wanting and unacceptable and Parliament, through Acts, has often given greater protection to the party with the weaker bargaining strength in certain types of contracts by the process of inserting or implying terms into the contracts irrespective of the express intentions of the parties.

Such a process is common in Acts governing consumer contracts, such as the Sale of Goods Act 1979 (as amended) and the Supply of Goods and Services Act 1982. It is also prominent in employment contracts with not only the Employment Rights Act 1996 but various Acts outlawing discrimination, such as the Sex Discrimination Act 1975, Race Relations Act 1976 and Disability Discrimination Act 1995, and many other Acts giving a wide variety of protection to employees by the process of implying terms into the contract of employment.

The importance of such terms is that they provide a statutory protection that can be constantly relied upon because they will usually apply regardless of what is said in the contract.

The Sale of Goods Act 1979

The Sale of Goods Act 1979 contains a number of these terms which provide a very clear example of the process and its benefits.

Section 12 – the implied condition as to title

In sale of goods contracts a term is automatically implied that the person selling the goods can pass on good title to the goods, in other words (s)he has the right to sell the goods.

> **NIBLETT LTD V CONFECTIONERS' MATERIALS CO. LTD (1921)**
>
> A seller sold 3,000 tins of condensed milk that were on consignment from America. The tins were marked 'Nissly' which Nestlé argued was too close to their brand name and therefore an infringement of their trademark. The goods were impounded as a result. The buyers then removed the labels as they were required to do and sold the goods on for whatever price they could get. They successfully sued the sellers under s.12. The sellers had been unable to legitimately sell the goods in their original state.

The implied term obviously can protect a buyer in those circumstances where the seller does not own the goods and the original owner wants their return.

> **ROWLAND V DIVALL (1923)**
>
> The claimant bought a car that turned out to be stolen. When the proper owner took the car back the claimant was able to recover the full price of the car from the seller.

Section 13 – the implied condition as to description

By this, goods sold in a sale of goods contract must correspond to any description applied to them, and this might even include the packaging.

> **RE MOORE & CO. AND LANDAUER & CO.'S ARBITRATION (1921)**
>
> A contract for a consignment of tinned fruit was described as being in cartons of 30 tins. When on delivery half of the cartons were of 24 tins there was a breach of s.13 even though the actual quantity of tins ordered was correct.

Section 14(2) – the implied condition that the goods are of satisfactory quality

Unlike s.12 and s.13 this implied term, as with s.14(3), applies only when the goods are sold in the course of a business.

Traditionally the requirement was that goods should be of 'merchantable' quality. Merchantability was a legal term with a fairly narrow meaning and as a consequence many parties might be left without a remedy.

> **BARTLETT V SIDNEY MARCUS LTD (1965)**
>
> In this case a car was bought with a defective clutch. The sellers offered either to repair the clutch or to reduce the price by £25. The buyer accepted the price reduction but very soon had to replace the clutch costing an extra £45 besides. Lord Denning nevertheless rejected the buyer's claim that the fact that the defect was more costly meant that the goods were not merchantable.

The Sale and Supply of Goods Act 1994 amended the section, replacing merchantable with satisfactory, a concept that should be easily understood by consumers generally. It also inserted a new s.14(2)(b) explaining what is satisfactory. The definition would include:

(a) *fitness for all purposes for which goods of the kind in question are commonly supplied*

(b) *appearance and finish*

(c) *freedom from minor defects*

(d) *safety and durability*

There is little case law on the new provisions but they should make it much easier for consumers to bring claims in respect of defective goods.

Section 14(3) – the implied condition that the goods are fit for their purpose

This provision will apply where the buyer 'either expressly or impliedly makes known to the seller any particular purpose for which goods are being bought regardless of whether or not that is a purpose for which goods of that kind are commonly supplied'.

So the provision mainly applies where the buyer is relying on the skill and judgement of the seller in buying the goods and has expressed a particular purpose for which the goods are required.

BALDRY V MARSHALL (1925)

Here the buyer claimed that a Bugatti car was not fit for the purpose. He had asked the seller to supply him with a fast, flexible and easily managed car that would be comfortable and suitable for ordinary touring purposes. The Bugatti that he was sold was not such a car.

It may also apply, however, in respect of purposes that are implicit in the contract rather than actually stated.

GRANT V AUSTRALIAN KNITTING MILLS LTD (1936)

Here the buyer contracted a painful skin disease from chemicals in underpants that he had bought. The court accepted that the buyer would have impliedly made known the purpose for which he was buying the underpants even if he had not actually stated it to the seller.

Section 15 – the implied condition that goods sold by sample should correspond with the sample

This provision is particularly appropriate when a seller is being sued by a customer for defective

GODLEY V PERRY (1960)

A boy was injured in the eye by a catapult bought from a retailer when the elastic snapped. The retailer had tested the sample but was able to show that the bulk did not match the quality of the sample.

goods and is able to argue that the defect was not apparent in the sample on which was based the decision to buy the bulk for resale. The seller uses s.15 to claim against the original supplier.

The Supply of Goods and Services Act 1982

Similar implied terms are contained in the Supply of Goods and Services Act 1982. Since the Act covers situations where goods as well as services are provided certain of the terms mirror those in the Sale of Goods Act 1979. These include an implied condition as to title (s.2); description (s.3); an implied condition of satisfactory quality and fitness for the purpose (s.4); and an implied condition in respect of sale by sample (s.5).

There are also three further significant implied terms of particular relevance to the supply of services:

Section 13 – 'In a contract for the supply of a service where the supplier is acting in the course of a business there is an implied term that the supplier will carry out the service with reasonable care and skill.'

LAWSON V SUPASINK LTD (1984)

Here the defendant was contracted to design, supply and install a fitted kitchen for £1,200. Plans were drawn up but the defendant failed to properly follow them. The claimants were able to recover their money. Since the work was shoddy there was no entitlement to payment less the price of repairing defects on the part of the defendant.

Section 14 – 'Where the time for the service to be carried out is not fixed … the supplier will carry out the service within a reasonable time.'

CHARNOCK V LIVERPOOL CORPORATION (1968)

The defendant took eight weeks to repair a car when a competent repair should have taken only five weeks and so was in breach of the implied term.

Section 15 – 'Where the consideration for the service is not determined … the party contracting to with the supplier will pay a reasonable charge.'

3.4 THE RELATIVE SIGNIFICANCE OF TERMS

3.4.1 INTRODUCTION

We have already considered how in representations made prior to the formation of the contract some are more important than others. As a result some are incorporated in the contract and others are not.

In the same way not all terms are equally important to the contract. Some are of critical importance and without them the contract could not be completed. On the other hand some terms are of lesser importance. They may, for instance, be purely descriptive and even if they are breached this will not mean that the contract cannot be carried out.

If terms are of different significance then the effects of a breach of those terms will also vary in significance and there are of necessity different remedies available to the parties in the event of a breach. The courts have traditionally dealt with the issue by classifying terms into different categories. Broadly speaking then the courts always distinguished between terms and determined their classification in two ways. Firstly, the term can be categorised according to its importance to the completion of the contract. Secondly, it can be categorised according to the remedies available to a party who is a victim of a breach of the term – a failure to honour the obligation.

3.4.2 CONDITIONS

Until fairly recently judges recognised only two classes of term. The most important of these was the condition, which can be considered in two ways.

Firstly, a condition is a term of a contract which is so important to the contract that a failure to perform the condition would render the contract

KEY FACTS

- Terms can be implied into a contract in one of three ways: (i) by fact, because of the presumed intention of the parties; (ii) by law, because the courts feel that such terms should always be present – *Liverpool City Council* v *Irwin* (1976); (iii) by law, because statutory provisions insert terms into contracts
- Terms will be implied by fact because of:
  - custom or common usage – *Hutton* v *Warren* (1836)
  - professional custom – *Walford's Case* (1919)
  - business efficacy – *The Moorcock* (1889)
  - past conduct of the parties – *Hillas* v *Arcos* (1932)
- Terms are implied by fact according to the 'officious bystander' test – if an officious bystander had asked the parties about a term that was missing from the contract they would have replied that it was obviously included
- Terms are implied by statute e.g. for consumer protection – Sale of Goods Act
- Sale of Goods Act terms 1979 include e.g. goods should correspond with description – s.13; and be of satisfactory quality – s.14(2); and fit for their purpose – s.14(3).
- Supply of Goods and Services Act 1982 implied terms include e.g. service to be carried out with reasonable care and skill – s.13; service to be carried out within a reasonable time – s.14; where price not stated party receiving service to pay a reasonable charge – s.15.

FIGURE 3.4 *Key fact chart for implied terms*

meaningless and destroy the purpose of the contract. As a result a condition is said to 'go to the root of a contract'.

Secondly, as a result of the significance of the term to the contract, the court allows the claimant who has suffered a breach of the term the fullest range of remedies. When a condition is unfulfilled the claimant will not only be able to sue for damages but will be able to repudiate his or her obligations, or indeed do both. Repudiation as a remedy is the right to consider the contract ended as a result of the other party's breach of contract. This may be particularly appropriate as it may mean that the claimant can contract with an alternative party, and treat himself or herself as relieved of his or her obligations under the contract, without fear of the defendant alleging a breach by the claimant instead.

POUSSARD V SPIERS AND POND (1876)

Here an actress was contracted to appear in the lead role in an operetta for a season. The actress was unable to attend for the early performances, by which time the producers had given her role up to the understudy. The actress sued for breach of contract but lost. She had in fact breached the contract by turning up after the first night. As the lead her presence was crucial to the production and so was a condition entitling the producers to repudiate and terminate her contract for her non-attendance at the early performances.

3.4.3 WARRANTIES

Warranties are regarded as minor terms of the contract or those where in general the contract might continue despite their breach. Almost by default, then, a warranty is any other term in a contract, one that does not go to the root of the contract.

It is a residual category of terms dealing with obligations that are ancillary or secondary to the major purpose of the contract.

As a result, the remedy for a breach of warranty is merely an action for damages. There is no right to repudiate for breach of a warranty.

BETTINI V GYE (1876)

In a case with similar circumstances to the last, a singer was contracted to appear at a variety of theatres for a season of concerts. His contract included a term that he should attend rehearsals for six days prior to the beginning of the actual performances. In the event he turned up only three days before but had been replaced. When the singer sued, the producers' claim that the obligation to attend rehearsals was a condition failed. The court held that it was only ancillary to the main purpose and only entitled the producers to sue for damages not to end the contract and replace the singer.

Thus it can be seen that the way in which the terms are classified is critical in determining the outcome of the contract and the remedies available in the case of a breach of the terms.

3.4.4 THE CONSTRUCTION OF TERMS

The remedies available to a party who has suffered a contractual breach depend on the classification given to the term that is not complied with. Parties to a contract do not always think to outline prior to the contract the nature of the terms they are incorporating in the contract or the precise remedies they are contemplating will be available in the event of a breach. Where the parties are silent on the classification of terms or the classifications are vague it will be for judges to construe what the terms are and their contractual significance.

Judges use a number of guiding principles:

- Where terms are implied into the contract by law then judges will apply the classification given to the terms in the statute, e.g. the implied terms in the Sale of Goods Act 1979 that we have already looked at are stated as conditions.

- Where the terms are implied by fact the judges will construe them according to the presumed intention of the parties.

- Where the terms have been expressed by the parties who have identified how the terms are to be classified or what remedies attach to them then the judges will usually try to give effect to the express wishes of the parties.

- Where the terms are express but the parties have not identified what type of term they are or what is the appropriate remedy in a breach then the judges will construe those terms according to what they believe is the true intention of the parties.

Inevitably it is very advantageous if a term is a condition since a greater range of remedies is available. This has the potential for unscrupulous parties to a contract to classify all of the terms of the contract as conditions. In view of the complexities of modern contracting, and particularly the use of the standard form contract, there may well be occasions when the judges feel that it is impossible to follow the express classification of the terms. In this way a term stated as being a condition may be construed in fact as a warranty.

SCHULER (L.) AG v WICKMAN MACHINE TOOL SALES LTD (1974)

In an agency contract Wickman was appointed sole distributors of Schuler's presses. It was stated as a condition of the contract that Wickman's representatives would make weekly visits to six large UK motor manufacturers to solicit orders for presses. A further term stated that the contract could be terminated for a breach of any condition that was not remedied within 60 days. The contract was to last more than four years, amounting to more than 1,400 visits. When some way into the contract Wickman's representatives failed to make a visit Schuler sought to terminate the contract. In HL Lord Reid felt that it was inevitable that during the length of the contract there would be occasions when maintaining weekly visits would be impossible. He also felt that the effect of accepting the term as a condition would be to entitle Schuler to terminate the contract even if there was only one failure to visit out of the 1,400. This would be unreasonable so the term could not be a condition.

Judges may, of course, be aided in their construction of terms by guidance given in statutory defi-

nitions, and referring to the market in which the particular contract operates may also assist them.

MAREDELANTO CIA NAVIERA SA v BERGBAU-HANDEL GMBH (1970) (*THE MIHALIS ANGELOS*)

A charter party repudiated their contract with shipowners when the contract contained an 'expected readiness to load' clause and it was clear that the vessel would not be ready to load on time. There was a clear breach of a term but the court had to decide of which type. HL, using guidance from statutory terms as well as from the commercial character of the contract, decided that the term was a condition justifying repudiation. The judges held that in commercial contracts predictability and certainty of relations must be the ultimate test.

So while in general a contract drafted by a lawyer should usually conform to the classification of terms given, nevertheless the courts may seek to preserve certainty in commercial contracts whatever the apparent intent of the parties.

HARLINGDON & LEINSTER ENTERPRISES LTD v CHRISTOPHER HULL FINE ART LTD (1990)

Here defendant dealers sold a painting as a Munter (a German expressionist painter). The sellers declared at the time of the contract that they had no expertise on such paintings whereas the buyers did have. When it was discovered that the painting was a forgery the buyers tried to claim a breach of description by the sellers. CA held that the sale was not one by description entitling the buyers to repudiate. There was no reliance by the buyers who had relied on their own superior judgment.

3.4.5 INNOMINATE TERMS

The problem of determining which category a term fits usually happens when the parties have been silent on the subject or where the contract is oral. The effect of the classification is to identify what the term was at the time of the formation of the contract, and therefore all later consequences depend on that classification.

A more recent approach of the courts has been to describe terms as 'innominate', or without specific classification, and in determining the outcome of a breach of the term to consider the consequence of the breach rather than how it is classified in deciding on the available remedy.

The purpose of distinguishing between different classes of term is ultimately to determine what remedies are available to the victim of the breach of the term. The modern concept of the innominate term has developed out of a desire that the right to repudiate a contract should only be available in the event of a breach when it is fair to both sides.

The rather simplistic process of classifying all terms as either conditions or warranties was not without its problems and the innominate term was first considered as an alternative method of deciding the appropriate remedy in the event of a breach of a term in:

HONG KONG FIR SHIPPING CO. LTD V KAWASAKI KISEN KAISHA LTD (1962) (THE HONG KONG FIR CASE)

The defendants chartered a ship from the claimants under a two-year charter contract. A term in the contract required that the ship should be 'in every way fitted for ordinary cargo service'. In fact the ship broke down as a result of the incompetence of the engine room staff, and in any case was in a generally poor state of repair and not seaworthy, a fact admitted by the claimants. As a result, 18 weeks' use of the ship was lost by the defendants and they claimed to treat the contract as repudiated and at an end. The claimants sued claiming that the term was only a warranty, only entitling the defendants to sue for damages. CA agreed. There were, however, some interesting points made in the judgments. Lord Diplock felt that not all contracts could be simply divided into terms that are conditions and terms that are warranties, and that many contracts are of a more complex character. He considered that 'all that can be predicted is that some breaches will, and others will not, give rise to an event which will deprive the party not in default of substantially the whole benefit which it was intended that he should obtain from contract; and the legal consequences … unless expressly provided for in the contract, depend on the nature of the event to which the breach gives rise and do not follow automatically from a prior classification … as a "condition" or a "warranty".'

The process seems simple enough. The available remedy is only discovered after the consequences of the breach have first been identified. The innominate term in this way could be particularly useful in contracts such as charters where the results of the breach can vary all the way from rendering the contract impossible to relatively trivial effects.

Nevertheless there is an uncertainty to the innominate term. Nobody can be really sure what the outcome of a particular situation will be until the term has been breached and the judge in the case has construed the term and declared what remedy is appropriate. The doctrine has, however, been accepted.

CEHAVE N.V. V BREMER HANDELSGESSELSCHAFT MBH (1976) (THE HANSA NORD)

A cargo of citrus pulp pellets to be used as cattle feed was rejected by the buyers because part had suffered overheating and did not conform to the term 'Shipment to be made in good condition'. As the sellers would not refund the price already paid the buyers applied to the Rotterdam court which ordered its sale. Another party then bought the cargo and sold it on to the original buyers at a much lower price than they had paid the original sellers. The cargo was then used for its original purpose, cattle feed. The buyers argued that the goods were not merchantable within the meaning of the Sale of Goods Act 1893, the term was a condition and therefore justified their repudiation. This was at first successful. CA, however, using the Hong Kong Fir approach, accepted that, since the goods had been used for their original purpose, there was not a breach of the contract serious enough to justify repudiation. Only an action for damages was appropriate in the circumstances.

The use of the innominate term is particularly appropriate where there is unequal bargaining strength between the parties or where breaches of the contract are technical rather than material and the traditional methods of classification would lead to an injustice.

However, the court may still classify a term as a condition, regardless of what the possible

REARDON SMITH LINE LTD V HANSEN-TANGEN (1976)

In a contract for the charter of a tanker the ship was described as 'Osaka 354', a reference to the shipyard at which the tanker would be built. In fact, because the shipyard had too many orders the work was sub-contracted to another yard and the tanker became known as 'Oshima 004'. When the need for tankers lessened the buyers tried to get out of the contract by claiming a breach of a condition that the tanker should correspond with its description. The court held that since the breach was entirely technical and had no bearing on the outcome of the contract it could not justify repudiation.

consequences of a breach might be, where it feels that the circumstances demand it.

BUNGE CORPORATION V TRADAX EXPORT SA (1981)

In a contract for the sale of soya bean meal the buyers were required to give at least 15 days' notice of readiness to load the vessel. In the event they gave only 13 days' notice. This would not necessarily prevent the sellers from completing their obligations. As a result, the first instance court held that since the consequences of the breach were minor it would not justify repudiation. HL, however, held that, since the sellers' obligation to ship was certainly a condition the obligation to give notice to load in proper time should also be a condition without regard to the consequences of the breach. Lord Wilberforce felt that stipulations as to time in mercantile contracts should usually be viewed as conditions.

3.5 COMMON LAW CONTROL OF EXCLUSION CLAUSES

3.5.1 INTRODUCTION

A clause in a contract that seeks to either limit or exclude liability for breaches of the contract is itself a term of the contract. It is therefore subject to all of the normal rules regarding terms, particularly those concerning incorporation of the term.

Such terms can be particularly harsh on the party

SELF ASSESSMENT QUESTIONS

1 In what ways does a term differ from a mere representation?

2 Why is it that some statements made before the contract attach no liability at all?

3 In what ways can expertise or specialist knowledge be important in determining what the terms of a contract are?

4 What are the benefits of putting a contract in writing?

5 What is the effect of signing an agreement that you have not read?

6 How are terms implied into a contract?

7 What is the difference between a term implied by fact and a term implied by law?

8 In what ways is the 'officious bystander test' ineffective?

9 What is the difference between a 'condition' and a 'warranty'?

10 When will a court give a different classification to a term than the one already given by the parties themselves?

11 What are the advantages and disadvantages of defining terms as innominate?

subject to them and they often highlight the inequality of bargaining that can exist between different parties, notably providers of goods and services and consumers. Historically the principle of caveat emptor gave a great deal of leeway to a seller and little protection to a consumer. Even

KEY
FACTS

- There are different types of term – which category a term falls into is determined by how important it is to the contract

- In this way terms also vary according to the remedy available if they are breached

- A condition is a term which 'goes to the root of the contract' – breach of a condition would render the contract meaningless, so that the party who is the victim of the breach can repudiate his or her obligations under the contract as well as or instead of suing for damages – *Poussard* v *Spiers and Pond* (1876)

- A warranty is any other term – only damages are available for a breach of a warranty – *Bettini* v *Gye* (1876)

- Where the parties are silent on what type the term is judges must construe it from the surrounding circumstances – while judges try to give effect to the express intentions of the parties, remedies for breach of a term will only be awarded if the condition operates like a condition – *Schuler* v *Wickman Machine Tool Sales* (1974)

- Judges sometimes also view terms as innominate i.e. the appropriate remedy is judged from the seriousness of the breach – *The Hong Kong Fir Case* (1962)

- This can prevent the wrong remedy being given for breaches which are purely technical in character – *Reardon Smith Line* v *Hansen-Tangen* (1976)

FIGURE 3.5 *Key fact chart for the relative significance of terms*

where statute intervened to create protections for the consumer, as in the Sale of Goods Act 1893, the sellers' superior position was generally preserved. Thus s.55 of the 1893 Act allowed sellers to exclude liability for breaches of the implied conditions in the Act.

As a result judges gradually developed rules to prevent sellers having an unfettered discretion to avoid liability for their contractual breaches. More recently a general trend towards consumer protection has seen the introduction of more effective statutory controls and the UK has also had to implement controls created in European law. Judicial controls, though, are still effective in limiting the use of exclusion clauses.

3.5.2 RULES ON INCORPORATING EXCLUSION CLAUSES INTO CONTRACTS

Judges have shown a willingness to redress the imbalance that exclusion clauses can give rise to. They have done so initially by insisting on strict

rules of incorporation of such clauses. The rules are generally interchangeable with rules regarding incorporation of other terms.

Signed agreements

As with terms in general, the initial proposition is that where a party has signed a written agreement then (s)he is prima facie bound by that agreement.

L'ESTRANGE V GRAUCOB (1934)

Here, as we know, the purchaser of the vending machine was bound by the exclusion clause in the contract regardless of the fact that she had not read it.

Express knowledge of the clause

The first principle adopted by the courts is that an exclusion clause will only be incorporated into a contract where the party subject to the clause has actual knowledge of the clause at the time the contract is made.

OLLEY V MARLBOROUGH COURT HOTEL (1949)

Mr and Mrs Olley booked into the hotel, at which point a contract was formed. When they later went out they left the key at reception as required. In their absence a third party took the key, entered their room and stole Mrs Olley's fur coat. The hotel claimed that they were not liable because of an exclusion clause in the contract that 'the proprietors will not hold themselves liable for articles lost or stolen unless handed to the manageress for safe custody'. CA rejected their claim. The clause was not incorporated in the contract since it was on a notice on a wall inside the Olleys' room.

On the other hand, where the parties have dealt on the same terms in the past it may be possible to imply knowledge of the clause from the past dealings, in which case it may be incorporated in the contract.

J. SPURLING LTD V BRADSHAW (1956)

The defendant had contracted to store goods in the claimant's warehouse over many years. On this occasion he had stored a consignment of orange juice that went missing. The defendant refused to pay and the claimant sued and the defendant counter-claimed the claimant's negligence. The claimant pointed to an exclusion for any 'loss or damage occasioned by the negligence, wrongful act or default' of them or their servants contained in a receipt sent to the defendants. They in turn argued that this was only sent out after the contract was formed. The court accepted the validity of the exclusion since the parties had dealt on the same terms in the past.

However the courts will not allow a party to rely on past dealings to imply knowledge of an exclusion clause in order to incorporate it into the contract unless the previous dealings represent a consistent course of action.

MCCUTCHEON V DAVID MACBRAYNE LTD (1964)

The claimant had used the defendants' ferries to ship his car from Islay to the Scottish mainland on many occasions. Sometimes he was asked to sign a risk note including an exclusion clause and on other occasions he was not. On the occasion in question the claimant's relative, McSporran took the car to the ferry. He received a receipt on which was printed the exclusion clause, but he did not read it, and he was not asked to sign a risk note. The ferry sank through the defendants' negligence and the car was a write off. The claimant claimed compensation and the defendants tried to rely on the exclusion clause in the risk note and on the receipt. They failed because there was not a consistent course of action that allowed them to assume that the claimant knew of the exclusion clause so it was not incorporated in the contract. As Lord Devlin put it 'previous dealings are only relevant if they prove knowledge of the terms actual and not constructive and assent to them'.

Sufficiency of notice of the exclusion clause

In general the courts will not accept that an exclusion clause has been incorporated into a contract unless the party who is subject to the clause has been made sufficiently aware of the existence of the clause in the contract.

The obligation then is firmly on the party inserting the clause into the contract to bring it to the attention of the other party before it can be relied on and the party who wishes to rely on the exclusion clause is relieved of liability for their contractual breach.

PARKER V SOUTH EASTERN RAILWAY CO. (1877)

The claimant left his luggage in the cloakroom of the station and was given a ticket on paying a fee. On the back of the ticket was a clause stating that the Railway Company would not be liable for any luggage that exceeded £10 in value. Mr Parker's luggage was worth more than that amount and when it was stolen he claimed compensation from the Railway Company. Their attempt to rely on the exclusion clause failed since they could not show that they had instructed the claimant to read the clause or otherwise brought his attention to the exclusion clause.

Clearly one of the issues in *Parker* would have been whether or not the claimant could have been expected to contemplate that the cloakroom ticket in fact formed the basis of a written contract. An exclusion clause will not be incorporated into the contract when on an objective analysis it is not contained in a document that would ordinarily be perceived as being a contractual document or having contractual significance.

CHAPELTON V BARRY URBAN DISTRICT COUNCIL (1940)

Here the claimant hired deckchairs on the beach at Barry, and received two tickets from the council's beach attendant on paying the cost of hiring the chairs. On the back of these small tickets were the words 'The council will not be liable for any accident or damage arising from the hire of the chair' though the claimant did not read it, believing it only to be a receipt. The canvas on one chair was defective and it collapsed injuring the claimant. He claimed compensation and the council tried to rely on their exclusion clause. Their defence failed since the existence of the clause was not effectively bought to the attention of the claimant. It was unreasonable to assume that he would automatically understand that the ticket was a contractual document, and the council was liable for the claimant's injuries.

The exclusion clause might not be incorporated either where reference to it is contained in another document given to the claimant prior to the formation of the contract but where insufficient is done to bring the claimant's attention to the existence of the clause.

DILLON V BALTIC SHIPPING CO. LTD (1991) (*THE MIKHAIL LERMONTOV*)

A woman booked to go on a cruise with her daughter. In the booking form there was a clause that the contract of carriage was 'subject to conditions and regulations printed on the tickets'. In fact the contract of carriage would only then be issued some time later at the same time as the tickets. The cruise ship sank and the claimant was injured as a result. In her claim for compensation the defendant shipping company sought to rely on the exclusion clause in the contract of carriage. They failed. The court held that there was insufficient notice given in the booking form to draw the claimant's attention to the existence of the exclusion clause.

One further question concerns the extent to which parties inserting exclusion clauses in con-

tracts must go in order to claim that they are bought sufficiently to the attention of the other party and therefore incorporated in the contract. This is graphically illustrated in a judgment of Lord Denning. The case is also relevant to the requirement that the party subject to the clause must be aware of the clause at the time of contracting. Finally, the case also puts into perspective some of the problems of modern forms of contracting such as dealing with vending machines, ticket machines or other situations where there is no contact with the party seeking to insert the clause or his/her agents at the time of contracting.

THORNTON V SHOE LANE PARKING LTD (1971)

The claimant was injured in a car park owned by the defendants. At the entrance to the car park there was a notice that, as well as giving the charges, stated that parking was at the vehicle owner's risk. On entering, a motorist was required to stop at a barrier and take a ticket from a machine at which point a barrier would lift allowing entry to the car park. On the ticket was printed the words 'This ticket is issued subject to the conditions of issue as displayed on the premises'. Notices inside the car park then listed the conditions of the contract including an exclusion clause covering both damage and personal injury. When the claimant claimed the defendants argued that the exclusion clause applied but their argument was rejected. Lord Denning identified that the customer in such situations has no chance of negotiating. He 'pays his money and gets a ticket. He cannot refuse it. He cannot get his money back. He may protest to the machine, even swear at it. But it will remain unmoved. He is committed beyond recall ... The contract was concluded at that time.' In consequence Lord Denning says the customer is bound by the terms of the contract 'as long as they are sufficiently bought to his notice before-hand, but not otherwise'. In other words, for the party including the clause in the contract a very high degree of notice is required for it to be effective. As he had previously stated in *Spurling* v *Bradshaw* (1956) when looking at what needs to be done to draw a clause to the attention of the party subject to it, 'Some clauses which I have seen would need to be printed in red ink with a red hand pointing to it before the notice could be held to be sufficient'.

One final point worth mentioning on this issue is that the courts have not always felt constrained to apply this strict approach only to exclusion clauses. In certain instances the courts have adopted the same position in contracts containing clauses which are particularly burdensome to the other side regardless of the clause not being an exclusion clause.

INTERFOTO PICTURE LIBRARY LTD V STILETTO VISUAL PROGRAMMES LTD (1988)

Here the defendants hired photographic transparencies for a visual aid in a presentation from a party with whom they had no previous dealings. In the claimants' delivery note, which the defendants did not read, was a clause referring to a holding fee and VAT for each day when the transparencies were not returned past a set deadline, 19 March. When the defendants returned the transparencies on 2 April they were presented with a bill for £3,783.50 in respect of the holding charge for late return. The claimants sued when the defendants refused to pay. Dillon LJ in CA held that 'if one condition in a set of printed conditions is particularly onerous or unusual, the party seeking to enforce it must show that that condition was fairly brought to the attention of the other party'.

3.5.3 OTHER LIMITATIONS IMPOSED BY THE COURTS

Inconsistent oral representations

A party is generally bound by a contract which (s)he has signed. In some circumstances, however, the party subject to the clause may have enquired about the existence of the clause or queried the consequences of a clause that they have already read. Where oral misrepresentations have then caused that party to enter the contract with confidence the exclusion clause may be ineffective because it is the misrepresentation that has induced the other party to enter the contract.

CURTIS V CHEMICAL CLEANING AND DYEING CO. LTD (1951)

The claimant took a wedding dress to be cleaned and was asked to sign a document that exempted the defendants from liability for any damage 'howsoever arising'. She sensibly questioned the nature of the document that she was being asked to sign. She was then informed that it only referred to the fact that the defendants would not accept liability for beads or sequins attached to the dress. When the dress was returned it had a chemical stain for which Mrs Curtis tried to claim. The defendants failed in their attempt to rely on the exclusion clause because of the oral assurances made to the claimant.

So, as we have already seen, an oral undertaking made before the contract is formed can override an inconsistent express written term.

J. EVANS & SON (PORTSMOUTH) LTD V ANDREA MERZARIO LTD (1976)

In this case the carriage of the goods was changed to the use of containers. The promise made by the defendants' representative to continue to carry the claimants' machinery below deck was binding and would override any later inconsistent term in the contract.

The same point will apply where a collateral promise or undertaking is made on which the claimant can rely. The effect of the collateral promise may be to prevent the party inserting an exclusion clause into a contract from relying on it in a subsequent dispute.

WEBSTER V HIGGIN (1948)

The defendant had negotiated to purchase a car from the claimant's garage under a hire purchase agreement. In a hire purchase contract while the goods are bought under one contract the hire purchase agreement itself is a separate contract. Here the garage owners promised that the car the defendant planned to buy was in good condition. The hire purchase agreement contained a clause that 'no warranty, condition, description or representation as to the state or quality of the vehicle is given or implied'. In fact the car was, as the court described it, 'nothing but a mass of second hand and dilapidated ironmongery'. When the buyer refused to pay the claimant sued for return of the car and the balance of instalments due. The action failed. There had been a breach of the collateral promise that the car was in good condition.

The effect of exclusion clauses on third parties to the contract

The doctrine of privity means that the terms of a contract are only binding on the parties to the contract themselves. We have already seen that in general a party trying to enforce third party rights under a contract will fail for lack of privity. In the same way, despite the existence of an exclusion clause in a contract, it may not offer protection to parties other than the parties to the contract.

SCRUTTONS LTD V MIDLAND SILICONES LTD (1962)

Carriers had a contract to ship a drum of chemicals for a company, the claimants in the case. The bill of lading contained a clause limiting the liability of the carriers in the event of a breach to $500. The defendants were stevedores who were contracted by the carriers to unload goods. Their contract with the carriers contained terms that they should have the benefit of the limitation clause in the bill of lading. When the stevedores through their negligence did $583 worth of damage to the drum of chemicals they were sued and tried to rely on the limitation clause in the contract between the claimants and the carriers. Their defence failed because they were not parties to the bill of lading so could not claim any rights under it.

The fact that the doctrine of privity prevents a third party to a contract from relying on exclusions contained in it may mean that a claimant still has a party to sue despite the existence of the clause, where the third party is responsible for the damage, and is financially worth bringing an action against.

COSGROVE V HORSEFELL (1945)

A passenger on a bus was injured through the negligence of the driver. The contract with the bus company contained a valid exclusion clause which thus protected them from liability. This did not, however, protect the bus driver from an action in negligence.

There have of course been occasions where a party has successfully claimed the protection of an exclusion clause even though not a party to the contract in which the clause was contained. The approach, which is not without its critics, is to argue an agency relationship, and thus to claim that a contractual relationship is created also with the third party.

NEW ZEALAND SHIPPING CO. LTD V A. M. SATTERTHWAITE & CO. LTD (1975) (THE EURYMEDON)

Here there was a contract between a consignor and a carrier to ship drilling equipment to New Zealand. The bill of lading contained an exclusion clause stating that 'it is hereby expressly agreed that no servant or Agent of the carrier (including every independent contractor from time to time employed by the carrier) shall in any circumstances whatsoever be under any liability whatsoever to the shipper, consignee or owner of the goods or to any holder of the bill of lading for any loss or damage or delay of whatsoever kind arising or resulting directly or indirectly from any neglect or default on his part ...' and also stating that 'every right, exemption, limitation, condition and liberty herein contained ... shall extend to protect every such servant or agent of the carrier ...'. In the event stevedores hired by the carriers negligently damaged the drilling equipment and were sued by the consignors. Their attempt to claim protection under the carriers' exclusion clause succeeded. PC felt that the issue centred on whether the stevedores had given consideration under the contract. The stevedores had accepted a unilateral offer by the consignors that in return for their promise to carry out duties the consignors would in turn exempt them from any liability. The stevedores had accepted this offer by unloading the ship and could therefore rely on the exclusion clause.

3.5.4 CONSTRUCTION OF THE CONTRACT AS A WHOLE

Even though an exclusion clause satisfies the above tests and therefore appears to have been successfully incorporated into a contract this does not mean that it will necessarily operate successfully in all cases. The clause might still fail on a construction of the contract as a whole for a number of reasons.

The contra preferentum rule

The *contra preferentum* rule is a device that is basically hostile to ambiguities in a contract. The

activity

QUICK QUIZ

Consider whether exclusion clauses notified in the following ways will be successfully incorporated into contracts and say why:

A A notice placed on the counter in a shop.

B A notice contained in a signed contract.

C A notice contained in a delivery note where the parties have regularly dealt on the same terms.

D A notice posted on a hotel bedroom wall.

E A notice contained in a receipt.

F A notice on the back of a cloakroom ticket.

G A notice posted on the machine at the entrance to a car park.

---

basic proposition is this. If a party wishes to secure an exemption from liability for contractual breaches by means of incorporation of an exclusion clause in the contract then the clause must be specific as to the circumstances in which the exemption is claimed otherwise the clause will fail.

ANDREWS BROS. (BOURNEMOUTH) LTD V SINGER & CO. (1934)

A contract for the purchase of 'new Singer cars' contained a clause excluding 'all conditions, warranties and liabilities implied by statute, common law or otherwise …'. One car delivered under the contract was, strictly speaking, a used car because a prospective purchaser had used it. CA held that the supply of 'new Singer cars' was an express term of the contract. Since the exclusion clause applied to 'implied terms' the *contra preferentum* rule would prevent it being used in relation to express terms.

The effect of the *contra preferentum* rule as applied to exclusion clauses then is that, where there is any ambiguity in the contract, ambiguity will work against the party seeking to rely on the exclusion clause. Having inserted the clause in the contract that party cannot rely upon it unless it is clear.

HOLLIER V RAMBLER MOTORS (AMC) LTD (1972)

Hollier left his car with the garage as he had done on previous occasions. The normal conditions of the contract were contained in a form that Hollier had signed on previous occasions but not on the one in question. This form contained a term that 'The company is not responsible for damage caused by fire to customers' cars on the premises'. The car was damaged in a fire caused by the defendants' negligence. CA firstly held that the form was not incorporated into the contract merely by the previous course of dealings in this case. They also concluded that for the garage to rely on the clause they must have stated in it without ambiguity that they would not be liable in the event of their own negligence. Otherwise the customer might rightly conclude when making the contract that the company would be liable except where the fire damage was caused by other than the defendants' negligence.

It is important also to remember that the *contra preferentum* rule is not limited in its application to exclusion clauses. It can be used in construing other clauses in the contract where the term itself is ambiguous.

VASWANI V ITALIAN MOTOR CARS LTD (1996)

In this case the principle was applied to a price variation clause in a contract for the supply of Ferrari cars. The price variation would apply only in limited circumstances. When on a proper construction of the contract the suppliers had increased the cost to the purchaser for a reason not falling within those limited circumstances the supplier was unable to enforce the price variation.

Fundamental breach

Traditionally the courts were reluctant to allow a party to escape liability for a serious breach by the device of the exclusion clause. One way in which they could control this was by strict construction of the clause and of the contract as a whole as we have just seen.

Another method that the courts devised and at one time employed to combat the effectiveness of exclusion clauses was the doctrine of fundamental breach. By this doctrine a party who had committed a serious breach by breaching a central term of the contract, a 'fundamental breach', would find their exclusion clause rendered ineffective by the court. The fundamental breach would be treated as a breach of the whole contract, and therefore the other party would be able to treat the contract as repudiated. The party inserting the exclusion clause would be unable to rely on it since, by the doctrine, (s)he would be treated as being in breach of every term.

KARSALES (HARROW) LTD V WALLIS (1956)

In this case the purchaser arranged to buy a second-hand car on a hire purchase agreement. In this agreement was a clause stating that 'No condition or warranty that the vehicle is roadworthy, or as to its age, condition or fitness for any purpose is given by the owner or implied herein'. Though the purchaser had previously examined the car and found it satisfactory, when it was delivered the cylinder head had been removed, valves in the engine had burnt out, two pistons were damaged, the tyres were damaged and the radio was missing. The purchaser not surprisingly rejected the car. When he was sued the claimants tried to rely on the exclusion clause in the hire purchase agreement. CA rejected the argument. There had been a fundamental breach of the contract. There was

such a substantial difference between the contract as formed and the contract as performed that the breach went to the root of the contract and the claimant could not rely on the exclusion clause.

This approach of the court did not gain universal popularity with judges who found it to be destructive to the general philosophy of freedom of contract. There was also uncertainty as to what actually amounted to a fundamental breach. In consumer contracts judges might be more disposed to accepting the doctrine than they were in commercial contracts where bargaining strength was more equal. As a result the courts gradually moved to a position of deciding that the doctrine was unsustainable in the form expressed above and was merely a method of construction rather than a rule of law negating what the parties had freely decided between themselves.

SUISSE ATLANTIQUE SOCIÉTÉ D'ARMEMENT MARITIME SA v NV ROTTERDAMSCHE KOLEN CENTRALE (1967) (THE SUISSE ATLANTIQUE CASE)

The owners of a ship sought to sue the party that had chartered the vessel and were to pay them on the basis of the number of journeys made. The owners claimed, and it was accepted by the court, that breaches of the term concerning loading and unloading meant that the party chartering the vessel had made only eight voyages instead of the 14 that they might have been expected to complete. The charter party argued that their liability was limited to a fixed amount of $1,000 per day by virtue of a limitation clause in the contract rather than the actual loss. The shipowners countered this arguing that there was a fundamental breach as a result of which the limitation clause could not apply. The case was decided on the basis that the clause was not a limitation clause but a genuine liquidated damages clause, and in any case it was felt that there was no fundamental breach. Nevertheless, HL expressed the view that the doctrine of fundamental breach was a restriction on freedom of contract. Lord Wilberforce was a little more guarded since he recognised that where a breach is so serious that it is almost the same as no performance then it is hard to limit liability and still have a contract left.

The enactment of the Unfair Contract Terms Act 1977 did mean that consumers now had protection against exclusion clauses. The courts have subsequently been prepared to take a more relaxed view towards exclusion and limitation clauses in commercial contracts where the parties contract on the basis of a more equal bargaining strength. In this way a clause may be upheld where the parties have freely and genuinely agreed it at the time the contract was formed.

PHOTO PRODUCTIONS LTD V SECURICOR TRANSPORT LTD (1980)

Securicor was under contract on its own standard terms to provide a night patrol service at Photo Productions' factory. A clause in Securicor's standard terms stated that 'Under no circumstances shall the Company be responsible for any injurious act or default by any employee of the company unless such act or default could have been foreseen and avoided by the exercise of due diligence on the part of the Company as his employer'. The duty security officer on the night in question started a fire that got out of control and as a result burnt down a large part of the factory. It was not disputed that he was suitable for the work and nor was it considered that Securicor was negligent in employing him. While the trial judge held with Securicor, CA applied the doctrine of fundamental breach and found in Photo Productions' favour. HL, however, disagreed. They affirmed that parties dealing in free negotiations were entitled to include in their contracts any exclusions or limitations or modifications to their obligations that they chose. Since the clause was clear and unambiguous there was nothing to prevent its use and it therefore protected Securicor from their employee's actions. It was also fairly critical of the continued use of the doctrine of fundamental breach.

The approach has since been followed. It seems that in common law it is now immaterial how serious the breach is. If the clause seeking to exclude or limit liability occurs in a contract made out of equal bargaining strength then the party inserting the clause can rely on it provided it is clearly and unambiguously stated in the contract.

AILSA CRAIG FISHING CO. LTD V MALVERN FISHING CO. LTD (1983)

Securicor were under contract to the Aberdeen Fishing Vessels Owners Association Ltd, who acted on behalf of various fishing boat owners, to provide a security service in the harbour where boats moored. Following negligence by the security guard one vessel fouled another vessel; both sank and became trapped under the quay. The contract was on Securicor's standard terms and in the ensuing action they sought to rely on a clause in the contract limiting liability 'for any loss or damage of whatever nature arising out of or connected with the provision of or failure in provision of, the services covered by this contract ... to a sum ... not exceeding £1,000 in respect of one claim ... and ... not exceeding a maximum £10,000 for the consequences of any incident involving fire, theft or any other cause of liability'. The sums are clearly very small when compared to the likely cost of the damage done to two ships. The court, however, rejected the argument that since Securicor had clearly failed to carry out the terms of their contract at all they should be unable to rely on the limitation clause. HL stated that limitation clauses are not to be regarded with the same hostility as exclusion clauses because they relate to the risks to which the defending party is exposed, the remuneration he may receive and the opportunity of the other party to insure against loss. As a result they held that the clause was sufficiently clear and unambiguous to protect Securicor in the case. (The contract was itself made before the enactment of the Unfair Contract Terms Act 1977, otherwise there may well have been a different result.)

These two cases, often referred to as the 'Securicor cases', seem to suggest that the doctrine of fundamental breach can no longer apply. They also suggest that, subject now to statutory controls, where there is equality of bargaining strength and free negotiation the parties can include terms however onerous provided that the other side accepts them. These terms will then bind the party agreeing to them even if remedies are lost as a result.

On that level it is probably the case that the statutory provisions in the Unfair Contract Terms Act 1977 may be more effective in controlling exclusion clauses than the common law is.

GEORGE MITCHELL LTD V FINNEY LOCK SEEDS LTD (1983)

Seed merchants agreed to supply farmers with 30lb of Dutch winter cabbage seed for £192. A limitation clause in the contract limited liability in the event of breach to the cost of the seed only or to replacement seed. The farmers planned to sow 63 acres with the seed and calculated that their return would be £61,000. The seed was the wrong sort and was not merchantable and there was no crop. The farmers sued for £61,000 in compensation for their lost production. Using the terminology of the Unfair Contract Terms Act 1977 HL held that the clause was unreasonable and could not be relied on.

3.6 STATUTORY CONTROL OF EXCLUSION CLAUSES

3.6.1 INTRODUCTION

Provisions created by statute or in regulations are clearly the most effective in controlling the operation of both exclusion and limitation clauses in contracts. This is not to say that the common law has no relevance. Quite simply, as we have seen, if an exclusion clause has not been successfully incorporated into a contract according to the normal rules then it will be inoperable anyway.

There are two principal provisions provided by Parliament, the Unfair Contract Terms Act 1977 and the Unfair Terms in Consumer Contracts Regulations 1994 which were based in order to comply with EC Directive 93/13.

The Unfair Contract Terms Act is an effective break on the operation of exclusion clauses and as such a serious inroad into the principle of freedom of contract when compared, for instance, with the 'Securicor cases'. The Act applies to exclusions for tort damage as well as contractual breaches.

The 1994 regulations are based on the directive which is obviously aimed at harmonising rules on consumer protection throughout the European Union in order to make the single market

activity

SELF ASSESSMENT QUESTIONS

1 For what reasons did judges develop rules to control the use of contractual terms limiting or excluding liability?

2 In what ways does a limitation clause differ from an exclusion clause?

3 In what ways can the rule in *L'Estrange* v *Graucob* (1934) be described as unfair?

4 What complications are created when a person uses a vending machine or a ticket machine, and how do the courts deal with these problems?

5 Why are the courts reluctant to accept that tickets or receipts can contain contractual terms that then bind the parties?

6 Why were the courts prepared to accept exclusions or limitations in the case of such extreme breaches as those in the 'Securicor cases'?

7 To what extent did the common law control of exclusion clauses make statutory intervention inevitable?

8 How does the *contra preferentum* rule help to control the use of exclusion clauses?

- An exclusion clause is a term of a contract that aims to avoid liability for breaches of the contract, a limitation clause is one which has the effect of reducing damages if there is a breach of contract

- Again a party is bound by terms where (s)he has signed an agreement – *L'Estrange* v *Graucob* (1934)

- Judges gradually developed controls on the use of exclusion clauses because of their potential unfairness to consumers

- An exclusion clause will not be recognised unless it is incorporated into the contract:

  – the party subject to it must be aware of it at the time of contracting – *Olley* v *Marlborough Court Hotel* (1949)

  – though it is possible for past dealings to be taken into account if relevant – *McCutcheon* v *David MacBrayne* (1964)

  – the party wishing to rely on the clause must bring it to the other party's attention effectively – *Thornton* v *Shoe Lane Parking* (1971)

- Misrepresentations about the clause may mean that the party inserting it in the contract cannot rely on it – *Curtis* v *Chemical Cleaning & Dyeing Co.* (1951)

- In general third parties to the contract cannot rely on the clause – *Scruttons* v *Midland Silicones* (1962), but see *New Zealand Shipping* v *Satterthwaite* (1975)

- If the clause is ambiguous it cannot be relied upon – *Hollier* v *Rambler Motors* (1972)

- In recent times the courts have been prepared to take a different view where the parties contract on equal terms – *Photo Productions* v *Securicor Transport* (1980)

- Providing the clause is clear and unambiguous – *Ailsa Craig Fishing* v *Malvern Fishing* (1983)

FIGURE 3.6 *Key fact chart for common law control of exclusion clauses*

more effective. The regulations are in some senses narrower than the Act. This is because existing UK law already provided many of the features of the directive. Nevertheless, in some ways the regulations are broader than the Act because the directive was intended to apply in a much broader range of circumstances than the Act, and often imposes stricter duties.

The consequence is that when construing a given exclusion clause it may be appropriate to have regard to the Act, the regulations, and the common law.

3.7.2 THE UNFAIR CONTRACT TERMS ACT 1977

When passed the Act was certainly one of the most significant areas of consumer protection. However, it should be remembered that the Act does not cover every exclusion or indeed every unfair term.

What the Act does try to achieve is to protect the consumer by removing some of the inequalities in bargaining strength. It does this by making certain exclusion clauses automatically invalid, by drawing a distinction between consumer dealings and inter-business dealings, and by introducing a test of reasonableness to apply in inter-business dealings and in certain other circumstances. As a result of this some of the problems caused by unequal bargaining strength are mitigated.

Exclusions and limitations rendered void by the Act

Certain types of exclusion clauses are invalidated by the Act and will therefore be unenforceable even where they have been successfully incorporated in the contract.

- By s.2(1) a person cannot exclude liability for death or personal injury caused by his or her negligence.

- By s.5(1) any consumer contract clauses seeking to exclude liability by reference to the terms of a guarantee will fail in respect of defects which have been caused by negligence in the manufacture or distribution of the goods.

- By s.6(1) there can be no valid exclusion of breaches of the implied condition as to title in s.12 of the Sale of Goods Act 1979.

- This same provision applies in respect of Schedule 4 of the Consumer Credit Act 1974 which concerns the same type of condition.

- Section 6(2) invalidates any exclusion clause inserted in a consumer contract to cover breaches of the implied conditions of description (s.13), satisfactory quality (s.14(2)), fitness for the purpose (s.14(3)), and sale by sample (s.15)) in the Sale of Goods Act 1979.

- Again the provision will invalidate breaches of the same conditions in Schedule 4 of the Consumer Credit Act 1974.

- By s.7(2) there can be no valid exclusion in any consumer contract for breaches of the implied terms of reasonable care and skill (s.13), reasonable time (s.14), and reasonable cost (s.15) in the Supply of Goods and Services Act 1982.

- Under s.7(1) similar principles to those in s.6 apply in respect of goods which are transferred under the Supply of Goods and Services Act 1982.

Definitions of consumer contract and inter-business dealing

The Act inevitably is designed to operate principally for the protection of consumers. As a result the term consumer has to be defined in the Act. The definition is found in s.12(1) which identi-fies that a party acts in a contract as a consumer when:

'(a) he neither makes the contract in the course of a business nor holds himself out as doing so; and

(b) the other party does make the contract in the course of a business; and

(c) … the goods passing under or in pursuance of the contract are of a type ordinarily supplied for private use or consumption.'

If the party inserting the exclusion clause in the contract wants to argue that the party subject to the clause is not a consumer then by s.12(3) (s)he must prove it.

Whether or not a contract involves a consumer dealing or not is clearly a matter of construction for the courts. There are many situations where a party might buy goods that are ordinarily for business use, or a businessman buys goods but not for business use, so that difficulties can arise. Besides which a consumer can fall outside the definition in s.12 and thus lose the protection it entails if (s)he holds himself or herself out as acting in the course of a business in order to acquire a trade discount.

Business on the other hand is defined in s.14 as including 'a profession and the activities of any government department or local or public authority'.

Exclusions depending for their validity on a test of reasonableness

The Act identifies a number of contractual situations in which an exclusion clause will be valid provided that it satisfies a test of reasonableness. If it fails to satisfy these criteria then it will be invalid.

- By s.2(2) a clause seeking to exclude liability for loss, other than death or personal injury, caused by the negligence of the party inserting the clause can only stand if it satisfies the test of reasonableness in the Act.

QUICK QUIZ

Consider which of the following may be consumer dealings:

1 A solicitor buys 200 square yards of carpet to carpet her offices.

2 A carpet salesman sells at cost price to his brother enough carpet to carpet the whole house.

3 A private individual who owns seven large chest freezers buys enough lambs, and pigs cut into joints to fill the freezers.

4 A young man buys an ambulance second-hand to use as a normal vehicle.

- By s.3 in those contracts where the party deals as a consumer, or deals on the other party's standard business forms, the party inserting an exclusion clause cannot rely on a clause excluding liability for his or her own breach, or for a substantially different performance, or for no performance at all except where to do so would satisfy the test of reasonableness in the Act.

- By s.6(3) a party can only exclude liability for breaches of the implied conditions in s.13, s.14(2), s.14(3) and s.15 of the Sale of Goods Act 1979 in inter-business dealings where the test of reasonableness is satisfied.

- This same principle operates in the case of private sellers (those not selling in the course of a business) in respect of exclusions for breaches of s.13 and s.15 of the Sale of Goods Act.

- By s.7(3) exactly the same requirement of reasonableness operates in respect of exclusions for breaches of the implied conditions in s.3, s.4 and s.5 of the Supply of Goods and Services Act 1982.

- Under s.8 a clause seeking to exclude liability for misrepresentations will be subject to the same requirement of reasonableness.

- By s.4 consumer contracts clauses requiring a party to indemnify the other against loss will only be valid where the clause satisfies the reasonableness test. Such a clause might require the consumer to indemnify the party inserting the indemnity clause for injury, loss or damage caused to third parties.

THOMPSON v T. LOHAN (PLANT HIRE) LTD AND J. W. HURDISS LTD (1987)

A plant hire company hired out a JCB and driver. The contract required that the driver supplied should be competent, but the party hiring them would be liable for all claims arising from the use of the equipment or the work of the driver. On top of this the contract required them to indemnify the plant hire company for any claims against them. When the claimant was killed as a result of the driver's negligence the defendants claimed that the clause was a void exclusion clause under s.2(1) of the Act. The court held that it was in fact an indemnity clause covered by s.4 and thus subject to a test of reasonableness in determining its validity.

The test of reasonableness

Guidelines on what can be classed as reasonable are contained in both s.11 and Schedule 2 of the Act. These are not absolutely definitive so that the test is one really for judicial interpretation, although there is not a great amount of a case law on the area.

Section 11(5) identifies that it is for the party who inserts the clause in the contract and thus seeks to rely on it to show that it is reasonable in all the circumstances.

WARREN V TRUEPRINT LTD (1986)

A contract contained a limitation clause where the defendants were responsible only for a replacement film and would only undertake further liability if a supplementary charge were paid. They were obliged to but were unable to show that this clause was reasonable when they lost a couple's silver wedding snaps.

There are in effect three tests of reasonableness.

(a) Under s.11(1) which concerns exclusion clauses in general the test is whether the insertion of the term in the contract is reasonable in the light of what was known to the parties at the time when they contracted.

SMITH V ERIC S. BUSH (1990)

Here surveyors negligently carried out a building society valuation, and a defect was missed which later resulted in loss to the purchaser. The purchaser was obliged to pay for the valuation report. This and the mortgage application contained clauses excluding liability for the accuracy of the valuation report. The attempt to rely on the exclusion clause failed since the court were unwilling to accept that its inclusion was reasonable.

(b) Section 11(2) concerns those exclusion clauses referred to in s.6(3) and s.7(3), those involving breaches of the implied conditions in the Sale of Goods Act 1979 and Supply of Goods and Services Act 1982 in inter-business dealings. In the case of these the court should consider the criteria that are set out in Schedule 2:

- Whether the bargaining strength of the two parties was comparable – for instance, if the buyer could easily be supplied from another source then it would be.

- Whether or not the buyer received any inducement or advantage from the supplier that might make insertion of the exclusion clause reasonable, particularly if such an advantage could not be gained from any other source of supply.

- Whether the goods were manufactured, processed or adapted to the buyer's specifications.

- Whether exclusions or limitations of liability were customary practice.

(c) Section 11(4) specifically concerns limitation clauses. Here the party inserting the clause must show that a capability exists to meet liability if it arose. Insurance will also be considered.

GEORGE MITCHELL LTD V FINNEY LOCK SEEDS LTD (1983)

Here HL considered that the clause limiting damages to the price of the seeds was unreasonable since the suppliers had often settled out of court in the past and could have insured against such loss without altering their profits substantially.

Contracts falling outside the scope of the Act

A number of contracts of specific types will not be covered by the provisions of the Act. These are to be found in Schedule 1.

- Contracts of insurance.

- Contracts for the creation, transfer or termination of interests in land.

- Contracts that involve patents, copyright and other intellectual property.

- Contracts for the creation or dissolution of companies.

- Contracts for marine salvage, charter parties, or carriage of goods by sea or air (except in the case of incidents falling within the scope of s.2(1).

3.6.3 THE UNFAIR TERMS IN CONSUMER CONTRACTS REGULATIONS 1994

The scope of the regulations

The regulations are straightaway significantly different in operation to the Act because they cover contractual terms in general not just exclusion clauses. Nevertheless, they will as their name suggests operate only in relation to consumer contracts.

Consumer dealing is defined in different terms in the regulations than in the Act:

- A seller or supplier is defined as 'any person who sells or supplies goods or services and who in making a contract is acting for purposes related to his business'. So this is wider than in the Act.

- A consumer is defined as 'any natural person who is acting for purposes which are outside his trade, business or profession'. So this is narrower.

According to Regulation 39(1) the regulations will only apply where the parties have not individually negotiated the term in question. So the regulations operate particularly in relation to standard form contracts. In order to avoid the operation of the regulations therefore the seller or supplier will need to show that the contract has been negotiated and is not standard form.

As with the Act the regulations will not operate in the case of certain types of contract. These are identified in Schedule 1 and include contracts relating to employment, succession, family law rights and partnerships and companies. The regulations will not cover either insurance contracts where the risk and the insured are clearly defined. Other than this the scope of the regulations seems to be much broader than the Act, though their exact scope is uncertain.

Terms falling within the scope of the regulations

The regulations operate in respect of 'unfair terms'. According to Regulation 4(1) an unfair term is 'any term which contrary to good faith causes a significant imbalance in the parties' rights and obligations under the contract to the detriment of the consumer'. As a result the regulations introduce a general concept of unfairness into the making of contracts, which is then subject to controls.

'Good faith' is considered in Schedule 2. This identifies a number of factors that must be looked at in order to establish good faith:

- The relative bargaining strength of the parties to the contract.

- Whether the seller or supplier gave the consumer any inducement in order that (s)he would agree to the term of the contract in question.

- Whether the goods sold or services supplied under the contract were to the special order of the consumer.

- The extent to which the seller or supplier has dealt fairly and equitably with the consumer.

As well as these general guidelines, the regulations in Schedule 3 list a great number of terms that may generally be regarded as unfair, though the list is not intended to be exhaustive:

(a) Terms which limit or exclude liability for the death or personal injury of the consumer arising from an act or omission of the seller or supplier.
(b) Terms which inappropriately limit or exclude liability for a partial performance, a non-performance, or an inadequate performance.
(c) Terms that include provisions binding the consumer but which are only at the discretion of the seller or supplier.
(d) Terms allowing the seller or supplier to retain sums already paid over by the consumer who cancels the contract where there is no reciprocal term in relation to a cancellation by the seller or supplier.
(e) Terms requiring a consumer who is in breach of the contract to pay excessive sums in compensation to the seller or supplier.
(f) Terms allowing the seller or supplier to dissolve the contract where the same facility is

not made available to the consumer by the contract.

(g) Terms that enable a seller or supplier to dissolve a contract that has only indeterminate duration without giving reasonable notice of the dissolution, except where there are serious grounds for doing so.

(h) Terms which automatically allow a seller or supplier to extend a contract of fixed duration where the consumer does not indicate otherwise, when the deadline set for the consumer to indicate the contrary desire not to extend the contract is set unreasonably early.

(i) Terms which irrevocably bind the consumer to terms which (s)he had no real opportunity to become acquainted with prior to the formation of the contract.

(j) Terms that allow the seller or supplier to unilaterally alter terms without any valid reason specified in the contract.

(k) Terms allowing the seller or supplier to unilaterally alter without any valid reason the character of the goods or services supplied.

(l) Terms enabling the price of goods to be determined at the time of delivery or which allow a seller or supplier to alter prices without the consumer having the opportunity to cancel the contract.

(m) Terms giving the seller or supplier the right to interpret terms of the contract or otherwise to determine whether the goods or services supplied correspond to the requirements of the contract.

(n) Terms which limit obligations or commitments made by the agents of the sellers or suppliers.

(o) Terms requiring the consumer to comply with all obligations under the contract but not imposing a similar obligation on the sellers or suppliers.

(p) Terms which grant the sellers or suppliers the right to transfer obligations under the contract which might then have the effect of reducing the consumer's rights under any guarantees.

(q) Terms which would have the effect of hindering the right of the consumer to take legal action or which would restrict the availability of evidence.

A further requirement under Regulation 6 is that the terms of a contract should be expressed in plain and intelligible language. If any term is found to be unfair under the regulations then it will not bind the consumer.

activity

SELF ASSESSMENT QUESTIONS

1 To what extent will the Unfair Contract Terms Act 1977 prevent the exclusion or limitation of liability for negligence?

2 In what ways are a consumer dealing and an inter-business dealing different?

3 For what reasons does the Unfair Contract Terms Act make certain exclusions automati-

cally invalid if inserted in a contract?

4 Under the Unfair Contract Terms Act what exactly does reasonable mean?

5 Is there any difference between who is protected by the Unfair Contract Terms Act and the Unfair Terms in Consumer Contracts Regulations 1994?

The regulations still have certain limitations. They do not apply to any term that has been individually negotiated. This quite sensibly preserves the principle of freedom of contract, but it also has the effect in some cases of presuming an equality of bargaining strength that does not in fact exist. In introducing the regulations, the Government construed the provisions indicated in the directive quite narrowly. As a result of this, while the Trading Standards department has the power to challenge the standard form contracts of companies and large corporations the same facility has not been extended to the consumer groups that may have wished to police contracts. In consequence the directive may not be given full effect.

KEY FACTS

- Common law controls of exclusion clauses have also been supplemented by statutory controls through the Unfair Contract Terms Act 1977 and through the Unfair Terms in Consumer Contracts Regulations 1994 (the latter to comply with European Directive 93/13)

- The Act draws a distinction between consumer dealings and inter-business dealings

- Clauses in certain types of contract are made void by the Act, e.g. exclusion of liability for death or injury caused by negligence – s.2(1); exclusions of liability for breaches of the implied terms in the Sale of Goods Act 1979 and Supply of Goods and Services Act 1982 – ss. 6(1), 6(2) and 7(2)

- Clauses in certain other circumstances depend for their validity on a test of reasonableness e.g. damage caused by negligence – s.2(2); standard term contracts – s.3; breaches of Sale of Goods Act and Supply of Goods and Services Act implied terms – ss. 6(3) and 7(3)

- Under s.11 what is reasonable depends on the knowledge of the parties at the time of contracting and a number of factors can be taken into account, e.g. whether the goods were freely available elsewhere, whether the goods were made to the buyer's specification etc.

- The regulations are much wider and refer to unfair terms generally, not just exclusion clauses, but apply in consumer contracts only

- In general they are aimed at remedying inequality in bargaining strength and remove unequal conditions

FIGURE 3.7 *Key fact chart for statutory control of exclusion clauses*

CHAPTER 4

VITIATING FACTORS

4.1 VOID AND VOIDABLE CONTRACTS

We have looked so far at the requirements made on parties when entering into contracts and also at the obligations that parties may make for themselves when they have in fact contracted. If the parties have not complied with all of the necessary requirements that we looked at in Chapter 1 then there will not be a contract in existence anyway.

Nevertheless, the mere fact that all of the rules of formation have been complied with does not make a contract perfect. For instance, where a party has contracted on the basis of false information this is a denial of freedom of contract. That party may clearly have been unprepared to enter the contract if only (s)he had known the true facts.

Thus, even though the various requirements of formation might have been fully met, a party may still have legal rights and remedies because of other defects that are later discovered that are to do with other 'imperfections' at the time the contract was formed. Indeed contracts affected in such a way are often referred to as 'imperfect contracts'.

The defects in question are known as vitiating factors. A vitiating factor is one that may operate to invalidate an otherwise validly formed contract, that is one that conforms to all the rules of formation already identified.

To vitiate basically means to impair the quality of, to corrupt or to debase. In contractual terms this means that factors present at the time of the formation of the contract, possibly unknown to one or either party, mean that the contract lacks the essential characteristic of voluntariness, is based on misinformation or is of a type frowned on by the law. As a result the role of the law is to provide a remedy to the party who may not have wished to enter the contract given full knowledge of the vitiating factor at the time of formation.

There can be two effects if a contract is vitiated: it may be void or it may be voidable. Whether the contract is void or voidable in a given case depends on the type of vitiating factor that is complained of.

4.1.1 VOID CONTRACTS

In the case of certain vitiating factors the effect of demonstrating the presence of the vitiating factor to the court's satisfaction is to render the contract void.

Stating that a contract is void is in many ways the same as stating that the contract does not exist. This is because identifying a contract as void is identifying it as having no validity and therefore no enforceability in law.

4.1.2 VOIDABLE CONTRACTS

Where a contract is voidable there are different possibilities. The vitiating factor is identified and acknowledged but this does not necessarily mean that the contract is at an end.

A party who has entered a contract that is void-able for a vitiating factor can continue with the contract if that is to his or her benefit. On the other hand, that party can avoid their responsibilities under the contract and in effect set the contract aside.

4.1.3 THE CLASSES OF VITIATING FACTORS

There are essentially four classes of vitiating factors which themselves are subject to sub-divisions:

- misrepresentation
- mistake
- duress and undue influence
- illegality

4.2 MISREPRESENTATION

4.2.1 GENERAL

We have already considered in Chapter 3 that statements made before or at the time of contracting are known as representations. These representations can, if they are incorporated into the contract, be terms of the contract and as such may be actionable if they are breached.

Representations that are not incorporated into the contract will have no contractual significance if they are truly stated. They will have acted to induce the other party into the contract but that is where they end. Alternatively, they may be 'puffs' having no contractual significance.

A falsely made representation, however, is a 'misrepresentation' and it can have contractual significance even though it does not form part of the contract. In order to be actionable therefore the statement must not only be false but have acted to induce the other party to enter the contract.

Misrepresentation may refer to the false statement itself or it may be the action of making the false statement. The statement may be false or merely incorrect for it is now possible to claim for an innocent misrepresentation.

The consequences of a contract having been formed on the basis of a misrepresentation are for the contract to be voidable at the request of the party who is the victim of the misrepresentation. It is not void because this denies that party the right to continue with the contract if that is in their interest.

Traditionally misrepresentation was not actionable at common law. Some relief was available in equity, subject to a certain qualifications, and later a remedy was available where fraud could be proved. In general, though, a party had little possibility of claiming against a misrepresentation until the passing of the Misrepresentation Act 1967. For this reason it was often critical in the past for a party to prove that a statement made to them before the contract was a term.

It may still be advantageous to a party to identify that a representation has been incorporated as a term, though this is obviously more difficult where the contract is written. So misrepresentation should still be viewed in the general context of pre-contractual statements and representations.

A final point about misrepresentation is that it also shares some features with common mistake. As a consequence it is not impossible to see both pleaded in a case.

4.2.2 WHEN WILL A MISREPRESENTATION OCCUR?

Definition

A misrepresentation occurs, as we have already said, when a representation made at or before the time of the contract is also falsely stated. A misrepresentation can therefore be defined as a statement of material fact, made by one party to a contract to the other party to the contract, during the negotiations leading up to the formation of the contract, which was intended to operate and did operate as an inducement to the other party to enter the contract, but which was not intended to be a binding obligation under the contract, and which was untrue or incorrectly stated.

This is a very precise definition and if not conformed to it will not give rise to a misrepresentation. The components of this definition then should be considered individually.

The statement complained of is required to be one of material fact

It cannot therefore have been a mere opinion, unless of course the opinion was not actually held at the time of the making of the statement.

BISSET V WILKINSON (1927)

A representation as to the number of sheep land could hold was not based on any expert knowledge so could neither be relied upon nor be actionable as a misrepresentation.

Neither can it be a statement expressing future intention which would be speculation rather than fact, though it could be if the statement was falsely representing a state of mind which did not exist.

EDGINGTON V FITZMAURICE (1885)

The directors of a company borrowed money representing that they would use the loan for the improvement of the company's buildings. In fact they had intended from the start to use the loan to pay off serious, existing debts. They had misrepresented what their actual intentions were.

It could not either be a mere 'puff' which attaches no weight and is not intended to be relied upon at all.

CARLILL V THE CARBOLIC SMOKE BALL CO. LTD (1893)

The company's argument that their promise to pay £100 to whoever contracted flu was only a puff failed. The maxim *simplex commendatio non obligat* could not apply where they had supported the promise by lodging £1,000 in a bank to cover possible claims.

The statement that is claimed to be a misrepresentation must have been made by one party to the contract to the other party

As a result it will not be a misrepresentation where the false statement that it is argued induced the other party to contract was made by a third party, unless that third party is the agent of the other party.

PEYMAN V LANJANI (1985)

The defendant took the lease of premises under an agreement requiring the landlord's permission. The defendant did not attend the meeting at which the agreement was struck but sent an agent who he thought would create a better impression with the landlord. He later decided to sell the lease on to the claimant and again this would require the landlord's permission. Once more he sent his agent. The claimant discovered the deception after he had paid over £10,000 under the agreement with the defendant. He then successfully applied to rescind the contract. Using the agent was a misrepresentation of the legitimacy of the lease which had never been agreed between the defendant and the landlord.

The statement complained of must have been made before or at the time of the contract

If the statement therefore was made after the agreement was reached then it cannot be actionable as a misrepresentation because it had no effect on the formation of the contract.

ROSCORLA V THOMAS (1842)

After a deal had been struck for the sale and purchase of a horse the seller represented that it was 'sound and free from vice'. In fact the horse was unruly but the purchaser could not claim since the promise was made after the agreement.

The statement has to be an inducement to enter the contract

Therefore it must be materially important to the making of the contract.

It will not matter that the representation would not generally be an inducement as long as it induced the claimant.

JEB FASTENERS LTD V MARKS BLOOM & CO. LTD (1983)

The claimant engaged in a takeover of another company in order to obtain the services of two directors of the other company. In investigating the company it relied on accounts which had been negligently prepared. There could be no claim of misrepresentation since the purpose of taking over the company was to secure the services of the directors and the accounts were no inducement. They were not material to the real purpose.

MUSEPRIME PROPERTIES LTD V ADHILL PROPERTIES LTD (1990)

Three properties were sold by auction. There was a misrepresentation as to the existence of an outstanding rent review which could result in increased rents and therefore increased revenue. The defendants unsuccessfully challenged the claimants' claim for rescission arguing that the statement could realistically induce nobody to enter the contract.

It cannot be an inducement where the other party is unaware of the misrepresentation.

It will not be a misrepresentation where the party to whom it is made already knows the statement to be false.

It will not be a misrepresentation where the party to whom it was made never actually relied upon the statement in entering the contract.

ATTWOOD V SMALL (1838)

A mine was purchased and certain information given as to its remaining capacity. This was in fact false. The claimant could not argue a misrepresentation, however, since in buying the mine he had actually relied on his own mineral survey which was also inaccurate.

The statement was not intended to form part of the contract

If it were intended to be contractually binding then it would be a warranty rather than a misrepresentation.

COUCHMAN V HILL (1947)

Here the statement that the heifer was 'unserved' could not be a misrepresentation because of the significance attached to it. It was a term incorporated into the contract.

The representation was falsely made

Clearly if the representation was true it would have no further contractual significance once the contract was formed.

4.2.3 THE DIFFERENT TYPES OF MISREPRESENTATION

The character of a misrepresentation

A misrepresentation can obviously arise in a number of different ways. It could be a merely inaccurate statement, made for instance in all innocence, the inaccuracy being unknown to the maker of the statement. This could happen where the maker of the statement is relying on information supplied in manufacturers' specifications for example, or oral statements made about goods by a previous owner. A misrepresentation can also be a quite deliberate lie, intended to deceive and stated in full knowledge that it is untrue. In between these points a misrepresentation can be carelessly made by assuming knowledge and failing to check on the actual details.

As a result, misrepresentations can be classified according to type. Since the passing of the Misrepresentation Act 1967 the significance is less marked than it was, but it can still be important in determining what remedy is available to a party who is the victim of the misrepresentation. Traditionally the character of the misrepresentation was vital since only a fraudulently made misrepresentation was actionable, and in the tort of deceit rather than in the law of contract.

Originally everything that was not a fraud was classed as an innocent misrepresentation and the only remedy was in equity for rescission of the contract. Now it is possible to identify fraudulent, negligent and innocent misrepresentations, and there are remedies available in common law and under statute.

Fraudulent misrepresentation

At common law traditionally the only action available for a misrepresentation was where fraud could also be proved. This action itself is fairly recent, coming only at the end of the last century. This demonstrates clearly how vital it was to many litigants in the past to show that a statement on which they had relied had been incorporated into the contract as a term, otherwise they might be left without any remedy at all.

DERRY V PEEK (1889)

A tram company was licensed to operate horse drawn trams by Act of Parliament. Under the Act they would also be able to use mechanical power by gaining the certification of the Board of Trade. They made an application and also issued a prospectus to raise further share capital. In this, honestly believing that permission would be granted, they falsely represented that they were able to use mechanical power. In the event their application was denied and the company fell into liquidation. Peek, who had invested on the strength of the representation in the prospectus and lost money, sued. His action failed since there was insufficient proof of fraud. Lord Herschell in HL defined the action as requiring actual proof that the false representation was made 'knowingly or without belief in its truth or recklessly careless whether it be true or false'.

So those are the three possibilities if an action in deceit is to be successful. Knowingly is straightforward, the representor knew the inaccuracy of his/her statement. In other words, there is a deliberate falsehood. If the representor acted without belief in the statement then this is also a statement falsely made. A recklessly made statement must be something more than mere carelessness. In all cases the essence of liability is the dishonesty of the defendant in making a statement which (s)he did not honestly know to be true. The motive for making the statement is largely irrelevant. If the claimant has suffered loss as a result then there is a claim.

The simplest defence available then is to show an honest belief in the truth of the statement. It would not have to be a reasonable belief provided it was honestly held, and as a result fraud is extremely difficult to prove.

Remedies for fraudulent misrepresentation

As we have said a party suffering loss as the result of a fraudulent misrepresentation can sue for damages in the tort of deceit. The method of assessing any damages awarded then will be according to the tort measure, i.e. to put the claimant in the position (s)he would have been in if the tort had not occurred, rather than the contract measure which is to put the claimant in the position (s)he would have been in if the contract had been properly performed.

This may result in more being recovered by way of any claim for consequential loss. As Lord Denning put it in *Doyle* v *Olby (Ironmongers) Ltd* (1969) 'the defendant is bound to make reparation for all the damage flowing from the fraudulent inducement'.

This point has been confirmed so that the defendant is responsible for all losses including any consequential loss providing a causal link can be shown between the fraudulent inducement and the claimant's loss.

SMITH NEW COURT SECURITIES V SCRIMGEOUR VICKERS (1996)

The claimants had been induced to buy shares in Ferranti at 82.25p per share as a result of a fraudulent misrepresentation that they were a good marketing risk. The shares were actually trading at 78p per share at the time of the transaction. Unknown to either party the shares were worth considerably less since Ferranti itself had been the victim of a major fraud. The claimants, on later discovering the fraud, chose not to rescind but to sell the shares on at prices ranging from 49p to 30p per share. HL held that the losses incurred were a direct result of the fraud that induced the claimants to contract. As a result any losses awarded should be based on the figure paid of 82.25p rather than the 78p.

The clear consequence of the judgment is that heavier claims can be pursued if fraud is alleged, and there is therefore an encouragement to do so if proof is available.

The claimant who is a victim suffering loss as the result of a fraudulent misrepresentation then has two choices on discovering the fraud. (S)he may affirm the contract and go on to sue for damages as indicated above. But the claimant might also disaffirm the contract and refuse further performance.

If this is the claimant's choice then there are two further possible courses of action. Firstly, if there is nothing at this point to be gained by bringing action against the other party, the claimant can discontinue performance of his or her obligations and do nothing. Then if he or she is sued by the maker of the fraud he or she can use the misrepresentation as a defence to that claim. Alternatively, the claimant might seek rescission of the contract in equity on discovering the fraud.

Negligent misrepresentation

Traditionally any misrepresentation that was not identifiable as a fraud would be classed as an innocent misrepresentation for which the only possible action was for rescission of the contract in equity. The reason there was no available action for a negligently made misrepresentation was that negligence falls short of the criteria identified by Lord Herschell in *Derry* v *Peek* (1889).

There have, however, been developments in both common law and statute meaning that an action is now possible for a negligent misrepresentation. A common law action is again only possible in tort rather than contract and is a much more limited action than that available under the Act.

Common law

An action for a negligent misstatement causing a pecuniary, that is a financial, loss to be suffered by the other party is now possible.

HEDLEY BYRNE & CO. LTD V HELLER & PARTNERS LTD (1964)

The claimants were asked to provide advertising work worth £100,000 for another company, Easipower, on credit. Sensibly they sought a reference as to creditworthiness from Easipower's bankers, the defendants. They wrote back confirming that Easipower were a 'respectably constituted company good for its ordinary business engagements'. The bankers also claimed to reply without any responsibility for the reference they had given. When Easipower went into liquidation with the claimants still unpaid they brought an action in the tort of negligence against the bankers. Their action failed because the bank had validly disclaimed any liability for their reference. Nevertheless, HL, *in obiter*, considered that such an action would be possible in certain 'special relationships' where the person making the negligent statement owed a duty of care to the other party to ensure that the statement was accurately made. In reaching this conclusion, HL approved Lord Denning's dissenting judgment in *Candler* v *Crane Christmas & Co.* (1951), where he felt that negligently prepared company accounts should be actionable.

Subsequent case law has both accepted and refined the *Hedley Byrne* principle. The requirements of the tort are threefold. The party making the negligent statement must be in possession of the particular type of knowledge for which the advice is required. There must be sufficient proximity between the two parties that it is reasonable to rely on the statement. The party to whom the statement is made does rely on the statement and the party making the statement is aware of that reliance.

It is also possible for the principle to apply to representations as to a future rather than a present state of affairs.

ESSO PETROLEUM CO. LTD V MARDEN (1976)

Esso developed a filling station on a new site near to a busy road and let it to Marden. During negotiations for the lease their representative indicated that the throughput would amount to 200,000 gallons per year. Marden queried this figure but contracted on the basis of the reassurance of the more experienced representative. In fact the local authority then required pumps and entrance to be at the rear of the site, accessible only from side streets. As a result throughput was never more than 86,502 gallons per year, and the petrol station uneconomical. Marden lost all his capital in the venture and gave up the tenancy. Esso sued for back rent and Marden counter-claimed with two arguments, both of which were successful. Firstly, he claimed that the estimate of throughput was a warranty on which he was entitled to rely. Secondly, he claimed that the relationship with Esso was a special one creating a duty of care. Esso's failure to warn him properly of the changed circumstances and the very different throughput resulting was negligence under *Hedley Byrne*.

Statute

The above case started before the Misrepresentation Act was in force, otherwise a simpler action may have been available.

The Misrepresentation Act was passed in 1967. Its benefit is that it is much broader than any of the actions previously available. It is particularly appropriate where the claimant is unable to prove fraud. It followed the recommendation of the Law Reform Committee that damages should be available for losses arising from a negligent misrepresentation. However, the Act in that sense was based on the law as it existed before *Hedley Byrne* and so takes no account of that principle but rather operates as an alternative to fraud.

Section 2(1) identifies the main means of taking action. By this section

'Where a person has entered into a contract after a misrepresentation has been made to him by another party thereto and as a result thereof he has suffered loss, then if the person making the misrepresentation would be liable to damages in respect thereof had the misrepresentation been made fraudulently, that person shall be so liable notwithstanding that the misrepresentation was not made fraudulently unless he proves that he had reasonable grounds to believe and did believe up to the time the contract was made that the facts represented were true.'

All that this basically means is that a party who is the victim of a misrepresentation has an action available without having to prove either fraud or the existence of a special relationship in order to fulfil *Hedley Byrne* criteria.

There are then some important differences with the past law:

● Firstly, the burden of proof is partly reversed. Where formerly the claimant would have been required to prove fraud, under the Act it will be for the defendant to show that (s)he in fact held a reasonable belief in the truth of the statement once it is shown to be a misrepresentation.

● If the misrepresentation is negligently made then the claimant has the choice of whether to sue under the Act or under the *Hedley Byrne* principle.

● If the Act is chosen then there is no need to show the relationship required for *Hedley Byrne* type liability.

HOWARD MARINE DREDGING CO. LTD V A. OGDEN & SONS (EXCAVATING) LTD (1978)

Contractors estimating a price for depositing excavated earth at sea sought advice from the company from whom they intended to hire barges as to their capacity. The Marine Manager negligently based his answer of 1,600 tonnes on dead weight figures from Lloyd's register rather than checking the actual shipping register which would have shown a figure of 1,055 tonnes. Delays resulted in the work and the contractors refused to pay the hire for the barges. When sued for payment they successfully counter-claimed using s.2(1) of the Misrepresentation Act 1967.

Remedies for negligent misrepresentation

Damages are available as a remedy both under the Act and at common law. If the *Hedley Byrne* principle is applied then damages are calculated according to the standard tort measure. This means that damages will only be awarded for a loss that is a foreseeable consequence of the negligent misrepresentation being made.

Under the Act damages are again calculated according to a tort measure since the Act is stated as being appropriate where fraud cannot be proved. It is more arguable whether damages will be according to the normal tort measure or whether the test applied in the tort of deceit is appropriate. The latter is more beneficial and has been accepted in *Royscot Trust Ltd* v *Rogerson* (1991).

One consequence of damages under the Act being calculated according to tort measures, of course, is that they can be reduced if contributory negligence can be shown.

The only remedy traditionally available if the misrepresentation was negligently made would be for rescission in equity and this is still possible.

Innocent misrepresentation

As has already been stated, any misrepresentation not made fraudulently was formerly classed as an innocent misrepresentation regardless of how it was made. There would be no action possible under the common law, only an action for rescission of the contract in equity.

The emergence of the *Hedley Byrne* principle and of s.2(1) of the Misrepresentation Act 1967 means that possibly the only misrepresentations that can be claimed to be made innocently are where a party makes a statement with an honest belief in its truth. The obvious example of this is where the party merely repeats inaccurate information, the truth of which (s)he is unaware.

In this case an action under s.2(1) of the Act would not be possible since this can be successfully defended by showing the existence of a reasonable belief in the truth of the statement. Nevertheless, the traditional action for rescission in equity is still a possibility. There is also a possibility of claiming under s.2(2) of the Act.

Remedies for innocent misrepresentation

As we have seen, since damages were not formerly available under common law they will not be available either under s.2(1).

However, the court has a discretion under s.2(2) to award damages as an alternative to rescission where it is convinced that to do so is the appropriate remedy. The court must consider that 'it would be equitable to do so, having regard to the nature of the misrepresentation and the loss that would be caused by it if the contract were upheld, as well as the loss that rescission would cause to the other party'

It is important to consider three significant points regarding s.2(2):

● There is no actual right to damages as there may be in a common law action. The award of damages is at the discretion of the court as an equitable remedy would be.

● Since damages are to be awarded as an alternative to rescission then only one remedy can be granted not both.

● The measure of damages to be awarded is uncertain but since it is in lieu of rescission then it is unlikely that consequential loss could be claimed.

Prior to the passing of the Act then the only available remedy was rescission. This remedy may be appropriate because, in the words of Sir George Jessell, 'no man ought to seek to take advantage of his own false statements'.

REDGRAVE V HURD (1881)

In this case rescission was ordered in a contract between two solicitors for the sale and purchase of one's practice. He had misstated the income from the practice and when the other backed out tried to claim specific performance of the contract. The other solicitor successfully counter-claimed for rescission.

4.2.4 EQUITY AND MISREPRESENTATION

The availability of damages for a misrepresentation varies, as we have seen, according to the nature of the misrepresentation and the nature of the action brought by the injured party. Rescission, on the other hand, may be available whatever the character of the misrepresentation.

QUICK QUIZ

Suggest what type of misrepresentation is involved in the following examples:

1 James is selling his car to Frank. Frank asks what is the capacity of the engine. James, after looking at the registration documents, tells him that it is 1299 c.c. Unknown to James, the documents are incorrect.

2 Sally, a saleswoman, tells Rajesh that a three-piece suite is flame-resistant in order to gain the sale, without checking the manufacturer's specification that would have revealed that it was not.

3 Howard, who has no qualifications at all, tells prospective employers at an interview that he has a degree in marketing.

Rescission is, of course, an equitable remedy and its award is subject to the discretion of the court. It must be remembered that an actionable misrepresentation makes a contract voidable rather than void, so the contract remains valid until such time as it is 'set aside' by the court for the injured party.

The right to rescind is not absolute and it may be lost in a number of circumstances:

- *Restitutio in integrum* (literally, restored with integrity) is vital to rescission. In essence this means that, since the party claiming is asking to be returned to the pre-contract position, known as the *status quo ante*, this in fact must be possible to achieve. If it is not then rescission of the contract will not be granted.

LAGUNAS NITRATE CO. V LAGUNAS SYNDICATE (1899)

A nitrate field was bought by the claimants on an innocent misrepresentation of the defendant as to the strength of the market for nitrates. They made profits for a period but were affected adversely by a general depression in prices, at which point they sought rescission. They failed because they had extracted the nitrates for some time and the field could not be restored to its pre-contract order.

- An affirmation of the contract after its formation by the party seeking rescission will defeat the claim.

LONG V LLOYD (1958)

A lorry was bought on the basis of a representation as to its 'exceptional condition'. Several faults were discovered on the first journey that the purchaser then allowed the seller to repair. When the lorry again broke down through its faulty condition the buyer's claim to rescission was unsuccessful. He had accepted the goods in a less than satisfactory condition and was unable to return them.

- Delay is said to 'defeat equity'. So a failure to claim rescission promptly may mean it is unavailable as a remedy.

LEAF V INTERNATIONAL GALLERIES (1950)

A contract for the sale of a painting of Salisbury Cathedral described it as a Constable. When the description later proved false the purchaser's claim to rescission failed because a five-year period had then elapsed.

● If a third party has subsequently gained rights in the goods then it would be unfair to interfere with those rights by granting rescission.

WHITE V GARDEN (1851)

A rogue bought 50 tons of iron from the claimant using a bill of exchange in a false name, and resold it on to a third party who acted in good faith. When the claimant discovered that the bill of exchange was useless he seized the iron from the innocent third party. This was illicit since the third party had gained good title to the iron.

● Under s.2(2) of the Misrepresentation Act 1967 the judge has a discretion which remedy to apply. Rescission will not therefore be available if the judge has decided that damages is a more appropriate remedy.

It is possible to be granted rescission and an indemnity for other expenses incurred as a result of the misrepresentation.

WHITTINGTON V SEALE-HAYNE (1900)

Poultry breeders took a lease of premises on the basis of an oral representation that the premises were in a sanitary condition. This was untrue. The water was contaminated and the buyer became ill and some poultry died. At the time the claimants were not entitled to consequential loss because they could not prove fraud. However, as well as their claim to rescission of the contract, they were awarded an indemnity representing what they had spent out in terms of rent and rates and other costs.

In granting rescission the court must always take into account the seriousness of the breach and the likely consequences of rescission for both parties.

4.2.5 WHEN NON-DISCLOSURE AMOUNTS TO MISREPRESENTATION

There is no basic obligation at common law to volunteer information that has not been asked for.

FLETCHER V KRELL (1873)

A woman who had applied for a position as a governess had not revealed that she had formerly been married. Despite the fact that single women were generally preferred her failure to reveal her marriage was not a misrepresentation.

In fact silence of itself cannot generally be classed as misrepresentation.

HANDS V SIMPSON, FAWCETT & CO. (1928)

A commercial traveller acquired employment without advising his new employers that he was disqualified from driving, even though this was an essential part of the work. Even so he was not obliged to volunteer the information without being asked.

However, there are a number of situations where the act of withholding or not offering information will amount to misrepresentation:

● Contracts which are *uberimmae fides* or where the 'utmost good faith' is required. This principle is commonly applicable to contracts of insurance on the basis that with full information the insurer may not have been prepared to accept the risk.

LOCKER AND WOOLF LTD V WESTERN AUSTRALIAN INSURANCE CO. LTD (1936)

The insured party had not revealed to the insurer when entering the contract that another company had refused him insurance. This was clearly material to the contract.

● Fiduciary relationships, where again good faith is required. These may include the relationship between trustees and beneficiaries. A failure to reveal certain information material to the contract may result in its being set aside under the doctrine of constructive fraud.

TATE V WILLIAMSON (1866)

A young man dreadfully in debt was persuaded by an adviser to sell his land to raise money to settle the debts. This adviser then bought the land having not revealed full details as to its value and thus obtaining at half value. The contract was set aside.

- Where a part truth amounts to a falsehood.

> ### DIMMOCK V HALLETT (1866)
>
> A person selling land revealed that the land was let to tenants but not that the tenants were terminating the lease and thus that the income from the land was reducing. This amounted to a misrepresentation.

- Where a statement made originally in truth becomes false during the negotiations. This will then be a misrepresentation.

> ### WITH V O'FLANAGAN (1936)
>
> A doctor selling his practice stated the true income at the beginning of negotiations but by the time of the sale this had dwindled to a negligible figure. Since he failed to reveal this it was a misrepresentation.

4.3 MISTAKE

4.3.1 INTRODUCTION

Mistake is sometimes considered to be a difficult area of law. There are certainly a number of reasons for this. It is quite closely related to the area of agreement since agreement is said to depend on a *consensus ad idem*, a voluntary arrangement mutually agreed by both parties. If a party enters a contract on the basis of a mistake then this is said to negate the *consensus ad idem*, since any consensus could not be genuinely held in that case.

Mistake, certainly common mistake, is also closely related to misrepresentation, since a party might claim that they are mistaken owing to the misrepresentation of the other party, however innocent. In consequence a claimant sometimes pleads both claims.

Where goods have passed to third parties following a contract that is made as a result of a mistake this can also have quite profound effects since one apparently innocent party is going to lack rights to the subject matter of the contract. If a purchaser under a contract has not been given full title and then sells on to a third party then the maxim *nemo dat quod non habet* might apply. This means that nobody can transfer title who does not already have good title himself. The result of this could be goods being reclaimed from a third party who has acquired the goods in innocence of the defective title. This will become

activity

SELF ASSESSMENT QUESTIONS

1 What is a misrepresentation?

2 How can a misrepresentation be distinguished from an opinion?

3 Why is it important to think of misrepresentation in the context of all pre-contractual statements?

4 Why would a party traditionally need to prove that a falsely-made representation was in fact a term of the contract?

5 Can a misrepresentation be actionable if it does not induce the other party to enter the contract?

6 How easy is it to prove fraud?

7 Which is the more advantageous action, that under *Hedley Byrne* principles or that under s.2(1) of the Misrepresentation Act 1967?

8 In what ways has equity been vital to the development of misrepresentation?

KEY FACTS

- A misrepresentation is a false statement of fact made by one party to the contract to the other at or before the time of contracting not intended to be part of the contract but intended to induce the other party to enter the contract
- It will have the effect of making the contract voidable
- A misrepresentation can be made: fraudulently; negligently; innocently
- If fraudulent there is an action in the tort of deceit – *Derry* v *Peek* (1889) – in which case it must have been made knowingly or deliberately; or without any belief in its truth; or recklessly as to whether it is true or not – an honest belief is a defence
- If negligent then there is a possible action in tort under *Hedley Byrne* – provided it is made in a special relationship, where the party making it has expert knowledge relied upon by the other party; or under s.2(1) Misrepresentation Act 1967 – *Howard Marine & Dredging Co.* v *Ogden & Sons Ltd* (1978)
- If innocent then traditionally the only remedy was for rescission in equity, now there is also an action for damages under s.2(2) Misrepresentation Act
- Rescission is only available if
  - *restitutio in integrum* applies *Lagunas Nitrate* v *Lagunas Syndicate* (1899)
  - the contract is not affirmed *Long* v *Lloyd* (1958)
  - there is no undue delay *Leaf* v *International Galleries* (1950)
  - and no third party has gained rights.
- Non-disclosure of information will also amount to misrepresentation
  - in contracts *uberimmae fides* (of utmost good faith) such as insurance – *Locker and Woolf* v *Western Australian Insurance* (1936);
  - where a part truth amounts to a falsehood *Dimmock* v *Hallett* (1866); and
  - where a true statement later becomes false *With* v *O'Flanagan* (1936).

FIGURE 4.1 *Key fact chart for misrepresentation*

apparent when considering a unilateral mistake as to the identity of the other party to the contract.

For these reasons judges have shown unwillingness in the past to accept a mistake as operative and therefore justifying a declaration that the contract is void. The result of the courts' attitude and the common law constraints imposed on mistake has been for the courts to use equitable solutions, but only in those situations where the common law rules cannot apply.

This is then the first distinction to make in mistake, whether it is the common law or equity that provides the remedy. For the common law to have any effect the mistake must have been an 'operative' one. It must have been a mistake fun-

damental to the making of the contract such that the contract was only formed because of the mistake.

If the mistake is recognised as being 'operative' then the contract will be void *ab initio* (literally, from the start). Not only will the parties be returned to their pre-contract position, but also any further rights coming out of the contract will have no effect, because the contract is as though it had never existed.

If the court cannot accept that the mistake is operative, in other words the mistake was not the reason that the contract was formed, then common law rules cannot apply but a solution in equity is possible, subject to the discretion of the court and the normal maxims.

If equity can be applied then the effect is for the contract to be voidable. The contract could continue but a party to the contract who has been the victim of the mistake can avoid his/her obligations and the contract may be set aside.

There are basically three classes of mistake, although these themselves subdivide to cover more specific circumstances:

- A 'common mistake' is one where both parties have made the same mistake. The mistake can concern either the existence of the subject matter of the contract, or its quality, with different consequences depending on which it is.

- A 'mutual mistake' again involves both parties being mistaken, but at cross-purposes over the nature of the agreement rather than making the same mistake.

- A 'unilateral mistake' is one where only one of the parties is mistaken. By implication the other party will usually know of the other party's mistake and be set to take advantage of it.

4.3.2 COMMON MISTAKE

Res extincta

Res extincta means literally 'the subject matter no longer exists', so this involves a mistake about the existence of the subject matter of the contract at the time that the contract was formed. If at that time the subject matter of the contract did not exist then the mistake is an operative one, because clearly neither party to the contract would contract for something that did not exist, and the contract will be void.

COUTURIER V HASTIE (1852)

The contract was for sale and purchase of a cargo of grain in transit and which both parties believed existed at the time of the contract. In fact the captain of the ship had sold the cargo, as was customary practice, when it had begun to overheat. When this was discovered the court (while not actually mentioning mistake) declared the contract

---

void, rejecting the seller's argument that the buyer had accepted the risk and should pay the price. This basic proposition is now contained in s.6 Sale of Goods Act 1979 – 'Where there is a contract for specific goods, and the goods without the knowledge of the seller have perished at the time when the contract is made, the contract is void'.

The above case involved specific goods. If, however, the contract is of a more speculative nature then the consequence of the goods not existing at the time of the contract may be different, since the buyer has only bought a chance.

MCRAE V COMMONWEALTH DISPOSALS COMMISSION (1950)

Here the contract was for the salvage rights to a wreck. The buyer went to considerable expense to locate the wreck at the approximate position given by the Commission, but could not find it. When they sued for breach of contract the Commission tried to rely on the principle in the last case but failed. There was no operative mistake. The claimants had bought the salvage rights on the clear representation by the Commission that the wreck did exist, the Commission therefore being liable for breach of contract.

If the goods have 'commercially perished' at the time the contract is formed unknown to either party then this still could be an operative mistake leading to the contract being void. Commercially perished would mean that the goods no longer had the value attached to them in the contract.

BARROW LANE AND BALLARD LTD V PHILLIPS & CO. LTD (1929)

Here the seller bought 700 bags of groundnuts in a particular warehouse and, without ever inspecting the goods, sold them on. When the buyer came to inspect the goods 109 bags had been stolen. The seller could not sue the owner of the warehouse who had become insolvent so he sued the buyer for the price but failed. The goods had ceased to exist in commercial terms and the contract was void.

The classical operation of the principle of *res extincta* will still apply in modern commercial transactions.

ASSOCIATED JAPANESE BANK (INTERNATIONAL) LTD. v CREDIT DU NORD SA (1988)

A sale and leaseback arrangement over four packaging machines was concluded between the bank and a man called Bennett. Credit du Nord guaranteed Bennett's obligations under the contract. The machines did not in fact exist and the bank was prevented from suing Bennett when he was declared bankrupt. They then sued on the guarantee. Steyn J held that the guarantee was subject to a condition precedent that the four machines existed at the time of the contract. Applying the test from *Bell* v *Lever Brothers* (1932), for the mistake as to the existence of the machines to be an operative one the subject matter of the contract must be radically different to that expected by both parties. The guarantee was an accessory contract. The non-existence of the machines was of paramount importance to the guarantor in granting the guarantee. The *res extincta* doctrine applied and the contract of guarantee was void.

Res sua

Res sua means literally 'the subject matter has already changed hands', so this principle applies to a mistake as to ownership of the goods. If a party enters a contract as a buyer when in fact, unknown to either party, he owns the title to the goods then the contract is void.

COOPER v PHIBBS (1867)

Cooper took a three-year lease for a salmon fishery from Phibbs. At the time of the contract both parties believed that Phibbs owned the fishery when in fact it was subsequently discovered that Cooper was life tenant of the property. He was unable to dispose of the property but was effective owner at the time of contracting. Cooper then tried to have the lease set aside. HL agreed to this but also granted Phibbs a lien in respect of the considerable expense he had gone to in improving the property. Although the case was decided on equitable rather than common law principles, Lord Atkin in *Bell* v *Lever Brothers* (1932) refers to it as an example of *res sua*. The case can be seen as *res sua*. Equity was applied and the contract declared voidable rather than void because firstly Cooper had only an equitable interest in the property, and secondly Phibbs had spent money on it.

Mistake as to the quality of the contract

This is inevitably a more complex area than either *res extincta* or *res sua*. Generally, however, where the mistake that is common to both parties is that the subject matter of the contract is of a quality different to that anticipated then the mistake has three consequences. The mistake will not be considered an operative one, it will have no effect in common law on the contract, and both parties are still bound by their original obligations.

BELL v LEVER BROTHERS LTD (1932)

Lever Brothers employed Bell as Chairman of a subsidiary company, Niger Co. Ltd, with the brief of rejuvenating the subsidiary. When he was successful in his task and the subsidiary was merged with another company Lever Brothers offered a settlement of £30,000 for the termination of his existing service contract. It was later discovered that Bell was in breach of a clause of the service agreement, having entered into private dealings on his own account. Lever Brothers then sued for return of the settlement claiming fraudulent misrepresentation, in which they failed, and breach of contract. CA then held that the settlement was invalid for common mistake, the mistake being that Lever were bound to pay the settlement when they could in fact have merely fired Bell. In HL Lord Warrington felt that the 'mistake' could have no effect on the contract unless it was 'of such a fundamental character as to constitute an underlying assumption without which the parties would not have made the contract they in fact made'. The mistake was not one affecting the consideration or that went to the root of the matter, so the contract of settlement could not be void. Lord Atkin stated that 'Mistake as to quality of the thing contracted raises more difficult questions. In such a case, a mistake will not affect assent unless it is the mistake of both parties and is as to the existence of some quality which makes the thing without the quality essentially different from the thing as it was believed to be...'. The settlement had not been given as a result of the breach or otherwise of the clause, but in recognition of the work already done by Bell. It was not an operative mistake. The mistake was not fundamental in any way to the making of the settlement agreement. Lever Brothers were merely upset because had they known of the breach before the settlement they could have fired Bell and avoided the expense.

The common law principle then is applied absolutely. Nevertheless, the fact that the mistake is not operative means that an action in equity may still result.

SOLLE V BUTCHER (1950)

In an agreement for the lease of a flat both parties mistakenly believed that the rent was not subject to controls under the Rent Restrictions Act. The rent was set at £250 per annum, though if subject to the Act it should have been £140. However, had the landlord realised that it was subject to those controls he might have applied to increase the rent because of considerable repairs and improvements he had made to what was otherwise war-damaged property. On discovering that the rent was subject to controls under the Act the tenant then sued for a declaration that the rent should be £140 and to recover the difference already paid. On appeal the landlord claimed that the contract was void for mistake. CA held that at common law the mistake had no effect on the contract. It was merely a mistake as to quality. This did not prevent the court from setting the agreement aside in equity.

In some situations parties will easily mistake the quality of the contract. This is particularly so in the case of art works where valuations are a matter of opinion rather than fact, and the attitude taken by the court to the effect of the mistake can vary enormously.

LEAF V INTERNATIONAL GALLERIES (1950)

The contract was for the sale and purchase of an oil painting of Salisbury Cathedral that was innocently represented as being a Constable. The buyer discovered that it was not a Constable when he tried to sell it five years later. His claim for rescission failed and he appealed. CA rejected his claim holding that an action for damages would have been the appropriate action, and also that he had delayed too long for rescission. Lord Denning made some interesting references to mistake: 'There was no mistake about the subject matter of the sale. It was a specific picture of "Salisbury Cathedral". The parties were agreed in the same terms on the subject matter, and that is sufficient to make a contract...'. So Lord Denning suggested that the identity of the painter was irrelevant. It was a mistake only as to the quality of the contract.

Nevertheless, the opposite view has been taken in

relation to the effect of a mistake as to quality where works of art are concerned.

PECO ARTS INC. V HAZLITT GALLERY LTD (1983)

The claimant bought a drawing from a reputable gallery that both parties mistakenly believed was an original. The contract included an express term that the work was an original inscribed by the artist. Eleven years later the claimant discovered that the work was a reproduction, and tried to claim return of the purchase price and interest. The court, distinguishing *Leaf*, allowed his claim. The time lapse was no problem since it was accepted that, even with due diligence the truth could not have been discovered at an earlier stage.

4.3.3 MUTUAL MISTAKE

A mutual mistake occurs where the parties to the contract are at cross-purposes over the meaning of the contract. One of the problems here is that it is doubtful whether any meaningful and sustainable agreement has ever been reached.

What the courts will do is to try to make sense of the agreement that does exist in order that it can continue. To do this they will implement an objective test and will try to identify a common intent if one exists.

If, however, the promises made by the two parties so contradict one another as to render any performance of the agreement impossible then the court will deem that an operative mistake exists and the contract will be declared void.

RAFFLES V WICHELHAUS (1864)

The contract was for the sale of cotton on board a ship named *Peerless* that was sailing out of Bombay. In the event there were two ships both named *Peerless* both sailing from Bombay on the same day. The seller was selling the cargo other than the one that the buyer was intending to buy. There was no way of finding a common intention. The contract could not be completed and was declared void.

So ambiguity surrounding the subject matter of the contract may well make a mistake operative and result in the contract being declared void.

SCRIVEN BROS. & CO. V HINDLEY & CO. (1913)

There are different qualities of hemp. One is called 'tow' and is generally of inferior quality. Auctioneers were selling hemp that was actually 'tow' though this was not made absolutely clear in the catalogue. The purchaser bid extravagantly under the mistake that he was actually bidding for the superior product. He rejected the goods on discovering the mistake. The auctioneer's action to enforce the contract failed owing to the mutual mistake. There could be no reconciling the situation to mutual satisfaction.

However, where one party is merely mistaken as to the quality of the contract then the mistake is not mutual. The contract can be continued, although it is not to the liking of that party and the contract will not be declared void.

SMITH V HUGHES (1871)

Smith was offered a consignment of oats that he examined a sample of and bought. On delivery he discovered that the oats were 'new oats' rather than oats from the previous year's crop. He refused delivery and when the seller sued for the price claimed that the contract should be void for mistake. He believed he had been offered 'good old oats' rather than 'good oats' as the seller claimed. The court felt that it could not declare a contract void merely because one party later discovered it was less advantageous than he believed it to be.

4.3.4 UNILATERAL MISTAKE

The cases in unilateral mistake show two particular lines: the mistake will either be as to the terms of the contract or will be as to the identity of the other party to the contract. In either case, the significant point is that only one of the parties to the contract is actually mistaken, hence unilateral mistake.

The basic principle is simple. Where one party contracts on the basis of a mistake known to the other party then the contract is void because there is no consensus in this instance. The mistake must obviously be a fundamental one. A mistake as to quality will not suffice.

Mistaken terms

If one party to the contract makes a material mistake in expressing his or her intention and the other party knows, or is deemed to know, of the mistake then the mistake may be operative with the result that the contract may be void.

HARTOG V COLIN & SHIELDS (1939)

The contract was for 30,000 Argentine hare skins. The price was stated at 10d and 1 farthing per lb. The regular practice was to sell per piece. Since there were about three pieces per lb. this would reduce the cost of each piece to a third. The buyers tried to enforce the contract on the basis of the mistaken term. The sellers countered that the offer was wrongly stated, as would be common knowledge in the trade. The court declared the contract void for the mistake.

The test of whether or not such a mistake is operative and therefore voids the contract appears to have three parts:

● One party to the contract is genuinely mistaken over a material detail that had the truth been known would have meant (s)he would not have contracted on the terms stated. (This was clearly the position of the sellers in the above case.)

● The other party to the contract ought reasonably to have known of the mistake. (Again the court accepted in the above case that the buyers were taking advantage of a situation that they would have been aware of because of usual custom in the trade.)

● The party making the mistake was not at fault in any other way.

SYBRON CORPORATION V ROCHEM LTD (1984)

Having opted for early retirement, a manager was awarded a discretionary pension. It was subsequently discovered that the manager together with other employees had engaged in a fraud on the company. The company sought to have the pension agreement set aside and succeeded. CA held that it was the manager's breach of duty that had induced the company to believe that they were obliged to grant him the pension. They had done so under a mistake of fact.

However, the mistake cannot be operative if the other party is unaware of it.

WOOD V SCARTH (1858)

A landlord agreed to lease premises to a tenant mistakenly believing that his clerk had made plain to the tenant before the agreement that a premium of £500 was expected as well as rent. The court held that the mistake could not be operative since the tenant contracted on terms not including the premium in good faith and without knowledge of the landlord's mistake. The contract for rent only was therefore not affected.

Mistaken identity

Again the area is at first sight complex and it raises different issues to those already considered. However, the occasions when the principle arises are not straightforward. The common scenario will be when a rogue has made off with property belonging to another party after making false representations as to his or her identity. This then is the mistake made by the other party. The goods will then usually have been transferred to an innocent third party from whom the original owner is trying to recover them.

The cases are distressing because the courts will have to decide between two seemingly innocent parties which to disappoint. If the contract is one covered by the Sale of Goods Act 1979 then the rogue, as a seller, has no title to pass in disposing of the goods. If the original owner identifies the title as only voidable sufficiently early then he may have rights as against a subsequent purchaser. If the third party buying the goods from the rogue does so in good faith and without notice of the defective title then (s)he may have a good title as against the party from whom the rogue acquired the goods.

The case law shows some confusion and contradictions. There are some basic requirements that the original owner must satisfy in order to claim that (s)he retains ownership.

- In order to claim a mistake on the basis of a mistaken identity the party seeking to claim rights in the goods must first of all show that (s)he intended to contract with a person other than the one with whom they did contract. So there must have been another person.

KING'S NORTON METAL CO. LTD V EDRIDGE, MERRETT & CO. LTD (1897) (THE KING'S NORTON METAL CASE)

Wallis contracted under the name Hallam & Co. for the purchase of expensive items of brass rivet wire. The goods were supplied but never paid for. The Metal Co. sued the party who eventually purchased them from Wallis to recover the goods. The court was not prepared to void the contract for mistake. The Metal Co. was not so much mistaking the identity of Wallis, since Hallam & Co. did not exist, as mistaking the creditworthiness of Wallis with whom they had in fact contracted.

- In order to claim that the mistake is operative and therefore makes the contract void the mistake must be shown to have been material to the formation of the contract.

CUNDY V LINDSAY (1878)

Blenkarn hired a room at 37 Wood Street, a street where a highly respectable firm, Blenkiron & Co., conducted its business at number 123. He then ordered a large number of handkerchiefs from Lindsay's with a signature designed to be confused with the reputable firm. The goods were supplied and Blenkiron billed. Blenkarn had sold some on to Cundy before the fraud was discovered. Lindsay then tried to recover the goods. On appeal HL held that the contract was void for mistake. The mistake was operable because Lindsay's were able to show that the identity of the party trading from 37 Wood Street was material to the formation of the contract. Unlike the King's Norton Metal case, there was a party here with whom the claimants wished to contract. The third party acquired the goods from Blenkarn without any title.

● If the one party is to be able to claim that the mistake is to be considered material then the other party to the contract must have known of it.

BOULTON V JONES (1857)

The defendant ordered certain goods from Brocklehurst in order to take advantage of a set-off (a legal means of keeping the goods in return for a debt already owed to the defendant). Unknown to the defendant Brocklehurst had assigned his business to the claimant. When the goods were delivered and the defendant refused to pay, the defendant then tried to have the contract set aside for mistake as to the identity of the party with whom he had contracted. The court would not void the contract. The other party knew nothing of the mistake and had merely responded to an order to supply goods. The mistake was not operative.

Mistaken identity and face to face dealing

Where a party negotiates a contract in person then the party is deemed to be contracting with the other party who is physically present at the negotiations, whatever the identity that the other party assumes. In this way the mistake is not as to the identity but as to the creditworthiness of the other party. This is not material to the forming of the contract so the mistake is not operative and the contract cannot be void.

PHILLIPS V BROOKS LTD (1919)

North, a rogue, selected jewellery in a shop including a necklace worth £2,550 and a ring worth £450. He wrote a cheque for £3,000 misrepresenting himself as Sir George Bullough, whose address the jeweller found in the directory. North persuaded the jeweller to let him leave with the ring, leaving the rest of the jewels until his cheque cleared. The cheque bounced and when the jeweller later discovered the ring in a pawnshop where North had sold it he tried to sue for its recovery. His argument that the contract with North was based on mistaking North's identity for that of Sir George Bullough failed. He could have only intended to contract with the party he met face to face. The pawnshop gained good title because they bought in good faith without notice of any defect in title.

One case actually cast doubt on this principle and caused some confusion.

INGRAM V LITTLE (1960)

Sisters jointly owned a car that they advertised for sale. The rogue who came to buy it offered to pay by cheque. The ladies initially refused the cheque but were persuaded when the rogue passed himself off as an important local figure, and found the name offered in the telephone directory. The cheque bounced and when the ladies discovered the car in the hands of an innocent third party to whom the rogue had sold it they sued to recover the car. CA, strangely, accepted that the mistake as to identity was material to the contract, as was shown when the ladies initially rejected the cheque and so relied on the identity of the important local figure.

The case is seen as being either decided on the particular facts or indeed wrongly decided, and subsequent cases have reiterated the original principle.

LEWIS V AVERY (1972)

A rogue buying a car represented himself as a famous actor of the time, Richard Greene, and showed a false studio pass after his cheque was at first rejected. When the cheque was dishonoured and the seller later discovered the whereabouts of the car he sued the new owner for recovery. His action failed. The claimant had been induced into believing that the party he contracted with was somebody different but had still contracted with that party. The mistake was not operative and the contract could not be void.

It follows that, for a party to claim that the identity of the other party is material to the making of the contract, he must have taken adequate steps to ensure the true identity of the other party.

CITIBANK NA V BROWN SHIPLEY & CO. LTD; MIDLAND BANK V BROWN SHIPLEY & CO. LTD (1991)

A rogue passed himself off as a company officer and persuaded a bank to issue a banker's draft to pay for large amounts of foreign currency he was buying from another bank. The currency was passed once the legitimacy of the banker's draft was established. When the fraud was discovered the issuing bank tried to recover from the other bank but failed. They had done insufficient to establish the bona fides of the rogue for his identity to be material and their mistake to be operative.

4.3.5 MISTAKE AND EQUITY

If a mistake has been shown to be operative then the common law rather than equity will apply. If it is not an operative mistake and therefore not void then an equitable solution may be sought in one of three ways:

● Rescission of the contract, with the contract being set aside and new terms substituted.

● A refusal to grant the other party's claim for specific performance of the contract.

● Rectification of a document containing a mistake which is material.

Rescission

If the party claiming rescission can show that it is against conscience to allow the other party to take advantage of the mistake then the court may allow rescission, though usually at the same time substituting more equitable terms as an alternative.

SOLLE V BUTCHER (1950)

At common law the mistake as to the application of rent review rules had no effect. Nevertheless, the court set aside the original terms that were unworkable in the circumstances and was prepared to allow the tenant the choice of terminating the lease or continuing it with the rent set at £250. This would be appropriate since the improvements justified the increase.

Rescission will often be the appropriate remedy in the contracts made as the result of an innocent misrepresentation.

Refusal of specific performance

As an equitable remedy, specific performance

MAGEE V PENNINE INSURANCE CO. LTD (1969)

An insurance agent had filled out the proposal form for the proposer, Magee. The details as to the people driving the car were inaccurately stated as including Magee, who was stated as having a provisional licence, and his eldest son, a police driver, since only his youngest son was to drive the car and Magee himself did not have a licence. When the car was in an accident, the insurance company agreed to pay £385 being the true value of the car. When the company later discovered the inaccuracies in the proposal they refused to pay and Magee sued to enforce the agreement. On appeal Lord Denning affirmed his own principle in *Solle v Butcher* (1950), held that the agreement to pay was made as a result of a common mistake and was voidable in equity.

depends on the discretion of the court. So it can also be refused where one party entered the agreement on the basis of a mistake and:

● it would be unfair or harsh to expect him or her to perform the contract; or

● the mistake was actually caused by the other party's misrepresentation; or

● the other party knew of the mistake and tried to take advantage of it.

WEBSTER V CECIL (1861)

Webster offered to buy land from Cecil and Cecil, who stated that the land had cost him more than that, rejected his offer of £2,000. Webster then tried to enforce a written agreement for sale of the land for £1,250. His claim to specific performance failed since the written agreement clearly ran contrary to any oral one.

The court will not, however, refuse an order merely because it means one party has made a worse bargain than they thought they had.

TAMPLIN V JAMES (1880)

James bought an inn at auction. He believed that he had also bought adjoining land but had not. He had made no check of the plans and he could not resist an order of specific performance of the contract.

Rectification of a document

The court can rewrite a written document that does not conform to the actual agreement between the two parties, as happened in *Webster v Cecil* (1861).

The two sides in dispute will usually have a different view of what the agreement is so the side seeking rectification must show that a complete and certain agreement was reached, and that the agreement remained unchanged up to the time of contracting.

CRADDOCK BROS. LTD V HUNT (1923)

Craddock agreed to sell his house to Hunt, not intending an adjoining yard to be included in the sale. By mistake the yard was included in the conveyance so Craddock immediately sought rectification of the document and succeeded.

4.3.6 NON EST FACTUM

This is literally translated as 'this is not my deed'. It is a doctrine that operates only in respect of written agreements. Usually the principle in *L'Estrange* v *Graucob* (1934) applies and a party is bound by written agreements that (s)he has signed.

However, in some circumstances a party is able to claim that they only signed as a result of a genuine mistake as to the nature of the document signed. The doctrine is subject to strict requirements. It will only be appropriate because the party signing is subject to some weakness that has been exploited by the other party, for instance blindness or senility. Also the other party must have represented that the document is something different than that which has been signed.

If this is so and the party signing has taken the precautions available to check on the authenticity of the document before signing then the contract is void. However, before the court will declare the contract void it must be satisfied that the document is of a kind materially different to what it was represented to be, and that the party has not been negligent in signing it.

SAUNDERS V ANGLIAN BUILDING SOCIETY (1970)

This case, which began as *Gaillie* v *Lee*, involved an elderly widow who decided to transfer her property to her nephew on the stipulation that she could live there for the rest of her life. She did this so that he could borrow money on the property in order to start a business. The document was drawn up by Lee, a dishonest friend of the nephew, and was in fact a conveyance to him rather than a deed of gift to the nephew. Lee then borrowed against the property and defaulted on the loan. The widow in answer to the claim for repossession initially succeeded with a plea of *non est factum*. On a later appeal HL rejected *her* plea. There was insufficient difference between the documents that she did sign and had intended to sign. Both gave up her rights to the property and she had not done enough to check its nature.

4.4 DURESS AND UNDUE INFLUENCE

4.4.1 INTRODUCTION

The courts have always been keen to preserve freedom of contract. A necessary element of this freedom is that the agreement should be reached voluntarily. This means that no force or coercion should be used in order to secure the agreement. If a party does enter a contract because of coercion by the other party then the law accepts that the contract should be set aside and the party coerced should be relieved of their own obligations.

Such principles have been developed so that there is an action under common law for duress, and an action in equity for undue influence. In the first a remedy will be automatic on proof of the duress. In the second the remedy is at the discretion of the court. In either case the contract will be voidable rather than void.

activity

SELF ASSESSMENT QUESTIONS

1 In what ways is mistake close to a) agreement and b) misrepresentation?

2 Why might a party prefer to sue for a mistake rather than for misrepresentation?

3 When will a contract be void in common law as a result of a mistake?

4 In what sense is it possible to say that a common mistake as to quality has no effect on the contract?

5 What is the difference between a common mistake and a mutual mistake?

6 What is meant by the requirement in unilateral mistake that the mistake must be a material one?

7 In what ways does the case of *Ingram* v *Little* (1960) seem to be wrongly decided?

8 In what circumstances might a plea of *non est factum* arise?

9 Suggest what type of mistake is involved in the following scenarios:

A I contracted with Farmer Giles to buy his horse called Silver. He has two horses called Silver. He believes that he has sold me his brown stallion with the white flash on the nose. I believed that I was buying his grey mare.

B A man calling himself Tony Blair knocked on my door one evening and bought my car by cheque. I accepted the cheque because I believed he was the Prime Minister but I have now discovered that this was not the case, as his cheque has been returned.

C In the pub tonight I agreed to sell my collection of Elvis records to a man called Stan. However, when I went home and asked my wife where they were she said that she had thrown them away years ago because they were never played.

4.4.2 DURESS

Duress is a common law area which was traditionally associated with intimidation that was real or at least sufficiently real and threatening to vitiate the consent of the other party, and mean that (s)he acted not by free will.

CUMMING V INCE (1847)

An inmate in a private mental asylum was coerced into signing away title to all of her property or she was threatened that the committal order would never be lifted. The contract was set aside. It was not made of her free will.

The law developed so that the threat vitiating the contract was associated with violence or even death.

BARTON V ARMSTRONG (1975)

A former chairman of a company threatened the current managing director with death unless the managing director paid a large sum of money for the former chairman's shares. It was shown in the case that the managing director was actually quite happy to buy the shares and would have done so without the threats. Nevertheless they had been made and were therefore sufficient to amount to duress vitiating the agreement they had reached as a result.

Threats to carry out a lawful action, however, cannot amount to duress.

KEY FACTS

- A mistake can occur in one of three principal ways:
  - both parties are making the same mistake – known as common mistake
  - the parties are at cross purposes and so are both mistaken but making different mistakes – known as mutual mistake
  - only one of the parties is mistaken and the other party knowingly takes advantage of this – known as unilateral mistake
- If a mistake is operative (i.e. the contract was only made because of the mistake) then the contract is void at common law
- It may be possible to rescind the contract or set it aside in equity only if the mistake is not operative
- A common mistake can void a contract where the mistake is as to the existence of the subject matter of the contract – *res extincta* – *Couturier* v *Hastie* (1852)
  - but it will not void the contract where the mistake is only as to the quality of the contract made – *Bell* v *Lever Brothers* (1932)
  - authenticity of art works is a difficult area – *Leaf* v *International Galleries* (1950)
- A mutual mistake will void the contract when the parties are so at odds that it is impossible to make any sense of the agreement – *Raffles* v *Wichelhaus* (1864)
  - but if the mistake is only about the quality of the contract then the contract will continue – *Smith* v *Hughes* (1871)
- With unilateral mistake the mistake can be about the terms of the contract or about the identity of the other party to the contract
  - if the mistake is about the terms of the agreement then it is operative and the contract void if the one party through no fault of his or her own is mistaken over a material detail and the other party knows or ought to know of the mistake – *Hartog* v *Colin & Shields* (1939)
  - if the mistake is the identity of the other party then that mistake must have been material to the formation of the contract – *Cundy* v *Lindsay* (1878)
  - if the parties contract face to face then they are said to be contracting with the party in front of them regardless of what identity they assume – *Lewis* v *Avery* (1972)
- Where the mistake is not operative equity can be used in one of three ways:
  - to rescind the contract or set it aside on terms – *Solle* v *Butcher* (1950)
  - to refuse a request for specific performance of the contract – *Webster* v *Cecil* (1961)
  - to rectify a document which contains the mistake – *Craddock Brothers* v *Hunt* (1923)
- It is possible to claim *non est factum* (this is not my deed) in relation to a document signed provided a party has some disability which is being taken advantage of and (s)he thinks (s)he is signing an entirely different type of document – *Saunders* v *Anglian Building Society* (1970)

FIGURE 4.2 *Key fact chart for mistake*

WILLIAMS V BAYLEY (1886)

A young man forged his father's signature on promissory notes (IOUs) which he gave the bank causing them to lose money. The bank approached his father and demanded that he should mortgage his farm to them to cover the son's debt or they would prosecute. The threat was for lawful action and so could not amount to duress. However, the court were disturbed by the manner of the threats and accepted that they did amount to undue influence.

Traditionally for there to be duress the threat should be made against the other party not against their property.

> ### SKEATE V BEALE (1840)
>
> A promise given in return for recovery of goods that had been unlawfully detained was not duress.

4.4.3 ECONOMIC DURESS

This last point had been the subject of some criticism. A doctrine has subsequently developed in the commercial field whereby a contract may be set aside not because of threats of violence but because extreme coercion has rendered the contract otherwise commercially unviable. It was first discussed in cases without actually being applied.

> ### D.C. BUILDERS V REES (1965)
>
> In this case, as we have already seen, the Rees's forced the small firm of builders to accept a cheque of £300 in full satisfaction of the actual bill of £462 or take nothing. They had no choice in the circumstances but to accept. Lord Denning considered the issue of inequality of bargaining strength and felt that coercion in such circumstances justified avoidance of the agreement.

The point was then taken further and a more formal doctrine was developed.

> ### OCCIDENTAL WORLDWIDE INVESTMENT CORPORATION V SKIBS A/S AVANTI (1976) (THE SIBOEN AND THE SIBOTRE)
>
> During a world recession in the shipping industry charterers demanded a renegotiation of their contract with the shipowners. They claimed that they would otherwise go out of business and that with no assets they were not worth suing. The shipowners had no choice but to agree. Because of the recession they would have little chance of other charters of their vessels. Kerr J suggested that the question to ask was 'was there such a degree of coercion that the other party was deprived of his free consent and agreement'. He also identified a two-part test to establish if economic duress had occurred: (i) did the party alleging the coercion

> protest immediately; and if so (ii) did that party accept the agreement or try to argue openly about it?

Lord Scarman then also accepted the basic doctrine in *Pao On* v *Lau Yiu Long* (1980)

'there is nothing contrary to principle in recognising economic duress as a factor which may render a contract voidable provided always that the basis of such recognition is that it must always amount to a coercion of will which vitiates consent'.

Lord Scarman also outlined the test for coercion:

'whether the person alleged to have been coerced did or did not protest ... did or did not have an alternative course open to him ... was independently advised ... took steps to avoid it'.

The doctrine and the tests have been subsequently and satisfactorily applied.

> ### ATLAS EXPRESS LTD V KAFCO (IMPORTERS AND DISTRIBUTORS) LTD (1989)
>
> Atlas, a national carrier, contracted with Kafco to deliver Kafco's basketwork to Woolworth stores. It was estimated that each load would be between 400 and 600 cartons and a price of £1.10p per carton was agreed. In fact the loads were only about 200 cartons each and Atlas refused to carry any more without a minimum £440 per load. Kafco had no immediate alternative and were forced to agree to protect their contract with Woolworth. However, they later failed to pay the agreed rate and Atlas sued. Tucker J held for Kafco and said 'I find that the defendant's apparent consent to the agreement was induced by pressure which was illegitimate ... In my judgement can properly be described as economic duress, which is a concept recognised by English law, and which in the circumstances of the present case vitiates the defendant's apparent consent...'.

The doctrine has been extended to apply wherever there is an intentional submission to improper pressure, although what the difference is between legitimate pressure and improper pressure is not always certain.

> **UNIVERSE TANKSHIPS INCORPORATED OF MONROVIA V INTERNATIONAL TRANSPORT WORKERS FEDERATION (1983) (THE UNIVERSAL SENTINEL)**
>
> One of a number of cases involving action by the ITWF in respect of a campaign to improve conditions on ships 'flying flags of convenience'. Here the ship was blacked by the union and forced to pay towards the ITWF welfare fund to secure the ship's release. This was economic duress, the pressure being illegitimate, though the court were undecided on the difference between what was legitimate pressure and what was not.

The doctrine is still developing and is subject to uncertainty. Even though the economic duress can be shown this is no guarantee of a remedy.

> **NORTH OCEAN SHIPPING CO. LTD V HYUNDAI CONSTRUCTION CO. LTD (1978) (THE ATLANTIC BARON)**
>
> A shipyard agreed to build a tanker for a shipping company, payment to be in five instalments. As part of the contract the shipyard opened a letter of credit for repayment of payments already made if they should fail to build the ship. After payment of the first instalment the shipyard demanded an increase in the price. The shipping company reluctantly agreed as they needed the ship to complete other contracts. The letter of credit was increased as a result. Months after completion of the ship the shipping company sued for return of the excess. While the court accepted that there was economic duress, it was felt that the increase in the letter of credit was sufficient consideration for the fresh promise, and also the delay meant that the contract was affirmed.

4.4.4 UNDUE INFLUENCE

Traditionally developed under equity, and so any remedy is at the court's discretion, undue influence developed to cover those areas where improper pressure prevents a party from exercising their free will in entering a contract. Since equity is inevitably more flexible than common law the doctrine could be applied whenever a party had exploited the other party to gain an unfair advantage.

Clearly there is nothing wrong with trying to induce another to enter a contract, so it is the degree of influence and the context in which it occurs that the court is concerned with in determining what is and is not acceptable.

Traditionally a distinction was made between those situations where undue influence was presumed from the relationship of the two parties and where undue influence had to be proved. The courts have recently redefined these classes.

> **BANK OF CREDIT AND COMMERCE INTERNATIONAL SA V ABOODY (1990)**
>
> Here a wife was able to avoid liability to the bank in respect of a surety transaction which she was induced to enter by her husband. She succeeded because the bank was said to have either constructive or actual notice of her husband's actions in either exercising undue influence over her or misrepresenting the amount of money he owed the bank. The court drew distinctions between the two classes of undue influence:
> *Class 1* – actual undue influence – representing the original situation where there was no special relationship between the parties and so the party alleging the undue influence is required to prove it.
> *Class 2* – presumed undue influence representing the traditional class where there was a special relationship and so undue influence is automatically presumed unless the contrary is proved.

The classifications have subsequently been approved in the leading case.

> **BARCLAYS BANK PLC V O'BRIEN (1993)**
>
> The bank granted an overdraft of £135,000 for O'Brien's failing business on the security of the jointly-owned marital home. The bank's representative failed to follow instructions to ensure that both O'Brien and his wife receive independent advice before signing. In the event the company went further into trouble and the bank then sought to enforce the surety to recover the debt. Mrs O'Brien succeeded in showing that she had been induced to sign as a result of her husband's undue influence and had an inaccurate picture of what she had signed. HL considered that:
>
> ● There was a presumption of undue influence against the husband.

- Such a presumption could also apply with cohabitees.

- A surety of this type could not be enforced where it had been gained by the presumed undue influence of the principal debtor.

- Unless the creditor took reasonable steps to ensure that the surety was entered into with free will and full knowledge then the creditor would be fixed with constructive notice of the undue influence.

- Constructive notice could be avoided by warning of the risks involved and advising of the need to take independent legal advice at a meeting not attended by the principal debtor.

Class 1: Actual undue influence

This type of undue influence applies where there is no special relationship between the parties. In this way it is impossible to show that an abuse of confidence or trust has occurred and as a result the party alleging the undue influence must show it.

Undue influence will be accepted in these circumstances where it is possible to show that the coercion amounted to a dominance to the extent that the party subjected to it was unable to exercise free will or act independently of the influence in contracting.

WILLIAMS V BAYLEY (1866)

A young man forged endorsements on promissory notes causing loss to a bank. His father was then approached by the bank to stand the son's debts. This was acceptable behaviour but the threat that they would have the son arrested and deported amounted to undue influence.

It was originally defined in *Allcard* v *Skinner* (1887) as 'some unfair and improper conduct, some coercion from outside, some overreaching, some form of cheating'.

Lord Denning felt it should apply where there is any inequality in bargaining strength.

LLOYDS BANK V BUNDY (1979)

An elderly farmer, his son, and a company owned by his son were customers of the same bank. The farmer was persuaded by his son and the bank manager to use his farm as security for a loan to the son's company. When the company defaulted on the loan and the bank sought possession of the farm, the farmer successfully pleaded undue influence. There was a clear conflict of interest because the bank represented all parties.

However, Lord Scarman subsequently rejected this in *National Westminster Bank plc* v *Morgan* (1985).

Lord Browne-Wilkinson in *CIBC Mortgages Ltd* v *Pitt* (1993) has more recently explained that 'actual undue influence is a species of fraud ... a man guilty of fraud is no more entitled to argue that the transaction was beneficial to the person defrauded than a man who has procured a transaction by misrepresentation'. He rejected the previously held view that the party claiming actual undue influence was required to show some manifest disadvantage.

Traditionally such relationships as husband and wife and banker and client were felt to fall within actual undue influence, but the class as a whole seems to be becoming more rare.

Class 2: Presumed undue influence

This class applies whenever the party claiming it can show a relationship of trust and confidence with the party against whom the undue influence is alleged. The claimant only need prove the relationship, and then undue influence is presumed and it is for the other party to disprove that it has in fact occurred. This can only be done by showing that the party alleging the undue influence entered the contract with full knowledge of its character and effect. In order to achieve this the party against whom undue influence is alleged will need to show that the other party had the benefit of independent, impartial advice before entering the contract.

Traditionally, presumed undue influence applied in relationships such as parent/child.

LANCASHIRE LOANS CO. V BLACK (1933)

A domineering woman induced her daughter to stand guarantor for a loan with a bank. When she defaulted on the loan and the bank sought to enforce the guarantee the daughter successfully claimed undue influence. She was dominated by her mother, did not properly know the nature of what she was signing and had been given no independent advice.

Also a relationship based on spiritual leadership gave rise to the presumption.

ALLCARD V SKINNER (1887)

A woman belonging to a religious sect was persuaded to join a closed order and to give up all of her property to the order. When she later left the order she then tried to recover railway stock that she had owned. While it was accepted that she had been subjected to undue influence her action failed because she waited until five years after leaving the order before claiming, and 'delay defeats equity'.

Other relationships such as trustee/beneficiary, doctor/patient, and other fiduciary relationships have been held to create a presumption of undue influence.

Such relationships are now identified as Class 2A, and arise automatically, merely because of the type of the relationship. It is also now possible to establish a relationship where the one party proves that (s)he has placed trust and confidence in the other where the presumption will apply even though not falling within one of the traditional categories. This is now known as Class 2B.

The most common case is that of husband and wife, which traditionally fell under the category of actual undue influence, requiring proof of the undue influence by the party alleging it, usually a wife. The court in *Bank of Credit and Commerce International SA* v *Aboody* (1990) rejected the proposition in *Midland Bank* v *Shepherd* (1988)

that the wife/husband relationship gave rise only to actual undue influence, and therefore proof of the undue influence by the husband was required.

It has been argued both that the party subject to undue influence in these cases is protected because the other party is seen as the agent of the creditor, or alternatively that the wife in such situations has a special protection in equity. The most common means of protecting the weaker party, however, is by application of the 'doctrine of notice'. That is the creditor, usually a bank or building society, will be unable to enforce the defaulted loan against the wife where it has actual or constructive notice of her equitable interest in the property which stands as surety for the loan.

Since *Barclays Bank plc* v *O'Brien* (1993) wives are able to show a relationship of trust and confidence in their husbands and thus qualify for presumed undue influence under Class 2B. The informality of the relationship, it is accepted, means that there is a greater risk of the wife being taken advantage of in order to secure a loan based on the surety of the matrimonial property. This is then sufficient to put the creditor on notice providing that the contract is not on the face of it to the wife's advantage, and there is a risk that the husband has unfairly induced the wife's acceptance. Lord Browne-Wilkinson, in the case, suggested that the principle should apply also to cohabitees where the relationship is actually known to the creditor.

So the creditor will be unable to enforce the surety against the loan unless he has 'taken reasonable steps to satisfy himself that the surety entered into the obligation freely and in knowledge of the true facts'. Reasonable steps might include personally interviewing the person standing surety for the loan in the absence of the principal debtor; explaining the full extent of the liability; explaining all of the risks involved; encouraging the person to seek independent legal advice before standing surety on the loan.

The creditor of course has no duty to enquire what goes on when the solicitor gives this independent advice.

MASSEY V MIDLAND BANK (1995)

Mrs Massey was persuaded to give the bank a charge on the property she shared with Potts, the father of her children, as security for his business overdraft. The bank suggested that Mrs Massey would need independent legal advice. This was arranged with Potts's solicitor, and Potts himself attended. Potts defaulted and the bank sought to enforce the charge. The bank had notice of the relationship, and of the risk that the charge was not to Mrs Massey's advantage. However, the solicitor confirmed to the bank that she had received independent advice, and they were not bound to make any further enquiries.

On this basis the creditor is entitled to assume that the solicitor will act honestly and competently. As Lord Justice Steyn put it in *Banco Exterior Internacional* v *Mann* (1994)

'I do not understand Lord Browne-Wilkinson to be laying down the only steps to be taken which will avoid a bank being faced with constructive notice … rather he is pointing out best practice.'

More recently *Royal British Bank of Scotland plc* v *Etridge* (1998) has considered the issue of whether a solicitor appointed by the bank to give the wife independent advice is agent of the bank. In this instance the wife clamed undue influence by the husband, and argued that the solicitor had not explained the charge to her alone, and that the bank was therefore fixed with constructive notice of the undue influence.

The effects of pleading undue influence

Where a claimant succeeds in a plea that undue influence has taken place then the contract is voidable by the party alleging the undue influence. The contract will be set aside subject to the principle of *restitutio in integrum*.

activity

SELF ASSESSMENT QUESTIONS

1 What is the main limitation on a claim to duress?

2 Why has the doctrine of economic duress developed?

3 When will a claim of economic duress fail?

4 What was the traditional difference between a claim of duress and a claim of undue influence?

5 What differences are there between actual undue influence and presumed undue influence?

6 Why is undue influence presumed in the case of certain relationships?

7 What is the difference between the new classes 2A and 2B in undue influence?

8 What is the role of the 'doctrine of notice' in undue influence?

9 When will a bank have constructive notice of the undue influence, and how can it avoid this?

10 What is the basic rule in *Barclays Bank* v *O'Brien* (1993), and what impact do cases such as *Massey* v *Midland Bank* (1995) and *Royal British Bank of Scotland* v *Etridge* (1998) have on the basic rule?

KEY
FACTS

- To preserve freedom of contract the courts have traditionally invalidated a contract which has been formed as the result of any coercion

- Duress is a common law action where a contract has been procured by violence or threats of violence – *Barton* v *Armstrong* (1975)

- Economic duress is a modern area where in a commercial contract a party is coerced into a change of arrangements under the threat of a commercially damaging course of action – *The Siboen and the Sibotre*

- The party raising it must have protested immediately, and shown a reluctance to enter the arrangement, otherwise any remedy may be lost – *The Atlantic Baron*

- Undue influence is traditionally an equitable area where one party has been induced by coercion to enter a contract – it is a question of degree what level of persuasion is acceptable and what amounts to undue influence

- There are now identified two types of undue influence – Class 1 or actual undue influence, and Class 2 or presumed undue influence – *Bank of Credit and Commerce International* v *Aboody* (1990)

- Actual is where there is no special relationship and the party alleging the undue influence must prove it – *CIBC Mortgages* v *Pitt* (1993)

- Presumed undue influence occurs in certain relationships such as parents and children – *Lancashire Loans* v *Black* (1933) – and spiritual adviser/follower – *Allcard* v *Skinner* (1887)

- The party against whom the undue influence is alleged must disprove it

- Class 2B now extends this type of undue influence to those situations where a wife is induced to place the family home as security for a loan made to the husband – *Barclays Bank* v *O'Brien* (1993)

- In such situations the creditor is put on notice of the possibility of the undue influence and must take reasonable care to ensure that the wife only agrees to the arrangement after having full knowledge of the risks involved, having been given independent legal advice

- Many cases such as *Massey* v *Midland Bank* (1995), *Banco Exterior International* v *Mann* (1994) and *Royal British Bank of Scotland* v *Etridge* (1998) concern whether or not the creditor has done sufficient to discharge their duty towards the wife to escape actual or constructive notice

FIGURE 4.3 *Key fact chart for duress and undue influence*

However, in certain circumstances a party may be denied an effective remedy despite a successful plea if the actual value of the property has changed.

4.5 ILLEGALITY

1.5.1 INTRODUCTION

Most vitiating factors represent some sort of defect in the formation, for instance that the

CHEESE V THOMAS (1994)

Cheese, who was aged 84, contributed £43,000 to the purchase of a property costing £83,000. His nephew provided the remaining £40,000 by way of a mortgage. The property went in the nephew's sole name, but was to be solely occupied by the uncle until his death. The nephew then defaulted on the mortgage. The uncle then sought return of his £43,000 fearful of his security. The court accepted a claim of undue influence and ordered the house sold. However, the slump in property prices meant that the house could only fetch £55,000 and the uncle was then only entitled to a 43/83 share.

agreement does not truly represent the consensus of the two parties because the agreement is based on a mistake or a misrepresentation. Illegality, on the other hand, is more about the character of the agreement itself. It is of a type that for some reason the law frowns on.

The basic principle involved is straightforward enough: the law will not enforce a contract that is tainted with illegality. However, the area is not a simple one for a number of reasons. Firstly, the types of contract that have been declared illegal are not only numerous but also diverse. Secondly, while judges frequently refer to contracts being illegal or void or unenforceable, they do not always fully distinguish between these terms. Thirdly, there is the added complication that over time both the common law and statute law have been used to render different types of contract illegal. Fourthly, the area is one that is heavily influenced by public policy.

Despite these difficulties, it is possible to identify some loose groupings in which to categorise such contracts:

● Certain contracts are said to be void and therefore unenforceable – in other words there is nothing to prevent their creation and so long as the parties comply with the terms of their agreement they create no problems, but if one party breaches a term of the agreement the other will have no redress in law.

● Certain other contracts are said to be illegal and therefore unenforceable – with these it is possible that they should not have been made at all, in any case other connected transactions may be tainted with their illegality.

Since contracts can be illegal by statutory provision or by common law it is possible to classify illegality into four groups:

● contracts void by statute;

● contracts declared illegal by statute (with the further division between contracts that are

illegal in their formation and those declared illegal because of the manner of their performance);

● contracts that are void at common law – an area that is heavily influenced by public policy;

● contracts that are illegal at common law – again for public policy reasons.

4.5.2 CONTRACTS VOID BY STATUTE

These are of two types:

Contracts of wager

Wager was defined in *Carlill* v *The Carbolic Smoke Ball Co.* (1893) as where 'two persons mutually agree that one shall win from the other money or other stake upon the determination of some event, neither party having an interest in the contract apart from the stake'.

By virtue of s.18 Gaming Act 1845 such contracts are null and void. So it is possible to make a contract of wager but not to enforce it. Money passed as a result of the wager is not recoverable and contracts that are associated with the wager may also be affected.

There are of course a number of contracts involving betting that are now regulated by various Acts and are consequently enforceable. These include the lottery and the pools, on-course tote betting, and casino gambling under the Gaming Act 1968.

Restrictive trade practices

Public policy originally prevented enforceability of agreements aimed at restricting free competition. Now such agreements fall under the Restricted Trade Practices Act 1976, and are regulated by the Director General of Fair Trading. They are also subject to the control of EU competition law in Articles 85 and 86 of the EC Treaty.

4.5.3 CONTRACTS ILLEGAL BY STATUTE

Here the contract could be illegal in one of two ways:

- It could be illegal to make such contracts at all – generally this would be for reasons of public policy: Parliament does not wish such contracts to be made.

- It could be legal to engage in such a contract but the manner in which the contract is performed is illegal.

Contracts illegal when formed

Where the contract is illegal as formed then the contract is void *ab initio* and unenforceable as a result.

> **RE MAHMOUD AND ISPAHANI (1921)**
>
> The Seed, Oils and Fats Order of 1919 prohibited unlicensed trading in linseed oil. One party had a licence and contracted to supply the defendant who did not but who falsely stated that he did. When the defendant backed out of the agreement the claimant sued for the failure to accept delivery. He was unsuccessful because the contract was void and unenforceable for the lack of the licence.

The justification for this is that the contract would be 'a transgression of the positive laws of our country' – Lord Mansfield.

> **COPE V ROWLANDS (1836)**
>
> An Act made it illegal for stockbrokers to deal without a licence. Cope set up business in London without obtaining a licence. As a result, when he sued Rowlands for payment for work done he failed. His lack of a licence made the contract illegal and unenforceable. The purpose of the provision was to protect the public from the harm that could be caused by unregulated brokers.

Sometimes, however, the contract will not be illegal because the provision in an Act is for a different purpose than to prevent the contract from being made.

> **SMITH V MAWHOOD (1845)**
>
> A tobacconist failed to get the appropriate licence to sell tobacco products. The purpose of the licensing was to impose a penalty for the revenue so the contract to sell tobacco was not unenforceable.

Contracts illegally performed

A contract may be created legitimately but become illegal and therefore unenforceable because the manner in which it is performed is illegal.

> **ANDERSON LTD V DANIEL (1924)**
>
> A statute provided that, in sales of fertilisers, an invoice listing chemicals contained in the product must be given to the buyer. Fertiliser was supplied without the proper invoice. When the buyer failed to pay for the goods, the seller's action for the price failed. The contract could be made lawfully but the absence of the invoice rendered it illegal and the seller could not enforce it.

But the fact that performance is not by the prescribed manner does not mean that it will be automatically unenforceable on all occasions.

> **ST JOHN SHIPPING CORPORATION V JOSEPH RANK LTD (1956)**
>
> The court refused to hold that a contract for the carriage of goods at sea was illegal and therefore unenforceable merely because the captain loaded his ship beyond the legal loading line. To do so would have allowed the other party to avoid payment with no justification.

The point that the case clearly makes is that the illegality must relate to the contract's central purpose if the contract is to be declared invalid and unenforceable.

4.5.4 CONTRACTS VOID AT COMMON LAW

The central issue here is again whether the type of contract offends public policy. Again as void contracts there is nothing to prevent parties agreeing to their formation but the parties will be unable to enforce the terms of the contract when there is any dispute.

Contracts unenforceable under this heading fall into three distinct categories:

Contracts seeking to oust the jurisdiction of the courts

Generally the courts will reject any attempt to remove their jurisdiction through clauses in contracts to that effect.

An exception to this are arbitration clauses, known as Scott Avery clauses. Many bodies will contain a clause referring any dispute, at least initially, to a qualified arbitrator expert in the specific field.

Also Parliament directs a number of contractual disputes to bodies other than the courts. An obvious example of this are employment disputes and Employment Tribunals.

Contracts prejudicial to the family

The courts have long seen themselves as the defenders of moral values and marriage is seen as a sacred institution requiring the protection of the courts. Traditionally then any arrangement which might have the effect of harming marriage would be deemed void by the courts. Obvious examples of this would be taking a fee not to marry or indeed procuring a marriage for a fee, or otherwise threatening a marriage.

Originally the courts would also view contracts which relinquished parental responsibility as void, as when a parent sold the child. Now this principle may be complicated by the practice of surrogacy.

Contracts in restraint of trade

These are clearly the most important category of contracts void at common law and they are probably also the most contentious.

A restraint of trade clause is a clause of a contract by which one party agrees to limit or restrict their ability to carry on their trade, business or profession.

Judges have always viewed such arrangements as prima facie void for two principal reasons. Firstly, the courts are reluctant to endorse an arrangement whereby one party effectively gives up their right to their livelihood as a requirement of the stronger party to the contract. Secondly, the judges are similarly reluctant to see the public deprived of that party's skill or expertise.

Nevertheless, the courts have always tried to protect the idea of freedom of contract and only intervene in a contractual relationship reluctantly. As a result, while restraint clauses are prima facie void, the courts will allow them to stand where they are demonstrated as reasonable.

Reasonable in this context is measured in two ways.

- Firstly the restraint must be reasonable as between the two parties to the contract. Reasonable here means that the restraint is no wider than is needed to protect the legitimate interests of the party inserting the restraint clause into the contract. Merely preventing legitimate competition through use of the restraint is unacceptable and the clause will fail.

- Secondly the restraint must be reasonable in the public interest. A restraint would not be considered reasonable that deprived the public of a benefit that might otherwise be enjoyed or that unduly restricted choice.

Restraint clauses generally operate in one of three distinct contexts:

Employee restraints

These are clauses contained in the contract of employment that restrict the activities of the employee on leaving the employment. The employer will be able to legitimately use such a clause to protect his or her trade secrets and client connections.

Such a clause cannot, however, be used merely to prevent legitimate competition and thus prevent the employee from exercising his or her trade or skill.

What is reasonable in relation to such clauses depends on a number of factors:

● Whether or not the work is specialised, in which case the restraint is more likely to be seen as reasonable.

FORSTER V SUGGETT (1918)

A clause in a glass blower's contract prevented him from working for any competitor of his employers on leaving. The court held that the skill was so specialised at the time that it amounted to a trade secret and the glass manufacturers were entitled to the protection of the clause.

● The position held by the employee in the employer's business. The higher up and more important it is the more likely that inclusion of the restraint is reasonable.

HERBERT MORRIS LTD V SAXELBY (1916)

The restraint clause prevented the ex-employee from involvement with the sale or manufacture of pulley blocks, overhead runways, or overhead travelling cranes for a period of seven years after leaving the employment. This covered the whole range of the employer's business and was too wide to succeed despite the key position held by the employee.

● The geographical area covered by the restraint – this must not be wider than necessary to protect the legitimate interest.

FITCH V DEWES (1921)

A restraint in a conveyancing clerk's contract prevented him from working in the same capacity for any firm within a seven-mile radius of Tamworth Town Hall for life. The restraint was reasonable because of the rural nature of the community and the clerk's contact with the solicitor's client base.

● The duration of the restraint – this must not be longer than necessary to protect the legitimate interest.

HOME COUNTIES DAIRIES LTD V SKILTON (1970)

A milk roundsman had an employment contract containing two restraints. Clause 12 prevented him from entering any employment connected with the dairy business. The second, Clause 15, provided that he should not work as a roundsman or serve any existing customer for a period of one year after leaving the employment. Clause 12 was too wide to be reasonable. Clause 15 was successful since it only protected legitimate interests and for only a short period of time.

It may also be unreasonable to attempt to achieve the restraint through other means than a direct restraint clause.

BULL V PITNEY BOWES (1966)

There was no restraint clause in the contract but there was a clause whereby employees forfeited their pension rights in the event that they took up work with a competitor of the employer. This was held to be void for public policy.

A similar line would be taken when employers agree among themselves on an arrangement that has the effect of a restraint of trade.

KORES MANUFACTURING CO. V KOLOK MANUFACTURING CO. (1959)

Two electronics companies reached an agreement not to employ the other's staff for five years in the event of their leaving. This had the same effect as a restraint clause and was held to be void.

Vendor restraints

These will occur where sellers of a business agree under the contract of sale not to compete unfairly with the purchaser of the business. Again such agreements are prima facie void. Declaring such restraints void has been justified as preventing an individual from negotiating away his or her livelihood, and also for preventing the public from losing a valuable benefit where the one party is prevented from trading by the other.

They are, however, more likely to be accepted as reasonable by the courts because the bargaining strength of the parties is more likely to be equal.

Again to be reasonable and enforceable they must protect only legitimate interests and not merely aim to prevent legitimate competition.

BRITISH REINFORCED CONCRETE CO. V SCHELFF (1921)

A business that specialised in the production of steel reinforcement for roads was sold. In the contract a restraint clause prevented the vendors of the business from engaging in any similar business. One of the vendors then entered another business as manager of the reinforced concrete section. The clause was held to be too wide to protect legitimate interests and could not be applied.

Again the same tests apply as for employee restraints and no clause will be enforced that is too wide in its application, though what is too wide is a question of fact dictated by the circumstances of each case.

NORDENFELT V MAXIM NORDENFELT CO. (1894)

Nordenfelt had established a worldwide business manufacturing and selling guns and ammunition. When he sold the business, it was subject to a clause in the contract preventing him from engaging in the armaments business anywhere in the world for a period of 25 years. This seems an unusually wide clause. However, the court was prepared to enforce it since the world was the appropriate market.

4.5.5 CONTRACTS ILLEGAL AT COMMON LAW

This is potentially a very wide group of contracts and it includes any type of agreement that is prejudicial to the general notion of freedom of contract. The basis for judges declaring such arrangements illegal is that to allow them to stand would be harmful to the public good. So like most aspects of illegality at common law the reason for the illegality is public policy.

The categories of such agreements are numerous and varied. The common characteristic seems to be some form of immorality in each case. They include:

A contract to commit a wrong

This might be a tort, a fraud, or even a crime.

DANN V CURZON (1911)

Here the claimant had been hired to start a riot in a theatre. When he sued for the unpaid fee of £20 he was unsuccessful. The judges as a matter of policy could not enforce an agreement to carry out a crime.

A contract to benefit from the crime of another

BERESFORD V ROYAL INSURANCE CO. LTD (1937)

Relatives were prevented from benefiting from the life insurance of a suicide.

A contract to defraud the revenue

NAPIER V THE NATIONAL BUSINESS AGENCY (1951)

Under his contract of employment the claimant received expenses of £6 per week where his actual costs were no more than £1. This was a deliberate agreement between the parties with the purpose of avoiding income tax. When he was dismissed he was unable to sue for back pay since the contract was unenforceable.

Contracts aimed at corruption in public life

PARKINSON V THE COLLEGE OF AMBULANCE (1925)

The claimant who was wealthy was asked to donate funds to a company in return for which the other party promised he would be able to gain him a knighthood. When the claimant made the donation but was not given any honour he sued for return of his money. He failed because this was purely a corrupt practice.

Contracts to interfere with justice

HARMONY SHIPPING CO. SA V DAVIS (1979)

An agreement by a witness not to give evidence in return for a cash payment was void and unenforceable.

Contracts to promote sexual immorality

PEARCE V BROOKS (1866)

A prostitute hit on the idea of conducting her trade from hired carriages. When she did not pay the fee owed the owner's action for the price failed. The contract was for immoral purposes and was unenforceable.

4.5.6 THE CONSEQUENCES OF THE CONTRACT BEING VOID

Where the contract is declared void the significant difference in effect is between contracts void under common law and contracts void because of statute.

Common law

Where the contract is declared void by the courts, as may be the case with a contract in restraint of trade, there are a number of possible consequences:

- Firstly, depending on the wording of the contract, the whole contract itself is not necessarily void, though the offending clause may be.

- Money that has been paid under the contract may be recoverable as a result of the contract being declared void as in *Hermann* v *Charlesworth* (1905) where the procurement of a marriage for a fee was declared void.

- It is possible to sever the clause that is void from the rest of the contract to avoid voiding the whole contract.

GOLDSOLL V GOLDMAN (1915)

A restraint in the sale of a jewellery business, specialising in the sale of imitation jewellery inside the UK, prevented the vendor from engaging in the sale of real or imitation jewellery throughout most of Europe and America. The court severed the word 'real' from the contract, and also the clauses relating to those areas outside of the UK, and the rest of the clause stood.

- But the court will not sever parts of a contract where to do so would alter the whole character of the agreement.

ATTWOOD V LAMONT (1920)

A tailor's cutter was restrained, on leaving his employment, from taking up work as 'tailor, dressmaker, general draper, milliner, hatter, haberdasher, gentleman's, ladies' or children's outfitter at any place within a ten mile radius'. The court saw this not so much as a list but a comprehensive description of the employer's whole business and as such severance was not possible and the contract was void and unenforceable.

- Also the court will not employ severance if to do so would defeat public policy which rendered the contract void in the first place.

NAPIER V THE NATIONAL BUSINESS AGENCY (1951)

Here, because of the tax avoidance mechanism, the contract was void and the claimant was unable to recover any of the money owing.

Statute

The effects if the contract is void because of a statutory provision may obviously vary and will depend on the wording of the Act itself.

However, where the statute itself is silent on the effects of the contract being declared void then the common law effects above will apply.

4.5.7 THE CONSEQUENCES OF THE CONTRACT BEING ILLEGAL

Here the principal difference is not between the common law and statute but between contracts that are illegal as formed and those that are legally formed and only become illegal by the manner of their performance.

Illegal as formed

Where statute or the common law has declared that a class of contract will be illegal if made then such a contract can never be legally formed or performed and will be illegal from the moment of formation. There are then a number of consequences for such agreements:

Since the contract is illegal it is also unenforceable by either party

> **DANN V CURZON (1911)**
>
> Since the agreement to start the riot was illegal then there was no legal way of enforcing payment.

Property or money transferred in advance of the agreement cannot generally be recovered

This was the case with the claimant in *Parkinson* v *The College of Ambulance* (1925) where the court would not permit recovery of the donation.

This may be the position even where the parties are unaware of the illegality of the agreement

> **J. W. ALLAN (MERCHANDISING) LTD V CLOKE (1960)**
>
> Fees to hire a roulette wheel for an illegal game under the Betting and Gaming Act 1960 were not recoverable although the parties were unaware that the game was illegal.

Exceptions to the basic rule

However, there are certain exceptions to this basic rule where property transferred may be recoverable:

- where not to allow recovery is 'an affront to public conscience'

> **HOWARD V SHIRLSTAR CONTAINER TRANSPORT LTD (1990)**
>
> The contract was to recover an aircraft impounded in Nigeria, so in effect it meant stealing it for the owner. When it was com-

pleted and the aircraft owner refused to pay claiming that the arrangement was void for illegality the court held that the claimant could recover in the circumstances.

- where the illegality is not vital to the cause

> **TINSLEY V MILLIGAN (1993)**
>
> The claimant and defendant bought a house putting it in the claimant's name so that the defendant could carry on claiming benefits, and thus an illegal agreement. The defendant later claimed a share of the property under a resulting trust arising out of the contribution to the purchase. The claimant argued illegality but HL accepted that the right arising out of the trust was enforceable.

- Where the party seeking recovery is not *in pari delicto* i.e. is not as culpable as the other party

> **KIRRI COTTON CO. LTD V DEWANI (1960)**
>
> A landlord demanded a premium from a tenant even though this was illegal under legislation. The tenant could recover the cost because he had no choice but to go along with the illegal arrangement.

- where the agreement has been induced by a fraud

> **HUGHES V LIVERPOOL AND VICTORIA LEGAL FRIENDLY SOCIETY (1916)**
>
> The claimant was induced by the fraud of an insurance agent to take out on parties who were not insurable by her. When the fraud was discovered she was entitled to return of the premiums paid.

- where the one party repents before the contract is performed

Illegal as performed

If both parties are equally culpable for the illegal performance then the rules are basically the same as for contracts illegal in their formation.

However, if one party is unaware of the illegality then (s)he may have remedies available including recovery of any money handed over in advance of the contract.

MARLES V TRANT (1954)

A seed supplier sold seed to Trant as 'spring wheat' seed which in fact it was not. Trant then sold it on to Marles, but without an invoice required by statute. When Marles discovered that the seed was 'winter wheat' seed he was able to sue despite the illegality of the contract.

activity

SELF ASSESSMENT QUESTIONS

1 In what ways does illegality differ from other vitiating factors?

2 How are restrictive trade practices regulated in modern times?

3 What is the difference between a contract illegally formed and a contract illegally performed?

4 How important do you think control of contracts prejudicial to marriage are in the present day?

5 Why are contracts in restraint of trade prima facie void?

6 When will a restraint clause be upheld?

7 What are the common characteristics of contracts declared illegal by the common law?

8 In what circumstances can a party recover money or property handed over under an illegal contract?

- Illegality is a difficult area because judges refer to contracts being illegal, void, and unenforceable, and also because a contract can be invalidated by statute or by the common law

- Contracts void by statute include contracts of wager, and restrictive trade practices

- A contract can be illegal by statute in its formation – *Re Mahmoud and Ispahani* (1921) – in which case it is unenforceable

- Or a legally formed contract can be illegal in its performance – *Anderson Ltd* v *Daniel* (1924)

- Contracts void at common law include:

  – contracts to oust the jurisdiction of the court

  – contracts harmful to family life

  – contracts in restraint of trade

- Contracts in restraint of trade are prima facie void but may be enforced if they are accepted as reasonable as between the parties, and in the public interest

- Reasonableness depends on:

  – geographical extent – *Fitch* v *Dewes* (1921)

  – duration of the restraint – *Home Counties Dairies* v *Skilton* (1970)

- A party is only able to protect legitimate interests – *British Reinforced Concrete* v *Scheff* (1921)

- A vendor restraint is more likely to be held reasonable than an employee restraint – *Nordenfelt* v *Maxim Nordenfelt* (1894)

- A party cannot try to use other means to effect a restraint – *Bull* v *Pitney Bowes* (1966)

- Contracts illegal at common law are all for reasons of public policy and include:

  – a contract to commit a wrong – *Dann* v *Curzon* (1911)

  – a contract to commit a crime – *Beresford* v *Royal Insurance Co.* (1937)

  – a contract to defraud the revenue – *Napier* v *The National Business Agency* (1951)

  – contracts aimed at corruption – *Parkinson* v *The College of Ambulance* (1925)

  – contracts to interfere with justice – *Harmony Shipping Co.* v *Davis* (1979)

  – contracts promoting immorality – *Pearce* v *Brooks* (1866)

- If a contract is void by statute the effect depends on what the statute says

- If a contract is void at common law then money paid over may be recovered – *Hermann* v *Charlesworth* (1905) – and sometimes the offending clause can be severed to save the rest of the agreement – *Goldsoll* v *Goldman* (1915)

- A contract illegal as formed is unenforceable and money paid over is generally unrecoverable though there are exceptions

- A contract legally formed but illegally performed will have remedies available to a party who is unaware of the illegality – *Marles* v *Trant* (1954)

FIGURE 4.4 *Key fact chart for illegality*

CHAPTER 5

DISCHARGING THE CONTRACT

5.1 DISCHARGE BY PERFORMANCE

5.1.1 INTRODUCTION

Discharge of the contract refers to the ending of the obligations under the contract, so that where we have thought of formation being the beginning of the contract discharge is concerned with its end.

In its simplest form discharge will be the point at which all of the primary obligations created by the contract have been met. However, the situation is not always that simple or straightforward and there are times when we refer to the contract being discharged even though the obligations under the contract remain uncompleted.

The obvious example of this latter point is where the contract has been breached. Secondary obligations in this case may be substituted for the primary obligations, and a party not carrying out his/her obligations under the contract may be required to pay damages.

Where all of the obligations under the contract have been carried out this is referred to as performance of the contract. The contract is discharged, but even then the area can be complicated by one party completing some but not all of the obligations.

5.1.2 THE STRICT RULE ON PERFORMANCE

The rule in Cutter v Powell

The starting point for performance of the contract, sometimes known as the 'perfect tender' rule, is that there should be complete performance of all of the obligations under the contract. If this is the case then the contract is in effect complete and discharged.

On the other hand it also means that where a party fails to meet all of his/her obligations the contract is not discharged and this may require the other party to be remedied.

The bare and potentially unjust simplicity of the rule can be seen in the case from which it emerges.

> **CUTTER V POWELL (1795)**
>
> Cutter was the second mate on a ship, *The Governor Parry*, sailing from Jamaica to Liverpool. The boat set sail on 2 August and reached Liverpool on 9 October. Cutter died during the voyage on 20 September. When his wages were not paid his wife sued on a *quantum meruit* (meaning 'for the amount owed'). Her action failed because her husband had signed on for the complete voyage. By dying he had failed to complete his contract and since it was an entire contract there was no obligation on the shipowners to pay.

An entire contract is one where all of the obligations are seen as a single transaction that cannot be broken down in any way. The case illustrates the effect of failing to perform such a contract. It also shows how it can work injustice since Cutter could hardly be said to have defaulted by dying, an event that was beyond his control.

Application of the rule

Application of the strict rule can be commonly seen in sale of goods contracts where the description applied to the contract may mean that all rather than part is essential to completion of the contract.

> **ARCOS LTD V E A RONAASEN & SON (1933)**
>
> A buyer of wooden staves, described in the contract as half an inch thick, was allowed to reject the consignment sent to him. Those delivered were a sixteenth of an inch narrower and so did not correspond to the contract description. The rule is shown for its strictness here since the staves could still be used for the purpose for which the buyer wanted them. Lord Atkin commented that 'a ton does not mean about a ton, or a yard about a yard. If a seller wants a margin he must, and in my experience does, stipulate for it …'.

The strict rule has been applied even in the case of ancillary obligations such as packaging.

> **RE MOORE & CO. AND LANDAUER & CO.'S ARBITRATION (1921)**
>
> Tinned fruit was sold described as being in cases of 30 tins. When delivered some of the cartons contained 24 tins, although the overall total number of tins ordered was correct. The buyer intended to resell the goods so the difference would have no impact on him. Nevertheless, CA, applying the strict rule, held that packaging could be included in description and that the buyer was correct in rejecting the goods and repudiating the contract.

Despite that, it is of course always possible that a judge in a case may apply the maxim *de minimis non curat lex* (literally, the law does not concern itself with trifles, in other words, the law will not grant a remedy for something that is too trivial).

> **REARDON SMITH LINE LTD V HANSEN-TANGEN (1976)**
>
> We have already seen in this case, using innominate terms, how the judges were not prepared to accept a repudiation of obligations where the term was a mere technicality describing the shipyard and job number.

This principle that a buyer should not be allowed to reject goods delivered when there is a slight shortfall or excess has now been incorporated in the Sale of Goods Act 1979 as s.30(2A).

5.1.3 WAYS OF AVOIDING THE STRICT RULE

The potential injustice of the rule, as seen in *Cutter* v *Powell* (1795), has led to judges accepting exceptions when the rule does not operate.

Divisible contracts

In these the contract can be seen as being made up of various parts. If each part can be discharged separately then it might also be enforced separately, and the strict rule need not apply. The rule here can be particularly appropriate for instance where there is delivery by separate instalments, except where the seller has stipulated for a single payment.

> **TAYLOR V WEBB (1937)**
>
> Premises were leased to a tenant for rent. A term in the lease required the landlord to keep the premises in good repair. In the event the landlord failed to maintain the premises and the tenant then refused to pay the rent. In the landlord's action the court held that the contract had divisible obligations, to lease the premises, and to repair and maintain. The contract was thus not entire and the tenant could not legitimately refuse payment.

Acceptance of part performance

Where one of the parties has performed the contract but not completely, if the other side has shown willingness to accept the part performed then the strict rule will usually not apply. Part performance may occur where there is a shortfall on delivery of goods or where a service is not fully carried out. This exception to the rule will only apply though when the party who is the victim of the part performance has a genuine choice whether or not to accept.

SUMPTER V HEDGES (1898)

A builder was hired to build two houses and stables. Certain of the work was done when the builder ran out of money and was unable to complete it. The landowner then had the work completed using materials left on the land. The builder was awarded the value of the materials that had been used. His argument that part performance had been accepted was rejected. The landowner had no choice but to complete the work. The alternative was to leave the partly completed buildings as an eyesore on his land.

Substantial performance

If a party has done substantially what was required under the contract then the doctrine of substantial performance can apply. That party can then recover the amount appropriate to what has been done under the contract, providing that the contract is not an entire contract.

DAKIN & CO. V LEE (1916)

Here a builder was bound by contract to complete major repair work to a building. He did complete all of the work but some of it was carried out so carelessly that the owner of the building refused to pay on the grounds that performance was in effect incomplete. The builder was able to sue for the price of the work less an amount representing the value of the defective work.

The price is thus often payable in such circumstances and the sum deducted represents the cost of repairing the defective workmanship.

HOENIG V ISAACS (1952)

A decorator was hired to decorate and furnish a flat for £750. He finished the work. The owner moved into the flat and paid £400 by instalments. Then, because of defects to a bookcase and a wardrobe that would cost about £55 to put right, he refused to pay the remaining £350. CA held that the contract was substantially performed and the balance was payable less the amount representing the defects.

However, what is deemed to be substantial performance is a question of fact to be decided in each case. It will largely depend on what remains undone and its value in comparison to the contract as a whole.

BOLTON V MAHADEVA (1972)

An electrical contractor was hired to install central heating. When completed it gave off fumes and did not work properly. When payment was refused as a result the contractor sued for the price. CA rejected his claim on the ground that there was not substantial performance. Part of the reasoning lay in the fact that there were £174 worth of defects in a system costing £560.

Prevention of performance

If the other party prevents a party from carrying out his or her obligations because of some act or omission then the strict rule cannot apply. In these circumstances the party trying to perform may have an action for damages.

PLANCHE V COLBURN (1831)

A publisher hired an author to write one of a series of books on a theme. When the publisher decided to abandon the whole series the author was prevented from completing the work through no fault of his own. He was entitled to recover a fee for his wasted work.

Tender of performance

A similar situation with slightly different consequences occurs where a party has offered to complete his or her obligations but the other side has unreasonably refused performance. In such a situation the party 'tendering' performance can sue and recover under the contract. He or she may also consider his or her own obligations discharged even though there has been no performance.

In the case of money owed which is tendered and refused, though the debtor is freed from making further offers to pay the debt will still exist.

STARTUP V MACDONALD (1843)

The contract was for 10 tons of linseed oil to be delivered by the end of March. The seller delivered at 8.30 p.m. on 31 March which was a Saturday, and the buyer refused to accept delivery. The seller was able to recover damages. (The answer might be different now under the Sale of Goods Act 1979 since delivery should be at a 'reasonable hour'.)

5.1.4 STIPULATIONS AS TO TIME OF PERFORMANCE

Traditionally a failure to perform on time would give only an action for damages but not to repudiate the contract. While under the common law it was accepted that time could be 'of the essence'

this principle was not generally accepted in equity, and this is now the general assumption.

There are three principal occasions when time will be considered to be 'of the essence' and a repudiation of the contract is therefore available as a remedy:

● Where the parties have made an express stipulation in the contract that time is of the essence.

● Where the surrounding circumstances show that time of performance is critical, as would be the case with delivery of perishable goods.

● Where one party has already failed to perform his or her obligations under the contract. In this case the other party is able to confirm that unless performance is then completed within a stated period repudiation will occur.

activity

SELF ASSESSMENT QUESTIONS

1 In what circumstances is a contract considered to be 'entire'?

2 How can the strict rule cause injustice?

3 What is a 'divisible contract'?

4 In what way can the *de minimis* rule be applied to performance?

5 What is the effect of a contract being only partly performed?

6 How is it possible to measure 'substantial performance'?

7 What effect does failing to perform on time have on a contract?

5.2 DISCHARGE BY AGREEMENT

5.2.1 INTRODUCTION

If a contract is formed following an agreement then it seems almost pure logic to suggest that the contract can also be ended by agreement

without necessarily having been performed. Inevitably what is required is mutuality.

There are in fact two ways in which the contract could be discharged by agreement:

● A bilateral discharge – here the assumption is that both parties are to gain a fresh but different benefit from the new agreement;

KEY
FACTS

- The strict rule on performance is that in an 'entire contract' all obligations must be performed, so there can be no payment for part performance – *Cutter* v *Powell* (1795)

- There are exceptions to this strict rule

- If obligations are 'divisible' then payment should be made for the part performed – *Taylor* v *Webb* (1937)

- Where a party has accepted part performance then this should be paid for – *Sumpter* v *Hedges* (1898)

- Where there has been substantial performance then the full price will be paid less the sum appropriate to what has not been done – *Hoenig* v *Isaacs* (1952)

- Unless too much remains to be done under the contract – *Bolton* v *Mahadeva* (1972)

- A party can sue for damages where his or her performance has been prevented by the other party – *Planche* v *Colborn* (1831)

- And also where he or she has offered to perform but this has been refused – *Startup* v *Macdonald* (1843)

- Time of performance is 'of the essence' when (i) it says so in the contract; (ii) the circumstances make it so; (iii) one party has already failed to perform

FIGURE 5.1 *Key facts chart for discharge by performance*

- A unilateral discharge – the benefit is probably only to be gained by one party, who is therefore trying to convince the other party to let him or her off the obligations arising under the original agreement. Lack of consideration is an inevitable problem if one party is merely promising to release the other from existing obligations.

So two problems are immediately apparent where a contract is discharged by agreement:

- absence of consideration for the fresh agreement;

- the possible lack of proper form for the new agreement in the case of speciality contracts.

5.2.2 BILATERAL DISCHARGES

Wholly executory arrangements

If neither side has yet performed any obligations under the contract it is possible that there is no problem at all. Each side can release the other from performance and there is consideration for the new promise in each case – not having to perform the obligations under the original agreement.

A further possibility occurs where the parties wish to continue the contractual arrangement but to substitute new terms for the old ones. In this case it is possible for the parties to 'waive' their rights under the old agreement and to substitute the new agreement.

Arrangements which are partly executory and partly executed

In this situation one of the parties wishes to give less than full performance and it is possible for the other to waive rights. However, the obvious problem with this is the absence of consideration.

Where form is an issue

Traditionally this would have been dealt with subject to the rule in s.40 Law of Property Act 1925 and the doctrine of part performance. Now an agreement to vary the terms in a contract requiring specific form may be invalid unless it is evidenced in writing. If a new agreement is to be substituted for an existing agreement then again this change will be unenforceable unless evidenced in writing.

5.2.3 UNILATERAL DISCHARGES

Where the contract is left unperformed by one party despite the willingness to contract of the other party there are a number of possible consequences.

Firstly, the party not in default might release the other from performing, but this would require a deed for validity otherwise it would fail for lack of consideration. However, as we have already seen, in consideration the principle in *Williams* v *Roffey Bros. & Nicholls Contractors* (1990) may be sufficient to discharge the other party's obligations in circumstances where there is an extra benefit gained.

Secondly, it is also possible to discharge the party in default from full performance where there is 'accord and satisfaction'. This could be as indicated in the rule in *Pinnel's Case* (1602) either by adding a new element which would count as consideration, or by making a smaller payment at an earlier time than the full payment is due.

Finally, by the equitable doctrine of promissory estoppel, where the party waiting for performance has agreed to waive rights under the contract, knowing that the other party is relying on this promise to forego performance, then the party making the promise may be prevented from going back on the promise.

activity

SELF ASSESSMENT QUESTIONS

1 Why should parties to a contract be able to discharge their obligations by agreement without actually performing?

2 What is the difference between a bilateral discharge and a unilateral discharge?

3 In what way is form a problem in discharge by agreement?

4 When is it easiest to discharge a contract by agreement?

5 What is the easiest way of discharging a contract in a unilateral discharge?

6 What exactly is 'accord and satisfaction'?

KEY FACTS

- Since a contract can be formed by agreement then it can also be discharged without performance by agreement of both parties
- There are two types of discharge by agreement: a bilateral arrangement and a unilateral agreement – the first is where both parties wish to back out of the arrangement, the second is where in effect only one does
- Bilateral discharge is simple where the contract is executory – the waiving of rights is given by the one party in return for the waiving of rights by the other
- Where form is an issue the discharge will need evidence in writing
- Where only one party wants to back out of the contract then that party will need to give some consideration, as in accord and satisfaction, unless estoppel applies

FIGURE 5.2 *Key fact chart for discharge by agreement*

5.3 DISCHARGE BY FRUSTRATION

5.3.1 INTRODUCTION

In the strictest sense effective discharge of a contract, as we have seen, requires performance of the obligations under the contract. Inevitably there will be times when the requirement for strict performance will lead to injustice.

This can be particularly the case where there is a factor preventing a party or parties from performing which is beyond the control of either party to the contract. It is because of this potential injustice that the doctrine of frustration developed in the nineteenth century.

The original common law rule was that a party was bound to perform his or her obligations under the contract regardless of the effect of intervening events making it more difficult or even impossible to perform.

PARADINE V JANE (1647)

Paradine sued Jane for rent due under a lease. Jane's defence was that he had been forced off the land by an invading army. The court held that he had a contractual duty to pay the rent due under the lease, which was not discharged by any intervening event. If he had wished to reduce his liability to take account of intervening events preventing his performance then he should have made express provision for that in the lease.

This was the strict rule and it would override any circumstances.

5.3.2 THE DEVELOPMENT OF A DOCTRINE OF FRUSTRATION

The clear injustice of the strict rule above led inevitably to exceptions. In the nineteenth century a doctrine was developed whereby a party bound by a contractual promises, in circumstances where (s)he was prevented from keeping the promise because of an unforeseeable, intervening event, would be relieved of the strict

obligation. As a result that party would not be liable for a breach of contract.

This is said to be the origin of the doctrine of frustration. The judges achieved the desired result by the fiction of implying into the contract a term.

TAYLOR V CALDWELL (1863)

Caldwell had agreed to rent the Surrey Garden and Music Hall to Taylor for four days for a series of concerts and fêtes. Before the concerts were due to start the music hall burnt to the ground and performance of the contract was impossible. The contract contained no stipulations as to what should happen in the event of fire. Since Taylor had spent money on advertising the concerts and other general preparations he sued Caldwell for damages under the principle in *Paradine* v *Jane*. The court held, however, that the commercial purpose of the contract had ceased to exist, performance was impossible, and so both sides were excused further performance. As Blackburn J stated 'in contracts in which performance depends on the continued existence of a given person or thing, a condition is implied that the impossibility of performance arising from the perishing of the person or thing shall excuse the performance ... that excuse is by law implied, because from the nature of the contract it is apparent that the parties contracted on the basis of the continued existence of the particular person or chattel ...'.

The doctrine then developed to cover those situations where the frustrating event meant that performance as envisaged in the contract was impossible.

DAVIS CONTRACTORS LTD V FAREHAM UDC (1956)

A building firm contracted to build houses for a local council for £92,450 over a period of eight months. In fact, due to a shortage of skilled labour, the work took some 22 months to complete and the builders wanted an extra £17,651. The council paid the contract price. The builders claimed that the contract was frustrated in order to claim the extra on a *quantum meruit*. HL held that the contract was not in fact frustrated, but Lord Radcliffe did explain those factors that would justify the doctrine when used: 'without default of either party, a contractual obligation has become incapable of being performed because the circumstances in which performance is called for would render it a thing radically different from that which was undertaken by the contract.'

The immediate consequence of application of the doctrine then is that both parties are relieved of the burden of further performance, and of liability for not performing. This will inevitably not remove all apparent injustice since the one party to the contract is still being denied the performance of the other party through no fault of his or hers, and may have incurred costs in anticipation of the contract being performed.

As a result operation of the doctrine is subject to a number of limitations, and parties may provide in their contracts for what happens if there are intervening frustrating events, the so-called *force majeure* clauses.

5.3.3 FRUSTRATING EVENTS

The doctrine has developed largely out of the case law, and will operate in three main types of circumstance:

● where the intervening event makes performance impossible

● where performance of the contract becomes illegal

● where the contract becomes commercially sterilised

Impossibility

The contract may be frustrated because of the destruction of the subject matter of the contract.

TAYLOR V CALDWELL (1863)

Here the destruction of the music hall was the cause of the impossibility and hence the frustration.

It may alternatively be the case that the subject matter becomes unavailable when the contract is to be performed.

JACKSON V UNION MARINE INSURANCE CO. LTD (1874)

A ship was chartered to sail from Liverpool to Newport and from there with a cargo of iron rails to San Francisco. The ship ran aground and could not be loaded for some time. The court accepted that there was an implied term that the ship should be available for loading in a reasonable time and the long delay amounted to a frustration of the contract.

Where a contract is for services the frustrating event may be the unavailability of the party who is to render the service due to illness.

ROBINSON V DAVIDSON (1871)

A husband, acting as agent for his wife, a celebrated pianist, contracted for her to perform. A few hours before her performance was due she became ill and the husband contacted the claimant to inform that she would be unable to attend. When the claimant sued the court held that the contract was conditional on the woman being well enough to perform and because of her illness she was excused. The contract was frustrated.

This principle of impossibility because of unavailability may apply even where there is only a risk that the party will be unavailable.

CONDOR V THE BARON KNIGHTS (1966)

A contract entered into by a pop music group allowed that the group should be available to perform for seven evenings a week if necessary. One member of the group became ill and was advised to rest and work fewer hours. Though he actually ignored this advice, the court still held that the contract was frustrated since it was necessary to have a stand in musician in case he fell ill.

In fact any good reason that will mean that a party is unavailable to perform his or her obligations may lead to a frustration of the contract.

MORGAN V MANSER (1948)

A music hall artiste was contracted to his manager for a ten-year period commencing in 1938. Between 1940 and 1946 he was in fact conscripted into the forces during the war years. His absence rendered the purpose of the contract undermined and both parties were excused performance.

An excessive but unavoidable delay in performing will often be classed as impossibility and mean that the contract is frustrated.

PIONEER SHIPPING LTD V BTP TIOXIDE LTD (1981) (*THE NEMA*)

A time charter of nine months was agreed which anticipated a possible seven voyages. In fact due to strikes at the port where the vessel was loaded this was reduced to two and the contract was held to be frustrated.

Outbreak of war is also a common frustrating event.

METROPOLITAN WATER BOARD V DICK KERR & CO. LTD (1918)

In July 1914 a contract was formed for the construction of a reservoir and a water works. The contract allowed that the work should be completed within a six-year period. In 1916 a Government order stopped the work and also requisitioned much of the plant. It was held that the contract was frustrated at the time of the Government order.

Subsequent illegality

A contract may be frustrated as the result of a change in the law that makes the contract illegal to perform in the manner anticipated in the contract.

DENNY, MOTT & DICKSON LTD V JAMES B. FRASER & CO. LTD (1944)

Lord Macmillan said that a contract to import certain goods to an English port would be frustrated if the law was changed so that importing goods of that kind became illegal.

Outbreak of war is an obvious time when laws may change rapidly and cause a contract to be frustrated.

RE SHIPTON ANDERSON & CO. AND HARRISON BROS. & CO. (1915)

A cargo of grain was sold but before it could be delivered war broke out. The Government requisitioned the cargo and the contract was frustrated.

Commercial sterility

Even where the contract is not impossible to perform, but the commercial purpose of the contract has disappeared as a result of the intervening event, then the contract might still be held to be frustrated. This is sometimes also known as frustration of the common venture, and it is commonly claimed when an event that is fundamental to the contract does not occur.

KRELL V HENRY (1903)

A contract was reached for the hire of a room overlooking the procession route for the coronation of King Edward VII. There was no specific mention of the purpose of the hire in the contract. However, when the coronation did not take place because of the King's illness and the defendant refused to pay for the room the court, applying the principle from *Taylor* v *Caldwell* (1863), accepted that the contract was frustrated. Watching the coronation procession was the 'foundation of the contract'; the defendant was relieved further performance.

All commercial purpose must be destroyed, however if any is left then the contract is not frustrated and obligations under it continue.

HERNE BAY STEAMBOAT CO. V HUTTON (1903)

This was another case arising from the delayed coronation. The defendant hired a boat from which to see the review of the fleet by the King. His claim that the contract was frustrated failed. One purpose had disappeared, but it was still possible to use the boat and to see the fleet.

5.3.4 LIMITATIONS ON THE DOCTRINE OF FRUSTRATION

Because one party to the contract is still left harmed there are a number of situations where the courts have stated that the doctrine cannot apply.

Self-induced frustration

Frustration demands that the event is beyond the control of either party so the doctrine is unavailable when the event is within the control of one party.

MARITIME NATIONAL FISH LTD V OCEAN TRAWLERS LTD (1935)

A fishing company owned two trawlers but wished to run three and so hired one. They required a licence for each vessel but were granted licences only for two. They used their own and, in failing to pay for the hire of the other trawler, claimed frustration. The court rejected their claim. They chose not to use the hired vessel rather than were prevented from doing so.

Contract more onerous to perform

There will be no release from obligations merely because the contract has become less beneficial as a result of the intervening event.

DAVIS CONTRACTORS LTD V FAREHAM UDC (1956)

Here, merely because the builders were unable to make the same profit was not accepted as justifying declaring the contract frustrated.

Foreseeable risk

If the event claimed as frustrating the contract was in the contemplation of the parties at the time of contracting then the plea will be rejected.

AMALGAMATED INVESTMENT & PROPERTY CO. LTD V JOHN WALKER & SONS LTD (1977)

The defendants contracted to sell a building to the investment company who wanted it for redevelopment. Unknown to either party, the Department of the Environment then listed the building, meaning that it could not be used for development resulting in a drop of £1.5 million from the contract price of £1.71 million. The court rejected a claim of frustration, holding that listing was a risk associated with all old buildings of which the developers should have been aware.

Provisions made in the contract for the frustrating event

If the parties have contemplated the possibility of a frustrating event and catered for that in the contract then there can be no release from obligations.

activity

QUICK QUIZ

Which of the following involve frustrating events and which do not:

1 A famous comedian dies just before he is due to appear on stage.

2 A plumber is contracted to fit central heating in a house. He underestimates the days needed to complete the work and as a result he will lose profit on the price agreed.

3 A car I had contracted to buy is destroyed when an explosion sets fire to it.

4 As a lecturer I have contracted to personally take 15 students on a trip to court. An Act is passed requiring teaching and lecturing staff to take no more than ten students per one member of staff on educational visits.

5 In a contract to supply a Far Eastern state with machinery one clause in the contract stipulates what happens in the event of war. In fact war is declared after the making of the contract.

FIBROSA SPOLKA AKCYJNA V FAIRBAIRN LAWSON COMBE BARBOUR LTD (1943) (THE FIBROSA CASE)

A contract for the sale of machinery to a Polish company could not be completed because of the German invasion. The contract contained a 'war clause'. The contract was still frustrated in the event because the clause only anticipated delays in delivery, not the effects of invasion.

So that if a *force majeure* clause does not specifically cover the event in question frustration may still be claimed.

An absolute undertaking to perform

Where the contract contains an undertaking that performance should occur in any circumstances then a frustrating event will not affect the obligations. This was the case with the lease in *Paradine* v *Jane* (1647).

5.3.5 THE COMMON LAW EFFECTS OF FRUSTRATION

The contract terminates at the point of the frustration. This means that the parties are released from their obligation to perform from that point on. Nevertheless, they would still be bound by obligations arising before the frustrating event occurred.

CHANDLER V WEBSTER (1904)

This was another case arising from the delayed coronation of Edward VII. Again a room was hired. However, unlike in *Krell* v *Henry* (1903), where the room was to be paid for on the day of the procession, in this case it was paid for in advance. Despite the frustration there could be no recovery of the money.

This is clearly an unsatisfactory situation because it means that the effect on the parties depends entirely on what point in the contract they have reached.

HL overruled this principle in the *Fibrosa Case* and modified the harshness of the rule. They held that a party could recover payments made prior to a frustrating event provided that there

was a total failure of consideration. This is an improvement, but of course it still means that one party will lose out and will receive no payment for work done in advance of a contract.

5.3.6 THE LAW REFORM (FRUSTRATED CONTRACTS) ACT 1943

Frustration is a common law doctrine originally developed to avoid some of the harshness of existing rules. Nevertheless, as has been shown, it can produce injustice itself. As a result the Act was passed specifically to deal with the consequences of frustrating events.

The Act covers three main areas:

● recovery of money paid in advance of a contract

● recovery for work already completed under the contract

activity

SELF ASSESSMENT QUESTIONS

1 What exactly is 'a frustrating event'?

2 How did *Taylor* v *Caldwell* (1863) help to modify the harshness in the law?

3 What are the differences between 'impossibility' and 'commercial sterility'?

4 In what ways is the doctrine still unfair on at least one party?

5 How does the *Fibrosa Case* 1943 modify the principle?

6 How does the Law Reform (Frustrated Contracts) Act 1943 modify the principle?

● financial reward where a valuable benefit has been conferred

In this way s.1(2) confirms the principle in the *Fibrosa Case* that money already paid over is recoverable despite the apparent lack of consideration. Money due under the contract also ceases to be payable.

Under s.1(2) the court also has the discretion to provide some form of reward for a party who has carried out work under the contract, thus mitigating the harshness of the rule in *Fibrosa*. The sum awarded is discretionary and is what the court believes to be fair, not what has actually been incurred in the way of expenses.

Finally, under s.1(3), a party is able to recover for a partial performance which has conferred a valuable benefit on the other party. Again application of this principle is at the court's discretion.

> ### BP EXPLORATION CO. (LIBYA) LTD V HUNT (NO. 2) (1979)
>
> Hunt had a concession to explore for oil in Libya. BP financed him in return for a half share of the concession. Their expenses would be three-eighths of the oil found until they had recovered 120 per cent of their outlay. Oil was discovered but Libya confiscated it. While BP had already spent $87 million they were awarded $35 million by the court.

The Act's effectiveness is limited because it does not apply in some circumstances. These include:

● contracts for the carriage of goods by sea, except time charter parties;

● insurance contracts (which in any case are all about risk);

● perishing of goods under the Sale of Goods Act 1979.

KEY FACTS

- A frustrating event is one that prevents performance of the contract but is beyond the control of either party
- The original rule on frustrating events was that a party was still bound by all obligations under the contract – *Paradine* v *Jane* (1647)
- A doctrine was developed in the nineteenth century so that in such cases obligations finished at the point of the frustrating event – *Taylor* v *Caldwell* (1863)
- Frustrating events include:
  - impossibility – which could be through the destruction of the subject matter – *Taylor* v *Caldwell*, or the unavailability of the other party – *Robinson* v *Davidson* (1871), or outbreak of war – *Metropolitan Water Board* v *Dick Kerr & Co.* (1918)
  - subsequent illegality – *Re Shipton Anderson & Co.* (1915)
  - commercial sterilisation – the commercial purpose in the contract is lost –*Krell* v *Henry* (1903)
- The courts will not recognise frustration where it is self-induced – *Maritime National Fish Ltd* v *Ocean Trawlers Ltd* (1935)
  - or the contract is merely more burdensome to perform *Davis Contractors Ltd* v *Fareham UDC* (1956)
  - or where the risk is foreseeable – *Amalgamated Investment & Property Co. Ltd* v *John Walker & Sons Ltd* (1977)
  - or has been provided for – the *Fibrosa case* (1943)
- The common law principle was changed so that payments made before the frustrating event could be recovered – *Fibrosa*
- And now the Law Reform (Frustrated Contracts) Act 1943 makes more complex provision.

FIGURE 5.3 *Key fact chart for discharge by frustration*

5.4 DISCHARGE BY BREACH

5.4.1 INTRODUCTION

Whenever a party fails to perform an obligation arising under a contract then that party can be said to be in breach of contract.

A breach of the contract can actually occur in one of two ways:

- By failing to perform obligations – this situation itself can occur in one of two ways: either the contract is not performed at all, or the contract is not performed to the standard required under the contract e.g. providing goods that are not of satisfactory quality.

- By repudiating the contract without justification.

Breach is described as a method of discharge although this seems slightly illogical since by definition a breach means that obligations under the contract have not been discharged.

Lord Diplock explained this position in *Photo Productions Ltd* v *Securicor Transport Ltd* (1980). He suggested that the terms of a contract, whether express or implied, are primary obligations. If a party fails to perform what (s)he has promised to do then this is a breach of a primary obligation which in consequence is then replaced by a secondary obligation, for instance to pay damages. So breach is not so much a discharge of the contract but a replacing of one set of obligations with a different set.

Lord Diplock also saw there being two basic exceptions to his proposition:

- The doctrine of fundamental breach – whereby if a breach of a term deprives the other party of substantially the benefit they were to receive under the contract then the whole contract is said to be breached. (It is unlikely of course that this doctrine has actually survived the *Securicor* cases.)

- Breach of a condition – where the term is so central to the contract that its breach renders the contract meaningless and thus entitles the other party to repudiate their obligations under the contract.

The significant difference between the two traditionally would have been that, while exclusion clauses would be rendered ineffective by the first, it would still be possible to successfully rely on an exclusion clause despite a breach of a condition. This is precisely what the *Securicor* cases demonstrate.

5.4.2 THE DIFFERENT FORMS OF BREACH

There are three identifiable forms of breach:

Breach of a term

Here in effect the character of a term is unimportant. Regardless of whether it is a condition or a warranty, if a term is breached there will always be available an action for damages.

Breach of a condition

A condition can either be expressed by the parties or indeed it can be implied by law, as in the case of the implied conditions in the Sale of Goods Act 1979. However it is identified as being a condition, it must of course conform to the nature of a condition to attract the range of remedies associated with a condition.

SCHULER (L.) AG V WICKMAN MACHINE TOOLS SALES LTD (1974)

Here the claimants could not rely on the term regarding the required frequency of visits by the defendants to the motor manufacturers to repudiate their obligations. They had accepted numerous similar breaches in the past. The term obviously did not go to the root of the contract.

A breach of a condition could also in effect include a breach of an innominate term where the effect of the breach was so serious as to justify repudiation by the other party.

If the doctrine has survived then it might also include a fundamental breach.

Anticipatory breach

An anticipatory breach can occur whenever one party to a contract gives notice, whether expressly or implied by conduct, that (s)he will not complete his or her obligations under the contract.

Again this does not necessarily mean that all obligations will remain unperformed. It may of course be that the obligations will be performed but not in the manner described in the contract. An obvious example of the latter would be late performance, as in delivery of goods after the contract date.

The doctrine can probably be more correctly described as a breach by an anticipatory repudiation, as this is in effect what is usually taking place.

> #### HOCHSTER V DE LA TOUR (1853)
>
> The claimant was hired to begin work as a courier two months after the contract date. One month later the defendants wrote to him cancelling the contract. In answer to his claim they argued that he could not sue unless he could show that on the due date he was ready to perform. The court disagreed. There was no requirement that the victim of a breach of contract should wait until the actual breach to sue.

5.4.3 THE EFFECTS OF BREACH

The consequences for the party who is the victim of a breach of contract and the remedies available will vary according to the categories of breach that we have already considered.

Breach of a term

An action for damages is always available for breach of any kind of term. If the term is only a warranty or, in the case of innominate terms the breach is not a serious one justifying repudiation, then only an action for damages is available. Any attempt to repudiate in such circumstances will itself amount to a breach of contract.

Breach of a condition

Where, on the other hand, a condition is breached or the breach is sufficiently serious the party who is the victim of the breach has more choice. (S)he may continue with the contract and sue for damages, or repudiate his or her own obligations under the contract, or indeed both repudiate and sue for damages.

Before repudiating, of course, a party should be certain that the term is in fact a condition entitling repudiation or the breach by the other party is so serious as to justify repudiation. Otherwise his or her own repudiation might be a breach.

> #### CEHAVE N.V. V BREMER HANDELSGES-SELSCHAFT MBH (1976) (*THE HANSA NORD*)
>
> Here the buyers' refusal to accept the animal feed was an unlawful repudiation. Using innominate terms it could be shown that, since they went on to buy the goods and use them for the same purpose, the effects of the breach could not have been sufficiently serious to justify repudiation.

Anticipatory breach

Here again the party who is victim of the breach has choices available once having discovered that the contract will be breached.

(S)he might immediately consider the contract at an end and sue for damages.

> #### FROST V KNIGHT (1872)
>
> At one time a broken promise to marry was actionable. Here the defendant had promised to marry his fiancée when his father died. Before his father did die he broke off the engagement. The claimant sued successfully for the breach of promise even though the date of the actual beach had not yet arrived since the father was still alive.

As an alternative it is possible to continue with the contract, wait for the due date of performance and, if the contract is not performed, sue at that point.

AVERY V BOWDEN (1855)

Bowden was contracted to load cargo onto a ship for Avery. When it was clear that Bowden would be unable to meet his obligations Avery could have sued. He waited, however, in the hope that the contract would be completed, and intending to sue if it was not completed. This actually turned out to be a mistaken strategy since the Crimean War then broke out frustrating the contract, and Avery thus lost out.

It is always a danger for a party to take this latter course of action. The contract remains live and as a result it is always possible for the party not only to lose their remedy but also to become liable for a breach themselves.

FERCOMETAL SARL V MEDITERRANEAN SHIPPING CO. SA (1989) (*THE SIMONA*)

A charter party contained an 'expected readiness to load' clause, entitling the charterers to repudiate if the ship was not loaded by 9 June. The shipowners asked for an extension on 2 June and the charterers then chartered another ship. The shipowners, instead of repudiating here for the breach by the charterers, gave notice of readiness to load instead. In fact this was not the case and the charterers continued to use the other vessel. The shipowners' action eventually failed in HL. Since they had elected to affirm the contract they were bound by their own original terms, of which they were in breach for not being ready to load on 9 June.

It is also possible that the fact of the innocent party having the right to affirm the contract can itself cause apparent injustice to the other party.

WHITE AND CARTER LTD V MCGREGOR (1962)

Under a contract one party was to supply litterbins for a local council. The bins were to be paid for from advertising revenue from businesses that would have advertisements placed on the bins for a three-year period. One such business backed out of the arrangement before the bins had been prepared. The supplier of the bins nevertheless prepared the advertising and continued to use it for the whole period of the contract and then sued successfully for the full price.

activity

SELF ASSESSMENT QUESTIONS

1 In what way does a breach of contract discharge the obligations under it?

2 What are Lord Diplock's 'primary obligations' and 'secondary obligations'?

3 How limited are the remedies available to a party who has suffered a breach of warranty?

4 Why is there a difference between the reme-

dies available for a breach of a condition and those available for a breach of a warranty?

5 What effect does breach of an innominate term have?

6 What possible problems are there in waiting until the actual breach when there is an anticipatory breach?

KEY FACTS

- A breach occurs when one party fails to perform at all, or does less than is required under the contract, or does not perform satisfactorily

- It will also be a breach where one party wrongly repudiates

- Breach of a warranty allows only an action for damages

- Breach of a condition allows for an action for damages and/or repudiation, but only if the term is really a condition going to the root of the contract – *Schuler* v *Wickman Machine Tool Sales Ltd* (1974)

- The same choice applies where the effect of breach of an innominate term is sufficiently serious – *The Hansa Nord* (1976)

- An anticipatory breach occurs where a party makes known before performance is due that the contract will not be performed – *Hochster* v *De la Tour* (1853)

- The victim of an anticipatory breach has the right to treat the contract at an end and sue immediately – *Frost* v *Knight* (1872)

- Or to wait until performance is due and then sue for the breach – *Avery* v *Bowden* (1855)

- The latter course can be unfair to the party in breach – *White & Carter Ltd* v *McGregor* (1962)

- Waiting for the actual breach can also mean losing the remedy – *Fercometal* v *Mediterranean Shipping Co.* (1989)

FIGURE 5.4 *Key fact chart for discharge by breach*

PART 2 THE LAW OF TORTS

CHAPTER 6

NEGLIGENCE

6.1 THE DUTY OF CARE

6.1.1 THE ORIGINS OF NEGLIGENCE AND THE NEIGHBOUR PRINCIPLE

The origins of negligence lie in other torts in a process known as an action on the case, a method of proving tort through showing negligence or carelessness. The modern tort of negligence begins with Lord Atkin's groundbreaking judgment in *Donoghue* v *Stevenson* (1932). A new approach was necessary in the case because no other action was available.

The judgment is important not just for the decision itself, or only for identifying negligence as a separate tort in its own right, but also for devising the appropriate tests for determining whether negligence has actually occurred.

DONOGHUE V STEVENSON (1932)

The claimant claimed to suffer shock and gastroenteritis after drinking ginger beer from an opaque bottle out of which a decomposing snail had fallen when the dregs were poured. A friend had bought her the drink and so she could not sue in contract. She claimed £500 from the manufacturer for his negligence and was successful. Lord Atkin's judgment contained five critical elements:

● Lack of privity of contract did not prevent the claimant from claiming.

● Negligence was accepted as a separate tort in its own right.

● Negligence would be proved by satisfying a three-part test:

  – the existence of a duty of care owed to the claimant by the defendant;

  – a breach of that duty by falling below the appropriate standard of care;

  – damage caused by the defendant's breach of duty that was not too remote a consequence of the breach.

● The method of determining the existence of a duty of care – the so-called 'neighbour principle'. As Lord Atkin put it 'You must take reasonable care to avoid acts or omissions which you can reasonably foresee would be likely to injure your neighbour. Who then in law is my neighbour? ... persons who are so closely and directly affected by my act that I ought reasonably to have them in my contemplation as being affected so when I am directing my mind to the acts or omissions in question'.

● A manufacturer would owe a duty of care towards consumers or users of his or her products not to cause them harm.

6.1.2 PROXIMITY AND POLICY – THE TEST IN *ANNS*

Over many years the tort of negligence developed incrementally, case by case, with a duty of care being established in numerous relationships.

Lawyers were able to use the neighbour principle to argue for the extension of negligence into areas previously not covered by the tort where damage was a foreseeable consequence of the defendant's acts or omissions.

The test was later simplified so that a duty of care would not be determined in a given case according to how the case fitted in with past law, but rather a duty would be imposed unless there were policy reasons for not doing so.

> **ANNS V MERTON LONDON BOROUGH COUNCIL (1978)**
>
> The local authority had failed to ensure that building work complied with the plans, and as a result the building had inadequate foundations. The claimant, a tenant who had leased the property after it had changed hands many times, claimed that the damage to the property threatened health and safety and sued successfully. The decision was clearly arrived at on policy grounds. Lord Wilberforce, in framing the 'two-part' test, suggested the appropriate method of determining whether or not the defendant owed a duty of care in a given case. First it should be established that there is sufficient proximity between defendant and claimant for damage to be a foreseeable possibility of any careless act or omission. If this was established then it was only for the court to decide whether or not there were any policy considerations that might either limit the scope of the duty or remove it altogether.

Lord Wilberforce's two-part test led to some significant developments in the law of negligence in the 1980s, particularly in relation to economic loss and nervous shock (see later, for instance, *Junior Books* v *Veitchi* (1983) in section 6.6.3 of this chapter). However, these developments were not always considered appropriate and the 'two-part' test caused distress among many judges.

In a series of cases in the 1990s criticism of the two-part test was expressed. Lord Keith in *Governors of the Peabody Donation Fund* v *Sir Lindsay Parkinson & Co. Ltd* (1985) suggested that whether or not it was just and fair to impose a duty was a more appropriate test than mere policy considerations. Lord Oliver in *Leigh and*

Sillavan Ltd v *Aliakmon Shipping Co. Ltd* (1985) (*The Aliakmon*) considered that the test should not be considered as giving the court a free hand to determine what limits to set in each case. In *Yeun Kun-yeu* v *Attorney-General of Hong Kong* (1988) Lord Keith also argued that the test had been 'elevated to a degree of importance greater than its merits …', which he also felt was probably not Lord Wilberforce's intention.

As a result of this the two-part test was later discarded and the case of *Anns* also overruled.

> **MURPHY V BRENTWOOD DISTRICT COUNCIL (1991)**
>
> A house had been built on a concrete raft laid on a landfill site. The council had been asked to inspect and had approved the design of the raft. The raft was actually inadequate and cracks later appeared when the house subsided. The claimant sold the house for £35,000 less than its value in good condition would have been and sued the council for negligence in approving the raft. HL held that the council was not liable on the basis that the council could not owe a greater duty of care to the claimant than the builder. In doing so the court also overruled *Anns* and the two-part test, preferring instead a new three-part test suggested by Lords Keith, Oliver and Bridge in *Caparo Industries plc* v *Dickman* (1990).

6.1.3 THE MODERN POSITION – THE THREE-PART TEST

In *Caparo* v *Dickman* HL had in fact shown some dissatisfaction with the two-part test and preferred a return to the more traditional incremental approach by reference to past cases. The test was able to change in *Murphy* v *Brentwood District Council* because they had identified an incremental approach with three stages.

> **CAPARO INDUSTRIES PLC V DICKMAN (1990)**
>
> Shareholders in a company bought more shares and then made a successful take-over bid for the company after studying the audited accounts prepared by the defendants. They later regretted the move and sued the auditors claiming that they had relied on accounts which had shown a sizeable

surplus rather than the deficit that was in fact the case. HL decided that the auditors owed no duty of care since company accounts are not prepared for the purposes of people taking over a company and cannot then be relied on by them for such purposes. The court also considered a three-stage test in imposing liability appropriate.

- Firstly, it should be considered whether the consequences of the defendant's behaviour were reasonably foreseeable.

- Secondly the court should consider whether there is a sufficient relationship of proximity between the parties for a duty to be imposed.

- Lastly, the court should ask the question whether or not it is fair, just and reasonable in all the circumstances to impose a duty of care.

Reasonable foresight

This is slightly confusing given the fact that a claimant must then go on and satisfy the remoteness of damage test. It operates of course in relation to whether or not there is a duty of care owed.

TOPP V LONDON COUNTRY BUS (SOUTH WEST) LTD (1993)

A bus company did not owe a duty of care when leaving a bus unattended and joyriders stole the bus and injured the claimant.

It is of course possible that attitudes to what is considered reasonably foreseeable can change, as can be seen from comparing the next two cases.

GUNN V WALLSEND SLIPWAY & ENGINEERING CO. LTD (1989)

There was held to be no duty of care to a woman who contracted mesothelioma from inhaling asbestos dust from her husband's overalls. At the time the risk was felt to be unforeseeable.

But a contrary line has since been adopted.

MARGERESON V J. W. ROBERTS LTD (1996)

Here the danger of children playing near an asbestos factory inhaling dust and contracting related illnesses was said to be foreseeable, even though the events in question were in 1933.

Proximity

Proximity was a major part of both the neighbour principle and Lord Wilberforce's two-part test and is still a major factor in identifying the existence of a duty of care.

JOHN MUNROE (ACRYLICS) LTD V LONDON FIRE AND CIVIL DEFENCE AUTHORITY (1997)

Here there was held to be insufficient proximity between a fire brigade and individual owners of property for a duty to respond to calls to be imposed.

Determining whether there is proximity also inevitably seems to be influenced by policy considerations.

HILL V CHIEF CONSTABLE OF WEST YORKSHIRE (1988)

There was insufficient proximity between the police and the public for a duty to protect individual members of the public from specific crimes to be imposed.

Fairness and reasonableness

This requirement is in reality identifying that there must be a limit to liability and no duty will be imposed unless it is just in all the circumstances.

HEMMENS V WILSON BROWNE (1994)

A man had instructed his solicitors to settle a sum of money on a third party. The deed was then negligently drafted so that the gift was unenforceable. There was no duty owed by the solicitors to the third party in question when it was in the power of the man to remedy the situation by instructing the drafting of another document but he had changed his mind and refused to do so.

POINTS FOR DISCUSSION

THE ROLE OF POLICY CONSIDERATIONS

Policy has always been a major consideration in determining liability in negligence. As *Winfield* puts it,

'the court must decide not simply whether there is or is not a duty, but whether there should or should not be one ...'.

Policy factors considered by judges

A great number of factors may be considered by judges in deciding whether or not to impose a duty of care on a defendant in a particular case:

- Loss allocation – inevitably judges are more likely to impose a duty on a party who is able to stand the loss, the role of insurance clearly is a major determining factor also.

- Practical considerations – for instance, courts may be willing to impose vicarious liability on companies that can then plan effective policies for the future avoidance of liability.

- Moral considerations – for instance, the public might be more prepared to accept a 'good Samaritan' law than would the judges.

- Protection of professionals – Lord Denning in particular has expressed concern here that professionals should not be prevented from working by restrictive rulings.

- Constitutional considerations – the judges are not keen to be seen as lawmakers which they acknowledge is Parliament's role.

- The 'floodgates' argument – judges are reluctant to impose liability where to do so might encourage large numbers of claims on the same issue.

- The beneficial effects of imposing a duty for future conduct – in *Smolden* v *Whitworth and Nolan* (1997) the court imposed a duty on a rugby referee who failed to control a scrum properly.

Policy and the refusal to impose a duty

Judges have often in the past identified policy reasons as the justification for refusing to impose liability in certain situations, and there are many examples.

- Liability of lawyers for court work:

RONDEL V WORSLEY (1969)

The claimant argued that he had only lost his case in court because of the negligent presentation of the case by the barrister. The court refused to impose a duty because fear of a negligence action might prevent the barrister from effectively carrying out his duties in court, and in any case could lead to cases being reopened thus ending certainty in litigation.

- Immunity of judges – declared in *Sirros* v *Moore* (1975)

- Liability of the police to the public – as we have already seen in *Hill* v *Chief Constable of West Yorkshire* (1988) – one argument here of course is that there is an alternative means of compensating through a claim to the Criminal Injuries Compensation Board.

- Specific types of claim e.g. the action for 'wrongful life':

MCKAY V ESSEX AREA HEALTH AUTHORITY (1982)

A pregnant woman was not advised that she had contracted German measles and that her child would thus be born severely disabled. The claim was obviously made so that the parents would have the means to support such a severely disabled child. The court would not impose a duty on a doctor to advise of the need for an abortion in such circumstances because that would interfere with the idea of the sanctity of life and policy would not allow that.

Policy and the three-part test

One of the major concerns expressed about Lord Wilberforce's test from *Anns* was that it put too much power in the hands of judges to decide cases on policy issues alone.

While the test may have been flawed it is almost inevitable that policy considerations will still have a part to play in determining liability. The major difference is that under *Anns* this was an open policy, whereas now there is the danger that it might be done much more secretly. Policy was clearly a consideration in the decision in *Hill* even while that very aspect of the test in *Anns* was subject to wider criticism.

Policy has been an issue then in determining the duty of care owed by public regulatory bodies.

PHILCOX V CIVIL AVIATION AUTHORITY (1995)

The Authority here was held not to owe a duty of care to the owner of an aircraft to ensure that he properly maintained that aircraft. Any duty arising out of the Authority's supervisory role was owed to the public.

It has also been a determining factor in the development of the immunity of actions enjoyed by professionals and lawyers in particular.

KELLEY V CORSTON (1997)

There was no duty of care owed by a barrister for negligent advice to settle prior to a court hearing on ancillary relief in divorce proceedings.

Policy also seems to have operated in protection of the public services.

CAPITAL & COUNTIES PLC V HAMPSHIRE COUNTY COUNCIL (1997)

A fire officer ordered sprinklers to be turned off and this then led to more extensive damage. While the employers were liable because of having caused extra damage, the court identified that there was in general no duty owed by a fire brigade for the negligent handling of a fire.

activity

SELF ASSESSMENT QUESTIONS

1 Why is *Donoghue* v *Stevenson* (1932) such an important case?

2 Who or what in the law of negligence is a 'neighbour'?

3 What are the three main ingredients that must be proved for a successful claim of negligence?

4 In what ways was the test in *Anns* (1978) such a radical change from before?

5 Why did HL discard this test and is the new test in fact any better?

6 What factors does a court now take into account in determining whether or not to impose a duty of care?

7 What is the role of policy in establishing a duty of care?

KEY
FACTS

- Negligence requires the existence of a duty of care, which is breached by the defendant and causes damage to the claimant that is not too remote a consequence of the breach – Lord Atkin in *Donoghue* v *Stevenson* (1932)

- The existence of a duty is established by reference to Lord Atkin's 'neighbour principle' – neighbours are those people who are so closely affected by our deeds that we should take care to avoid harming them

- A development of the test was Lord Wilberforce's 'two-part' test from *Anns* v *Merton London Borough Council* (1978) – first see if there is sufficient proximity between claimant and defendant to impose a duty, second decide whether policy reasons will prevent a duty being imposed

- This test was overruled in *Murphy* v *Brentwood District Council* (1991)

- A new 'three-part' test for establishing a duty from *Caparo Industries plc* v *Dickman* (1990) is now used – is there proximity, is the damage foreseeable, is it just and reasonable to impose a duty?

- Policy has always played a part in deciding whether to impose a duty, e.g. immunity of barristers from negligence actions for work done in court – *Rondel* v *Worsley* (1969)

- And e.g. the 'floodgates' argument has been a regular justification for not imposing a duty of care

- A dislike for deciding cases purely on policy grounds was one of the reasons for overruling *Anns*

- Now policy may still be a factor, only a more hidden one – *Hill* v *Chief Constable of West Yorkshire* (1988)

FIGURE 6.1 *Key fact chart for the duty of care*

6.2 THE BREACH OF DUTY

6.2.1 THE STANDARD OF CARE AND THE 'REASONABLE MAN' TEST

We have already seen how negligence occurs where a person owing a duty of care to another person breaches that duty and causes damage which is not too remote a consequence of the breach of duty.

This second element, breach of duty, actually refers to the standard of care that is appropriate to the duty owed. A breach of the duty simply occurs when the party owing it falls below the particular standard of behaviour that is required by the duty in question.

The judge in the case will determine the standard of care and whether or not the defendant's behaviour has fallen below that standard. While the standard in any situation is a question of law, whether or not the defendant has fallen below the standard is a question of fact that will be determined by reference to all of the circumstances of the case.

The standard of care required is generally measured according to an objective method of testing. In this way, while what is the appropriate standard is obviously determined factually according to the circumstances of the case, it is nevertheless the standard that would have been adopted by a 'reasonable man' confronted by the same circumstances that will be taken as the measure by which the defendant's actions will be judged.

The 'reasonable man' test

The objective standard measured according to

the standards of the 'reasonable man' was first identified in:

BLYTH V PROPRIETORS OF THE BIRMINGHAM WATERWORKS (1856)

A water main was laid in which there was a 'fire plug'. This was a wooden plug in the main that would allow water to flow through a cast iron tube up to the street when necessary. A severe frost loosened the plug and water flooded the claimant's house, the cast iron tube being blocked with ice. The frost was beyond normal expectation. There was nothing that the defendants could have reasonably done to prevent the damage and there was no liability. Alderson B explained that 'Negligence is the omission to do something which a reasonable man, guided upon those considerations which ordinarily regulate human affairs, would do, or doing something which a prudent and reasonable man would not do.'

The test on the face of it seems simple enough. The question is, who is the reasonable man by whose standards we are supposed to judge our behaviour?

Judges have over time attempted to define the character of the reasonable man in order that the objective standard can be more closely understood. In *Hall* v *Brooklands Auto-Racing Club* (1933) Lord Justice Greer defined the reasonable man in the following terms: 'The person concerned is sometimes described as "the man on the street", or, as I recently read in an American author, the "man who takes the magazines at home and in the evening pushes the lawnmower in his shirt sleeves" '.

The precise characteristics associated with the reasonable man have also been considered:

GLASGOW CORPORATION V MUIR (1943)

Here small children were scalded when a tea urn was dropped. The urn was being carried through a narrow passage where the children were buying ice creams when the corporation allowed a church picnic to come inside on a rainy day. MacMillan LJ concluded that, 'The standard of foresight of the reasonable man is an impersonal test. It eliminates the

---

personal equation and is independent of the idiosyncrasies of the particular person whose conduct is in question. Some persons are by nature unduly timorous and imagine every path beset by lions; others, of more robust temperament, fail to foresee or nonchalantly disregard even the most obvious dangers. The reasonable man is presumed to be free from both over-apprehension and from over-confidence.'

In fact, the breach of duty is another way of saying that the defendant is at fault and is therefore liable for the damage caused. The issue of whether liability should always be based on fault or whether there should be a no-fault liability system is a controversial question and one that we will return to.

Certainly in practice who or what is the reasonable man, and what constitutes an objective standard, are concepts determined by the judges in a case. Judges in reaching a decision will also base their judgment on either policy or expediency as the need arises.

Policy considerations that can influence a judge include:

● Who can best stand the loss – clearly a claimant needs to claim from a party who can afford to pay. The key rule in deciding whether or not to bring a case is 'never sue a man of straw' (a person of no means).

● Whether or not the defendant is insured – in most circumstances in the modern day it will be an insurance company rather than the actual defendant who will pay the compensation. This would be so, for instance, in the case of motorists, employers, professional bodies, manufacturers, etc.

● The extent to which the decision will prevent similar behaviour in the future – the tort system is mainly about compensating for loss and damage suffered but it should also have a deterrent element.

● Whether or not the decision would 'open the floodgates' to further cases.

- Whether or not particular types of actions should be discouraged – for instance, against the police or administrators of the law.

- Whether or not there are alternative means of gaining a remedy.

6.2.2 PRINCIPLES IN DETERMINING THE STANDARD OF CARE

Through the cases judges have developed a number of rules concerning those things that should be taken into account in determining the standard by which the defendant's behaviour should be measured.

Foreseeability of risk

There is no obligation on the defendant to guard against risks other than those that are within his or her reasonable contemplation. It would be unfair to make a defendant responsible for the unforeseeable.

> **ROE V MINISTER OF HEALTH (1954)**
>
> A patient became paralysed after being injected with nupercaine, a spinal anaesthetic. This had been stored inside glass ampoules themselves stored in a sterilising fluid, phenol. Evidence at the trial showed that the phenol solution had entered the anaesthetic through hairline cracks in the ampoules, contaminating it and causing the paralysis. There was no liability because such an event had not previously occurred and was unforeseeable as a result.

Nevertheless, if the defendant is aware of the possibility of harm (s)he must guard against it, and it will be a breach of the duty of care to fail to.

> **WALKER V NORTHUMBERLAND COUNTY COUNCIL (1995)**
>
> Here a senior social worker had suffered a nervous breakdown. His employers knew that he might suffer another breakdown when he returned to work if the pressures of his work were too severe and stressful. They took insufficient steps to reduce the pressures of his workload and, when he was again made ill, they were in breach of their duty to take reasonable steps to avoid psychiatric injury knowing of his state of health.

The magnitude of the risk

We must all guard against the risk of doing harm. This is only reasonable. The degree of caution that we must exercise will obviously be dictated by the likelihood of the risk. The magnitude of the risk then can be balanced against the extremes that must be taken in order to avoid it.

> **BOLTON V STONE (1951)**
>
> Miss Stone was standing outside a cricket ground and was hit by a cricket ball that had been hit out of the ground. She was actually 100 yards from where the batsman had struck the ball. The batsman was 78 yards from a 17 foot high fence over which the ball had travelled. This was quite incredible and it was shown that balls had only been struck out of the ground six times in 28 years. In Bolton's appeal there was held to be no negligence. The cricket ground had done everything reasonably possible to avoid risks of people being hit.

The defendant though must take into account any factors that might increase the risk.

> **HALEY V LONDON ELECTRICITY BOARD (1965)**
>
> Here a hole was being dug along a pavement and a hammer was left propped up on the pavement to warn passers-by of the presence of the hole. A blind man was passing and his stick failed to touch the hammer and he tripped and fell which left him deaf. It was held that there was a sufficiently large proportion of blind people in the community for precautions to be taken that would protect them also, and the cost would be very low. The defendants were liable for negligence.

The extent of the possible harm (the 'thin skull' rule)

The court will not only be concerned with the likelihood that harm will occur but with the risk that the harm will be great if it does occur. In this sense the defendant must 'take the claimant how he finds him', the so-called 'thin skull' rule.

PARIS V STEPNEY BOROUGH COUNCIL (1951)

The claimant here, who was a mechanic, was already blind in one eye. He was then blinded in the other eye in an accident at work when his employers had failed to supply him with safety goggles that they were actually legally required to do. They were then liable to the defendant to the extent of causing his total blindness rather than merely for the loss of the sight in the one eye. The claimant's partial sight meant that the duty towards him was necessarily greater than normal.

The same principle can apply even though the foreseeable harm is psychiatric rather than physical.

WALKER V NORTHUMBERLAND COUNTY COUNCIL (1994)

An area social services officer had particularly onerous and stressful responsibilities and suffered a nervous breakdown. He returned to work after three months on the understanding that there would be a lighter workload and less pressure. He was nevertheless expected to clear up the backlog and suffered a further breakdown leading to eventual dismissal on the grounds of ill health. The employers were held to have breached their duty to protect his psychiatric well-being and health.

It is also possible for the characteristic in question to be to do with other than the claimant's health or physical characteristics.

MATTOCKS V MANN (1993)

Here the claimant was able to recover the cost of hiring a replacement vehicle used during a delay caused by the insurers' negligent failure to pay for repairs to her vehicle. She was unable to pay for the repair costs herself, and it was foreseeable that she would hope that the insurers would meet those costs.

The social utility of the activity

A defendant can sometimes escape liability in a case because it is possible to show that there was a justification for taking the risk in question. This might be so, for instance, where the defendant acts to avoid a potentially worse event.

WATT V HERTFORDSHIRE COUNTY COUNCIL (1954)

A woman was trapped in a car crash. The fire station summoned to the incident had a special heavy jack for using in such circumstances. It would normally be taken to the scene properly secured in its own vehicle, but the vehicle was elsewhere. The jack was taken unsecured in another vehicle because of the emergency and when the driver was forced to brake sharply the jack moved injuring a fireman. There was no negligence because the situation was an emergency and justified the risk.

However, this will not mean that the taking of any risk at all can be justified. Only the precise circumstances can justify the taking of the risk.

GRIFFIN V MERSEY REGIONAL AMBULANCE (1998)

There was liability when an ambulance crossing a light on red crashed. However, 60 per cent contributory negligence was held on the part of the other motorist.

The practicability of precautions

The reasonable man only has to do what is reasonable in order to avoid risks of harm. This means that there is no obligation to go to extraordinary lengths, particularly if the risk is slight.

LATIMER V AEC LTD (1953)

A factory became flooded after a torrential rainstorm. The water mixed with oil and grease on the floor, making the surface very slippery and dangerous. When the water subsided sawdust was spread over the floors in order to make them secure. There was not enough to cover the whole floor and Latimer slipped on an uncovered patch and was injured. HL held that everything reasonable had been done in the circumstances and, balancing out the possible risks, it was unreasonable to expect the factory to be closed. There was no negligence.

Common practice

A negligent activity cannot be excused merely because it is common practice. Nevertheless, the fact that something is generally practised may be strong evidence that it is not negligent, otherwise it would not normally be carried out. This, of course, is not an absolute principle and it will not necessarily be negligent merely to fail to follow common practice.

BROWN V ROLLS-ROYCE LTD (1960)

An employee contracted dermatitis. The employers provided adequate washing facilities but they did not provide a barrier cream that was commonly used in the industry. They were not negligent in not providing the barrier cream because it could not be shown in the case that using the cream was guaranteed to prevent the condition.

6.2.3 THE STANDARD OF CARE AND DIFFERENT CLASSES OF DEFENDANT

The standard of care is measured objectively but the courts have often looked at whether the standard may differ according to the type of person who it is owed by.

Children

Traditionally there was little case law involving the standard of care owed by children. Case law from other jurisdictions indicated that a child was not expected to have the same skill or understanding as an adult and therefore the standard of care owed was that appropriate to the age of the child in question.

MCHALE V WATSON (1966)

A 12-year-old boy injured a girl in the eye when he threw a steel rod at a post. There was held to be no negligence.

This seems to be more of a subjective than an objective test but the English courts have tended to follow it.

MULLIN V RICHARDS (1998)

Here two 15-year-old schoolgirls were 'fencing' with plastic rulers. One ruler broke and one of the girls was injured in the eye. CA held that since such games were commonplace and would normally not lead to injury then the injury was unforeseeable to girls of that age and there was no negligence.

However, the judges have been willing on occasions to make awards of contributory negligence against child claimants.

ARMSTRONG V COTTRELL (1993)

The judge in this case was prepared to reduce damages for a 12-year-old by a third because he felt that children of that age should know the Highway Code.

And this can even be to a high level of reduction with quite young children.

MORALES V ECCLESTON (1991)

Damages were reduced by 75 per cent when an 11-year-old ran into the road to recover his football.

The disabled

Where a person is sick or suffering from a disability it is likely that the standard of care owed is what would be appropriate in the case of the reasonable man suffering the same illness or disability. It is inevitable that the same degree of care will not be expected as would be for a person in normal health.

A person suffering from a disability of the mind may be liable for the torts (s)he commits if sufficiently aware of the quality of the act.

MORRIS V MARSDEN (1952)

Here the defendant was a schizophrenic who attacked the claimant and was thus accused of battery. It was held that persons suffering from a mental illness could be liable for intentional torts even if unaware that their actions were wrong provided they knew the quality of the act they committed.

Motorists

In general the same standard of care is expected of all motorists regardless of their age or experience, and even of learner drivers.

NETTLESHIP V WESTON (1971)

A learner driver on her third lesson crashed into a lamp-post injuring the person teaching her to drive. CA found that she was liable despite being a learner driver. As Lord Denning put it, 'The learner driver may be doing his best, but his incompetent best is not enough. He must drive in as good a manner as a driver of skill, experience and care ...'.

Lord Denning identified in the case that this is probably to do with the fact that motorists are obliged to carry compulsory insurance and therefore the degree of risk associated with the particular class of driver can be reflected in the insurance premium they are expected to pay.

The principle might even extend to a motorist who becomes physically incapable of controlling the vehicle because of a physical impairment.

ROBERTS V RAMSBOTTOM (1980)

A driver crashed into a stationary vehicle after suffering a cerebral haemorrhage (a stroke). He continued to drive after the seizure and the court felt that he was negligent for doing so. The court accepted that a defendant would have a defence if his actions were entirely beyond his control, but that here the driver should have stopped driving immediately.

However, a motorist will not be liable if (s)he is unaware of the disabling condition that causes the loss of control.

MANSFIELD V WEETABIX LTD (1997)

Here it was held that the driver could not have reasonably known of the infirmity that led to his loss of control and the subsequent accident so there was no fault. The last case was said to be wrongly decided on this point but was still correct in that the driver continued to drive when he should have known that he was unfit to do so.

People engaged in sport

The standard of care appropriate to participants in sport is the ordinary standard of reasonable care. The level of care required will depend on the circumstances of the case including whether the player is a professional or an amateur.

CONDON V BASI (1985)

Here the ordinary standard of reasonable care was applied when a footballer was injured in a dangerous and unacceptable tackle during an amateur football match. Sir John Donaldson MR suggested in the case that a much higher degree of care would be expected of a professional footballer.

While participants in sport are inevitably aware of the risks of engaging in sporting activities, particularly contact sports of any kind, they are nevertheless to be protected from unnecessary harm by the officials in the game. In this way a referee in a sporting contest owes a duty of care to the players.

SMOLDEN V WHITWORTH AND NOLAN (1997)

In a colts' rugby match, that is one involving young and inexperienced players, the referee had been approached by the coaches about repeated collapsing of the scrum by players on the other side. He failed to properly control the scrums and eventually one player was seriously injured, leading to paralysis, when the scrum collapsed. CA agreed that the referee had fallen below the standard of care that he owed to the players. They were, however, eager to emphasise that the judgment was appropriate to the colts but not to the senior game where the players would be more experienced.

A spectator at a sporting contest is generally said to consent to the risks associated with being present at the sport. A person engaged in the sport, then, will not be liable in negligence to a spectator for any injuries or damage caused in the normal course of the sport unless the sportsman has shown a blatant and reckless disregard for the safety of the spectator.

WOOLDRIDGE V SUMNER (1963)

A photographer stood behind a line of shrubs marking the perimeter of the arena at the National Horse Show at White City Stadium. The defendant tried to take a corner too fast on his horse with the result that the horse plunged through the shrubs and injured the claimant. CA held that the defendant was not liable for negligence, but had merely made an error of judgment in how fast he should be going at the time.

People lacking specialist skills

If a person carries out a task requiring a specialist skill (s)he will be judged according to the standard of a person reasonably competent in the exercise of that skill, though this does not mean that an amateur will be expected to show the same degree of skill as would a professional.

WELLS V COOPER (1958)

A tradesman delivering fish was injured when a door handle fitted by the householder came off in his hand. CA held that the appropriate standard of care was that of a reasonably competent carpenter. The claimant's complaint was that the handle was fixed to the door with three-quarter-inch screws that he claimed were inadequate. Since these were the screws that a carpenter would have used there could be no negligence.

Nevertheless, a person not possessing specialist skills will not be expected to exercise the same standard of care as a skilled person unless that standard is appropriate to the circumstances.

PHILLIPS V WHITELEY (1938)

A jeweller pierced ears in a whitewashed room using sterilised equipment. When the claimant contracted a blood disorder the jeweller was not negligent. He had taken all reasonable steps in the circumstances to avoid the risk of harm and could not be fixed with the same standard of care as a surgeon performing an operation. The appropriate standard of care was the degree of care that should be taken by a jeweller carrying out the procedure, not that which would be appropriate to a surgeon.

6.2.4 THE STANDARD OF CARE AND EXPERTS AND PROFESSIONALS

The 'Bolam test'

Professionals do not conform to the usual rules on the breach of duty in negligence and therefore are more appropriately considered as a special category on their own.

The standard of care appropriate to professionals is not judged according to the reasonable man test, so his or her actions are not compared with those of the 'man on the Clapham omnibus'. On the contrary a person exercising specialist skills is to be judged by comparison with his or her peers, other people exercising the same skill. The standard test is found in a case alleging medical negligence but it is equally appropriate to all professionals.

BOLAM V FRIERN HOSPITAL MANAGEMENT COMMITTEE (1957)

Mr Bolam suffered from depression and entered hospital to undergo electro-convulsive therapy. The practice, as the name suggests, causes possibly quite severe muscular spasms. The doctor giving the treatment failed to provide either relaxant drugs or any means of restraint during the treatment. The claimant suffered a fractured pelvis, and the question for the court was whether there was negligence in the practice of providing neither restraint nor relaxants. The court received evidence that a number of different practitioners carrying out the type of treatment took different views on the use of restraints or relaxant drugs. McNair J established the standard of care appropriate to professionals, concluding that 'where you get a situation which involves the use of some special skill or competence, then the test as to whether there has been negligence or not is not the test of the man on the top of a Clapham omnibus, because he has not got this skill'. The actual test was 'the standard of the ordinary skilled man exercising and professing to have that special skill'. Since there were doctors who would have carried out the therapy in the same manner, the doctor here had acted in accordance with a competent body of medical opinion and there could be no negligence.

Applying the test

The test not surprisingly has caused controversy. Nevertheless, HL has subsequently approved it in relation to various aspects of medical treatment and responsibility. It has, for instance, been accepted as appropriate in determining the level of information a doctor should give when obtaining consent from a patient.

SIDAWAY V GOVERNORS OF THE BETHLEM ROYAL & MAUDSLEY HOSPITALS (1985)

Mrs Sidaway had suffered persistent pain in her right arm and shoulder and had on advice of her surgeon consented to a spinal operation to relieve the pain. On obtaining consent, the doctor had accurately informed her that there was a less than 1 per cent risk of something going wrong. What Mrs Sidaway claimed the doctor had not told her was the potentially catastrophic consequences if something did go wrong. In the event, while the operation was carried out without negligence, the damage did occur and she was left paralysed. She sued on the grounds that the surgeon had been negligent in failing to properly warn of the possible extent of the damage. HL held that the degree of information given by the doctor conformed to 'a practice accepted as proper by a responsible body of neuro-surgical opinion ...' so that there was no negligence. They also rejected the idea that there should be a doctrine of 'informed consent' as there is in other jurisdictions because this would make operation of the 'Bolam test' impossible.

The rule has also been accepted and held to apply to diagnosis of illness.

MAYNARD V WEST MIDLANDS REGIONAL HEALTH AUTHORITY (1985)

Here consultants operated before the results of certain tests they had ordered became available. They both considered that the patient had pulmonary tuberculosis, but also felt that she might have Hodgkin's disease, and decided to operate immediately without benefit of the information from the tests. She claimed that the operation damaged her vocal cords unnecessarily. There was no negligence because they had followed a practice approved by a responsible body of medical opinion even if conflicting practices were possible at the time. Lord Scarman stated that 'There is seldom any one answer exclusive of all others to problems of professional judgment. A court may prefer one body of opinion to the other; but that is no basis for a conclusion of negligence'.

It is also long since accepted that the test applies to medical treatment, so that all aspects of medicine fall within the scope of the rule.

WHITEHOUSE V JORDAN (1981)

A senior registrar had carried out a forceps delivery of a baby. The baby had become wedged and suffered asphyxia and brain damage. The allegation was that the doctor had used the forceps with too much force and that was the cause of the damage. In fact, the mother gave evidence that she had been lifted off the bed when the forceps were applied to the baby's head. In HL Lord Edmund-Davis rejected the view put forward by Lord Denning in CA that an error of clinical judgement should not necessarily be the same as negligence. He considered that 'while some errors may be completely consistent with the due exercise of professional skill, other acts or omissions ... may be so glaringly below proper standards as to make a finding of negligence inevitable'. Nevertheless, he confirmed that the 'Bolam test' was the appropriate test by which to measure standards of professional activity.

The rule that the appropriate standard of care in relation to professionals is measured against the standard held by a reasonable, competent body of professional opinion is not a rule exclusive to doctors. It can be applied to professionals generally. A person professing to exercise a particular professional skill will be expected to act in accordance with the standards accepted by a competent body of opinion expert in that skill.

LUXMOORE-MAY V MESSENGER MAY AND BAVERSTOCK (1990)

Auctioneers sold paintings at auction for £840. Some months later the paintings were then resold for £88,000. It was alleged that the auctioneers were negligent in failing to recognise that the paintings were the work of a famous artist. CA held that the auctioneers should be judged according to the standards of a competent body of opinion skilled in the profession of the auctioneers. In the event they were not negligent because it was shown that there could be divergence of opinion on the origins of the paintings.

The standard is that appropriate to the professional exercising and professing to possess the skill in question. It is not, therefore, possible to argue that the standard is reduced because the defendant lacks experience. So the junior doctor must exercise the same degree of skill as the experienced doctor.

WILSHER V ESSEX AREA HEALTH AUTHORITY (1988)

A baby was born prematurely and with an oxygen deficiency. A junior doctor then administered excess oxygen by mistake. The junior doctor inserted a catheter in an artery rather than a vein and a registrar failed to spot the mistake. The baby was later found to be nearly blind. A possible cause of the blindness was the excess oxygen. HL rejected the Health Authority's argument that the standard of care expected should be reduced because it was a junior doctor. Accepting such an argument would then mean that the care a patient was entitled to would depend on the experience of the doctor who treated them. This was unacceptable and negligence was held to have occurred in the case.

The standard expected of the professional is that of a competent body of professional opinion, not of professional opinion generally, so that it is possible for the practice of the professional in question to be accepted in fact by only a minority of professionals.

DEFREITAS V O'BRIEN AND CONNOLLY (1995)

A doctor specialising in spinal surgery considered an intricate exploratory operation necessary. The argument that there was negligence because, as it was shown, only eleven out of over 1,000 surgeons who regularly performed the operation would have operated in the case was rejected. CA held that the number involved was capable of being seen as a competent body of medical opinion in the circumstances.

Common practice amongst a profession is often cited as indicating that the practice is acceptable and not negligent. There are, of course, some practices that can be seen as negligent regardless of whether they are commonly carried out or not.

RE *HERALD OF FREE ENTERPRISE* (1987)

It was argued that it was standard practice for the bow doors of roll-on roll-off ferries to be left open on leaving ports. It was still, however, seen as being a dangerous practice and negligent on the part of the master of the ferry.

One final aspect of the standard of care expected of professionals is that they should keep reasonably abreast of changes and developments in their profession. They would not, however, be expected to be immediately aware of all new ideas.

CRAWFORD V BOARD OF GOVERNORS OF CHARING CROSS HOSPITAL (1983)

Here a patient suffered brachial palsy following an operation. It was argued that this was due to the position of his arm during a blood transfusion, and that the anaesthetist should have been aware of the risk because of a recent article in *The Lancet*, a journal for doctors. The court rejected the argument. There was no negligence because the reasonable doctor cannot be expected to keep up with every new development.

However, it is important that where guidelines are issued by Government or by the professional bodies governing the professions that indicate best practice, then professionals should act according to those guidelines.

THOMSON V JAMES AND OTHERS (1996)

A GP failed to follow Government guidelines in advising parents on vaccinations for rubella, measles and mumps. A child was then not vaccinated following the advice of the GP and contracted first measles and later meningitis, and was brain damaged as a result. The doctor was negligent in failing to issue proper advice.

Criticism of the 'Bolam test'

Although the test is the appropriate method of determining whether a professional has fallen below an appropriate standard of care and is therefore negligent in a given case it has not been without its critics. Indeed there are numerous problems with the rule.

- The test allows professionals to set their own standard in negligence actions – in the case of people other than professionals the standard is an objective one, measured against the 'reasonable man'. In this case the court will decide what the appropriate standard is. In the case of professionals, however, the standard is measured subjectively according to what other professionals, brought to court as expert witnesses, say it is.

- As such it protects professionals to a greater degree than is the case for anyone else – it is sufficient for a professional to bring to court a fellow professional to say that he would have done the same in the circumstances for the allegation of negligence to fail.

- Practices that are only marginal may be accepted as a result – the danger is that the test can legitimise practices that are highly experimental without real credibility, or at the least practices that few other responsible practitioners would carry out.

- There is a danger that professionals will close ranks – even if this is not the case, the criticism will certainly be made and this can have the obvious effect of undermining confidence in the profession.

- It is impossible to say what a reasonable, competent body of professional opinion is – in some cases this can just amount to a question of numbers. The judges in any case are in effect leaving the definition to be made by those accused of the negligence.

There have in fact been a number of cases where doubt has been cast on how appropriate the test is, and where judges have preferred to take a more objective view.

LYBERT V WARRINGTON HEALTH AUTHORITY (1996)

Evidence was introduced to show that a warning given by a gynaecologist concerning the possibility of a sterilisation operation failing conformed to established practice. Nevertheless, CA was prepared to declare that the warning was inadequate and therefore negligent.

Most recently HL has suggested that it is for the court in each individual case to determine what is the standard of care appropriate to the professional against whom the negligence is alleged, and not for professional opinion.

BOLITHO V CITY AND HACKNEY HEALTH AUTHORITY (1997)

A two-year old boy was in hospital being treated for croup. His airways became blocked and, despite being summoned on more than one occasion by nursing staff, a doctor failed to attend. The boy suffered a cardiac arrest and brain damage as a result. This could have been avoided if a doctor had intubated and cleared the obstruction. The hospital admitted that the doctor was negligent in failing to attend. Nevertheless, they claimed that they were not liable because the doctor stated that even if she had attended she would not have intubated and so the cardiac arrest and brain damage would in any case have occurred. Evidence was introduced to show that there were at the time two schools of thought as to whether or not to intubate in such circumstances. The case is ultimately one of causation and whether the 'Bolam test' applies at that point, but HL rejected the view that because certain medical opinion accepted the practice of the doctor in question they were bound to accept it because of Bolam. Lord Browne-Wilkinson suggested that 'if, in a rare case, it can be demonstrated that the professional opinion is not capable of withstanding logical analysis, the judge is entitled to hold that the body of opinion is not reasonable or responsible'.

POINTS FOR DISCUSSION

FAULT LIABILITY AND THE NEED FOR REFORM

Fault liability, particularly in the case of medical negligence as we have seen, seems unfair to claimants because of the problems associated both with amassing evidence and of actually proving fault.

It seems obviously wrong to impose liability on a body such as a health authority unless that body can be shown to have done wrong. The fact that the defendant satisfies legal tests on fault is nevertheless scant comfort to a person who places his or her safety in the hands of professional people and finds himself or herself later to have suffered irreversible and disabling damage.

Fault liability can also be seen as unfair to victims who have suffered harm because the degree to which a person can easily gather evidence and therefore present a winnable case may depend on the degree of publicity that the case has produced. Inevitably people involved in an event gaining media attention or involving a number of claimants may be in a better position to find suitable evidence.

In this way fault liability can also be unfair to society generally in not providing an adequate means of remedying wrongs since the fault-based system can create classes of victims who can be compensated and classes who cannot. This can be particularly true of the victims of pure accidents and those suffering from genetic disorders.

It can also be seen as unfair to defendants since there are no identified degrees of culpability. This in turn means that a defendant will not be penalised according to the degree of negligence shown.

The rules concerning the standard of care as well as the imposing of duties mean that very often a claimant's ability to recover for the wrong suffered is determined according to the whims of policy and therefore can be subject to arbitrary and often inconsistent reasoning.

In fairness to the fault-based system, its major justification is that it does punish the wrongdoer and so is said to have some deterrent value.

However, no-fault systems have been advocated on a number of occasions. The Pearson Committee in 1978 suggested such a system in the case of personal injury claims, though this has never been accepted or implemented. Two no-fault based medical negligence bills have also been introduced unsuccessfully. The principle is not without precedent since such a system has operated in New Zealand.

activity

SELF ASSESSMENT QUESTIONS

1 Who exactly is a 'reasonable man'?

2 In what ways does a 'reasonable man' differ from an average man?

3 How big a part does policy play in determining the standard of care in negligence?

4 To what extent must a person owing a duty weigh up the risks associated with his or her acts and omissions?

5 What exactly is the 'thin skull' rule?

6 When will a standard of care be lowered

because of the inexperience of the person owing the duty?

7 What standard of care does a child usually owe?

8 What effect does the fact that the acts leading to the damage were common practice have?

9 How does the test used for measuring the standard of care appropriate to a professional differ from the normal test?

10 What is the value of expert witness evidence in determining whether or not a professional has breached his or her duty of care?

11 In what ways has *Bolitho* v *City and Hackney HA* (1997) altered the principle in *Bolam* v *Friern Hospital* (1957)?

KEY FACTS

- A breach of duty occurs where a person falls below the standard of care appropriate to the duty (s)he owes
- The standard of care is that appropriate to the 'reasonable man' – *Blyth* v *Birmingham Waterworks* (1856)
- The reasonable man is free from both over-apprehension and over-confidence – *Glasgow Corporation* v *Muir* (1943)
- Policy considerations often govern what the standard will be e.g. the floodgates argument
- Many factors are taken into account in determining whether the duty is breached:
    - foreseeability of harm – *Roe* v *Minister of Health* (1954)
    - the magnitude of the risk – *Bolton* v *Stone* (1951)
    - the 'thin skull rule' – *Paris* v *Stepney BC* (1951)
    - the social utility of the act – *Watt* v *Herts CC* (1954)
    - the practicability of precautions – *Latimer* v *AEC* (1953)
- And consideration will be made for different types of defendant e.g.
    - children – are expected to be less cautious – *Mullin* v *Richards* (1998)
    - motorists – all owe the same duty even if inexperienced – *Nettleship* v *Weston* (1971)
    - sportsmen – will depend on rules of sport being observed – *Smolden* v *Whitworth and Nolan* (1997)
- The standard appropriate to professionals is judged according to the standards of a competent body of professional opinion – *Bolam* v *Friern Hospital Management Committee* (1957)
    - this is because the 'reasonable man' does not share those skills
    - and all aspects of medicine are tested against this rule – *Whitehouse* v *Jordan* (1981)
    - though there is no lowering of standard to take account of inexperience – *Wilsher* v *Essex AHA* (1988)
    - the rule is criticised for allowing doctors to set their own standards while standards generally are measured according to an objective standard
    - it is felt that the standard should not be applied to hypothetical situations – *Bolitho* v *City & Hackney HA* (1997)
- There are alternative systems where no-fault principles operate

FIGURE 6.2 *Key fact chart for the breach of duty*

6.3 CAUSATION IN FACT

6.3.1 INTRODUCTION

Once the claimant has shown the existence of a duty of care and proved that it has been breached by falling below the appropriate standard of care, (s)he must still prove that the defendant's negligent act or omission caused the damage.

As with the other two elements the burden is on the claimant to prove the causal link on a balance of probabilities. This may actually be quite difficult, particularly where the incident has been the result of multiple causes or where the damage suffered is of an unusual type.

Causation is also clearly appropriate to other torts, even those that are strict liability and where the claimant as a result is relieved only of the burden of proving fault.

Causation is necessarily measured against the facts of the individual cases. Nevertheless, as in the other areas, policy can still play a big part in decisions. Causation is measured in two ways:

- According to the 'but for' test, that the defendant's negligent act or omission did in fact cause the claimant's damage (causation in fact).
- By establishing that the damage is still sufficiently proximate in law to hold the defendant liable to compensate the victim (remoteness of damage).

Remoteness of damage will be examined in Section 6.4.

6.3.2 THE 'BUT FOR' TEST

The simplest proposition, and the effective starting point in establishing causation, is to say that the defendant will only be liable in negligence if the claimant would not have suffered the damage 'but for' the defendant's negligent act or omission.

The test was explained simply and precisely by Lord Denning in *Cork* v *Kirby MacLean Ltd* (1952)

'if the damage would not have happened but for a particular fault, then that fault is the cause of the damage; if it would have happened just the same, fault or no fault, the fault is not the cause of the damage'.

In many cases the facts allow the test to operate simply and straightforwardly.

BARNETT V CHELSEA & KENSINGTON HOSPITAL MANAGEMENT COMMITTEE (1969)

Three nightwatchmen from a college went to the casualty ward of the hospital at around 5.00 a.m. on the morning of New Year's Day complaining of vomiting and stomach pains after drinking tea. The doctor on duty refused to attend to them and told them to call on their own doctors. A few hours later one of the men died, as it was discovered later, through arsenic poisoning. The hospital was not liable for the failure to treat, even though this was a clear breach of their duty, because it was shown that the man would not have recovered even with treatment.

However, the facts of a case will not necessarily always be straightforward. So there can be difficulties in establishing causation.

6.3.3 PROBLEMS IN PROVING CAUSATION

Very often the problem is not purely one of fact, and the process of establishing cause is not so much scientific enquiry as attributing blame. Inevitably interpretation of the factual evidence may still depend on the value judgements used by the court. For instance, a pedestrian runs onto the road into the path of an oncoming vehicle that is travelling over the speed limit for the area and is injured. In purest scientific terms the cause of the accident is both parties being present on the road at the same time. It is possible in the circumstances to feel that the pedestrian has done as much as, if not more than, the motorist in causing his own injuries. Inevitably however, even allowing for a successful claim of contributory negligence, the motorist would be held to have caused the victim's injuries, because he is blameworthy by exceeding the speed limit.

Greater problems may occur where the level of knowledge available to the court makes it impossible to pinpoint a precise cause. This may be particularly appropriate where medicine and medical technology is concerned.

WILSHER V ESSEX AREA HEALTH AUTHORITY (1988)

Here the baby after delivery was given excess oxygen as a result of the admitted error of the doctor and then suffered blindness through retrolental fibroplasia. HL identified that the excess oxygen was just one of five possible causes of the condition and therefore it could not be said to fall squarely within the risk created by the defendants.

The difficulty of identifying precise cause means that the case law is often inconsistent. The risk then is that the decision will appear on the surface to be unfair to the claimant. This again is common where the chance of recovery may have been lost through negligence in medical treatment or diagnosis.

HOTSON V EAST BERKSHIRE AREA HEALTH AUTHORITY (1987)

A young boy suffered a fractured hip when he fell out of a tree. The hospital negligently delayed a correct diagnosis so that he later developed avuncular necrosis, a deformity of the hip. It was shown that he would have had a 75 per cent chance of the deformity even without the failure to diagnose promptly and CA awarded him 25 per cent of the damages they would have considered appropriate. HL allowed the Health Authority's appeal and would not consider the slim chance of recovery an issue of causation.

The reverse possibility is that the court accepts the chance of a causative link between the defendant's acts and the damage, and risks the possibility of unfairly penalising the defendant.

MCGHEE V NATIONAL COAL BOARD (1973)

Here the claimant worked in a brick kiln where he was exposed to brick dust, a possible cause of the dermatitis he contracted. The Board was not liable for exposure during working hours. They were held liable for increasing the risk of contracting the disease because of their failure to provide washing facilities, even though it could not be shown that he would have avoided the disease if there had been.

The problems that the courts have in determining cause can be added to by being asked also to

decide the possible outcomes of hypothetical situations.

BOLITHO V CITY AND HACKNEY HEALTH AUTHORITY (1997)

The doctor here argued that, even if she had attended the child with the breathing difficulties, she would not have intubated and thus the same damage would have occurred. HL rejected the idea that the *Bolam* test should be applied to the issue of causation in order that the Health Authority should escape liability.

Nevertheless, there are occasions where the courts appear to take a pragmatic approach where proof of causation is difficult.

BONNINGTON CASTINGS LTD V WARDLAW (1956)

The claimant contracted pneumoconiosis after years of working in dusty conditions and without adequate washing facilities. There were two principal causes of dust, the one requiring no extraction system and the other which did but for which no extractor was provided. It was impossible to prove accurately which dust the claimant had inhaled most of. Since the dust which should have been extracted legally was at least a partial cause of his illness the court were prepared to award compensation.

The courts are also at times prepared to accept the chance of a causal connection with the damage or the chance of damage being avoided without the defendant's negligent act or omission.

STOVOLD V BARLOWS (1995)

It was claimed that a house sale was lost through the negligence of the solicitors. CA felt that there was at least a 50 per cent chance that the deal would otherwise have gone through and so awarded half damages.

6.3.4 MULTIPLE CAUSES

The problem of proving a causal link between the defendant's negligent act and the damage is always made more difficult where there is the possibility of more than one cause. Multiple causes can arise generally in one of two types of circumstances.

Multiple concurrent causes

If the damage is caused by multiple causes that are acting concurrently then the 'but for' test appears to be incapable of providing an absolute test of causation. The case law demonstrates the difficulties faced by the courts.

The court may decide that the negligence has 'materially increased the risk' and that the defendant should therefore be liable for damages.

McGHEE v NATIONAL COAL BOARD (1973)

Here, as we have already seen, the court was prepared to make the employer liable for the dermatitis suffered by the worker in the brick kiln. It did so because it considered that the risk of the particular damage occurring had been materially increased, even though it was impossible to pinpoint the lack of washing facilities as the exact cause of the condition.

In comparison, where there are a number of possible concurrent causes of the damage and it is impossible to identify the specific one causing the damage then it is unlikely that the court will hold one cause ultimately responsible.

WILSHER v ESSEX AREA HEALTH AUTHORITY (1988)

Here the court identified that there were at least five possible causes of the baby's blindness, and the claimant thus could not establish the necessary causal link with the defendant's negligence.

Multiple consecutive causes

Where causes leading to the loss or damage suffered come one after the other then ordinarily the liability will remain with the first event unless subsequent events have added to the damage. The 'but for' test will be applied to the original defendant.

PERFORMANCE CARS LTD v ABRAHAM (1962)

The defendant negligently collided with a Rolls-Royce car. When the Rolls was later negligently struck by another car this did not relieve the original defendant of liability for a respray that had in any case been made necessary by the first collision.

However, a court in determining where liability lies in the case of consecutive causes has inevitably at times been influenced by the desire to avoid in any way undercompensating the victim.

BAKER v WILLOUGHBY (1970)

The claimant was knocked down by a car and suffered a permanently stiff leg as a result. He was then forced to take work on a reduced income. At a later time he was shot in the injured leg during an armed robbery causing it to need amputation. HL rejected the driver's claim that he was then only liable for damages up to the point of the amputation. The loss of earnings was a permanent state of affairs and had resulted from the original injury. The armed robbery and amputation of the leg had not altered this fact.

Nevertheless, the picture is even less straightforward because the courts have also at times been keen to ensure that the victim is not overcompensated at the expense of the defendant.

JOBLING v ASSOCIATED DAIRIES (1982)

In 1973, and as a result of his employer's negligence, the claimant slipped on the floor of a refrigerator in his employer's butcher's shop, injuring his back and losing 50 per cent of his earning capacity as a result. Then in 1976 he later developed spondylotic myelopathy, a crippling back disorder unrelated to the fall. The defendant employer was liable for damages only up to the condition developing in 1976. While not overruled *Baker* was heavily criticised in the case.

6.3.5 NOVUS ACTUS INTERVENIENS

Even though the defendant can be identified as negligent and the 'but for' test satisfied in some senses, the chain of causation may be broken by a subsequent, intervening act. If the court accepts that this intervening act is the true cause of the damage suffered then the defendant may not be liable despite his or her breach of duty.

Such a plea by the defendant is known as *novus actus interveniens*. Translated it means 'a new act intervenes', and it is an effective defence. If, however, the intervening act is not accepted by the court as being the true cause of the damage then the chain is unbroken and the defendant remains liable for his or her breach.

> ### KIRKHAM V CHIEF CONSTABLE OF GREATER MANCHESTER (1990)
>
> Police who had transferred a prisoner to Risley remand centre had failed to inform the authorities there that the prisoner was a known suicide risk. When the prisoner did in fact commit suicide the police were held liable for their failure to warn the prison authorities. Their plea of *novus actus interveniens* by the prisoner failed, since he was suffering from clinical depression, not in full control, and therefore the suicide was not as such a voluntary act.

The area is full of difficulties and the possibility of the plea succeeding is entirely dependent on the facts of the individual case. The case law seems, however, to fall into three definable categories.

An intervening act of the claimant

This is very closely interwoven with contributory negligence. Unlike contributory negligence, however, the plea here is that the claimant is actually responsible for his or her own damage and therefore the chain of causation is broken and the defendant has no liability at all.

> ### McKEW V HOLLAND & HANNEN & CUBITTS (SCOTLAND) LTD (1969)
>
> The claimant suffered an injury to his leg leaving it seriously weakened as a result of the defendants' negligence. When he later tried to climb a steep flight of steps with no handrail without asking for help he fell and suffered further serious injuries. The defendants were not liable for this fall. The claimant's act was a *novus actus interveniens*.

However, if the defendant's original breach is still the operating cause of the later damage and the claimant was not acting unreasonably then the plea that the chain of causation is broken will fail.

> ### WIELAND V CYRIL LORD CARPETS LTD (1969)
>
> Mrs Wieland suffered an injury following the defendants' negligence causing her to have to wear a surgical collar. She wore bifocals and wearing the collar restricted her head movement and meant her use of her spectacles was also seriously impaired. When she then fell down a flight of stairs and sustained further injuries the defendants were liable for those injuries. There was no break in the chain of causation. The risk to Mrs Wieland in the circumstances was said to be foreseeable. The obvious difference compared with the last case was that the claimant did nothing unreasonable.

An intervening act of nature

A plea that an act of nature has broken the chain of causation will rarely succeed. The reason is that the claimant in this instance is then left without any means of gaining a remedy for the wrong suffered.

However, the defendant might be relieved of liability in those situations where he or she can show that the act of nature he or she argues is breaking the chain of causation is unforeseeable and independent of his or her own negligence.

> ### CARSLOGIE STEAMSHIP CO. V ROYAL NORWEGIAN GOVERNMENT (1952)
>
> The claimant's ship was damaged following a collision with a vessel of the defendant's navy and through the defendant's fault. After a delay for repairs the ship then embarked on a voyage it would not otherwise have taken. On that voyage it suffered further damage in a heavy storm. The argument that the defendant should be liable for this damage also failed. The storm was a genuine break in the chain of causation.

An intervening act of a third party

In order to succeed with a plea of *novus actus interveniens* in these circumstances the defendant must show that the act of the third party is of such magnitude that it does in fact break the chain of causation. Furthermore, the consequences of the third party's act must be foreseeable and the defendant must not have any duty to guard against such an act.

KNIGHTLEY V JOHNS (1982)

The defendant, through negligent driving, crashed and blocked a tunnel. The police officer in charge at the scene then negligently sent a police officer against the flow of traffic to block off the tunnel at the other end. The defendant was not liable for the injuries sustained by this policeman. They were the fault of the other police officer.

Nevertheless, it is possible that in such circumstances both the defendant and the third party have in fact contributed to the damage caused, and will be held individually liable accordingly.

ROUSE V SQUIRES (1973)

The defendant driver negligently caused an accident on a motorway in which many vehicles were involved. Another driver then negligently collided with some of the stationary vehicles from the first incident killing the claimant. Despite the obvious responsibility of the later driver, the chain of causation was held not to be broken. The damage in the second incident was held to be a foreseeable consequence of the first and the first driver was held to be 25 per cent responsible for the death of the claimant.

6.3.6 CONTRIBUTORY NEGLIGENCE

Causation also needs to be considered when determining whether or not the claimant has contributed to his or her own damage by taking insufficient care for his or her own safety. In this way in road traffic accidents there may be contributory negligence, for instance, where the claimant has failed to wear a seat belt or, in the case of an accident involving a motorbike, where the claimant failed to wear a crash helmet.

If on the other hand the claimant has contributed so much to the damage suffered as to be entirely responsible then this will probably result in a successful plea of *novus actus interveniens*.

Contributory negligence then will only apply where the claimant has contributed to his or her own harm without being solely responsible. The effect is a reduction in the damages awarded.

SAYERS V HARLOW URBAN DISTRICT COUNCIL (1958)

A lady became trapped in a public lavatory when through negligent maintenance the door lock became jammed. She then stood on the toilet roll holder in an effort to climb out of the cubicle. She had to catch a bus so it was reasonable for her to try to get out in the circumstances, and so her act did not break the chain of causation. The council was liable but the damages were reduced by 25 per cent because of the careless manner in which she tried to get out.

activity

SELF ASSESSMENT QUESTIONS

1 What is the difference between causation in fact and causation in law?

2 How does the 'but for' test work?

3 In what ways is causation a problem to a claimant trying to prove medical negligence?

4 What exactly is the effect of the judgment in *Hotson* v *East Berkshire Area Health Authority* (1987)?

5 How will the courts react when there are multiple causes for the damage suffered?

6 What are the necessary requirements for a successful claim of *novus actus interveniens* by a defendant?

7 What is the difference between a plea of *novus actus interveniens* and one of contributory negligence?

KEY FACTS

- A defendant may be liable in negligence if 'but for' his act or omission the damage would not have occurred – *Barnet* v *Chelsea & Kensington Hospital Management Committee* (1969)

- It may be difficult at times to prove causation and courts will not impose liability where the cause is uncertain – *Wilsher* v *Essex AHA* (1988)

- And are reluctant to base liability on loss of a chance – *Hotson* v *East Berks AHA* (1987)

- Where there are multiple causes the court may feel that the defendant's act has materially increased the risk – *McGhee* v *National Coal Board* (1973)

- Where there are multiple consecutive causes the liability remains with the first defendant unless the later cause increased the damage – *Performance Cars* v *Abraham* (1962)

- Though they are careful not to undercompensate or to overcompensate – *Baker* v *Willoughby* (1970) and *Jobling* v *Associated Dairies* (1982)

- A defendant will not be liable where there is a *novus actus interveniens* (a new act intervening) – this could be:

  – an intervening act of the claimant – *McKew* v *Holland & Hannen & Cubitts* (1969)

  – an intervening act of nature – *Carslogie Steamship Co.* v *Royal Norwegian Government* (1952)

  – an intervening act of a third party – *Knightley* v *Johns* (1982)

- Damages may be reduced where there is contributory negligence – *Sayers* v *Harlow UDC* (1958) – Law Reform (Contributory Negligence) Act 1945

FIGURE 6.3 *Key fact chart for causation of fact*

6.4 REMOTENESS OF DAMAGE

6.4.1 THE TESTS OF REMOTENESS

The final element of proof in negligence is whether there is causation in law, otherwise known as remoteness of damage. Even though a causal link can be proved factually according to the 'but for' test, the claimant may still be prevented from winning the case if the damage suffered is too remote a consequence of the defendant's breach of duty.

The test is a matter of law rather than fact and like other aspects of negligence is much influenced by policy considerations. The principle justification for the rule is that the defendant should not be overburdened by compensating for damage linked to the breach that is of a kind that is unlikely or unforeseeable.

The original test of remoteness, however, was that the claimant could recover in respect of a loss that was a direct consequence of the defendant's breach regardless of how foreseeable.

RE POLEMIS AND FURNESS, WITHY & CO. (1921)

Charterers of a ship filled the hold with containers of benzine that then leaked during the voyage filling the hold with vapour. In port the ship was being unloaded when a stevedore negligently dropped a plank into the hold. A spark then ignited the vapours and the ship was destroyed. The arbitrator held that this was too unlikely a consequence of dropping the plank though some damage was of course foreseeable. CA held that the charterers, as employers of the stevedores, were liable. Scrutton LJ stated that 'if the act would or might probably cause damage, the fact that the damage it in fact causes is not the exact kind of damage one would expect is immaterial, so long as the damage is in fact directly traceable to the negligent act'.

The test was then criticised for its failure to distinguish between degrees of negligence. As a result the test was later changed to one of liability for damage only that was a reasonably foreseeable consequence of the breach.

OVERSEAS TANKSHIP (UK) LTD V MORTS DOCK & ENGINEERING CO. (1961) (*THE WAGON MOUND* (NO. 1))

Due to the defendant's negligence bunkering oil was leaked into Sydney harbour from a tanker. The oil floated on the water to the claimant's wharf mixing with various flotsam and jetsam, including patches of cotton wadding. Welding was taking place in the wharf and the claimant's manager enquired whether there was a risk of the oil igniting. This was considered unlikely since the oil had an extremely high flash point. Welding then continued and sparks did in fact ignite the oil-soaked wadding and then set fire to ships being repaired in the wharf. The oil also caused fouling to the wharf. The trial judge held that since some damage, the fouling, was foreseeable the defendants were liable also for the fire damage which was a direct consequence of their breach of duty in allowing the spillage. PC reversed this decision holding that the defendant could not be liable for the fire damage since the correct test for remoteness was reasonable foreseeability and, because of the improbability of the oil igniting, the fire damage was unforeseeable.

6.4.2 APPLYING THE REASONABLE FORESEEABILITY TEST

The critical element of the test is foreseeability of the general rather than the specific type of damage. It is not therefore necessary for the full extent of the damage to be foreseen.

BRADFORD V ROBINSON RENTALS (1967)

The claimant suffered frostbite when sent on a long journey by his employers in severe winter weather in a van without a working heater. The defendant argued that the type of damage was too remote and unforeseeable. The court disagreed. It was certainly foreseeable that some cold-related illness was a possibility. It was immaterial that the actual damage was frostbite and the defendant was held liable.

It is not therefore necessary for the defendant to have contemplated the precise consequences of the negligent act or omission provided (s)he is aware of the possibility of damage resulting.

MARGERESON V J W ROBERTS LTD (1996)

The court in this case considered that the owner of an asbestos works should have been aware of the dangers of inhaling asbestos dust even in 1933. In consequence it was prepared to impose liability in respect of mesothelioma contracted by children who played in dust from the factory collecting in and around the entrance to the factory.

Neither is it necessary, when the defendant is negligent, for the precise consequences of the act or omission to be foreseen when damage is a foreseeable consequence.

HUGHES V THE LORD ADVOCATE (1963)

Post Office employees negligently left a manhole uncovered inside a tent and the tent unattended. They left four lit paraffin lamps at the corners of the tent. A boy entered the tent with a lamp and when it fell into the hole there was an explosion, the boy fell in also and was burnt. This was an unlikely chain of events but the defendants were nevertheless liable since some fire-related damage was a foreseeable consequence of leaving the scene unattended.

The 'thin skull' rule will also apply so that the defendant will be liable for the full extent of the damage if damage of the type is foreseeable.

SMITH V LEECH BRAIN & CO. LTD (1962)

An employee suffered a burnt lip following his employers' negligence. He later died from cancer which had developed following the burn. His lip had actually been in a pre-malignant state at the time of the burn. Harm from the burn was foreseeable though death from cancer was not, but the defendants were liable.

The test of reasonable foreseeability and claims for personal injury

In general, cases such as the above seem to indicate that the courts take a fairly broad view of what is reasonably foreseeable in the event that the damage suffered is personal injury.

Nevertheless, there are occasions when the court has taken a narrower view and this appears on the surface to work unfairly on the claimant.

TREMAIN V PIKE (1969)

The claimant, a herdsman, suffered Weil's disease. This is a rare disease only contracted through contact with rats' urine. This, he said, in fact happened when he worked with hay and washed with water that was contaminated with rats' urine. It was accepted that the defendant had allowed the rat population on his farm to grow too large, and that there was some risk of damage from rats. Nevertheless, the defendant was not held liable since the court considered that the disease was so rare in humans that it was unforeseeable.

On occasions it also appears that the test in *Hughes* can be contradicted if the court focuses too closely on the circumstances in which the damage occurs.

DOUGHTY V TURNER MANUFACTURING CO. LTD (1964)

Here, due to negligence, a cover over a cauldron of heated sodium cyanide was allowed to slide into the liquid. The cover was made of asbestos compound. There was a chemical explosion and the claimant was burned. It was previously unknown that there would be such a chemical reaction between the asbestos and the sodium cyanide and CA held that the defendants were not liable. The chemical reaction was unforeseeable and the damage was thus too remote. However, there certainly seems to be merit in the claimant's argument that damage from the liquid if splashed would be foreseeable.

The test of reasonable foreseeability and claims for property damage

With the exception of the last two cases the courts in general appear to adopt a narrower approach to what is foreseeable when the damage in question is to property rather than being personal injury.

OVERSEAS TANKSHIP (UK) LTD V MORTS DOCK & ENGINEERING CO. (1961) (*THE WAGON MOUND* (NO. 1))

The trial judge acknowledged that some damage was foreseeable in the circumstances. The type of damage that was foreseeable though was fouling by the oil, not fire, so he concluded that the defendants were not liable.

Even degree of risk of the type of damage actually caused has been considered narrowly thus avoiding imposing liability.

OVERSEAS TANKSHIP (UK) LTD V MILLER STEAMSHIP CO. PTY (1967) (*THE WAGON MOUND* (NO. 2))

The owners of the two ships that were being repaired in the wharf and were damaged in the fire brought this case. The trial judge showed a very narrow approach to foreseeability in relation to an action for property damage. While he accepted, unlike the trial judge in *Wagon Mound (No. 1)*, that fire was a foreseeable consequence of the defendant's negligence, he nevertheless felt that it was so remote as not to give rise to any liability. He was reversed by PC which held that provided the type of damage was foreseeable then liability must result, and the degree of likelihood irrelevant.

POINTS FOR DISCUSSION

It is difficult in some ways to see a real difference between the test based on direct consequences and the test based on reasonable foreseeability. In many instances, certainly, damage that is reasonably foreseeable will also be a direct consequence of the defendant's breach. It is similarly difficult to contemplate situations that are totally unforeseeable and yet are still a direct consequence.

Besides this the difference may well be unimportant. The effect of the 'thin skull' rule is to compensate many victims for damage that the defendant will probably not have contemplated at all. On top of this many areas of quite remote damage are in any case within the scope of insurance and so a claimant may still gain some form of compensation.

activity

SELF ASSESSMENT QUESTIONS

1 When will damage be too remote to be compensated?

2 How exactly is reasonable foreseeability measured: in other words, what has to be foreseen?

3 Do the attitudes of the courts generally vary according to the type of damage caused?

4 What precisely is the difference between damage that is a direct consequence of the defendant's negligence and damage that is reasonably foreseeable?

5 What is the effect of a claimant's peculiar sensitivities on the issue of remoteness of damage?

KEY FACTS

- At one time a defendant was liable for all damage that was a direct consequence of his negligent act or omission – *Re Polemis and Furness, Withy & Co.* (1921)

- Now the modern test is one of liability for reasonably foreseeable damage – *The Wagon Mound (No. 1)* (1961)

- Only the general, not the actual, type of damage needs to be foreseen – *Bradford* v *Robinson Rentals* (1967)

- Nor do the precise consequences of the negligent act or omission have to be foreseen – *Hughes* v *The Lord Advocate* (1963)

- The 'thin skull' rule applies – *Smith* v *Leech Brain* (1962)

- The courts generally, but not always, seem to take a broader view of remoteness in personal injury cases than they do with property damage

FIGURE 6.4 *Key fact chart for remoteness of damage*

6.5 *RES IPSA LOQUITUR*

6.5.1 INTRODUCTION

One of the common threads throughout all law is the general maxim that 'he who accuses must prove'. In this way the party claiming the negligence has the burden of proof and must show the defendant's breach of the duty of care. The burden of proof can work very harshly on a claimant who will be bound to collect all of the necessary evidence to show the negligence. This can be particularly difficult, for instance, in medical negligence cases where a mass of highly technical evidence may need to be produced.

There are certain, rare circumstances in which this burden of proof can be made less demanding. The first of these is under the Civil Evidence Act 1968 by which under s.11 it is possible to introduce criminal convictions as evidence.

A second area, which relaxes the burden of proof, is an old common law maxim *res ipsa loquitur*. Literally translated *res ipsa loquitur* means 'the thing speaks for itself'. So it is a mechanism whereby the claimant can be relieved of the burden of proving the negligence and the court can infer negligence in those situations where the factual circumstances of the case would make proving it almost impossible.

6.5.2 THE EFFECT OF THE DOCTRINE

There is some argument as to the exact means by which the principle works. In simple terms it is often explained as reversing the burden of proof, and in effect putting the burden on the defendant to prove that (s)he was not negligent. In *Wilsher* v *Essex Area Health Authority* (1988) on the other hand it was suggested that the maxim does not in fact reverse the burden of proof. Here it was suggested that invoking the maxim raises a prima facie presumption of negligence. The defendant is then required to rebut that presumption by the introduction of evidence to the contrary. Nevertheless, it was said that the burden remains throughout with the claimant. This, though, does not appear to be the standard view.

Whatever the precise mechanism is, it does at least give a claimant alleging negligence the opportunity to demand some contrary proof from the defendant in circumstances where the collection of evidence is difficult if not impossible.

Inevitably the effect of the maxim can be equally harsh on the defendant so the maxim is very narrowly construed and it will only be considered as appropriate if the facts of a case fit specific criteria laid down by the courts.

SCOTT V LONDON AND ST KATHERINE'S DOCK CO. (1865)

Here the claimant was standing outside the defendant's warehouse when several large bags of sugar fell on him. There was little or no explanation for the incident and no evidence that anybody had been negligent. The trial judge initially found for the defendant since there was no proof of negligence. On appeal the criteria for dealing with such claims were established.

There are three specific criteria for successfully pleading *res ipsa loquitur*:

- At all material times the thing causing harm must have been in the control of the defendant.

- The incident is of a type that could only have been caused by negligence.

- The cause of the incident is not known and there is no other obvious explanation for the incident.

The incident was in the control of the defendant

Inevitably the defendant must be in control of the situation that has led to the damage or there can be no liability.

What falls within the defendant's control is a question of fact in each case for the court to decide.

GEE V METROPOLITAN RAILWAY CO. (1873)

A passenger leaned on a train door shortly after it left the station. The door opened and the passenger fell out and was injured. The defendants were responsible for ensuring that all doors were properly closed before the train left the station, so they were in control at the material time and were liable.

And clearly circumstances may show that it would be unfair to suggest that the defendant had actual control.

EASSON V LONDON AND NORTH EASTERN RAILWAY (1944)

Here a boy passenger fell through the door of a train when it was a long way from its last stop. It was possible that another passenger had opened the door. It was certainly felt to be impossible to say that the doors were under the control of the railway company throughout the journey and *res ipsa* could not apply.

It seems only fair that if the defendant is in control of the circumstances in which the damage occurred (s)he should be called on to give some explanation of the incident.

The incident is of a type usually associated with negligence

It is crucial also to show that the incident causing the damage is of a type that would not normally occur if proper care were taken. If this is so then the incident can be seen as one of a type commonly caused by negligence.

SCOTT V LONDON AND ST KATHERINE'S DOCK CO. (1865)

Large bags of sugar are inanimate objects and it is unlikely that they could fall from a hoist without a lack of care being taken.

Res ipsa is often pleaded in medical negligence cases because the claimant is entitled to an explanation of how the damage occurred if not by negligence.

GLASS V CAMBRIDGE HEALTH AUTHORITY (1995)

A man with a normal healthy heart went into cardiac arrest while under a general anaesthetic. The maxim was held to have been appropriately pleaded in the case although the Health Authority was able to introduce evidence to show why they had not been negligent.

In medical negligence cases the plea may often be used because the precise party responsible is unknown.

MAHON V OSBORNE (1939)

Here after an operation a patient later died and a swab was found inside him. It was clear that the swab could not have been there but for negligence although the person actually responsible could not be identified. Scott LJ, however, felt that some positive evidence of neglect of duty in the operation was needed in such cases.

The maxim in such cases may be used when the claim is that a particular body is vicariously liable for the acts of the tortfeasor (the wrongdoer).

WARD V TESCO STORES LTD (1976)

A customer slipped on yoghurt that had been spilt onto the supermarket's floor. Tesco claimed that they had a procedure in place whereby the floors were cleaned regularly throughout the day and staff were instructed to stay with such spillages when they were found until they were cleaned. Nevertheless, the customer was also able to show evidence of other spillages that were not immediately cleaned up. The court accepted that such occurrences could only result from negligence.

There is no other explanation for the incident causing damage

The third and final criterion is that it is impossible to give any explanation of the incident. If the circumstances of the incident are capable of explanation by the claimant then the usual burden applies and the claimant should show how the facts prove negligence.

A claim of *res ipsa loquitur* can only apply because there are no other means available to explain the true cause of the incident. It is thus fairer in the circumstances to ask the defendant to introduce some evidence to rebut the presumption that negligence has occurred.

BARKWAY V SOUTH WALES TRANSPORT CO. LTD (1950)

A bus mounted a pavement and resulted in injury to the claimant. A tyre had burst through a defect in the wall of the tyre that could not have been discovered earlier. *Res ipsa* was shown to be inappropriate, however, when it was discovered that the bus company gave no instructions to drivers to report heavy blows suffered by the tyres. As a result negligence could be shown and the defendants were liable.

6.5.3 *RES IPSA LOQUITUR* AND MEDICAL NEGLIGENCE

We have already seen that there is debate amongst the judiciary as to the proper role of the maxim in relation to medical negligence.

There is a strong argument to say that the maxim should always apply because the three criteria will generally be satisfied and the claimant may face a very difficult time gathering the appropriate evidence.

The courts have been reluctant to accept such widespread application of the maxim. The Pearson Report in 1978 also rejected general application because of the fear of an escalating number of claims resulting and the consequent rise in insurance premiums for medical staff.

6.5.4 STRICT LIABILITY IN NEGLIGENCE

Res ipsa was formerly very often used in cases involving foreign bodies in foodstuffs. Clearly while it may be difficult to show how the material got there it is nevertheless something that should not happen if proper care is taken.

EU law is fairly explicit on such issues and has traditionally imposed stricter standards than English law. English law is now very much in line with European law since the passing of the Consumer Protection Act 1987, enacted to comply with EU directives. The Product Safety Directive has also subsequently been implemented in the form of regulations.

The Consumer Protection Act allows that any person within the chain of distribution of a product is strictly liable if a consumer suffers harm as the result of defects in the product.

While fault is in a sense abolished in the Act causation is still an issue.

activity

SELF ASSESSMENT QUESTIONS

1 *Res ipsa loquitur* means 'the thing speaks for itself', but what does this mean precisely in relation to the incident in question?

2 What three elements must always be present for a judge to accept that the doctrine applies in the case?

3 To what extent is it accurate to speak of a reversal of the burden of proof?

4 What sorts of things indicate that the loss or damage suffered could only have been the result of negligence?

5 Why has the doctrine regularly been pleaded in medical negligence cases?

6.6 NOVEL DUTY SITUATIONS

6.6.1 INTRODUCTION

We have already seen how the tort of negligence is based on the existence first of a duty of care owed by the defendant to the claimant. The law

has developed over time to include many instances where a duty of care exists.

There are numerous obvious or straightforward relationships where we might naturally expect a duty of care to exist. These would include between fellow motorists, between doctor and

KEY
FACTS

- *Res ipsa loquitur* means 'the thing speaks for itself' – it is a means of establishing negligence where proof is hard to come by

- The doctrine in effect means that the defendant has to prove that he or she was not negligent if the plea is raised successfully

- There are three essential aspects to the plea:

  - at all material times events leading to the damage were under the control of the defendant – *Gee* v *Metropolitan Railway* (1873)

  - the incident is of a type usually associated with negligence – *Scott* v *London and St Katherine's Dock* (1865)

  - there is no other explanation – *Barkway* v *South Wales Transport* (1950)

- It can be particularly appropriate to medical negligence claims

FIGURE 6.5 *Key fact chart for* res ipsa loquitur

patient, between employer and employee, between manufacturers of products and their consumers, and many others. We have already seen examples in the case law of all of these.

There are also certain situations that are less obvious that have had to be considered by the courts. They have proved more controversial but in some of them the courts have held that a duty of care does in fact exist. They include the following four examples:

- negligent misstatement

- pure economic loss

- nervous shock

- omissions

6.6.2 NEGLIGENT MISSTATEMENT

The law of torts is concerned mainly with compensating for physical damage or personal injury, not for loss that is only economic. The obvious justification for this stance is that economic loss, or for instance loss of a profit or bargain, is more traditionally associated with contract law and the judges have always been eager to separate out the two.

An action for an economic loss caused by a statement was traditionally available in tort, but in the tort of deceit and only in the case of fraudulently made statements.

DERRY V PEEK (1889)

A representation in a share prospectus that a tram company could use motive power led to loss when the Board of Trade refused the company a licence to use motorised trams. The company had fully expected to be granted the licence so their misstatement was not considered to be fraudulent.

The origins of liability

An action in respect of an economic loss caused through reliance on a negligently made statement was reaffirmed even more recently, although not without some fundamental disagreement being expressed.

CANDLER V CRANE CHRISTMAS & CO. (1951)

Accountants negligently prepared a company's accounts and investors then lost money. In the absence of a contractual relationship or fraud the court was not prepared to declare the existence of a duty of care. Lord Denning, dissenting, felt that there should be a duty of care to the investor and to 'any third party to whom they themselves show the accounts, or to whom they know their employer is going to show the accounts so as to induce them to invest money ...'.

HL eventually accepted this dissenting judgment a long time afterwards, and initially only *in obiter*.

HEDLEY BYRNE & CO. LTD V HELLER & PARTNERS LTD (1964)

An advertising company was approached with a view to preparing a campaign for a small company, Easipower, with whom they had not previously dealt. The advertisers then did the most sensible thing in the circumstances and approached Easipower's bank for a credit reference. The bank gave a satisfactory reference without checking on their current financial standing and the advertisers produced the campaign. They then lost money when Easipower went into liquidation. They sued the bank for their negligently prepared advice. They failed because the bank had included a disclaimer of liability in the credit reference. Nevertheless, HL, approving Lord Denning's dissenting judgment in the last case, held that such an action should be possible, and this has subsequently been accepted as law.

The interesting point of the court's approval of the principle in the case is that they were holding that such a duty could apply despite there being no contractual relationship, and despite the fact that, in effect, they were accepting imposing liability for economic loss.

As a result HL in the case laid down strict guidelines for when the principle could apply.

- There must be a special relationship between the two parties.

- The person giving the advice must be possessed of special skill relating to the type of advice given.

- The party receiving the advice has acted in reliance on it.

The subsequent case law has in general followed these requirements.

Special relationship

The precise meaning of 'special relationship' was never really examined in *Hedley Byrne* and so it has become an area for judicial policy making. The original leaning was towards a narrow interpretation that would then only include a relationship where the party giving the advice was in the business of giving advice of the sort in question.

However, it has since been suggested that a business or professional relationship might in general give rise to the duty if the claimant is genuinely seeking professional advice.

HOWARD MARINE & DREDGING CO. LTD V A. OGDEN & SONS (EXCAVATING) LTD (1978)

Dredging took a lot longer because the hirers of the barges had misstated the payload weight to the party hiring them. It was accepted that the relationship, while a standard business one, could give rise to a special relationship for the purposes of imposing a duty.

A purely social relationship should not normally give rise to a duty of care, but has done so when it has been established that carefully considered advice was being sought from a party with some expertise.

CHAUDHRY V PRABHAKER (1988)

A woman asked her friend, who, while not a mechanic, had some experience of cars, to find her a good second-hand car that had not been in an accident. When it was later discovered that the car advised on had been in an accident and was not completely roadworthy the friend advising on its purchase was successfully sued.

The common relationships in which a duty will be identified, though, are those where valuers or accountants are providing the advice.

YIANNI V EDWIN EVANS & SONS (1982)

A building society surveyor was held to owe a duty to purchasers of a property valued at £12,000 where it was later discovered that repairs worth

£18,000 were required. The duty was imposed because it was shown that at the time less than 15 per cent of purchasers would have their own independent survey carried out, and therefore it was foreseeable that they would rely on the standard building society survey.

The possession of special skill or expertise

Ordinarily, then, a claim is only possible if the party giving the advice is a specialist in the field which the advice concerns.

MUTUAL LIFE AND CITIZENS ASSURANCE CO. LTD V EVATT (1971)

A representative of an insurance company gave advice about the products of another company. The court held that there could only be a duty in such circumstances if the party giving the advice had held himself or herself out as being in the business of giving the advice in question.

So advice given in a purely social context could not usually give rise to liability. Clearly the defendant in *Chaudhry* v *Prabhaker* was unfortunate in this way, though the result was justified on the basis that he should have applied the same caution in advising on the car that he would have if he had been buying it himself.

Reasonable reliance on the advice

It is only fair and logical that if there has been no reliance placed on the advice given then there should be no liability on the defendant for giving it.

JEB FASTENERS LTD V MARKS BLOOM & CO. (1983)

A negligent statement of the value of a company's stock did not give rise to a duty. This was because the party buying the company was doing so only to secure the services of two directors, and so placed no reliance on the stock.

So it will not be foreseeable reliance if the claimant belongs to a group of potential claimants that is too large.

GOODWILL V BRITISH PREGNANCY ADVISORY SERVICE (1996)

Here a man had not been properly advised of the possibility that his vasectomy could automatically reverse itself. It was held that there could be no duty of care owed to a future girlfriend of the man.

But whenever there is foreseeable reliance on advice given then there will be a duty of care owed.

SMITH V ERIC S. BUSH (1990)

A building society valuation had identified that chimney breasts had been removed, but the valuer had failed to check whether the brickwork above was properly secured. It was not and after the purchase it collapsed. There was a duty of care because, on the same basis as *Yianni* v *Edwin Evans*, even though the contract was between building society and valuer, it was reasonably foreseeable that the purchaser would rely on it.

Foreseeable reliance by the party seeking the advice might also prevent an exclusion of liability clause in a contract from operating successfully.

HARRIS V WYRE FOREST DISTRICT COUNCIL (1989)

Here in the sale of a council house a negligent survey had been carried out for the local authority. Even though the purchaser did not see the valuation he could rely on it and a disclaimer of liability inserted in the valuation was ineffective because it was not reasonable within the terms of the Unfair Contract Terms Act 1977.

The current state of the law

In *Caparo* v *Dickman* (1990) HL had the opportunity to consider the principles involved in liability under *Hedley Byrne*. The financial booms and rapid development in property markets had not only led to a greater increase in home ownership and share ownership, it had also led on to a great number of claims for negligent misstatement, particularly against property surveyors and accountants.

HL preferred an incremental approach to

establishing the duty of care, as we have already seen. They also made a number of observations regarding the circumstances in which the *Hedley Byrne* type duty will be owed.

- The advice must be required for a purpose described at the time to the defendant at least in general terms.

- This purpose must be made known either actually or by inference to the party giving the advice at the time it is given.

- If the advice is to be subsequently communicated to the party who relies on it then this fact must be known by the advisor.

- The advisor must be aware that the advice will be acted upon without benefit of any further independent advice.

- The person alleging to have relied on the advice must show actual reliance and consequent detriment suffered.

This is a very narrow approach to the duty and subsequent cases have tended to take a more relaxed view.

Some cases certainly seem to be at odds with the general principle and liability has been imposed apparently to prevent a party being without any remedy.

WHITE v JONES (1995)

Solicitors who negligently failed to draw up a will before the testator's death were held to owe a duty to the intended beneficiaries who consequently lost their inheritance. Any contractual relationship was with the testator, and since a will can be changed a beneficiary is not necessarily ensured the inheritance. Nevertheless, HL were prepared to identify both a special relationship in the circumstances and reliance.

However, in some instances this is because the court is uncertain whether the principle in *Hedley Byrne* or that in *Donoghue* v *Stevenson* (1932) is the appropriate one to apply. The latter is certainly less restrictive.

SPRING v GUARDIAN ASSURANCE PLC (1995)

An employee of an insurance company was dismissed and then prevented from gaining a position with another company because of a negligently prepared and highly unfavourable reference provided by the first company. HL held that the first employers were liable because of the reference, but were split on whether *Hedley Byrne* should apply.

activity

SELF ASSESSMENT QUESTIONS

1 Why did HL in *Hedley Byrne* alter the previous rule in *Candler* v *Crane Christmas & Co* (1951)?

2 What exactly is a special relationship?

3 How can the decision in *Chaudhry* v *Prabhaker* (1988) be justified?

4 Against what standards is reasonable reliance measured?

5 To what extent does the case of *Caparo* v *Dickman* (1990) limit the rule?

6 How do cases like *White* v *Jones* (1995) and *Spring* v *Guardian Assurance* (1995) fit in with the normal rule?

6.6.3 PURE ECONOMIC LOSS

The *Hedley Byrne* case introduced the concept that a claimant could recover for economic loss arising from negligently made statements. However, the courts have always distinguished

▼ KEY FACTS

- Originally there was only an action available for misrepresentations if they were made fraudulently – *Derry* v *Peek* (1889)

- And an action for negligence was originally specifically rejected in *Candler* v *Crane Christmas* (1951)

- But HL eventually accepted *in obiter* that such an action was possible in *Hedley Byrne* v *Heller & Partners* (1964)

- But only subject to certain requirements:

  – the existence of a special relationship – *Yianni* v *Edwin Evans* (1982)

  – where the party giving the advice has specialist skill and knowledge of the type sought – *Mutual Life & Citizens Assurance* v *Evatt* (1971)

  – the other party acts in reliance of the advice which is known to the other party – *Smith* v *Eric S. Bush* (1990)

- Limitations on these requirements have since been made – *Caparo* v *Dickman* (1990)

- But there are also cases that do not fit the principle neatly – *White* v *Jones* (1995) and *Spring* v *Guardian Assurance* (1995)

FIGURE 6.6 *Key fact chart for negligent misstatement*

such an action from 'pure economic loss' arising out of negligent acts. The position here was traditionally very clear: there was no liability for a 'pure economic loss'.

In the past this was based on policy and the idea that 'economic loss', for instance a loss of profit, was a concept applicable to contract law rather than tort. The principle has been quite clearly stated and illustrated in past cases.

SPARTAN STEEL V MARTIN & CO. (CONTRACTORS) LTD (1973)

An electric power cable was negligently cut by the defendants resulting in a loss of power to the claimants who manufactured steel alloys. A 'melt' in the claimants' furnace at the time of the power cuts had to be destroyed to stop it from solidifying and wrecking the furnace. The claimants were able to claim for physical damage and the loss of profit on the 'melt' in the furnace. The court refused to allow their claim for lost profits for four further 'melts' they argued they could have completed while the power was still off. The loss was foreseeable. Nevertheless, Lord Denning held that a line must be drawn as a matter of policy, and that the loss was better borne by the insurers than by the defendants alone.

There appears to be an artificial distinction here created for policy reasons purely for the purpose of restricting any extension of liability. The distinction has the obvious potential to create unfair anomalies in the law. For instance it might mean that an architect giving negligent advice leading to the construction of a defective building could be liable where the builder whose negligence leads to a defect in a building may not be.

Nevertheless other cases have confirmed the principle that a pure economic loss arising from a negligent act is unrecoverable.

WELLER & CO. V FOOT AND MOUTH DISEASE RESEARCH INSTITUTE (1966)

Auctioneers' regular income from sale of cattle was disrupted as the result of a ban on the movement of livestock following an escape of a virus from the defendant's premises. No liability could be accepted for their loss of profit.

However, there have also been situations where an economic loss was recovered, although in less clear-cut situations where the difference between a negligent statement and a negligent act was less obvious.

DUTTON V BOGNOR REGIS URBAN DISTRICT COUNCIL (1972)

A local authority was responsible for a building inspection negligently carried out that resulted in defective foundations having to be repaired at great financial cost to the owner of the building. CA held that, since a local authority were under no duty to carry out an inspection then they could not be held liable for a negligent inspection. Nevertheless, they were prepared to impose liability on the basis of physical damage, that the defective foundations were a risk to the health and safety of the occupants. The claimant as a result was awarded damages to restore the building to a state where it was no longer a danger. Clearly it is difficult to distinguish between a negligent inspection (an act) and a satisfactory report based on the inspection (a statement). The case did not fit easily under either *Hedley Byrne* (1964) or *Donoghue v Stevenson* (1932), which perhaps explains the court's reasoning.

Pure economic loss and the 'Anns test'

Further erosion of the basic principle that pure economic loss is unrecoverable came as a result of Lord Wilberforce's 'two-part' test.

ANNS V MERTON LONDON BOROUGH COUNCIL (1978)

Here the negligent building inspection had failed to reveal that the foundations were too shallow. On the basis of the two-part test, and that there were no policy grounds to avoid imposing a duty, the tenant was able to recover the cost of making the flat safe, economic loss in other words.

Because of the availability of the *Anns* two-part test the so-called 'high water mark' was then reached in respect of recovery for a pure economic loss.

JUNIOR BOOKS LTD V VEITCHI CO. LTD (1983)

The claimants' architects nominated the defendants to lay the floor in the claimants' new print works. As a result they sub-contracted to the main builders to complete the work. In the event the defendants laid a thoroughly unusable floor which then had to be relaid. The claimants could not sue the builders who had hired the floor layers at the

claimants' request, and they had no contractual relationship with the floor layers. Nevertheless, they succeeded in winning damages not just for the cost of relaying the floor, but also for their loss of profit during the delay. There were said to be three key issues:

● The claimants had nominated the defendants and so they relied on the defendants skill and judgment.

● The defendants were aware of this reliance at all material times.

● The damage caused was a direct and foreseeable consequence of the defendant's negligence.

Lord Brandon dissented and criticised the other judges for creating obligations in a non-contractual relationship only appropriate as between contracting parties.

The retreat from 'Anns'

Almost immediately judges considered that the relaxation of the principle concerning recovery for economic loss had now gone too far. A long line of cases followed which tried to limit the scope of the above cases.

GOVERNORS OF THE PEABODY DONATION FUND V SIR LINDSAY PARKINSON & CO. LTD (1985)

The court would not accept that there was liability owed for a negligent council inspection that resulted in a drain having to be relaid because it did not conform to regulations. The council's duty in inspecting was to protect the health and safety of the public.

The cases had often arisen because an action in contract was not available and the reliance test from *Junior Books* argued.

MUIRHEAD V INDUSTRIAL TANK SPECIALITIES LTD (1985)

Fish merchandisers bought lobsters while they were cheap to sell on when their price increased. They bought storage tanks in which to hold the lobsters and lost money when the French-built pumps in the tanks were defective and the lobsters could not be stored. They originally succeeded against the supplier of the tanks in contract but when they went into liquidation bought an action in tort against the manufacturers of the pumps. Their claim that the test of proximity and reliance in *Junior Books* applied failed. The court held that reliance had only been possible in that case because the claimants nominated the defendants. The case was therefore distinguished.

The argument for costs of repairing defects in property that could lead to a danger to health or safety, approved in *Anns*, was also gradually rejected.

D & F ESTATES V CHURCH COMMISSIONERS (1989)

Liability against builders was rejected when plaster cracked, fell off walls, and had to be replaced as the result of the negligence of sub-contractors. The builders had satisfied their duty by hiring competent tradesmen and, in the absence of injury or an actual risk to health, any loss was purely economic and not recoverable.

These represent only a few of the cases where *Anns* was argued to allow economic loss and rejected or the case distinguished. The general unease that was felt at Lord Wilberforce's test in *Anns* and at the extension of liability for economic loss led eventually to the overruling of *Anns*, and thus back to a more restrictive attitude towards economic loss.

MURPHY V BRENTWOOD DISTRICT COUNCIL (1991)

HL would not impose liability on a council that had approved plans for a concrete raft on which properties were built and which then moved causing cracks in the walls. The claimant was forced to sell the house for £35,000 under its value if not defective but, in the absence of any injury, loss was purely economic. So the *ratio* in *Anns* (i.e. the principle of law that decided the case) was overruled and the principle of law now is that a local authority will not be liable for the cost of repairing dangerous defects (in the case gas pipes had broken during the settlement of the property) until physical injury is actually caused.

The case has subsequently been followed.

DEPARTMENT OF THE ENVIRONMENT V THOMAS BATES & SONS LTD (1990)

Here the claimant failed to recover the cost of repairing a building that had been built of concrete that was of insufficient strength to support its intended load, although it was not dangerous to carry its existing load. Such cost was purely economic and thus unrecoverable.

So the present policy of the courts in relation to economic loss appears to be that recovery for such loss should be through the normal insurance of the injured party rather than through the courts using negligence.

MARC RICH & CO. V BISHOP ROCK MARINE CO. LTD (1995)

A vessel was negligently classed as seaworthy and then sank. The classification society did not owe a duty of care to the owners of a cargo that sank with the ship. This was economic loss. HL applied the three-part test from *Caparo v Dickman* (1990) and determined that it was not just and reasonable in the circumstances of the case to impose a duty.

activity

SELF ASSESSMENT QUESTIONS

1 What exactly is a 'pure economic loss'?

2 Why are the courts more willing to accept an economic loss caused by a negligently made statement?

3 Why were judges in later cases nervous about the judgment in *Junior Books* v *Veitchi* (1983)?

4 What is the difference between physical damage to property and the cost of repairing defects in property?

5 How would the courts now prefer a claimant to recover compensation for an economic loss?

KEY FACTS

- The courts have always been reluctant to allow liability for 'pure economic loss' because it is felt that it is more to do with contract – *Spartan Steel* v *Martin* (1973)

- Although claims have been successful where there has been a risk also to health – *Dutton* v *Bognor Regis UDC* (1972)

- And the position on economic loss was drastically relaxed as the result of Lord Wilberforce's two-part test in *Anns* – *Junior Books* v *Veitchi* (1983)

- But this caused anxiety for the judges and *Anns* and the two-part test were eventually overruled – *Murphy* v *Brentwood DC* (1991)

FIGURE 6.7 *Key fact chart for pure economic loss*

6.6.4 NERVOUS SHOCK

This is another area of negligence that has been the subject of uncertain development. The extent to which liability has been imposed has expanded or contracted according to:

- the state of medical knowledge, i.e. psychiatric medicine and the recognition of psychiatric disorders has developed dramatically over the past 100 years, the great concern expressed in recent years over soldiers who were executed in the First World War is an interesting example of that;

- policy considerations on the part of judges, particularly the 'floodgates' argument, that to impose liability in a particular situation may lead to a rush of claims, and so should be avoided whatever the justice of the case.

Actions failed in the last century for three reasons. Because psychiatric illness or injury was not properly recognised there could be no duty if the type of damage concerned was not recognised. Another problem, of course, was the fear that a person making such a claim could actually be faking the symptoms. Finally, there was the 'floodgates' argument, that once one claim was accepted it would lead to a multitude of claims.

VICTORIAN RAILWAY COMMISSIONERS V COULTAS (1888)

Nervous shock resulting from involvement in a train crash did not give rise to liability not least because of the 'floodgates' argument.

Even from the start there were two aspects to determining whether liability should be imposed:

- Firstly, the injury alleged must conform to judicial attitudes of what constitutes nervous shock, a recognised psychiatric disorder.

- Secondly, the person claiming to have suffered nervous shock must fall into a category accepted by the courts as being entitled to claim.

Definition of nervous shock

The claim must then involve an actual, recognised psychiatric condition capable of resulting from the shock of the incident, and recognised as having long-term effects.

REILLY V MERSEYSIDE REGIONAL HEALTH AUTHORITY (1994)

No liability could be imposed when a couple became trapped in a lift as the result of negligence and suffered insomnia and claustrophobia after they were rescued.

In the modern day, conditions such as post-traumatic stress disorder and acute anxiety syndrome would be recognised whereas the courts would be reluctant to allow a claim purely for a temporary upset such as grief or distress or fright from which we all suffer at times.

TREDGET V BEXLEY HEALTH AUTHORITY (1994)

Unusually, parents of a child born with serious injuries following medical negligence and then dying two days later succeeded in their claim. They were held to be suffering from psychiatric injuries despite the argument that their condition was no more than profound grief.

The courts in recent times have been prepared to accept a claim that is partly caused by grief and partly by the severe shock of the event.

VERNON V BOSELY (NO. 1) (1997)

Here a father had witnessed his children being drowned in a car negligently driven by their nanny. He recovered damages for nervous shock that was held to be partly the result of pathological grief and bereavement, but partly also the consequence of the trauma of witnessing the events.

Development of a test for who can recover damages for nervous shock

Originally claims were first allowed purely on the basis of foreseeability of real and immediate fear of personal danger (the so-called 'Kennedy' test) so that the class of possible claimants was at first very limited.

DULIEU V WHITE & SONS (1901)

The court accepted a claim when a woman suffered nervous shock after a horse and van that had been negligently driven burst through the window of a pub where she was washing glasses. She was able to recover damages because she had been put in fear for her own safety (the 'Kennedy' test).

This limitation was later extended to include a claim for nervous shock suffered as the result of witnessing traumatic events involving close family.

HAMBROOK V STOKES BROS. (1925)

A woman recovered damages for nervous shock when she saw a runaway lorry going downhill towards where she had left her three children, and then heard that there had indeed been an accident involving a child. The court disapproved the 'Kennedy' test and considered that it would be unfair not to compensate a mother who had feared for her children's safety when she could have claimed if she only feared for her own safety.

This principle was even extended at one point to include shock suffered on witnessing events involving close but not related people.

DOOLEY V CAMMELL LAIRD & CO. (1951)

A crane driver claimed successfully for nervous shock when he saw a load fall and thought that workmates underneath would have been injured.

Indeed, claims have even been allowed where harm to the person with whom the close tie exists would be impossible.

OWENS V LIVERPOOL CORPORATION (1933)

Here relatives recovered for nervous shock when the coffin fell out of the hearse that they were following.

One restriction on this development was to prevent a party from recovering who was not within the 'area of impact' of the event.

KING V PHILLIPS (1953)

A mother suffered nervous shock when from 70 yards away she saw a taxi reverse into her small child's bicycle and presumed him to be injured. Her claim failed because the court said she was too far away from the incident and outside of the range of foresight of the defendant.

In contrast the same principle of reasonable foresight has allowed recovery for nervous shock where the damage was to property.

ATTIA V BRITISH GAS (1987)

A woman who witnessed her house burning down when she arrived home was able to claim successfully for nervous shock. She was within the area of impact. The claim was said to be within the reasonable foresight of the contractors who negligently installed her central heating, causing the fire.

An alternative measure to the area of impact test is whether the claimant falls within the area of shock.

BOURHILL V YOUNG (1943)

A pregnant Edinburgh fishwife claimed to have suffered nervous shock after getting off a tram, hearing the impact of a crash involving a motorcyclist, and later seeing blood on the road, after which she gave birth to a still-born child. HL held that, as a stranger to the motorcyclist, she was outside of the area of foreseeable shock.

It has also been well established in the case law that a rescuer will be able to recover when suffering nervous shock.

CHADWICK V BRITISH RAILWAYS BOARD (1967)

When two trains crashed in a tunnel a man who lived nearby was asked because of his small size to crawl into the wreckage to give injections to trapped passengers. He was able to claim successfully for the anxiety neurosis he suffered as a result. This was largely explained on the basis that he was a primary victim, at risk himself in the circumstances.

Usually only professional rescuers will be able to claim or those present at the scene or the immediate aftermath.

HALE V LONDON UNDERGROUND (1992)

A fireman claimed successfully for post-traumatic stress disorder he suffered following the Kings Cross fire.

However, claims for shock suffered at the scene of disasters will not be successful in the case of those people considered only to be bystanders.

MCFARLANE V E E CALEDONIA (1994)

A person who was helping to receive casualties from the Piper Alpha oil rig failed in his claim because he was classed as a mere bystander rather than a rescuer at the scene.

As we have seen, the tests developed above involve the proximity of the claimant in time and space to the negligent incident or the closeness of the relationship with the party who is present. The widest point of expansion of liability came under the two-part test from *Anns*, and allowed for recovery when the claimant was not present at the scene but was at the 'immediate aftermath'. Inevitably the meaning of 'immediate aftermath' was open to an interpretation based on policy.

MCLOUGHLIN V O'BRIAN (1982)

A woman was summoned to a hospital about an hour after her children and husband were involved in a car crash. One child was dead, two were badly injured, all were in shock and they had not yet been cleaned up. HL held that since the relationship was sufficiently close and the woman was present at the 'immediate aftermath' she could claim.

The foreseeability test mentioned earlier has allowed a claimant to succeed in nervous shock even though not present at the scene or the immediate aftermath.

HEVICAN V RUANE (1991)

A claimant who identified his son's body at the mortuary recovered damages for nervous shock even though the identification was many hours after the death.

Restrictions on the scope of the duty not to cause nervous shock

HL has subsequently had the opportunity to review all aspects of the duty and to identify fairly restricted circumstances in which a claim can succeed.

ALCOCK V CHIEF CONSTABLE OF SOUTH YORKSHIRE (1992)

At the start of a football match at Hillsborough police allowed a large crowd of supporters into a caged pen as the result of which 95 people in the stand suffered crush injuries and were killed. Since the match was being televised much of the disaster was shown on live TV. A number of claims for nervous shock were made. These varied between those present or not present at the scene, those with close family ties to the dead and those who were merely friends. HL refused all of the claims and identified the factors important to consider in determining whether a party might recover. These were:

- The proximity in time and space to the negligent incident – there could be a claim in respect of an incident or the immediate aftermath that was witnessed or experienced directly, there could be none where the incident was merely reported.

- The proximity of the relationship with a party who was a victim of the incident – a successful claim would depend on the existence of a close tie of love and affection with the victim, or presence at the scene as a rescuer.

- The cause of the nervous shock – the court accepted that this must be the result of witnessing or hearing the horrifying event or the immediate aftermath.

The case then identifies for the future the classes of claimants who will be successful and those who will not:

- Primary victims. Those present at the scene and themselves injured:

PAGE V SMITH (1996)

Here Page was involved in a car accident caused by the defendant's negligence. Although he actually suffered no physical injury he suffered a recurrence of 'chronic fatigue syndrome' which he had suffered some years before. HL held that the defendant was liable for the psychiatric injury caused to the claimant.

- Primary victims. An alternative is those who were present at the scene and their own safety was threatened, as in *Dulieu* v *White* (1901) where the woman could have been hurt by the horse coming through the glass window, and did in fact suffer a miscarriage.

- Secondary victims. These are people who are not primary victims of the incident but who are able to show a close enough tie of love and affection to a victim of the incident and witnessed the incident or its 'immediate aftermath' at close hand. The probable limit of this is in *McLoughlin* v *O'Brian*. In *Alcock* the judges were reluctant to allow claims there in respect of both proximity in time and space to the incidents at Hillsborough and turned down claims from people who had identified bodies in the morgue some time after the events of the match.

- Rescuers. These may well, of course, be primary victims and at risk in the circumstances of the incident causing the nervous shock:

HALE V LONDON UNDERGROUND (1992)

A fireman who had been involved in the rescue of victims at the Kings Cross fire suffered post-traumatic stress disorder and recovered damages for nervous shock.

However, the question of who qualifies as a rescuer seems uncertain.

DUNCAN V BRITISH COAL (1990)

There was surprisingly no liability where a miner saw a colleague crushed in a roof fall, the fault of the employers, and tried to resuscitate him.

HL certainly seems to be hostile towards claims by the emergency services for psychiatric injury suffered while dealing with the aftermath of a disaster in the course of their duties.

WHITE V CHIEF CONSTABLE OF SOUTH YORKSHIRE (1999)

Police officers who claimed to have suffered post-traumatic stress disorder following their part in the rescue operation at the Hillsborough disaster were denied a remedy by HL. The reasoning seems to be that they did not actually put themselves at risk, and that public policy prevented them from recovering damages when the relatives of the deceased in the disaster could not. This altered the position originally taken in *Frost* v *Chief Constable of South Yorkshire*, also involving police officers attending the Hillsborough disaster.

- Secondary victims watching the events on live TV in contravention of broadcasting standards may claim from the broadcasting authority.

Those who cannot claim

Bystanders

The law has always made a distinction between rescuers or people who are at risk in the incident and those who are merely bystanders and have no claim.

McFARLANE V E E CALEDONIA LTD (1994)

A person on shore receiving survivors from the Piper Alpha oil rig disaster was not classed as a rescuer and therefore had no valid claim.

No close tie of love and affection

Workmates who witness accidents involving their colleagues will not be able to claim because any ties are not close enough to involve foreseeable harm.

ROBERTSON AND ROUGH V FORTH ROAD BRIDGE JOINT BOARD (1995)

Three workmates had been repairing the Forth Bridge during a gale. One of them was sitting on a piece of metal on a truck when a gust of wind blew him off the bridge and he was killed. His colleagues who witnessed this were unable to claim. They were held not to be primary victims and had insufficient ties with the dead worker for injury to be foreseeable.

Gradual rather than sudden shock

If the psychiatric injury is the result of a gradual appreciation of events rather than a sudden shock then there will be no liability.

SION V HAMPSTEAD HEALTH AUTHORITY (1994)

A father claimed to have suffered psychiatric injury as the result of watching his son over the space of 14 days gradually deteriorate and then die, when there was the possibility of the death resulting from medical negligence. There could be no claim because there was no sudden appreciation of a horrifying event.

activity

SELF ASSESSMENT QUESTIONS

1 What exactly is 'nervous shock'?

2 Why were courts originally reluctant to allow a claimant to recover damages for nervous shock and why has this changed?

3 Has there been any logical kind of development to nervous shock?

4 What is the difference between a 'primary victim' and a 'secondary victim'?

5 To what extent is policy a determining factor?

6 How do the 'area of impact' and the 'area of shock' differ?

7 To what extent does *McLoughlin* v *O'Brian* (1982) fit in with other cases?

No causal link between the incident and the damage

If the psychiatric injury can be attributed to an event other than the horrifying incident in question then there is no causal link and no possible claim.

CALASCIONE V DIXON (1994)

The defendant was responsible for the death of a 20-year-old in a motorcycle accident. He was not liable, however, for the psychiatric injuries suffered by the mother of the young man. It was shown that the psychiatric illness was more the result of the stress of the inquest and a private prosecution rather than the incident itself.

MULTIPLE CHOICE QUESTIONS

In the following series of situations in each case suggest which of the statements may raise a successful claim of nervous shock:

1

A James is present when his dog is run over by Carl's negligent driving and suffers nervous shock.

B James hears his mother has been run over by Carl's negligent driving four days ago and suffers nervous shock.

C James is a passenger in a car when his friend Andrew, the driver, is killed by Carl's negligent driving and suffers nervous shock.

D James hears screams when Carl crashes his car and suffers nervous shock.

2

A Sally hears that a friend has died in a car crash caused by negligence and suffers from profound grief.

B Sally sees her friend killed in an accident at work caused by the employer's negligence and cannot sleep.

C Sally is called to the hospital to identify her mother's body after a car driver has negligently run her over and it makes her very angry.

D Sally is with her father when he drowns as a result of negligence when a ferry sinks and she suffers post-traumatic stress disorder.

LEGAL ESSAY WRITING

Consider the following essay title:

Compare and evaluate the rules applied by the courts to different types of claimants in cases of nervous shock.

Answering the question:

There are usually two key elements to essays in law:

- Firstly, you are required to reproduce a series of factual information on a particular area of law as identified in the question.

- Secondly, you are required to answer the question set, which usually is in the form of some sort of critical element, i.e. you may very probably see the words discuss, analyse, critically consider, explain etc.

Students for the most part seem quite capable of doing the first, and also generally seem less skilled at the second. The important points in any case are to ensure that you only deal with relevant legal material in your answer and that you do answer the question set, rather than one you have made up yourself, or the one that was on last year's paper.

For instance, in the case of the first, in this essay while you might say that nervous shock is an area of negligence, and that negligence requires proof of the existence of a duty of care, the breach of that duty, and damage caused by the defendant that is not too remote a consequence of the breach, you do not need to treat the examiner to everything that you know about the standard of care, or the 'but for' test etc., because none of it is relevant.

In the case of the second the essay asks you to 'compare and evaluate' the rules applicable to different types of claimant in nervous shock cases. This clearly indicates that you must compare the different rules for dealing with primary and secondary victims, and since you are asked to evaluate you will need to pass some sort of comment on whether the law treats both fairly, adequately etc.

Relevant law:
- The appropriate law appears to be:

- That nervous shock is one of those novel duty situations in negligence and thus all the other rules of negligence apply.

- Nervous shock involves recognised psychiatric illnesses such as PTSD but not mere grief or other distress – compare *Reilly* v *Merseyside RHA* (1994) and *Tredget* v *Bexley HA* (1994).

- The rules on who can recover in what situation are now contained in *Alcock* (1992).

- The law distinguishes between primary victims: those present at the scene of an incident and directly affected or injured by the defendant's negligent act or omission, and secondary victims: those indirectly affected by the trauma caused by the defendant's negligent act or omission.

- Primary victims can recover damages if they suffer physical as well as psychiatric injury, or if physical harm is foreseeable and they suffer nervous shock as a result – *Dulieu* v *White* (1901) or *Page* v *Smith* (1996).

- Secondary victims must show a close tie of love and affection with a primary victim, and close proximity in time and space to the traumatic event or its immediate aftermath – *McLoughlin* v *O'Brian* (1982) – or be a professional rescuer – *Chadwick* v *British Railways Board* (1967) and *Hale* v *London Underground* (1992). Note also that such people must be of reasonable fortitude – *Bourhill* v *Young* (1943) – and that the psychiatric injury must result from the trauma being witnessed by their own unaided senses, either seeing or hearing.

Evaluation

The commentary in the essay requires you to compare the treatment of primary and secondary victims and to evaluate their treatment. Relevant comments might include:

- That the range of injuries that will allow liability is limited, although 'floodgates' argument and state of medical knowledge may justify this and it has had some expansion – *Vernon* v *Bosely (No. 1)* (1997).

- That primary victims generally have no problem recovering damages.

- Consideration of whether rescuers should be treated as primary victims?

- That close tie of love and affection is quite limited in scope – *Alcock*.

- And perhaps unfairly does not include close friendships or working relationships – *Robertson and Rough* v *Forth Road Bridge* (1995) and *Duncan* v *British Coal* (1990).

- That immediate aftermath is quite narrowly defined – *Alcock* – and the widest point predates the test now – *McLoughlin* v *O'Brian*.

- That bystanders are treated unfairly in comparison to professional rescuers although they might suffer the same psychiatric injuries – *McFarlane* v *E E Caledonia* (1994).

- That professional rescuers are apparently treated more fairly in determining liability than are the relatives of primary victims – *Alcock* – but that the courts are aware of the possible injustice of this position and have changed their stance somewhat on professional rescuers in relation to the 'Hillsborough' litigation – compare *Frost* v *Chief Constable of South Yorkshire* in CA and HL, and also the different approach in *White* v *Chief Constable of South Yorkshire* (1999).

- That public policy plays an important role in deciding on liability in nervous shock, particularly the 'floodgates' argument.

- That numerous cases seem to be out of line with the 'strict' rules – e.g. *Attia* v *British Gas* (1987) and nervous shock following witnessing damage to property, *Owens* v *Liverpool Corporation* (1933) and primary victim being a corpse, *Dooley* v *Cammell Laird* (1951) and primary victim being a work colleague of the claimant, *Tredget* v *Bexley Health Authority* (1994) where the nervous shock seemed to be based on profound grief at the death of a child, *Hevican* v *Ruane* (1991) where the nervous shock following the claimant being informed of the death of his son and witnessing the body was long after the immediate aftermath.

KEY FACTS

- Originally courts were unwilling to allow actions for nervous shock – *Victorian Railway Commissioners* v *Coultas* (1888)
- This was because of the primitive state of psychiatric medicine
- So the key requirement is always that the illness amounts to a recognised psychiatric disorder – *Vernon* v *Bosely (No. 1)* (1997)
- An action was first accepted only because the claimant was also in physical danger – *Dulieu* v *White* (1901)
- But this was then extended to include a person who was in the area of shock, i.e. witnessed the accident and had some close tie with the victim – *Hambrook* v *Stokes* (1925)
- The widest extent of the duty was to include witnessing the immediate aftermath of the accident – *McLoughlin* v *O'Brian* (1982)
- Now basic rules identify a restricted range of people who can claim – *Alcock* v *Chief Constable of South Yorkshire* (1992) – which include:
– primary victims – present and either injured or at risk
– secondary victims – close tie of love and affection to the victim, and a witness of the incident or its immediate aftermath
– rescuers – where the rescuer is put at risk by the incident, but there is now no general category of liability to a rescuer
– those witnessing it on live TV in contravention of broadcasting requirements
- There are a number of classes of people who could not claim:
– mere bystanders – *McFarlane* v *E E Caledonia* (1994)
– secondary victims without close ties to the victim – *Robertson and Rough* v *Forth Road Bridge Joint Board* (1995)
– those not suffering a recognised psychiatric disorder – *Reilly* v *Merseyside Regional Health Authority* (1994)
– those outside of the area of foreseeable shock of the accident – *Bourhill* v *Young* (1943)

FIGURE 6.8 *Key fact chart for nervous shock*

6.6.5 OMISSIONS

English law does not include any general liability for non-feasance, or failing to act. There are of course those that believe in the idea of a 'good neighbour' principle, but this idea has generally not been accepted.

There are two fairly obvious reasons for this historically:

- The problem of showing causation – showing that somebody failed to prevent harm is much more difficult than showing that they caused it.

- The problem of imposing onerous burdens – it is hard to define the burdens on a defendant and when they should act, and there is the distinct possibility of unfairness in doing so. For instance should a person who sees someone drowning be obliged to jump in to attempt a rescue even if they cannot swim themselves?

The law has, however, recognised a number of exceptions:

- the defendant owes a duty by contractual or other undertaking

- the defendant owes a duty because of a special relationship with the defendant

- the defendant owes a duty because of damage caused by a third party who is within his or her control

- the defendant owes a duty because of control over land or some other dangerous thing

These have all been identified and categorised by the court in the following case.

SMITH V LITTLEWOODS ORGANISATION LTD (1987)

The defendant bought a cinema to demolish and rebuild as a supermarket. It was then left empty and vandals broke in and set fire to it, the fire spreading and causing damage to adjoining property. There was no liability since the defendant was not responsible for the acts of strangers. As Lord Goff in HL stated, 'In such a case it is not possible to invoke a general duty of care; for it is well recognised that there is no general duty of care to prevent third parties from causing such damage'. Further than this he discussed the situations in which the law will impose a duty for a failure to act.

The defendant owes a duty by a contractual or other undertaking

The defendant may owe a contractual duty to act.

STANSBIE V TROMAN (1948)

A decorator was given the key to the premises he was decorating and told to lock the door when he left. He failed to do so and a thief entered the house and stole property. The decorator was liable for failing to lock the door.

The duty might also arise from the character of an undertaking.

BARNETT V CHELSEA & KENSINGTON HOSPITAL MANAGEMENT COMMITTEE (1969)

Here the hospital casualty department undertook to diagnose ailments and injuries and treat their patients. They were therefore in breach of their duty when the doctor negligently failed to diagnose the condition of a patient who later died of arsenic poisoning.

However, policy considerations may prevent a duty from being imposed.

HILL V CHIEF CONSTABLE OF WEST YORKSHIRE (1988)

A powerful argument by the mother of the Yorkshire Ripper's last victim that her murder might have been avoided with adequate policing was rejected. It was held that the police have no duty to the victims of crime to prevent the crime, or to catch the criminal according to any set timescale.

The defendant owes a duty because of a special relationship with the claimant

Clearly in certain situations the nature of the defendant's duty arises because of the potential danger to the public presented by the activity carried out by the defendant. In such cases the defendant may have a duty to act.

HOME OFFICE V DORSET YACHT CO. LTD (1970)

Borstal boys escaped due to the negligence of the warders. These young offenders then did considerable damage to neighbouring property. The Home Office was then liable for their employees' failure to control the offenders in their charge.

There can be a duty in such a relationship leading to liability for its breach despite the fact that the claimant has contributed to his or her harm.

BARRETT V MINISTRY OF DEFENCE (1995)

Employers were liable for the death of a naval airman who became so drunk on cheap alcohol provided in the mess that he fell into a coma and drowned in his own vomit. CA would not impose liability for supplying the drink since the claimant had a responsibility for his own safety. The defendants were liable, however, for a failure to call a doctor or to look after him properly when he had collapsed. Damages were reduced by two-thirds to account for the man's contributory negligence.

The defendant owes a duty because of damage caused by a third party who is within his or her control

If the defendant can in fact be said to be responsible for a third party then there may be liability for a failure to properly exercise that control.

HAYNES V HARWOOD (1935)

A driver left his horse-drawn van unattended in a street. Boys then threw stones at the horses that bolted injuring a policeman trying to prevent harm to pedestrians. The driver was liable. He had failed to leave the horses in a secure state and the boys' act was entirely foreseeable.

The defendant owes a duty because of control over land or some other dangerous thing

If the defendant is in control of premises then there is a duty to ensure that visitors to the premises use them safely without risk to others.

CUNNINGHAM V READING FOOTBALL CLUB LTD (1992)

Here the football club was liable for the injuries caused by football hooligans breaking lumps of concrete off the premises and using them as missiles. They had failed to exercise proper control over these visitors.

In this way a defendant might owe a duty even for damage caused by acts of nature where he has failed to deal properly with the hazard arising.

GOLDMAN V HARGRAVE (1967)

Here a tree was struck by lightning on the defendant's land and ignited. When the defendant failed to deal with the fire and it spread to neighbouring property he was liable.

activity

SELF ASSESSMENT QUESTIONS

1 What exactly is 'non-feasance'?

2 Why did English law traditionally reject the idea of liability for a failure to act?

3 What is the common factor in those situations where the courts will impose liability for a failure to act?

activity

LEGAL PROBLEM SOLVING

Which of the following is an omission creating a duty of care?

1 A man sees another man bleeding to death in the street and walks past.

2 A doctor refuses to attend to a sick patient who then dies.

3 An electrician paid to fit new lights for a householder leaves some bare wires overnight and a child of the house is electrocuted.

4 A person who has borrowed a book from a friend leaves the book on the bus and it is lost.

5 I could help my nephew revise for his A Level Law but I do not and he fails.

- There is no general liability for a failure to act
- But there can be liability where there is a positive duty to act
- A defendant may be liable for an omission where:
  - there is a contractual duty to act – *Stansbie* v *Troman* (1948)
  - there is a duty based on a special relationship – *Home Office* v *Dorset Yacht Co.* (1970)
  - the defendant has a duty to control another's acts – *Haynes* v *Harwood* (1935)
  - the defendant has a duty to control events on his or her land – *Goldman* v *Hargrave* (1967)

FIGURE 6.9 *Key fact chart for omissions*

CHAPTER 7

TORTS AFFECTING LAND AND THE USE OF LAND

7.1 TRESPASS TO LAND

7.1.1 THE DEFINITION, PURPOSE AND CHARACTER OF THE TORT

Trespass is one of the oldest torts, originating with the medieval writ: *quare clausum fregit*, literally meaning by way of taking an enclosed area. So even within the general heading of trespass a trespass to land is still the oldest form of the tort.

The tort is defined fairly straightforwardly: a trespass to land occurs where there is an intentional (or negligent), unlawful entry onto or direct interference with the land in the possession of another.

Again, the purposes of bringing an action in trespass to land seem quite straightforward: a claimant may wish to remove unwanted intruders from his or her land; there may be a dispute as to title; the claimant may be seeking to regain entry to land from which (s)he has been unlawfully ejected; and above all of these the claimant may be seeking an award of damages for any loss or physical damage caused by the trespasser.

Before identifying the various ingredients of the tort there are a number of important general points to make:

● Trespass is actionable per se – this means that there is actually no need for the claimant to prove that (s)he has suffered any damage – it is enough merely that the defendant has trespassed onto the land.

● Nevertheless, if damage has occurred then the claimant is entitled to make a claim for compensation.

● While usually a trespass is committed consciously and intentionally it does not have to be – a negligent trespass might occur for example where picnickers stop on land on which they are unaware they have no right to be.

● A defendant in a trespass claim might have entered onto the land perfectly lawfully but become a trespasser by going beyond the legitimate purpose for which (s)he is on the land.

7.1.2 WHO CAN SUE IN TRESPASS? (POTENTIAL CLAIMANTS)

Deciding who is eligible to sue in trespass to land can seem quite complex, since it is not based on pure ownership or on pure possession. If only an owner of land could sue then this would prevent a legitimate tenant from ejecting trespassers or suing for damage they may have caused. If the right to sue came purely with possession then this might prevent a rightful owner from recovering land from a squatter or even on termination of a lease.

Possession involves some form of occupation or physical control over the land. Any action in trespass then, is said to be in favour of a person in possession at the actual time of the trespass as against the wrongdoer. So the right to sue implies some superior right over the land enjoyed by the possessor in comparison to the defendant or alleged trespasser.

So it is generally possible to use trespass against someone with a lesser right to be on the property.

GRAHAM V PEAT (1861)

The claimant was allowed to sue despite his lease being void by statute.

Whereas an action against a party with superior rights of occupation would fail:

DELANEY V T. P. SMITH & CO. (1946)

Under an oral agreement the claimant would acquire a tenancy of the defendant's property. Before the lease was executed the claimant secretly entered the premises. When the claimant was then ejected he sued in trespass and failed. The agreement had not been reduced to writing and the defendant still had superior rights of occupation.

Since exclusivity of possession is necessary it would for instance be possible for a tenant to use trespass against the freehold owner but impossible for a lodger to succeed against a landlord, since the lodger has only a licence.

WHITE V BAYLEY (1861)

The claimant was paid £75 a year for managing and living in premises rented by his employers. When the defendants gave the claimant notice to quit and took possession the claimant forcibly re-entered. The defendants sought an injunction. The claimant's counter-action in trespass failed. He was entitled to 'the use but not the occupation of the premises …'.

7.1.3 WHAT ACTS CAN AMOUNT TO A TRESPASS?

The first and most significant point about a trespass to land is that the interference, whatever it is, must be direct. Indirect interference may well be actionable but as nuisance or negligence not as trespass.

ESSO PETROLEUM CO. V SOUTHPORT CORPORATION (1956)

Oil discharging into an estuary when a tanker beached, while possibly the result of negligence, was felt by Lord Denning to be too indirect to amount to a trespass.

Clearly there has to be some entry onto the land.

PERERA V VANDIYAR (1953)

The claimant's gas and electricity meters were situated in the defendant's cellar. When the defendant switched off both supplies, while there was a clear interference with the claimant's premises, there was no direct entry so there was no trespass.

It does not, however, have to be the claimant who is responsible for the entry.

SMITH V STONE (1647)

Stone successfully defended a trespass action when he had been carried onto the land by force.

So any unwanted presence on the land might amount to a trespass. This might include walking, running, riding, cycling or driving on the land. Besides these, however, it is always possible for a trespass to occur where the defendant is responsible for things being placed or even thrown onto the land. It is interesting to note, then, that while rocks or balls thrown onto the land might be a trespass, rubbish which is blown onto the land might not be. Compare *Smith* v *Stone* and *Esso Petroleum Co.* v *Southport Corporation* in this respect.

It will be common for the trespass to involve an active interference.

BASELY V CLARKSON (1681)

Here the cutting and carrying away of a neighbour's grass was held to amount to a trespass even though it was carried out by mistake.

It could, however, involve a mere passive state of affairs.

> ### KELSEN V IMPERIAL TOBACCO CO. LTD (1956)
>
> The trespass here involved an advertising hoarding which overhung the neighbouring land.

Even this could be a purely temporary state of affairs.

> ### WOOLERTON & WILSON V RICHARD COSTAIN LTD (1970)
>
> In this case the defendant's crane swung out over the claimant's land and was sufficient to amount to a trespass.

Indeed even the merest contact might be seen as a trespass.

> ### WESTRIPP V BALDOCK (1938)
>
> A ladder leaning against the claimant's wall was a trespass.

Finally a trespass might occur even though the original entry onto the land was lawful, as when a postman veers off the path to pick flowers from the garden.

7.1.4 WHAT COUNTS AS LAND FOR THE PURPOSES OF TRESPASS?

There is no single definition of what counts as land that a claimant can then protect legitimately against a trespass. It will quite obviously include the land itself and any structure that has been erected upon it. Significantly, it can also include the boundary as seen in *Westripp* v *Baldock*.

A traditional principle applied to rights in land is *cujus est solum ejus est usque ad coleum et ad inferos*. Roughly translated this means that the rights in the land extend to the air space above the land as well as to the subsoil below it.

In the case of airspace then it has been held to be a trespass where:

- signs overhang land – *Kelsen* v *Imperial Tobacco Co.* (1956)

- cranes swing out over land – *Woolerton & Wilson* v *Costain* (1970)

- cables overhang land – *Wandsworth Board of Works* v *United Telephone Co.* (1884) (though of course in modern times this would be subject to any statutory authority)

However, balloons passing overhead have been held not be a trespass – *Pickering* v *Rudd* (1815) and *Saunders* v *Smith* (1838).

It has been further considered that rights over airspace cannot extend so far as to interfere with proper, legitimate use of air transport.

> ### LORD BERNSTEIN OF LEIGH V SKYWAYS & GENERAL LTD (1977)
>
> Here aerial photographers flew over the claimant's land, took photographs, and then tried to sell them to him. It was held not to be a trespass. The claimant's rights over airspace should only extend to a height 'reasonably necessary for the enjoyment of the land'.

This point is also confirmed in the Civil Aviation Act 1982.

In the case of the subsoil, where subterranean rights were crucial to the growth of industry in the eighteenth and nineteenth centuries, most under-soil activities are now authorised specifically by statute.

However, some interesting principles have developed within the common law, so that under-soil rights might extend under a highway which passes through the claimant's land.

> ### HARRISON V THE DUKE OF RUTLAND (1893)
>
> The Duke held grouse shoots on his land. When protesters who were on the highway tried to scare off the grouse they were held to be trespassing.

This principle has also been extended where the defendant has been using an adjoining highway for improper purposes.

HICKMAN V MAISEY (1900)

There was a trespass where the defendant used the highway to spy on the claimant's race horses in training.

It will not apply where a trespass follows a legitimate use of the highway.

RANDALL V TARRANT (1955)

The defendant parking on the highway was no trespass when it was followed by a trespass onto the claimant's land.

7.1.5 TRESPASS *AB INITIO*

One final problem concerning trespass is the old common law doctrine of trespass *ab initio*.

As we have seen already, wherever a person abuses the limits of their right of entry onto land that person might become a trespasser from that point on. The common law doctrine of trespass *ab initio* was developed in relation to those people who entered onto land with a legal right rather than by the claimant's permission. Where such a person, for instance a police officer, enters the land, if the person exercising the right of entry does go beyond the legitimate purpose then (s)he will be said to have trespassed from the beginning (*ab initio*) – *The Six Carpenters' Case* (1610).

This legal fiction operates quite simply in order to protect the claimant from abuses of authority.

OXLEY V WATTS (1785)

Here the doctrine was used when the defendant improperly worked a horse that he had taken under a distraint order.

It will, however, not apply where any ground justifying entry remains.

ELIAS V PASMORE (1934)

Police took documents that would help them in their case when they arrested the claimant. There was no trespass *ab initio* because the arrest was lawful.

Lord Denning has cast doubt upon this principle and upon the doctrine itself.

activity

QUICK QUIZ

Consider whether I have trespassed on land in the following situations:

1 While playing frisbee with my small nephew, the frisbee has landed in my next door neighbour's garden.

2 While waiting for a bus I have sat on a garden wall next to the bus stop.

3 In a high wind my washing has blown off the line and onto my neighbour's garden.

4 While paragliding I have flown over a farmer's land.

5 Roofers replacing tiles on my roof have erected scaffolding that juts out over my neighbour's land.

6 I hide in a tree near to the house of a famous actress to take pictures of her sunbathing.

CHIC FASHIONS LTD V JONES (1968)

Removing goods for evidence that were believed stolen was held by CA not to be a trespass *ab initio* and CA also doubted the continued existence of the doctrine.

However, the same judge has since applied the doctrine to mini-cab drivers touting for business – *Cinnamond* v *British Airport Authority* (1980).

7.1.6 DEFENCES

A number of specific defences may apply in the case of a trespass.

- A customary right to enter – this might apply where rights have been gained according to prescription or long use.

MERCER V DENNE (1905)

The owner of a beach was prevented from building on it because local fishermen had a customary right to dry their nets on it.

- A common law right to enter – which itself may be lost if the legitimate entrant goes beyond his or her legal rights.

CLISSOD V CRATCHLEY (1910)

Here a solicitor entered land to enforce collection of a debt owed to his client. Since, unknown to the solicitor, the debt had already been paid there was a trespass.

- Statutory right to enter land – which might apply for instance where a police officer enters to search under the Police and Criminal Evidence Act 1984 or where gas and electricity meter readers enter under the Rights of Entry (Gas and Electricity Boards) Act 1954.
- *Volenti non fit injuria* (consent, literally, to a willing person no wrong is done) – so that it is always possible to come onto land with the permission of the owner.

- Necessity – which may operate for instance where the defendant comes onto land to avert a worse disaster. For example, coming onto the land to rescue a child from a fire in the house.

- Licences – people are constantly granted licences in a variety of contexts e.g. visiting the cinema or a football match, buying from a shop, visiting friends, contractors doing work. It must be remembered though that the licence ends where the person entering goes beyond its strict terms.

7.1.7 REMEDIES

Different remedies may be available depending on whether the land is in the possession of the claimant or the defendant at the time the trespass is complained of. Generally, if the claimant is in possession of the land then he or she will be suing for the interference with his or her rights of possession, and also for any loss that has arisen as a result of the trespass. In this case the claimant might recover damages for the loss and also an injunction to prevent further trespasses.

If the defendant is in possession of the land then the claimant will probably want to sue for ejectment of the defendant and recovery of the land, as well as claiming for any consequent loss, in this instance known as mesne profits. However, a more common and quicker remedy is under RSC Order 113 or CCR Order 26.

It is possible to claim purely nominal damages, and exemplary damages are also possible. In relation to specific losses damages can be based on actual deterioration. They can also take into account any costs of repossession.

Two further remedies are worthy of mention. Distress damage feasant is an old common law remedy that involves keeping an object associated with damage caused to the land until such time as the damage is made good. This could, for instance, apply in the case of straying livestock,

SELF ASSESSMENT QUESTIONS

1 What damage, if any, must a defendant cause to be liable for trespass?

2 Must a claimant claiming in trespass be the owner of the land?

3 Does a trespass have to be a conscious act?

4 In what circumstances can a defendant be liable for trespass without a positive action?

5 How far above and below the land itself do the claimant's rights extend?

6 What remedy will usually be the most appropriate in trespass?

7 When will it be possible to become a trespasser, despite having entered the land for a legitimate purpose?

8 What exactly is trespass *ab initio*? Does it still have any practical significance?

- Trespass is a direct interference with someone's land

- Anybody with an interest can sue a person with an inferior interest in the land but a person cannot sue someone with a superior interest – *Delaney* v *T.P. Smith* (1946)

- There must be a direct entry onto the land – *Perera* v *Vandiyar* (1953)

- Though it may be only temporary – *Woolerton & Wilson* v *Richard Costain* (1970)

- Trespass is actionable per se so no damage need be done

- The land can include the subsoil – *Harrison* v *The Duke of Rutland* (1893)

- And the air space above except in the case of preventing air traffic – *Lord Bernstein of Leigh* v *Skyviews* (1977)

- Defences include: a customary or a common law or a statutory right to enter, consent, necessity, licences

- Remedies include: a right of ejectment, repossession, and damages

FIGURE 7.1 *Key fact chart for trespass to land*

though in this case the police must be notified within a specific time.

A declaration can be obtained from the court where rights are unclear or uncertain.

> **ACTON BC V MORRIS (1953)**
>
> A door was locked which deprived the occupiers of access to their upper floor flat. Rights of entry were then established by declaration of the court.

7.2 NUISANCE

7.2.1 INTRODUCTION

The tort of nuisance is the second tort to deal with interference with the land; however, in this case it involves indirect rather than direct interference. Nuisance is sometimes seen as a quite complex tort. There are a number of reasons for this.

- Firstly, there are two distinct types – private nuisance and public nuisance. These are very different to one another. Besides this, many aspects of nuisance are now found in statutory form.

- Secondly, the tort covers a more diverse range of situations than do most other torts.

- Thirdly, the tort has itself, in specific circumstances been developed to create the separate tort of *Rylands* v *Fletcher*.

- Finally, many of the situations involved can appear to be indistinguishable from ones which might now be covered by the tort of negligence.

7.2.2 THE CHARACTER AND AIMS OF PRIVATE NUISANCE

The usual definition of private nuisance is *Winfield's*

'an unlawful interference with a person's use or enjoyment of land or some right over, or in connection with it'

To this must be added the word 'indirect', because any direct interference would be actionable under trespass.

Nuisance is very much a tort of neighbourhood. It will almost always involve the competing claims of neighbours to do as they wish on their own land. A number of points stand out in this respect.

- Firstly, neighbourhood is a continuous state of affairs, and clearly a problem created by one neighbour could affect another neighbour over a period of time in this way.

- Secondly, it is not unreasonable to expect to be able to do whatever you like on your own land. Problems only arise when this affects your neighbour's ability to enjoy his or her land.

- Thirdly, disputes between neighbours can be as trivial as disputes within families. It would be an intolerable waste of court time to have to deal with all complaints no matter how trivial they were.

For these reasons nuisance is very often called the 'law of give and take'. It involves balancing the competing interests of individuals, and as the author Rogers says

'each of us must put up with a moderate amount of inconvenience caused by others as the price of being able to inflict some inconvenience upon others in the conduct of our own activities'

So not every intentional interference with the enjoyment of land will be classed as a nuisance, only that which is also classed as unreasonable. What is reasonable in this respect then, depends not so much on the conduct of the defendant but on whether the interference caused by that conduct is sufficient to give rise to a legal action.

7.2.3 WHO CAN SUE IN PRIVATE NUISANCE? (POTENTIAL CLAIMANTS)

Since nuisance involves the competing rights of neighbours to use their land how they wish, then the basic rule is that anyone who has the use or enjoyment of the land and is affected by the interference may claim. This will obviously include an owner and an occupier, but also can be any holder of a legal or equitable title.

It could then include an owner not in possession who is suing with respect to permanent damage done to the land by the interference.

A tenant can also sue, though there are some gaps in the law here regarding landlords' responsibilities to their tenants for the condition of the property.

HABINTEG HOUSING ASSOCIATION V JONES (1994)

Here, following an appeal by the landlord, a tenant was unable to claim compensation for damage caused by a cockroach infestation when there was no vermin control responsibility in the tenancy agreement and the tenant was unable to prove that the infestation began in the landlord's flat.

The Law Commission in its *Report No. 238* in 1966 has recommended that the implied covenant of fitness for human habitation in the Landlord and Tenant Act 1985 should be updated to cover such eventualities.

Traditionally it was felt that, while the tenant would be able to bring an action his or her family could not.

MALONE V LASKEY (1907)

Here the wife of the householder was unable to sue in respect of personal injury sustained when vibrations from machinery caused the cistern to fall on her in the lavatory.

A recent innovation modified this principle somewhat.

KHORASANDJIAN V BUSH (1993)

The right to sue was granted to an occupier's family where they had suffered harassing telephone calls.

However, HL has overturned this principle in *Hunter and Another* v *Canary Wharf* (1997) preferring the principle that the right to sue in nuisance is linked to a proprietary right in the land.

7.2.4 THE REQUIREMENTS FOR PROVING PRIVATE NUISANCE

There are three key elements in proving the existence of a nuisance:

- an unlawful (meaning unreasonable) use of land

- which leads on to an indirect interference

- with the claimant's use or enjoyment of land

The unreasonable use of land

Mere interference on its own is insufficient to found an action. The claimant must prove that the defendant's activity amounts to an unlawful use of land. Unlawful is not used here in the usual sense of illegal but rather means that the court accepts that the defendant's use of land is unreasonable in the way that it affects the claimant.

The proper question for the court is – in all of the circumstances is it reasonable for the claimant to have to suffer the particular interference? The courts in assessing the defendant's conduct are really analysing fault but with a more flexible approach than might be the case with negligence.

SOLLOWAY V HAMPSHIRE COUNTY COUNCIL (1981)

Here the council were not liable for trees on the highway which damaged the claimant's property because they lacked the resources to do anything about it.

However, the opposite answer has been given in *Hurst and Another* v *Hampshire County Council* (1997) for consistency with other cases.

Because the tort is all about balancing competing interests a number of factors will have to be considered by the court in deciding whether the use of land by the defendant is unreasonable.

Locality

Nuisance has to do with use of land, and land can be used in very different ways according to the area concerned. Thus, as Lord Justice Thesiger stated it in *Sturges* v *Bridgman* (1879) 'what would be a nuisance in Belgrave Square would not necessarily be so in Bermondsey'.

- Thus the nuisance might be as simple as an acceptable activity carried out in the wrong area

LAWS V FLORINPLACE LTD (1981)

Here the claimant succeeded in gaining an injunction where a shop in a residential area was converted into a sex shop and cinema club.

- So the customary use of the area is important in determining liability.

MURDOCH V GLACIER METAL CO. LTD (1998)

The claimant failed in showing that his use and enjoyment of land was interfered with when he lived close to a busy bypass.

- Usually the result may be different in an industrial area where claimants might naturally expect noise and pollution, though this will not prevent success in a nuisance action where damage is caused rather than mere interference with comfort.

ST HELENS SMELTING CO. V TIPPING (1865)

Copper smelting, even in an industrial area, could be classed as a nuisance when it resulted in smuts from the process damaging the claimant's shrubs.

- Often in any case it is possible for the court to reach a compromise between the competing interests of the two parties.

DUNTON V DOVER DISTRICT COUNCIL (1977)

Here the opening hours of a local authority playground were reduced following a successful complaint by a neighbouring old people's home.

The duration of the interference

To be actionable the interference should be continuous. In this way a noisy one-off party to celebrate A Level results may not be a nuisance,

where the continuous vibration of machinery may.

- Usually it will be necessary for both the interference as well as its cause to be continuous for there to be liability.

BOLTON V STONE (1951)

There was no liability when a cricket ball hit Miss Stone and the pitch was 78 yards from the road, she herself 100 yards away, and the fence 17 feet above the pitch. Significantly it was shown that only six balls had been hit out of the ground in 28 years.

- However, isolated instances have been accepted as nuisances where they arose from a continuing state of affairs.

SPICER V SMEE (1946)

Fire that began as the result of faulty wiring spread to a neighbour's house. This was accepted as nuisance, the faulty wiring being a continuous state of affairs.

- This principle has more recently been extended to cover an event lasting no more than fifteen or twenty minutes.

CROWN RIVER CRUISES LTD V KIMBOLTON FIREWORKS LTD (1996)

Here a barge was set alight by flammable debris resulting from a firework display lasting only 20 minutes.

- Indeed *Rylands* v *Fletcher* (1868) has been described as a specific form of nuisance covering isolated escapes.

CAMBRIDGE WATER CO. V EASTERN COUNTIES LEATHER PLC (1994)

Chemicals from the tanning process eventually filtered through the ground and polluted the claimant's borehole.

The seriousness of the interference

The law sensibly makes a distinction here between mere inconvenience and actual physical damage.

- In the case of mere discomfort or inconvenience then the test is all about balancing the competing interests and about what is reasonable. The appropriate test is whether the interference is 'an inconvenience materially interfering with the ordinary comfort physically of human existence, not merely according to elegant or dainty modes and habits of living, but according to plain and sober and simple notions among the English people', Knight Bruce Vice Chancellor in *Walter* v *Selfe* (1851).

- Generally where the interference causes damage to the claimant it will be sufficient to class the use of land as unreasonable.

HALSEY V ESSO PETROLEUM CO. LTD (1961)

Here the claimant was successful in complaining about the noise coming from the defendant's depot, but also in relation to the damage which smuts caused to the washing.

- However, even damage may be insufficient cause to claim if the activity is for the public benefit.

MILLER V JACKSON (1977)

The majority of CA held cricket balls coming onto Miller's land from the local cricket club to be a nuisance. Nevertheless, they were not prepared to grant an injunction since it was not in the public interest.

- The use of land in any case might not be considered unreasonable where such use is an absolute right.

STEPHENS V ANGLIAN WATER AUTHORITY (1987)

Because the right to appropriate water is an absolute right it could not be classed as unreasonable even though it caused subsidence in the claimant's property.

The sensitivity of the claimant

- The claimant cannot engage in a use of land that in itself is hypersensitive and then complain of damage caused by normal activities.

ROBINSON V KILVERT (1889)

There was no liability when the heat required in the manufacture of the defendant's boxes downstairs in a building damaged the brown paper made by the claimant upstairs as it would not damage any other paper.

Malice shown by either party

- Deliberately harmful acts will ordinarily be nuisances.

HOLLYWOOD SILVER FOX FARM V EMMET (1936)

The defendant, objecting to the claimant's use of his land as a mink farm, fired shotguns near to the property. Normally this would not be unreasonable use of land. However, mink eat their young when frightened. The act was meant to cause harm and was unreasonable.

- Acts of revenge taken in response to unreasonable behaviour can themselves be classed as unreasonable and therefore a nuisance and any action that might have been brought may in turn be defeated.

CHRISTIE V DAVEY (1893)

The defendant became annoyed by the noise from music lessons next door and responded by banging on the walls, beating trays and shouting. An injunction was granted against him.

The state of the defendant's land

- It is not possible for the defendant to simply ignore nuisances that arise on his or her land, however they are created.

LEAKEY V THE NATIONAL TRUST (1980)

The defendants were liable when a large mound, the Burrow Mump, on their land subsided and damaged the claimant's cottages.

- So defendants owe a duty to prevent the spread of those things on their land which might create a nuisance.

> **BRADBURN V LINDSAY (1983)**
>
> The owner of a semi-detached property was held to be liable to his neighbour for the spread of dry rot which he should have prevented.

An indirect interference

The boundaries between trespass to land and nuisance are found in the character of the interference.

If the interference involves a direct physical intrusion then the action should be fought in trespass. Nuisance will only be available where the interference is indirect. In this way a variety of things have been held to be actionable as nuisances:

- fumes drifting over neighbouring land – *Bliss* v *Hall* (1838)
- loud noises including gunfire – *Hollywood Silver Fox Farm* v *Emmet* (1936)
- vibrations from industrial machinery – *Sturges* v *Bridgman* (1879)
- hot air rising into other premises – *Robinson* v *Kilvert* (1889)
- smuts from factory chimneys – *Halsey* v *Esso Petroleum* (1961)
- fire – *Spicer* v *Smee* (1946)
- continuous interference from cricket balls – *Miller* v *Jackson* (1977)
- pollution of rivers – *Pride of Derby and Derbyshire Angling Association* v *British Celanese* (1953)

The use and enjoyment of land

We have already seen how courts will draw a distinction between an interference with the mere enjoyment of the land and actual physical damage.

In this way there has been some judicial control over the extent to which enjoyment of land is protected within the tort. This is where the courts are called on most to balance competing interests. It means that certain activities will be beyond protection.

Generally the courts have refrained from protecting purely aesthetic interests.

> **BRIDLINGTON RELAY LTD V YORKSHIRE ELECTRICITY BOARD (1965)**
>
> Here there was no nuisance when overhead power cables ruined television reception.

This is because, as Lord Hoffman has stated, the inconvenience involved in such cases should be in relation to the land itself rather than merely the landowner.

> **HUNTER AND ANOTHER V CANARY WHARF LTD (1997)**
>
> Families of tenants were denied an action in private nuisance where they complained of dust and poor television reception caused by the erection of a tall building nearby because they lacked *locus standi* (the right to bring an action). HL overruling CA also stated that such interference could not be classed as a nuisance.

It is logical to assume, therefore, that there could be no action for lowering the tone of a neighbourhood, and yet that seems to be the substance of the case in *Laws* v *Florinplace* (1981).

In a recent verdict, interference with a functional use of land supporting a purely entertainment or leisure purpose has been identified as an interest capable of protection – *Crown River Cruises Ltd* v *Kimbolton Fireworks Ltd* (1996).

7.2.5 WHO CAN BE SUED IN PRIVATE NUISANCE? (POTENTIAL DEFENDANTS)

Clearly the creator of the nuisance can be a defendant, and this might be the case whether or not the creator of the nuisance is also occupier of the land.

SOUTHPORT CORPORATION v ESSO PETROLEUM CO. LTD (1953)

Here the defendant's oil tanker beached in the estuary and leaked oil that subsequently drifted to local beaches. The court held that there was no reason why a defendant who is not the occupier of neighbouring land but misuses it so as to cause a nuisance should not be liable.

Even though an occupier has not created the nuisance (s)he might nevertheless be liable in law for authorising it.

TETLEY v CHITTY (1986)

Here a landlord was liable in nuisance by permitting go-kart racing on his premises.

However, the authorisation must apply to the nuisance not just to the use of land by the creator of the nuisance.

SMITH v SCOTT (1973)

A local authority was not liable for letting a flat to a 'problem family'. The lease specifically prohibited the creation of nuisances by tenants.

In other circumstances where the occupier is not responsible for creating the nuisance (s)he might still be liable as a result of 'adopting' the nuisance, i.e. of failing to deal with the nuisance.

This principle can apply where a stranger has created the nuisance.

SEDLEIGH DENFIELD v O'CALLAGHAN (1940)

Here strangers had blocked a culvert pipe on the defendant's land. He knew about it but failed to deal with it so that when it led to flooding on the claimant's land he was liable.

It can also apply even where the nuisance is the result of natural causes.

LEAKEY v THE NATIONAL TRUST (1980)

Here the large mound slipping onto the claimant's cottage was the result of natural causes.

There are also a number of more complex provisions under landlord and tenant law, that are connected with the obligation to repair.

7.2.6 POSSIBLE DEFENCES

A number of defences may be particularly appropriate to an allegation of private nuisance.

Statutory authority

Since many of the activities that are likely to be the cause of a nuisance are now regulated or licensed by environmental or other laws then statutory authority is likely to be one of the most effective defences.

HAMMERSMITH RAILWAY v BRAND (1869)

Vibrations from trains were an inevitable consequence of the existence of the railway. As Lord Cairns said, it would be a *reductio ad absurdam* (literally, reduction to absurdity), to grant injunctive relief since this would prevent the railway from operating.

However, the defence may not be available where a discretion to act is exercised improperly.

METROPOLITAN ASYLUM DISTRICT HOSPITAL v HILL (1881)

Here there was a general power to build a smallpox hospital. The defence was unavailable when it was sited in a place that would cause a nuisance.

The defence will not be available either where there is negligence.

DORSET YACHT CO. LTD v HOME OFFICE (1970)

In this case the Home Office could not avoid liability for the damage done by Borstal boys who had been taken to Poole by their warders.

Local authority planning permission can in some circumstances act as lawful justification for a nuisance

> **GILLINGHAM BOROUGH COUNCIL V MEDWAY (CHATHAM) DOCK CO. (1993)**
>
> Planning permission was granted to use part of a dockyard as a commercial port. Neighbours then suffered disturbance from heavy vehicles using the access 24 hours a day. It was held not to be an actionable nuisance because of the planning permission.

However, local authorities have no power to authorise nuisances, so that planning permission will only be granted where the nuisance is the inevitable result of a change in the character of a neighbourhood which Parliament itself has expressly authorised.

> **WHEELER V SAUNDERS (1996)**
>
> A pig farmer was granted planning permission to expand by building two more pig houses each containing 400 pigs. One pig house was only 11 metres from the cottage of a neighbour who then took action in nuisance. The defendant's appeal on the point of planning permission failed because the defence was said to operate only in respect of those nuisances that Parliament had authorised.

Prescription

This is a defence that is unique to nuisance. If the nuisance has continued for 20 years without complaint then the right to complain will lapse.

> **STURGES V BRIDGMAN (1879)**
>
> The vibrations from the defendant's machinery disturbed the claimant who had bought land next door and was using it as a doctor's consulting room. The defence of prescription actually failed since the court held that the nuisance only began when the consulting room was built.

Act of a stranger, or in other words of a trespasser, may be a defence

This will not apply, however, where the defendant adopts the nuisance – *Sedleigh Denfield* v *O'Callaghan* (1940).

Volenti non fit injuria

A claimant may always consent to the nuisance.

> **KIDDLE V CITY BUSINESS PROPERTIES LTD. (1942)**
>
> A tenant will generally be said to consent to the risk of nuisances arising from the condition of the premises that are not the result of the landlord's negligence. Here, then, the tenant failed in his action when gutters had become blocked and flooded over onto the tenant's stock.

Public policy

The tort, as we have said, is about competing interests. The courts will not then grant a nuisance action where it is not in the public interest.

> **MILLER V JACKSON (1977)**
>
> Here the court refused to grant an injunction to the neighbour of a cricket ground that had been in existence for more than 70 years, despite the damage the claimant had suffered, rather than cause the community to lose the cricket ground.

However, the mere fact that something is of public benefit does not mean that it will automatically escape liability for nuisance.

> **ADAMS V URSELL (1913)**
>
> A fish and chip shop in a residential area was still a nuisance despite the fact that it was patronised by local people.

The fact that the claimant is coming fresh to the nuisance is not a defence

> **BLISS V HALL (1838)**
>
> The claimant bought a house close to the defendant's candle works. This had been there for three years but was still held to be a nuisance.

7.2.7 REMEDIES

Damages are available as a remedy where the claimant has suffered some loss. The test of remoteness will be that in *The Wagon Mound (No. 2)*, based on reasonable foreseeability. The claimant will be able to recover for any physical loss, for depreciation in value and for a business loss.

The common remedy for nuisance will be an injunction. This will be prohibitory, ordering the defendant to refrain from the nuisance. The injunction may be coupled with damages where a loss has occurred.

One further remedy available to a claimant is 'abatement'. This may well involve entering the defendant's premises in order to prevent further nuisance. In this way a claimant might enter a defendant's land in order to chop down over-hanging branches, although these would need to be returned to the defendant. One possible difficulty with this remedy is that it could lead to a counter-injunction, as in *Stanton* v *Jones* (1995) that involved a dispute over a high hedge.

The remedy in any case may not always be possible.

> ### BURTON V WINTERS (1993)
>
> In a dispute over a boundary a wall was found to be a few inches over the boundary. When the injured party was awarded damages instead, and then damaged the other party's garage she was prosecuted for criminal damage.

7.2.8 THE DEFINITION AND CHARACTER OF PUBLIC NUISANCE

Public nuisance is very different to private nuisance. For one thing it extends beyond neighbours.

It has been defined by Lord Justice Romer, in *Attorney-General* v *PYA Quarries Ltd* (1957), as

'something which affects a reasonable class of Her Majesty's citizens materially or in the reasonable comfort and convenience of life'

Public nuisance does not have to be an interference with the use and enjoyment of land, so it is not based on proprietary rights. For this reason it has also developed as a crime in which respect it will commonly be prosecuted by the Attorney-General.

7.2.9 REQUIREMENTS FOR PROVING PUBLIC NUISANCE

It is essential for an action to be successful in public nuisance for there to be a substantial class of people affected by the nuisance.

> ### ATTORNEY-GENERAL V PYA QUARRIES LTD (1957)
>
> Here the nuisance complained of was the noise and vibrations caused by quarrying. The defendant's argument that too few people were affected failed. It was sufficient that a representative class was affected.

To succeed a claimant must be able to show special damage suffered over and above that which other members of the class have suffered.

> ### TATE & LYLE INDUSTRIES LTD V GREATER LONDON COUNCIL (1983)
>
> HL characterised an interference with navigation rights in the River Thames as physical damage making it actionable public nuisance.

● Special damage might include personal injury.

> ### CASTLE V ST AUGUSTINE LINKS (1922)
>
> A taxi driver was hit in the eye by a sliced golf ball. The golf club was liable. In comparison to *Bolton* v *Stone* (1951) the links straddled the highway so the risk of harm was much greater.

● It can also include damage to goods, as with the washing in *Halsey* v *Esso Petroleum Co. Ltd* (1961).

● It can also include financial loss.

> ### ROSE V MILES (1815)
>
> The defendant's barge blocked a navigable river. As a result the claimant was forced to empty his barge and pay for alternative transport. The defendant was liable for the cost.

- One further example of special damage might be a loss of trade connection as when shops lose trade during a long-term blockage of the highway such as road repairs – *Wilkes* v *Hungerford Market Co.* (1835).

Most commonly the tort involves use and abuse of the highway. Interference can be in a number of ways.

- It might involve obstructions to the highway. This might occur as the result of queues for which the defendant is responsible as at a football match or concert or theatre performance *Lyons* v *Gulliver* (1914). It may apply to a picket line – *Thomas* v *National Union of Mineworkers (South Wales Area)* (1985).

- It can apply to projections over the highway which cause damage. These could be clocks, hoardings, signs and other artificial structures.

In this case an occupier is liable to ensure that structures do not fall into disrepair. In the case of natural things the position may be less clear.

NOBLE V HARRISON (1926)

Here a branch from a tree on the defendant's land fell onto a bus. The defendant was not liable because the defect in the tree was latent and probably beyond his control.

- It will also apply to the condition of the highway, particularly since a local authority will usually have a duty to maintain the highway.

GRIFFITHS V LIVERPOOL CORPORATION

Here it was a nuisance when a person tripped on a flagstone that was standing up by half an inch.

activity

SELF ASSESSMENT QUESTIONS

1 Why is the nuisance sometimes referred to as 'the law of give and take'?

2 When will an action in nuisance be unavailable to a person who has suffered from the nuisance?

3 In what ways will locality affect an action for nuisance?

4 In what circumstances is it possible for an act that is not continuous to be an actionable nuisance?

5 What is the effect of malice in the tort of nuisance? How does this compare with other torts?

6 Why should a person's excessive sensitivity prevent them from claiming?

7 In what circumstances is a person liable in nuisance for a nuisance actually caused by someone else?

8 What is generally the most effective defence in nuisance, and why?

9 What factors will determine a claimant's choice of remedy in nuisance?

10 Why would a claimant bring an action in nuisance rather than negligence?

11 What are the significant differences between private and public nuisance?

12 What exactly is special damage in public nuisance?

KEY
FACTS

- It is possible to have private nuisance, public nuisance, and now statutory nuisance also
- A private nuisance is defined as an unlawful indirect interference with a person's use or enjoyment of his land
- Unlawful means unreasonable, and what is unreasonable can depend on:
  - locality – what is a nuisance in Belgravia need not be a nuisance in Bermondsey – *St Helens Smelting* v *Tipping* (1865)
  - duration of the nuisance – whether the nuisance is continuous or only short-lived – *Bolton* v *Stone* (1951)
  - sensitivity of the claimant – *Robinson* v *Kilvert* (1889)
  - the seriousness of the nuisance – whether or not damage is caused or merely inconvenience – *Halsey* v *Esso Petroleum* (1961)
  - malice can also play an important role – *Christie* v *Davey* (1893)
- The interference must be indirect, direct interference would be a trespass
- It is insufficient that the interference is with a purely recreational use of land – *Hunter and Another* v *Canary Wharf* (1997)
- Defences include: statutory authority, prescription, act of a stranger, consent and public policy
- Public nuisance is defined as an interference with the material comfort of a class of Her Majesty's subjects
- It must involve damage to the defendant over and above that caused to the public generally – *Tate and Lyle* v *GLC* (1983)
- It involves the highway, i.e. damage caused by obstructions to the highway, projections over the highway, and the condition of the highway

FIGURE 7.2 *Key fact chart for nuisance*

7.3 *RYLANDS* V *FLETCHER* AND STRICT LIABILITY

7.3.1 THE DEFINITION, PURPOSE AND CHARACTER OF THE RULE

The tort *Rylands* v *Fletcher* comes from the case of the same name (1868) and the rule was defined in the case in the Court of Exchequer Chamber by Blackburn J who said,

'We think that the true rule of law is, that the person who, for purposes of his own, brings on his land and keeps there anything likely to do mischief if it escapes, must keep it in at his peril, and, if he does not do so, he is prima facie answerable for all the damage which is the natural consequence of its escape.'

This basic definition contains the major ingredients of the tort which were then added to by Lord Cairns in the appeal to HL with the further requirement that for the claimant to succeed the thing brought onto the land must then amount to a 'non-natural' use of land.

The tort is identified as a form of strict liability to deal with dangerous activities and dangerous substances. However, it is arguable how much it can actually be seen as a tort of strict liability or how much it is rather a particular type of nuisance dealing with isolated but hazardous escapes rather than with continuous interference.

Whichever it is, the tort is not straightforward and it is not simple to bring an action. In fact there are so many defences available to a claim that it is hard to see that it is strict liability at all.

Traditionally it could be said that the liability was strict because there was no particular requirement to show fault, and the defendant could be made liable even if (s)he had taken care to avoid the escape. The tort was also seen as distinguishable from nuisance because there was a requirement in nuisance that harm of the type caused by the nuisance should be foreseeable, but no such requirement was apparent in *Rylands* v *Fletcher*.

This is not now the case since HL has identified the tort as a type of nuisance, and subject therefore to the same test of foreseeability.

> ### CAMBRIDGE WATER CO. V EASTERN COUNTIES LEATHER PLC (1994)
>
> The claimant Water Company used a borehole from which to extract water for domestic consumption and use. The defendants at their nearby tannery used a solvent for degreasing the animal skins. Sometimes this solvent would spill onto the concrete floor. Unknown to the defendants, over a period of time the spilt solvent seeped into the ground and eventually filtered through into the borehole contaminating the water. Since the contamination was not foreseeable at the time of the spillages HL held that there could be no liability.

There are other factors that make the tort difficult to prove. Lord Cairns added the requirement that there be a non-natural use of land. So the simplest way to defeat a claim is to show that the use of land in question is a natural use.

Moreover, the judges have shown hostility to the general principle of strict liability in the tort and have restricted the application of the rule still further.

- Firstly, according to *Read* v *Lyons* (1947), there can only be liability where the thing brought onto the defendant's land escapes from that land.

- Secondly, according to *Rickards* v *Lothian* (1913), there must be a 'special use of land bringing with it increased danger to others'.

- Thirdly the recent return to foreseeability of

type of damage as in *Cambridge Water Co.* v *Eastern Counties Leather plc* (1994).

Despite all this the tort can still not be seen as a straightforward extension of nuisance. Claimants have recovered damages despite not being occupiers of land as in *Hale* v *Jennings Bros.* (1938). The tort has similarly been said to apply to both accidental and intentional releases of the thing that 'causes mischief' – *Crown River Cruises Ltd* v *Kimbolton Fireworks Ltd* (1996).

7.3.2 THE INGREDIENTS OF THE TORT

There are essentially four elements that must be proved for there to be a successful claim under *Rylands* v *Fletcher*:

- a bringing onto the land and accumulating

- of a thing likely to cause mischief if it escapes

- which amounts to a non-natural use of the land

- and which does escape and causes damage.

In the case itself all elements were present and the defendants were liable.

> ### RYLANDS V FLETCHER (1868)
>
> The defendant, a mill-owner, hired contractors to create a reservoir on his land to act as a water supply to the mill. The contractors carelessly failed to block off disused mineshafts that they came across during their excavations. Unknown to the contractors these shafts were connected to other mineworks on adjoining land. When the reservoir was filled water then flooded the neighbouring mines. All elements of the modern tort were present. The large volumes of water were not naturally present in that form but were brought onto the land. Such a large volume of water could quite obviously do damage if it escaped. Lord Cairns identified that storage of water in these quantities did amount to a non-natural use of land. Finally, in the event, the water did escape through the mineshafts causing considerable damage to the claimant.

Each of the four elements requires proof and so should be considered individually.

The bringing onto the land

Clearly the starting point here is that if the thing in question is already naturally present on the land then there can be no liability.

> **PONTARDAWE RDC V MOORE-GWYN (1929)**
>
> In this case there was no liability for the damage caused by the escape of rocks in an avalanche.

Neither could there be liability if the thing in question was already growing on the land.

> **GILES V WALKER (1890)**
>
> There was no liability for weeds spreading onto neighbouring land.

Neither will there be liability for a thing that naturally accumulates on the land.

> **ELLISON V THE MINISTRY OF DEFENCE (1997)**
>
> Rainwater that accumulated naturally on an airfield at Greenham Common did not lead to liability when it escaped and caused flooding on neighbouring land.

However, it is still possible for there to be an action in nuisance where the defendant is aware of the thing causing the nuisance and has in effect 'adopted it' by failing to do anything about it.

> **LEAKEY V THE NATIONAL TRUST (1980)**
>
> Here the hill from which the mound slipped was particularly subject to cracking and slipping in bad weather. The defendants knew of this and were liable because they failed to do anything to prevent it.

Besides this, the person who brings the thing onto the land does not have to be the owner or occupier of the land. In this way a mere licensee could come within the scope of the rule.

> **CHARING CROSS ELECTRIC SUPPLY CO. V HYDRAULIC POWER CO. (1914) (THE CHARING CROSS CO. CASE)**
>
> Here the defendants had a statutory power to lay water mains, which were then situated above electric cables. They were liable to the claimants, however, when the water main burst and flooded the electric cable causing a blackout in large parts of London.

The thing brought onto the land must be brought onto the land for the defendants' purposes.

> **DUNNE V NORTH WESTERN GAS BOARD (1964)**
>
> The Gas Board was bound by statute to supply gas to its consumers. It was held, however, not to have collected the gas onto land for its own purposes.

But the fact that the thing is brought onto the land for the purposes of the defendant does not mean that it has to be accumulated there for the defendant's benefit.

> **SMEATON V ILFORD CORPORATION (1954)**
>
> A local authority collected sewage under a statutory authority. It was held that it did so for its own purposes even though it was accepted that it derived no benefit from collecting the sewage.

One final and quite significant point here is that the thing that is brought onto the land does not necessarily have to be the thing that escapes and causes mischief.

> **MILES V FOREST ROCK GRANITE CO. (LEICESTERSHIRE) LTD (1918)**
>
> The claimant brought the action in respect of injuries suffered when rocks flew onto the highway from the defendants' land where they were blasting. It was the explosives that had been brought onto land that actually caused the rock to escape, but there was still liability.

The thing is likely to do mischief if it escapes

It is not the escape itself that must be likely only

that mischief is likely if the thing brought onto land does escape.

MUSGROVE V PANDELIS (1919)

Here the rule was applied when a garaged car with petrol in its tank caught fire and the fire spread to the next door neighbour's house. The fire was unlikely but would certainly cause mischief if it escaped.

Neither must the thing that escapes be dangerous in any intrinsic sense. It is sufficient that it becomes dangerous by the manner of the escape.

SHIFFMAN V ORDER OF THE HOSPITAL OF ST JOHN OF JERUSALEM (1936)

Here the thing that 'escaped' and caused the damage was a flagpole.

However, the thing must be a source of foreseeable harm if it does escape.

HALE V JENNINGS BROS. (1938)

A car from a 'chair-o-plane' ride on a fairground became detached from the main assembly while it was in motion and injured a stallholder as it crashed to the ground. The owner of the ride was liable. Risk of injury was foreseeable if the car came loose.

Strangely enough, even people who 'escape' have been held to be dangerous and a potential mischief under the rule.

ATTORNEY-GENERAL V CORKE (1933)

Here a landowner allowed gypsies to camp on his land. When they then committed nuisances and trespasses against his neighbours the landowner was liable. The gypsies were held to be 'likely to do mischief if they escaped'. One potential problem here is whether or not the landowner would have been in a position to lawfully restrict the gypsies' free movement.

A non-natural use of land

Lord Cairns in HL in *Rylands* v *Fletcher* itself indicated the requirement of a non-natural use of land. He said

'*if the defendants, not stopping at the natural use of their close, had desired to use it for any purpose which I may term a non-natural use ... and in consequence of doing so ... the water came to escape ... then it appears to me that which the defendants were doing they were doing at their own peril*'

This concept of non-natural use was developed and explained by Lord Moulton in *Rickards* v *Lothian* (1913):

'*it is not every use of land which brings into play this principle. It must be some special use bringing with it increased danger to others, and not merely by the ordinary use of land or such a use as is proper for the general benefit of the community*'

The question of what is a non-natural use of land is by necessity a complex concept and one which inevitably changes to take into account technological change and changes in lifestyle. It is inconceivable, for instance, that leaving a car garaged with petrol in the tank could be seen as a non-natural use of land today though it was seen as such in 1919 at the time of *Musgrove* v *Pandelis*.

The case law suggests that we must consider that non-natural is something more than artificial and refers to some extraordinary use of land.

In general as a result, things associated with a domestic use of land will not be classified as non-natural even though they may be potentially hazardous.

● So fire in a domestic context has been held a natural use:

SOCHAKI V SAS (1947)

There was no liability for a fire that started from a spark from a domestic grate and spread to the claimant's premises.

● As has electric wiring:

Collingwood v Home & Colonial Stores (1936)

Defective wiring caused a fire to start that then spread to the claimant's premises. It was impossible to show negligence and the defendants escaped liability.

- And a domestic water supply has also been held to be a natural use of land for the purposes of the rule:

Rickards v Lothian (1913)

Here the defendant was not liable when an unknown person turned on water taps and blocked plugholes on his premises so that damage was caused in the flat below.

Even owners of commercial premises may be exempt from the rule because the activity leading to the escape is held to be a natural rather than a non-natural use of land.

Peters v The Prince of Wales Theatre (Birmingham) Ltd (1943)

The claimant occupied part of the premises of the theatre. A sprinkler system in the theatre caused flooding and damaged the claimant's stock. There was no liability since the use of land was not non-natural.

Where such facilities are in question it will often be the volume, size or quantity involved that will lead to the thing being classed as a non-natural use of land. In the *Charing Cross Co. Case* for instance it was the volume of water in the main and the pressure at which it was held that made the use of land non-natural rather than the storage of water itself. This, as we have already seen, is capable of being viewed as a natural use.

It is also at times the context in which the thing is brought onto land and accumulated that leads to the court holding that it is a non-natural use of land.

Mason v Levy Auto Parts of England (1967)

Large quantities of scrap tyres were stored on the defendants' land. These then were ignited and the resultant fire spread and caused damage to the claimant's premises. The storage of such large quantities of a combustible material, the casual way in which they were stored and the character of the neighbourhood were all then considered by the judge in determining that there was a non-natural use of the land.

On the other hand the fact that the public may derive a benefit from the particular use of land that is in question may mean that the court holds it to be a natural use of land.

British Celanese v A. H. Hunt (Capacitors) Ltd (1969)

Here the defendants stored strips of metal foil, which were used in the process of manufacturing electrical components. Some of these strips of foil blew off the defendants' land and onto an electricity substation causing power failures. The court held that the use of land was natural, partly because of the benefit derived from the manufacture by the public, and there was no liability under the rule as a result.

And the fact that an activity is associated with war does not mean that it constitutes a non-natural use of land merely because it occurs in peacetime.

Ellison v The Ministry of Defence (1997)

Here bulk fuel installations on a military airfield were held not to be a non-natural use of land when rainwater that naturally gathered on the airfield ran off flooding neighbouring land.

However, the courts have been prepared to accept that certain activities may be seen as always leading to a potential level of danger that amounts to a non-natural use of land regardless of the benefit to the public derived from the activity that has led to the danger.

CAMBRIDGE WATER CO. V EASTERN COUNTIES LEATHER PLC (1994)

Here the storage of particular chemicals on an industrial site was held to be a classic example of a non-natural use of land. HL, therefore, rejected the defendants' plea that the activity being an important source of local employment made it a natural use of land.

The thing must actually escape

Blackburn J's original rule in the case of *Rylands* v *Fletcher* does not appear to contain any specific application of the word 'escape'. It is unlikely, therefore, that it was intended at that point that the requirement should be for the thing to escape onto land in which the claimant held a proprietary interest. If this were the case then it would support the general idea of a strict liability tort for the control of dangerous activities.

However, the rule was seen as a development of the law of nuisance in which there is a clear requirement for the claimant to have an interest in land. This explains the opinion expressed by Lord MacMillan that there must be such an escape since the rule derives 'from a conception of mutual duties of adjoining or neighbouring landowners'.

READ V J. LYONS & CO. LTD (1947)

A munitions inspector was inspecting a munitions factory and was injured, along with a number of employees, one man dying, when certain shells exploded. HL held that the rule did not apply because there was 'no escape at all of the relevant kind'. Viscount Simon explained that an escape in *Rylands* v *Fletcher* means 'an escape from a place where the defendant has occupation or control over land to a place which is outside his occupation or control'.

This is obviously a very restrictive limitation on the operation of the rule. However, this interpretation of the meaning of escape for the purposes of the rule has not always been accepted as an absolute requirement. In *British Celanese* v *A. H. Hunt (Capacitors) Ltd* (1969) Lawton J felt that

the escape in question should be 'from a set of circumstances over which the defendant has control to a set of circumstances where he does not'. The test here is far less restrictive and far more appropriate to a tort of strict liability.

Certainly there are cases that appear to operate according to this reasoning rather than that in *Read* v *Lyons*.

HALE V JENNINGS BROS (1938)

Here both stalls operated on the same piece of land. Neither the 'chair-o-plane' operator nor the other stallholder owned the land.

A similar principle has been seen where both parties are operating on the same stretch of river.

CROWN RIVER CRUISES LTD V KIMBOLTON FIREWORKS LTD (1996)

Here inflammable material from a firework display fell onto barges used as a jetty for pleasure cruisers causing fire damage

7.3.3 WHO CAN SUE AND WHO CAN BE SUED UNDER THE RULE

Potential defendants

The question of the identity of potential defendants depends very much on the test of an escape that is accepted and used in the case.

According to Viscount Simon's test in *Read* v *Lyons* a defendant to an action in *Rylands* v *Fletcher* will be either the owner or occupier of land who satisfies the four ingredients of the tort which must all be present for liability.

On the other hand, according to the test as described by Lawton J in *British Celanese* v *Hunt*, a potential defendant is one who satisfies the four ingredients of the rule where the escape is from a set of circumstances over which (s)he has control to a set of circumstances over which (s)he does not.

The natural development of the less restrictive rule is to include a claim where the defendant is merely in control of the highway and not the occupier of land.

RIGBY V CHIEF CONSTABLE OF NORTHAMP-TONSHIRE (1985)

Here the defendant was liable for the damage caused by the negligent release of CS gas canisters on the highway.

Potential claimants

The question of who can sue is not necessarily quite so clear cut. In the original case we have already seen that Blackburn J made no suggestion of any requirement for a claimant to have a proprietary interest in land. Nevertheless, Lord MacMillan in *Read* v *Lyons* suggested that there is such a requirement.

Lawton J in the *British Celanese* case felt that Lord MacMillan's requirement was too restrictive, and his test would necessarily include a wider class of potential claimants. Indeed, in the case it was a third party who had suffered damage as a result of the loss of power when the foil landed on the power station.

The logical development of a less restrictive test here is to allow a claim for accumulations that escape causing damage to the claimant regardless of where the damage occurs.

CROWN RIVER CRUISES LTD V KIMBOLTON FIREWORKS LTD (1996)

Here the claimant was able to recover in nuisance and negligence despite the fact that the damage caused was to barges moored on the river. However, the opportunity to extend the rule here to cover the escape was rejected.

7.3.4 TYPES OF RECOVERABLE LOSS AND REMOTENESS OF DAMAGE

If MacMillan's test is accepted as correct then this has the effect of limiting claims to recovery only for damage to the land owned or occupied by the claimant and to damage to property found on that land. MacMillan also expressed doubts as to whether a claim for personal injuries was possible under the rule.

On the other hand, if Lawton's test is preferred then damages that can be recovered for are much wider, and indeed wide enough to include personal injury claims. Certainly there were cases before *Read* v *Lyons* including both *Shiffman* and *Hale* v *Jennings* in which the court found no problem in granting damages for personal injury.

Nevertheless, since the modern view following *Cambridge Water* is to accept *Rylands* v *Fletcher* as a form of nuisance, and since in *Hunter and Another* v *Canary Wharf Ltd* it was doubted whether personal injury was recoverable in nuisance, then this issue might also be settled in *Rylands* v *Fletcher*.

It is certainly unlikely that a claim for economic loss will be successful.

WELLER V FOOT AND MOUTH DISEASE RESEARCH UNIT (1966)

Auctioneers sued for their loss of usual income when there was a ban on the movement of livestock following the escape of a virus from the defendant's premises. In the case there was in fact held to be no liability because the claimants had no proprietary interest in land. It is unlikely that they would have succeeded in any case in respect of the type of damages claimed.

The tort is not actionable per se and this means that any claimant must show damage in order to succeed. So there can be no liability for the mere interference with the enjoyment of land.

EASTERN & SOUTH AFRICAN TELEGRAPH CO. LTD V CAPE TOWN TRAMWAYS CO. LTD (1902)

Electric emissions interfered with the transmission of telegraphic messages sent down underground cables. The claimants' action failed because of their 'hypersensitive' use of land. It was also suggested *in obiter* that the damage could not be classified as damage to property.

The rule on remoteness of damage was only recently settled. Blackburn J's original remarks refer to 'the natural consequence of the escape' suggest that the test of direct consequence in *Re Polemis and Furness, Withy & Co.* (1921) is applicable. However, HL in *Cambridge Water* have now stated that reasonable foreseeability of damage is a prerequisite of liability. In other words, the defendant must have known or ought reasonably to have foreseen that damage of the relevant type might be a consequence of the escape of the thing likely to cause mischief.

7.3.5 POSSIBLE DEFENCES

Despite the tort being described as strict liability a number of defences are possible in the event of a claim. Blackburn J identified some of these at the time of the original case, others have developed since.

Volenti non fit injuria *(consent)*

There will be no liability where the claimant has consented to the thing that is accumulated by the defendant.

Consent is a commonly available defence in the case of multiple occupation of buildings, particularly tall buildings. The claimant will be said to consent when the thing accumulated is for the common benefit of the occupants.

> **PETERS V PRINCE OF WALES THEATRE (BIRMINGHAM) LTD (1943)**
>
> Here the claimant's stock was damaged by water from the defendant's sprinkler system. The water supply was nevertheless for the benefit of both and so there was no liability for the escape.

Common benefit

There will in any case be no liability on a defendant when the source of the potential danger is something that is maintained for the benefit of both claimant and defendant.

> **DUNNE V NORTH WESTERN GAS BOARD (1964)**
>
> A gas mains exploded without any negligence on the part of the Gas Board. The court doubted whether the Board had accumulated the gas for their own benefit, it was for the benefit of the consumers and there was no liability.

Act of a stranger

If a stranger over whom the defendant has no control has been the cause of the escape causing the damage then the defendant may not be liable.

> **PERRY V KENDRICKS TRANSPORT LTD (1956)**
>
> The defendants parked their bus on their parking space having drained the tank of petrol. When an unknown person removed the petrol cap a child was then injured when another child threw in a match which ignited the fumes in the tank. CA considered that the burden of proof here was on the claimant to show that such an eventuality was foreseeable. There was a valid defence and no liability.

Nevertheless, in other jurisdictions the strict liability of the rule can mean that there is liability regardless of who causes the escape or whether it was foreseeable – *Mehta* v *Union of India* (1987), which concerned the chemical leak disaster in India.

Act of God

This defence may succeed where there are extreme weather conditions that 'no human foresight can provide against'. So the nature of the defence is that it is only possible in the case of unforeseeable weather conditions.

> **NICHOLS V MARSLAND (1876)**
>
> The defendant here made three artificial, ornamental lakes by damming a natural stream on his land. Freak thunderstorms accompanied by torrential rain broke the banks of the artificial lakes that then caused the destruction of bridges on the claimant's land. There was no liability because the weather conditions were so extreme.

Statutory authority

A statute on construction may provide a defence if the escape is a direct result of the carrying out of the duty contained in the statute.

> **GREEN V CHELSEA WATERWORKS CO. (1894)**
>
> The defendants were obliged by statute to provide a water supply. The court held that from time to time burst pipes were an inevitable consequence of this duty and there could be no liability in the absence of negligence.

In the absence of a duty there may still be liability when the thing escapes.

> **CHARING CROSS ELECTRIC SUPPLY CO. V HYDRAULIC POWER CO. (1914) (THE CHARING CROSS CO. CASE)**
>
> There was liability here because there was only a power rather than a duty to provide the water supply.

Fault of the claimant

A defendant will not be liable when a claimant is in fact responsible for the damage that (s)he suffers.

> **EASTERN & SOUTH AFRICAN TELEGRAPH CO. LTD V CAPE TOWN TRAMWAYS CO. LTD (1902)**
>
> Here the defendants were not liable because the interference with the telegraphic transmissions was said to be the fault of the excessive sensitivity of the telegraphic process.

Contributory negligence

Where the claimant is partly responsible then the provisions of the Law Reform (Contributory Negligence) Act 1945 will apply and damages may be reduced according to the amount of the claimant's fault.

POINTS FOR DISCUSSION

PROBLEMS WITH THE TORT

The rule in *Rylands* v *Fletcher* has a number of problems associated with it. The modern perception of the rule seems to be that it is a more particular development of the law of nuisance and therefore it not only has all the shortcomings of that tort but also would seem to be far from being strict liability in any straightforward sense. It is certainly unlikely that there is a future possibility of the tort being used as a general means of controlling dangerous activities or things by the use of strict liability.

In other jurisdictions, such as India, the tort has been expanded but that has not been the case in England. On the contrary, the rule has been constantly limited in its scope by the decisions in the cases.

- Lord Cairns limited it immediately in the actual case in HL when he imposed the requirement that the thing brought onto land should be a non-natural use of land for there to be liability.

- The tort was further restricted in its development by the requirement of proprietary interest in land established by Lord MacMillan in *Read* v *Lyons*. This inevitably limits the circumstances in which a claimant can recover for damage caused by dangerous things accumulated on land.

- The *Cambridge Water* case even seems to be taking the tort towards a negligence-style fault liability with the requirement of foreseeability.

The court in *Crown River Cruises Ltd* v

Kimbolton Fireworks Ltd expressly rejected suggestions that the tort could or should be developed. The very breadth of the defences that have been made available in the tort seem in any case to be at odds with the principle of strict liability.

The tort then seems to be of questionable significance in the modern day. The judges are reluctant to allow claims under the tort to succeed. Most claims that could be bought under the tort could probably just as easily be brought under negligence instead and indeed the requirement of foreseeability means that a claimant has similar concerns in some aspects.

The tort is rarely used and almost never successfully. Indeed shortly after the *Cambridge Water* case the Australian High Court in effect abolished the rule, claiming that the rule had been absorbed by the general rules of negligence.

Most areas of activity that could be affected or controlled by the rule are probably dealt with in the modern context by statutory controls. Certainly there are few hazardous activities that are not controlled by some form of statutory regulation.

BLUE CIRCLE INDUSTRIES PLC V MINISTRY OF DEFENCE (1998)

Here the Nuclear Installations Act 1965 was used in respect of contamination caused to land by radioactive materials even though the actual damage involved was economic.

Since the rule was first devised the judges appear to have missed a golden opportunity to have a real strict liability tort to deal generally with dangerous activities and substances. They instead have developed a tort that is so limited in its application as to be relatively unusable.

activity

SELF ASSESSMENT QUESTIONS

1 What are the key ingredients of the rule in *Rylands* v *Fletcher*?

2 To what extent is liability under the rule really 'strict liability'?

3 What exactly is a 'non-natural' use of land?

4 Which things situated on land that are dangerous will lead to liability if they escape?

5 What must escape for the tort to operate?

6 Does the rule help the victims of damage caused by dangerous activities in general?

7 Who will be liable under the rule?

8 What are the different consequences of the tests in *Read* v *Lyons* (1947) and in *British Celanese* v *Hunt* (1969)?

9 How limiting are the defences to a successful claim under the rule?

10 How are personal injuries covered under *Rylands* v *Fletcher*?

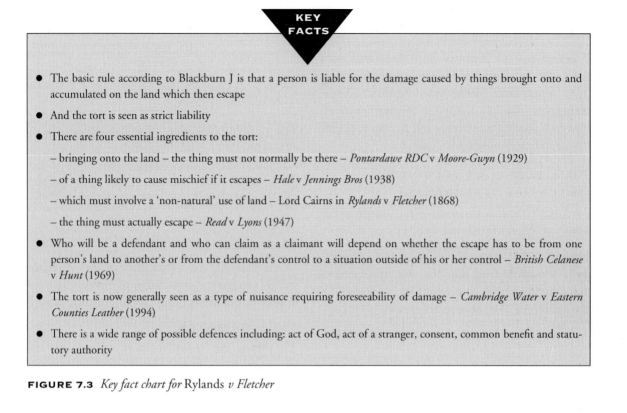

KEY
FACTS

- The basic rule according to Blackburn J is that a person is liable for the damage caused by things brought onto and accumulated on the land which then escape
- And the tort is seen as strict liability
- There are four essential ingredients to the tort:
  – bringing onto the land – the thing must not normally be there – *Pontardawe RDC* v *Moore-Gwyn* (1929)
  – of a thing likely to cause mischief if it escapes – *Hale* v *Jennings Bros* (1938)
  – which must involve a 'non-natural' use of land – Lord Cairns in *Rylands* v *Fletcher* (1868)
  – the thing must actually escape – *Read* v *Lyons* (1947)
- Who will be a defendant and who can claim as a claimant will depend on whether the escape has to be from one person's land to another's or from the defendant's control to a situation outside of his or her control – *British Celanese* v *Hunt* (1969)
- The tort is now generally seen as a type of nuisance requiring foreseeability of damage – *Cambridge Water* v *Eastern Counties Leather* (1994)
- There is a wide range of possible defences including: act of God, act of a stranger, consent, common benefit and statutory authority

FIGURE 7.3 *Key fact chart for* Rylands *v* Fletcher

7.4 OCCUPIERS' LIABILITY

7.4.1 INTRODUCTION AND ORIGINS

Occupiers' Liability concerns the liability of an 'occupier' of land for the claimant's injury or loss or damage to property suffered while on the occupier's 'premises'. Therefore it must be distinguished from damage caused by the defendant's use of his or her land, which the claimant suffers on his or her own land. This would lead to an action in nuisance or possibly *Rylands* v *Fletcher*.

It is a fairly recent tort, and is found in two statutes, the Occupiers' Liability Act 1957 (concerned with the duty of care owed to lawful visitors) and the Occupiers' Liability Act 1984 (concerned with the duty owed to trespassers).

While in statutory form, the tort has developed out of negligence, and so much of the terminology and many of the principles are the same. Indeed,

though the Acts do contain extensive definition, where definitions are not supplied in the Acts these are to be found in the common law.

Inevitably there is some overlap with negligence. The basic liability arises from the loss or injury caused by the 'state of the premises'. Loss or damage that arises other than because of the state of the premises then should be claimed for under negligence where this is possible.

OGWO V TAYLOR (1987)

Here there was no liability under the 1957 Act when a fireman was injured in a fire on the defendant's premises. The fire did not result from the state of the premises, so liability was in negligence.

It is possible to argue that the 1957 Act should apply in the case of damage caused other than by the state of the premises since s.1(1) states that the Act should apply 'in respect of dangers due to the state of the premises or to things done or omitted to be done on them'.

While the 1957 Act has been described as a particularly well-drafted statute it possibly suffers from under-use. While the Pearson Report recognised that as many as 27 per cent of reported accidents occur in the home, very few claims follow domestic accidents.

7.4.2 WHO IS AN OCCUPIER? (POTENTIAL DEFENDANTS)

Potential defendants are the same under either Act – occupiers of premises.

There is in fact no statutory definition of 'occupier'. Section 1(2) of the 1957 Act merely states that the rules apply 'in consequence of a person's occupation or control of premises …'.

The established test for determining occupation then is found in common law.

WHEAT V E. LACON & CO. LTD (1966)

A manager of a public house was given the right to rent out rooms in his private quarters even though he had no proprietary interest in the premises. When a paying guest fell on an unlit staircase, HL held that both the manager and his employers could be occupiers for the purposes of the Act. In the event neither had breached their duty since it was a stranger who had removed the light bulb.

So there can be dual or multiple occupation of premises, and the identity of the defendant, which party was in control of the premises, may depend on the circumstances in which the damage or injury was suffered.

COLLIER V ANGLIAN WATER AUTHORITY (1983)

Here a promenade formed part of the sea defences for which the Water Authority was responsible. The Local Authority owned the land, and was responsible for cleaning the promenade. When the claimant was injured as a result of its disrepair it was the Water Authority rather than the Local Authority which was liable, though both were occupiers.

Occupation does not require either proprietary interest or possession, so the position is quite different to trespass. All that is required for liability is that the defendant has sufficient control of the premises at the time that the damage was caused to be responsible for it.

HARRIS V BIRKENHEAD CORPORATION (1976)

Here a four-year-old child had been injured in an empty house, which was not boarded up or secured in any way. Even though the council had not yet taken possession of the house they were liable since they had served a compulsory purchase notice and were effectively in control of the premises.

In the final analysis the identity of the defendant will be influenced by the ability to meet a successful claim whether through insurance or other means.

7.4.3 PREMISES

The Acts are again relatively silent on the meaning of premises. Some limited reference is given in s.1(3)(a) 1957 Act which refers to a person having occupation or control of any 'fixed or moveable structure, including any vessel, vehicle and aircraft …'.

So the common law again applies, and besides the obvious such as houses, buildings and the land itself, premises has also been held to include:

- ships in dry dock – *London Graving Dock* v *Horton* (1951)
- vehicles – *Hartwell* v *Grayson* (1947)
- lifts – *Haseldine* v *Daw & Son Ltd* (1941)
- and even a ladder – *Wheeler* v *Copas* (1981)

7.4.4 POTENTIAL CLAIMANTS UNDER THE OCCUPIERS' LIABILITY ACT 1957

The 1957 Act was passed in order to simplify a fairly complex common law, whereby the duty owed to a person entering premises varied according to the capacity in which that person entered. The Act introduced a common duty to be applied to all lawful visitors.

By s.1(2) the classes of people to whom the occupier owes a duty remains as it was under common law. These are called visitors under the Act, and as a result of s.1(2) include:

- all invitees and licensees. Invitees can be for example friends making a social call or people whose entry is to the material interest of the occupier, e.g. customers. Licensees can include anyone with permission to be on the premises for whatever purpose (licensees were treated somewhat harshly by the common law, being entitled to no more than warnings of danger) – visitors under an implied licence will need to prove that the conduct of the occupier amounted to a grant of a licence;

LOWERY V WALKER (1911)

Certain members of the public used a short cut across the defendant's land for many years. While he objected he took no legal steps to stop it. When he loosed a wild horse on the land which savaged the claimant he was liable. The claimant by the defendant's conduct had a licence.

- those entering under a contractual agreement – in which case the terms of the contract might determine the extent of the duty;

- those not requiring permission to enter because of a legal right to enter, e.g. meter readers.

No duty is owed under the 1957 Act to trespassers. A more limited duty is owed to trespassers under the Occupiers' Liability Act 1984. Certain other categories of entrants are also not covered by the 1957 Act. These include:

- those using a private right of way

- those entering under an access agreement under the National Parks and Access to the Countryside Act 1949 (both of the above classes are also dealt with under the 1984 Act)

- those using a public right of way – these are excluded by both Acts and will fall under common law with the tortfeasor (the wrongdoer) being liable for misfeasance (actively

activity

QUICK QUIZ

Consider which of the following potential claimants would be able to class themselves as visitors for the purposes of the Occupiers' Liability Act 1957:

1 Trevor is a milkman delivering milk to Archie's door.

2 Gordon, a football fan with a season ticket for the Wanderers, arrives at the ground on Wednesday night for the match with United.

3 Hannah regularly crosses Farmer Giles's field using a well-known public path.

4 Greg is at Mavis's house on Monday morning as agreed, painting it.

5 Ali is a police officer who has called at Brian's house for some routine enquiries.

6 Tom regularly climbs over his neighbour's back fence and comes through his back garden on his way home, knowing that his neighbour works late so will be out.

doing wrong) but not nonfeasance (doing wrong by omission)

7.4.5 THE SCOPE OF THE OCCUPIER'S DUTY UNDER THE 1957 ACT

The extent of the duty of care is set out in s.2(1): 'An occupier owes the same duty, the common duty of care, to all his visitors except insofar as he is free to do and does extend, restrict, modify or exclude his duty to any visitors by agreement or otherwise'.

The nature of the duty is found in s.2(2). It is to 'take such care as in all the circumstances ... is reasonable to see that the visitor will be reasonably safe for the purpose for which he is invited ... to be there ...'.

Three key points need to be made straightaway:

● Firstly, the standard of care is that generally applied in negligence, the standard of the 'reasonable man'. As a result the occupier is merely obliged to guard against the foreseeable.

● The duty in the 1957 Act only applies so long as the visitor is carrying out activities which are authorised within the terms of the visit. So if the visitor strays (s)he may lose protection under the 1957 Act, although the 1984 Act might still apply.

● The duty is to keep the visitor safe, not necessarily to maintain safe premises. If the latter were the case it would make industry unworkable. But because of the scope and potential limitations of the duty the Act sensi-

bly makes some different rules for different classes of visitor.

7.4.6 CHILDREN AND THE 1957 ACT

Under s.2(3) the occupier 'must be prepared for children to be less careful than adults ...' and as a result 'the premises must be reasonably safe for a child of that age ...' demonstrating that in the case of children the standard of care is measured subjectively.

The reasoning is perfectly logical: what may pose no threat to an adult may nevertheless be very dangerous to a child.

Similarly, a child is unlikely to appreciate risks as an adult would and indeed might be attracted to the danger anyway. As a result an occupier should guard against any kind of 'allurement' which places a child visitor at risk of harm.

Nevertheless, the mere existence of an allurement on its own is insufficient ground for liability.

In fact, even though an allurement exists there

will be no liability on the occupier if the damage or injury suffered is not foreseeable.

JOLLEY V LONDON BOROUGH OF SUTTON (1998)

The council failed to move an abandoned boat for two years. Children regularly played in the boat and it was clearly a potential danger. When two young boys of fourteen jacked the boat up to repair it, the boat fell on one injuring him. The action for compensation failed, since nobody could have contemplated that the boys would follow this course of action.

In any case the courts will sometimes take the view that very young children should be under the supervision of a parent or other adult. In this case the occupier might find that (s)he is relieved of liability.

PHIPPS V ROCHESTER CORPORATION (1955)

A five-year-old child was injured having fallen down a trench dug by the defendant where the child frequently played. The defendant was not liable because the court concluded that the parents should have had the child under proper control.

7.4.7 PEOPLE CARRYING OUT A TRADE OR CALLING ON THE OCCUPIER'S PREMISES AND THE 1957 ACT

Sensibly the Act also has a more particular attitude to professional visitors, taking the view that, by s.2(3)(b), in relation to activities carried on within their trade, they should 'appreciate and guard against any special risks ordinarily incident to it …'.

So an occupier will not be liable where tradesmen fail to guard against risks which they should know about.

ROLES V NATHAN (1963)

There was no liability on the occupiers when chimney sweeps died after inhaling carbon monoxide fumes while cleaning flues. The sweeps should have accepted the advice of the occupiers to complete the work with the boilers off.

But tradesmen might still have an action against their employer if the latter has agreed to an unsafe system of work.

GENERAL CLEANING CONTRACTORS V CHRISTMAS (1953)

Occupiers were not liable for an injury sustained when a window cleaner fell after a window closed on him but the employers were.

However, the existence of a skill is not proof per se that the occupier is not liable. It depends whether the normal safeguards associated with the trade could have averted the loss or injury.

SALMON V SEAFARERS RESTAURANTS LTD (1983)

Owners of a chip shop were liable for the injuries caused to a fireman which were unavoidable because of the character of the fire.

7.4.8 LIABILITY FOR THE TORTS OF INDEPENDENT CONTRACTORS UNDER THE 1957 ACT

Generally the occupier will be able to avoid liability for loss or injuries suffered by his or her visitors when the cause of damage is the negligence of an independent contractor hired by the occupier. This is under s.2(4)

It is a sensible rule because a reputable contractor will in any case be covered by his or her own insurance, and so the claimant will still be able to recover compensation.

However, three requirements will apply:

● Firstly, it must be reasonable for the occupier to have entrusted the work to the independent contractor:

HASELDINE V DAW & SON LTD (1941)

The occupier was not liable for negligent repair of a lift, a highly specialist activity.

● Secondly, the contractor hired must be competent to carry out the task:

FERGUSON V WELSH (1987)

The claimant was employed by demolition contractors, hired by the local authority. When he was injured as a result of their unsafe working systems the local authority was liable.

- If possible the occupier must check the work (obviously the more complex and technical the work and the less expert the occupier the less reasonable it is to impose this obligation):

WOODWARD V THE MAYOR OF HASTINGS (1945)

Occupiers were liable when a child was injured on school steps which were negligently left icy after cleaning off snow. The danger should have been obvious to the occupiers.

7.4.9 AVOIDING LIABILITY UNDER THE 1957 ACT

As we have already seen in s.2(1) the occupier is free to extend, restrict, modify or exclude his duty to visitors. The occupier may achieve this in one of three ways:

Warnings

Under s.2(4)(a) a warning will not absolve the occupier of liability unless 'in all the circumstances it was enough to enable the visitor to be reasonably safe'. What is sufficient warning then will be a question of fact in each case.

Sometimes, for instance, a mere warning may be insufficient to safeguard the visitor and the occupier may be obliged to set up barriers instead.

RAE V MARS (UK) LTD (1990)

A warning was ineffective in respect of a deep pit inside the entrance of a dark shed, so the occupier was liable.

But a choice of words which are nothing more than an attempt to avoid liability will not be accepted as a warning.

Some risks are possibly so obvious that no additional warning is needed.

STAPLES V WEST DORSET DC (1995)

Danger of wet algae on a high wall at Lyme Regis should have been obvious.

Exclusion clauses

These are allowed by s.2(1) so they can be a term in a contractual licence.

ASHDOWN V SAMUEL WILLIAMS & SONS LTD (1957)

The claimant was unable to recover for injuries sustained in a shunting yard because notices excluding liability were sufficiently bought to her attention and she was no more than a contractual licensee when she entered.

Use of exclusion clauses will, however, be subject to various restrictions:

- they will be unavailable in the case of persons entering under a legal right

- they will not apply in the case of strangers e.g. a tenant's visitors, because they will have had no chance to agree the exclusion

- they will probably fail against children, who may be unable to read or to fully understand their implications

- they will not be allowed in respect of death or personal injury caused by the occupier's negligence by virtue of s.2(1) Unfair Contract Terms Act 1977

- there is also an argument that, since the Occupiers' Liability Act 1984 imposes a minimum standard of care owed to trespassers, then this minimum standard should be beyond exclusion, or trespassers have better rights than lawful visitors

General defences

There are two possibilities:

- The claimant's contributory negligence under the Law Reform (Contributory Negligence)

Act 1945, which has the effect of reducing awards of damages.

- *Volenti non fit injuria* – consent. Section 2(5) allows that the occupier 'has no liability to a visitor in respect of risks willingly accepted as his by the visitor ...'.

The risk must, however, be fully understood by the visitor:

SIMMS V LEIGH RFC (1960)

There was no liability to a rugby football player when the injury was sustained within the normal rules of the game.

Mere knowledge of the risk is also insufficient, it must be accepted:

WHITE V BLACKMORE (1972)

General knowledge that 'jalopy racing' was dangerous did not mean that the claimant had accepted inadequate safety arrangements.

If the claimant has no choice then there is no consent:

BURNETT V BRITISH WATERWAYS BOARD (1973)

A claimant on a barge entering the defendant's dry dock had no choice but to be there so there was no defence of consent available.

Express warnings that the claimant enters at his/her own risk may well be caught by the Unfair Contract Terms Act 1977

7.4.10 THE BACKGROUND TO THE 1984 ACT AND THE 'COMMON DUTY OF HUMANITY'

The 1984 Act was introduced to provide a limited duty of care mainly towards trespassers. The Act came about because traditionally at common law an occupier owed such entrants no duty at all, other than possibly to refrain from deliberately or recklessly inflicting damage or injury.

BIRD V HOLBRECK (1828)

This case finally outlawed mantraps. It prevented deliberately harming the trespasser but did not impose any duty to act to prevent the trespasser from being harmed.

CLAYTON V DEANE (1817)

This case accepted that an occupier was entitled to use reasonable deterrents to keep trespassers out, in this case broken glass on top of a wall.

The common law could be particularly harsh when applied to child trespassers:

ADDIE V DUMBRECK (1929)

Children frequently played on colliery premises and near to dangerous machinery. When one was injured there was no liability since he was a trespasser.

Because of the growth of more dangerous premises, and taking into account the difficulties of making children appreciate danger, the law was changed.

BRITISH RAILWAYS BOARD V HERRINGTON (1972)

A six-year-old was badly burned when straying onto an electrified railway line, through vandalised fencing. HL, using the Practice Statement to overrule past precedent, established the 'common duty of humanity', a limited duty owed when the occupier knew of the danger, and of the likelihood of the trespass.

Because of some of the impracticalities of this rule the 1984 Act was passed.

7.4.11 THE SCOPE AND NATURE OF THE 1984 ACT

By s.1(1)(a) a duty applies in respect of people other than visitors (who are covered by the 1957 Act) for 'injury on the premises by reason of any danger due to the state of the premises or things done or omitted to be done on them'.

Thus the 1984 Act provides compensation for injuries only. Damage to property is not covered, reflecting an understandable view that trespassers are deserving of less protection than are lawful visitors.

The occupier will only owe a duty under s.1(3) if (s)he:

'(a) … is aware of the danger or has reasonable grounds to believe it exists;

(b) … knows or … believes the other is in the vicinity of the danger; and

(c) the risk is one against which … he may be expected to offer … some protection.'

The character of the duty owed is, by s.1(4), to 'take such care as is reasonable in all the circumstances …' to prevent injury to the non-visitor.

So the standard of care is an objective negligence standard. What is required of the occupier depends on the circumstances of each case. The greater the degree of risk the more precautions the occupier will have to take. Factors to be taken into account include the nature of the premises, the degree of danger, the practicality of taking precautions, and of course the age of the trespasser.

7.4.12 AVOIDING THE DUTY IN THE 1984 ACT

Again, as with the 1957 Act, it is possible for the occupier to avoid liability.

Under s.1(5) the occupier could do so by taking 'such steps as are reasonable in all the circumstances …'. This might, in the case of adult trespassers, be achieved by use of effective warnings.

> ### WESTWOOD V THE POST OFFICE (1973)
>
> A notice that 'Only the authorised attendant is permitted to enter' placed on the door of a motor room was held a sufficient warning for an intelligent adult.

But again it is unlikely that such warnings will succeed in the case of children.

Section 1(6) also preserves the defence of *volenti*. Again the claimant must appreciate the nature and degree of the risk, not merely be aware of its existence.

There is no reference to exclusions in the Act. It is argued that exclusions should be impossible since the Act creates a minimum standard of care which would then be thwarted. However, this then creates the unhappy situation where a trespasser might be entitled to more care than a lawful visitor.

7.5 LIABILITY FOR ANIMALS

7.5.1 INTRODUCTION

Liability for animals stretches as far back as medieval times. Such liability developed for two reasons. Firstly, livestock in particular at that time was a major source of wealth and may have been crucial to survival so attitudes to straying livestock were very different. Secondly, though animals are personal property, they have always been placed in a separate category of civil liability because they are mobile and 'have a will of their own'.

The common law originally provided two basic actions in respect of animals:

● A scienter action. This was an action for knowingly keeping a dangerous animal that escaped and caused damage. The animal could be of a dangerous species or if not it might have dangerous characteristics known to its keeper.

● Cattle trespass. This was an action in respect of cattle or similar animals that strayed and caused damage.

In both actions liability was strict. This was justified on two levels. Firstly, in the case of dangerous

SELF ASSESSMENT QUESTIONS

1 Who exactly is a visitor?

2 What sorts of people are non-visitors?

3 What decides whether a person is an occupier?

4 Why should children have a different duty of care applied to them?

5 When will a tradesman be able to successfully sue an occupier?

6 How can an occupier avoid being liable to a lawful visitor?

7 Is it possible for an occupier to legitimately protect against intruders?

8 Does the 'duty of common humanity' and the duty owed to trespassers under the 1984 Act differ at all?

9 What difficulties are created by the minimum standard of care in the 1984 Act?

activity

PROBLEM SITUATIONS

Alsopp Towers is a large pleasure theme park. At the entrance gate there is a sign which reads 'All of the rides are dangerous and customers enter entirely at their own risk'. Using your understanding of the rules on Occupiers' Liability, consider the liability of Alsopp Towers in the case of the four claimants below:

A Jasbir catches her heel in a gap between the boards while getting off 'The Screw', falls several feet, and injures herself badly.

B Sean, who is a delivery driver, leaves his lorry to pick flowers from one of the ornamental borders and tears his shoe and sock and cuts his foot quite badly on broken glass.

C Pedro, an electrical contractor who is repairing one of the rides, is electrocuted and badly burnt when Daisy, who operates the ride, carelessly plugs it in.

D Tom and Jerry, two ten-year-old boys, have sneaked in by climbing over a fence. They are both injured when they walk across the rails on one of the rides and are hit by one of the cars.

animals, it was only fair that the keeper should be expected to be liable for any damage caused. That is the risk of keeping dangerous animals. Secondly, in the case of trespassing livestock, it was sensible to keep the dispute within the community rather than a further recourse to law.

Whatever liability formerly existed has now been replaced by the Animals Act 1971 which retains

KEY FACTS

- Occupiers' Liability is covered by two Acts: The Occupiers' Liability Act 1957 in the case of lawful 'visitors', and the Occupiers' Liability Act 1984 in the case of trespassers
- An 'occupier' is anybody in actual control of the land – *Wheat* v *Lacon* (1966)
- Premises is widely defined and has included even a ladder – *Wheeler* v *Copas* (1981)
- By s.2(1) 1957 Act a 'common duty of care' is owed to all lawful visitors
- By s.2(2) the duty is to ensure that the visitor is safe for the purposes of the visit
- Under s.2(3) an occupier must take extra care for children, who are less careful than adults, and not put extra danger in their path – *Glasgow Corporation* v *Taylor* (1922)
- Although it is assumed that parents should keep control of young children – *Phipps* v *Rochester Corporation* (1955)
- A person carrying out a trade or calling on the occupier's premises must prepare for the risks associated with the trade – *Roles* v *Nathan* (1963)
- The occupier will not be liable for damage which is the result of work done by independent contractors if it is reasonable to entrust the work; a reputable contractor is chosen; the occupier is not obliged to inspect the work – *Haseldine* v *Daw* (1941)
- It is possible to avoid liability where:
  – adequate warnings are given – *Rae* v *Mars* (1990)
  – exclusion clauses can be relied on – subject to the Unfair Contract Terms Act (1977)
  – consent or contributory negligence apply
- A common duty of humanity is owed to trespassers – *BR Board* v *Herrington* (1972)
- By the Occupiers' Liability Act 1984 this is only in respect of personal injury or death

FIGURE 7.4 *Key fact chart for occupiers' liability*

the essentials of both of the above torts. It is still possible to sue under different types of liability where the Act does not in fact apply.

Although actions involving animals are rare that is not to say that the damage caused by animals is also rare. The Pearson Committee in 1978 for instance found that animals are responsible for up to 50,000 injuries annually.

7.5.2 COMMON LAW ACTIONS

Although actions involving animals would most likely be brought under the Animals Act, if the ingredients of a tort are met by the situation in question then it is clearly possible to use that tort to seek compensation for the wrong suffered. A variety of actions illustrate this point.

Trespass to goods

MANTON V BROCKLEBANK (1923)

A defendant who taught his dog to steal golf balls was liable under this tort.

Trespass to land

LEAGUE AGAINST CRUEL SPORTS LTD V SCOTT (1985)

A keeper of foxhounds was liable for allowing the hounds to trespass onto the land owned by another person.

Private nuisance

RAPIER V LONDON TRAMWAYS CO. (1893)

The owner of horses that created 'foul stenches' was liable to neighbours in private nuisance.

Rylands *v* Fletcher

BRADY V WARREN (1900)

The keeper of a captive fox was liable when he allowed it to escape and it caused damage.

Defamation

It has been suggested that if an owner of a parrot or similar creature taught it to repeat defamatory remarks that were then overheard then this could create liability on the owner.

Trespass to the person

It has also been suggested that a party who taught animals to attack another party could be liable for assault and battery.

Negligence

Perhaps more importantly than most of these, because it may have more widespread application, an action is possible in negligence for a failure to control an animal where there is a foreseeable risk of it causing harm.

GOMBERG V SMITH (1962)

An owner of a dog who failed to control it was liable for the damage caused when the dog bolted across the road on a dangerous bend.

This will be particularly so where the owner knows of the characteristics of the animal that are likely to result in harm.

BIRCH V MILLS (1995)

A farm manager was liable for injuries done by a herd of Charolais cattle in an unfenced field. The cows were known to be frisky and, since they chased dogs, it was likely they would injure anyone walking close by.

Negligence is in any case particularly useful and appropriate in dealing with non-dangerous species where, under the Animals Act, liability will only result if the keeper knows of the animal's dangerous characteristic, so that there may often be no statutory cause of action.

DRAPER V HODDER (1972)

A child was savaged by a pack of Jack Russell terriers that were rushing from their owner's house next door. They had never acted this way before, so there could be no liability under the Act. However, this breed characteristically attacks in packs so there was foreseeable risk of harm and negligence.

So a keeper of animals has a duty to guard against foreseeable risks.

SMITH V PRENDERGAST (1984)

A scrapyard owner was liable for an attack by a stray Alsatian that had been in his yard for three weeks. While the dog had done nothing vicious up to the point of the attack the owner of the scrapyard had done nothing to remove it or to control it.

It is also always possible for a party to bring an action in more than one tort.

PITCHER V MARTIN (1937)

A dog owner was liable in both negligence and public nuisance when his dog tripped and injured a pedestrian while it was chasing a cat.

7.5.3 THE ANIMALS ACT 1971

In determining when to fix liability the Act distinguishes between animals of a dangerous species, *ferae naturae*, and species which are domesticated or ordinarily not dangerous, *mansuetae naturae*.

Dangerous species

Under s.6(2) of the Act a dangerous species is one:

(a) Which is not commonly domesticated in the British Isles.

(b) *Whose fully grown animals have such characteristics that they are likely, unless restrained, to cause severe damage or that any damage they may cause is likely to be severe.'*

What is dangerous then is a question of law rather than fact.

> **BEHRENS V BERTRAM MILLS CIRCUS LTD (1957)**
>
> When a circus elephant injured the claimant it was irrelevant that the animal was said to be as docile as a domestic cow. It was still classed as dangerous under the previous common law and would be so now under the Act.

This means that under s.6(2) a species may be classed as dangerous even though it is ordinarily classed as domestic in its country of origin.

> **TUTIN V CHIPPERFIELD PROMOTIONS LTD (1980)**
>
> A camel was classed as dangerous under the Act although it would ordinarily be a means of transport and beast of burden in its country of origin.

Very few animals that are natives of the British Isles would be likely to satisfy the test in s.6(2)(b). Therefore the provision applies mainly to imported animals.

This subsection also offers alternative tests – likely to cause severe damage, or damage caused is likely to be severe – so it can include animals such as the elephant in *Behrens* that because of its size could cause harm.

According to s.2(1), the duty in respect of such animals lies on any 'keeper'. Keeper is defined in s.6(3) as a person who:

(a) ... owns the animal or has it in his possession; or

(b) ... is head of a household of which a member under the age of sixteen owns the animal or has it in his possession.'

So it is possible for there to be more than one keeper at any time, and the Act makes for example a parent responsible for the animals kept by his or her children. So a claimant may have a choice of people to sue.

Under the Dangerous Wild Animals Act 1976 keepers of dangerous species of animals are required to be licensed by the local authority to keep the animal and are also required to carry third party insurance.

Non-dangerous species

The duty owed in respect of species that are not classed as dangerous is contained in s.2(2) and is much more complex. There are three characteristics identified in the subsection and all must be demonstrated for a successful claim. The keeper will be liable if:

'(a) *the damage is of a kind likely to be caused by the animal if unrestrained, or if caused by that type of animal is likely to be severe; and*

(b) *the likelihood of the damage being caused or being severe is due to characteristics peculiar to the animal in question – which are either not common to that species or only common to that species at particular times; and*

(c) *the particular characteristics of the animal causing the damage were known to the keeper, a servant of the keeper, or a person under sixteen who is the keeper and a member of the keeper's household.'*

The subsection obviously creates problems for interpretation and the correct approach is to consider each part in turn according to Lord Justice Start-Smith in *Curtis* v *Betts* (1990).

Section 2(2)(a) then is widely stated. It inevitably points to breeds of dogs that, for instance because of their size, if they should bite or attack people are likely to cause severe damage even if they are breeds that do not commonly attack.

This might include the bites of particular breeds such as an Alsatian in *Cummings* v *Grainger*

(1977) and a Bull Mastiff in *Curtis* v *Betts* (1990). It could also include infectious animals.

While the kind of damage caused should be likely, the way in which it is caused is not necessarily important.

SMITH V AINGER (1990)

The claimant's leg was broken when the defendant's dog attacked his own dog.

Section 2(2)(b) identifies the causal link between the damage and the characteristics of the animal causing it. There can be no liability if the damage was not due to the characteristics in question.

JAUNDRILL V GILLETT (1996)

The keeper of horses that had been released onto a highway by a stranger acting in malice was not liable to a motorist who was injured in collision with the horses. CA held that the real reason for the damage was the release of the horses. It was doubted whether horses panicking because they were loose on a road at night amounted to an abnormal characteristic rather than just abnormal circumstances.

The subsection also draws distinctions between permanent and temporary characteristics, and between the animal in question and its breed or species.

In this way, while we would accept that dogs in general do not attack people there would be liability for a dog that regularly did attack people or for one that attacked people at certain times or in certain circumstances.

An example of the first point could be *Smith* v *Ainger* (1990) where the dog in question was known for regularly attacking other dogs.

Examples of the latter point might include a bitch that was known to attack to protect her litter. It might also include dogs left freely to roam to act as guard dogs in the event of anyone intruding on the premises.

CUMMINGS V GRAINGER (1977)

An owner of a scrapyard allowed an untrained Alsatian to roam free at night. The dog savaged a woman who entered with her boyfriend who worked there. The circumstance in which the dog would attack was when being used as a guard dog.

By s.2(2)(b) the knowledge of the animal's characteristics required of the keeper is actual knowledge. It is not sufficient that the keeper ought to have known. If (s)he did not know then there can be no liability under the Act, though there may be liability in negligence if the damage is foreseeable, as we have already seen with the Jack Russells in *Draper* v *Hodder* (1972).

Defences

Available defences are provided by s.5 of the Act. Under s.5(1) the keeper of the animal is not liable for any damage suffered which is 'due wholly to the fault of the person suffering it'.

SYLVESTER V CHAPMAN LTD (1935)

There was no liability on the keeper for injuries sustained by the claimant who had entered a leopard's pen to recover a lighted cigarette.

By s.5(2) there will be no liability either in respect of a person who has voluntarily accepted the risk of some harm caused by the animal.

CUMMINGS V GRAINGER (1977)

Here the girl had entered the scrapyard knowing that the dog was dangerous. In fact she admitted that she was frightened of the dog.

By s.5(3) a keeper will not be liable to a trespasser if (s)he can prove either that the animal was not kept for the purposes of protecting people or property or, if it was, that it was not unreasonable to do so. In *Cummings* v *Grainger* for instance it was not considered unreasonable to have a guard dog in a scrapyard in the East End of London. This point is in any case quali-

activity

QUICK QUIZ

In the following instances suggest whether and why the animal in question would fall under the Act as a dangerous species, or as a non-dangerous species, or not fall under the Act at all:

1 Jeff, aged 15, has a pet hamster that regularly bites his friends when they hold it or stroke it.

2 Jasvinder owns a cat that has just had its first litter of kittens. The cat scratches Raj when she goes to pick up one of the kittens.

3 Ali owns an Anaconda that he allows to roam freely round his house.

4 Ernie, a postman, takes his pet Rotweiler with him on his round to exercise it. Ernie's dog bites another dog on the round one day, though it has never fought with or attacked any animal before.

5 Lucretia keeps a herd of goats for milk. One day one of the goats kicks the boy who is delivering the newspaper.

fied by the Guard Dog Act 1975 and 1995 which require a guard dog to be under the control of a handler at all times and which impose criminal sanctions for non-compliance.

Contributory negligence is also possible under the Act as identified in s.10 and if a plea is accepted then damages will be reduced accordingly.

Trespassing livestock

The Act abolishes the former action of 'cattle trespass' and replaces it with a new statutory action under s.4. The owner of livestock that strays onto the land in the ownership or possession of another is liable for any damage done by the livestock or for reasonable expenses incurred in keeping the animal until it can be returned to the owner.

The section specifies physical damage and reasonable expenses so that claims for personal injury would be bought under s.2(2).

Livestock is defined in s.11, the interpretation section. The definition includes cattle, horses, asses, mules, hinnies, sheep, pigs, goats and poultry, and deer that are not wild, and pheasants, partridges and grouse in captivity. So this is a wide group of animals.

There are a number of defences available under the Act. Under s.5(1) a person is again not liable if the damage was wholly the fault of the party suffering it. Again under s.10 damages can be apportioned if a claim of contributory negligence is accepted.

Older defences are also preserved. A person will not be liable where the livestock strayed from the highway and its presence on the highway was lawful, in other words for passage from one place to another. What is considered lawful is a question of fact in each case.

MATTHEWS V WICKS (1987)

Sheep allowed to roam free on the highway damaged the claimant's garden. This was held to be an unlawful use of the highway and so the owner of the sheep was liable. This contrasts with older attitudes that damage from straying livestock was a natural consequence of living next to the highway.

The owner of livestock may still owe a duty of care in negligence so that an action of some sort is still possible.

Section 5(6) identifies that there is no general duty to fence land to keep livestock in or out. So an owner of livestock will not have a defence merely because it was possible for the other party to avoid the damage by fencing the land. However, if there is an obligation to fence land arising from custom, easements or contract, then there may be a defence if the other party has failed in that duty.

Under s.7 there are powers to detain and even sell livestock that has strayed onto land. The section in effect replaces the old remedy of 'distress damage feasant'. The person on whose land the livestock has strayed must notify the police within 48 hours. They may also detain the animal until compensated for damage or expenses of keeping the animal until it is collected are paid under s.4. After 14 days the animal may also be sold at public auction and the damages or expenses under s.4 recovered, the remainder being passed on to the owner. The person detaining the animal, of course, must properly feed and maintain it.

Liability for injury to livestock caused by dogs

Under s.3 of the Act the owner of a dog that kills or injures livestock is liable for that damage. There is no requirement to show any abnormal characteristics of the dog in question, so in this sense livestock is given a greater degree of protection than people are.

The normal defence under s.5(1) is available, that the damage was wholly the cause of the owner of the livestock. Contributory negligence can also be pleaded under s.10. It may also be a defence under s.5(4) that the livestock killed or injured had strayed onto the land of the dog owner, and the dog was therefore entitled to be on the land.

Owners of livestock are entitled to protection from dogs that kill or injure their livestock and

so under s.9 it is lawful to kill or injure such dogs to protect livestock in certain circumstances:

- The person harming the dog must be entitled to act for the protection of the livestock.
- The dog must be 'worrying' or about to 'worry' the livestock, or has already done so and has not left the vicinity and there is no way of ascertaining who owns the dog.
- There must be no other way of dealing with the situation.
- The person harming the dog must then report it to the police within 48 hours.

Animals straying onto the highway

Prior to the passing of the Act there was no particular liability for animals that strayed onto the highway. This was in the past seen as an inevitability in a rural community. The Act abolishes any immunity from liability that might have existed formerly in the common law. Under s.8 there is now a duty of care and therefore liability in negligence.

Liability is, however, limited by s.8(2). A person will not be liable merely for placing an animal on unfenced land and allowing it to stray provided that: (a) the land is common, or fencing is customarily not required, or the land is a town green or village green; and (b) (s)he had a right to place the animal there.

Any duty that exists is inevitably only to do what is reasonable. So it would not be reasonable, for instance, to require someone to fence a moor.

It is easier to prove now whether a person has a right to graze animals freely. The Registration of Commons Act 1971 required that everyone entitled to such use of common land was to register the right or lose it.

Remoteness of damage

This issue is not dealt with in the Act as the ordinary principles of negligence will apply.

activity

SELF ASSESSMENT QUESTIONS

1 How limited was the law on animals prior to the passing of the Animals Act 1971?

2 When will it be particularly appropriate to bring an action under negligence for damage caused by animals?

3 Why does the law distinguish between dangerous and non-dangerous species of animals?

4 In what ways is the distinction a sensible one?

5 What happens if my Golden Retriever bites someone and has never done so before?

6 Would the answer be different if my dog was an Alsatian left guarding my property?

7 How would the law deal with an animal that gave somebody a disease?

8 Why has the law on animals straying onto the highway been completely reversed by the Act?

KEY FACTS

- The common law originally provided strict liability actions for damage caused by dangerous species of animals and for damage caused by straying livestock

- These have now been replaced by the Animals Act 1971

- Though it is possible to bring actions under many other torts, e.g. negligence – *Draper* v *Hodder* (1972)

- The Animals Act draws a distinction between 'dangerous species' and 'non-dangerous' species

- A dangerous species is one not domesticated in the UK and which is likely to cause severe damage unless restrained – s.6(2)

- A keeper of such an animal is liable for all the damage it causes

- A keeper of a non-dangerous animal will only be liable if: damage is likely if the animal is unrestrained, or damage is likely to be severe; because of characteristics not normally associated with the species, or only at specific times or in specific circumstances; and these characteristics were known to the keeper

- It may particularly apply to guard dogs and large dogs – *Cummings* v *Grainger* (1977)

- Defences under s.5 include consent, damage caused wholly by the claimant's own fault and contributory negligence

- Section 4 of the Act also provides an action for damage caused by straying livestock

- Under s.3 there is also an action for livestock killed by dogs, including the right to kill the dog in some circumstances to protect the livestock

- Under s.8 there is also a limited duty to prevent livestock from straying onto the highway

FIGURE 7.5 *Key fact chart for liability for animals*

Section 2(2), however, states that the keeper is liable for 'any damage'. This suggests the test is one of direct consequences rather than foreseeable damage.

Animals are taken to have several features in common with the tort of *Rylands* v *Fletcher* (1868), and indeed the damage caused is often due to their 'escape'. The tort was specifically excluded in the foreseeability test in the *Wagon Mound (No. 1)* (1961), which tends to reinforce the point.

Damage caused by non-dangerous species under s.2(2) of the Act is limited to such damage as is the result of unusual characteristics known to the keeper.

CHAPTER 8

TORTS AFFECTING CIVIL LIBERTIES

8.1 TRESPASS TO THE PERSON

8.1.1 THE ORIGINS AND CHARACTER OF TRESPASS

Trespass is as old as the English legal system itself. The word trespass most literally comes from the Latin *trans* (meaning through) and *passus* (meaning a step). So its most natural connections are with land.

Ever since biblical times, however, the term has been used quite generally to indicate an 'interference'. So an action for trespass traditionally was an action about an infringement of personal rights whether over land, personal property, or personal security and liberty.

It is not difficult to see how and why trespass to the person developed. In medieval times a person might be subject to all sorts of personal interference from footpads, highwaymen, robbers and burglars. There were no sophisticated, separate systems of civil and criminal law, and no organised police force to enforce the law. Victims of wrongs might have little choice other than to bring actions themselves under writs of trespass to protect themselves from attack, or to ensure their liberty.

One of the key characteristics of trespass is that it is actionable per se. This means that the claimant is not obliged to show that damage has been caused. So in this case it is sufficient to show that the trespass has taken place.

Traditionally, then, a trespass only occurred if it was the direct consequence of the defendant's positive act. Omissions are not covered by trespass. If an action arose indirectly from the defendant's act then a claimant would need to bring an action 'on the case' and show damage. These days the appropriate action for the latter would be in negligence.

Trespass to the person can be committed in one of three ways, as Figure 8.1 shows.

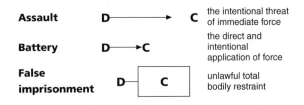

FIGURE 8.1 *The various types of trespass to the person*

Interestingly all three are also represented in the criminal law. This is possibly inevitable since it is of no great comfort to the injured victim of a serious assault that his or her attacker has been punished under the criminal law when compensation might be needed. The use of the Criminal Injuries Compensation scheme is available in modern times, but an action in tort is still available.

While the basic elements of all three are similar, in both tort and crime defences might differ in their application. For example, consent is a common defence in the case of sporting injuries in claims in tort, but is unavailable in certain circumstances in crime.

R v Brown and Others (1993)

In this case HL prevented sadomasochists from using consent as a defence when they inflicted on each other various harm and wounding in order to heighten their sexual pleasure.

8.1.2 Assault

It is not uncommon for assault to be mistaken for battery, and indeed in the criminal law the distinctions between the two things are more blurred.

The older view of assault was that it was merely an incomplete battery. Certainly there is no requirement for any physical contact for an assault to have occurred, and the claimant need not have suffered any harm.

I de S et Ux v W de S (1348)

W, in attempting to break into I's inn, swung his axe at her and missed. There was still liability for an assault.

The modern view, however, is that the tort requires intention also.

Letang v Cooper (1965)

Here the claimant was sunbathing on a verge by a car park. The defendant ran over her legs injuring her. There was direct harm caused by the defendant's negligence, but there was no intention.

So a more accurate definition, from Baker on *Tort*, might now be that

'a person commits assault where he intentionally and directly causes the claimant to apprehend that he is to be the victim of a battery …'

The intention involved is the intention to create apprehension or fear in the claimant, not as to what the defendant will actually do. So, in effect, it does not matter whether the defendant will inflict violence or not or indeed whether there is any contact with the other party at all.

Blake v Barnard (1840)

The defendant pointed a gun at the claimant causing reasonable apprehension of an imminent battery. The gun was in fact unloaded so that, even if he had fired, the defendant could not have harmed the claimant. There was still an actionable assault because the claimant was put in fear.

It is generally accepted, however, that an assault does require some form of active behaviour, so that a passive state is insufficient for an action.

Innes v Wylie (1844)

There was no assault where a policeman merely stood at a door and barred the claimant's entry.

Threatening behaviour can amount to an assault, provided that it includes some form of action.

Read v Coker (1853)

The claimant owed the defendant rent. When the defendant told the claimant to leave the premises the claimant refused. The defendant then ordered some of his employees to see the claimant off the premises. These men then surrounded the claimant, rolled their sleeves up and told him that if he did not leave they would break his neck. There was an assault.

Where there is an attempt to commit a battery but this is thwarted or prevented then it may still amount to an assault if the party threatened is put in fear of a possible battery.

Stephens v Myers (1830)

At a political meeting the defendant tried to attack the claimant, a speaker. He was prevented from doing so since he was apprehended as he launched himself towards the claimant. There was still an assault present in the attack.

Words

Whether or not words on their own can amount to an assault is more problematic. The traditional view was straightforwardly that they could not.

On the other hand it is always possible for words on their own to show that there is no assault.

TUBERVILLE V SAVAGE (1669)

There was no assault in this case because the words used showed that the claimant should not fear an impending battery. In an argument the defendant did actually handle his sword and said: 'If it were not Assize time I would not take such language from you'. Clearly the defendant had no intention to harm the claimant at that time so he could not be put in fear of personal violence.

However, there are circumstances where little more than a mere threat can be taken to be assault. In *Read* v *Coker* the men did little more than issue the threat. In the contract case *Barton* v *Armstrong* (1975) a threat of violence made over the telephone was accepted as leading to a possible cause of action since it could lead to immediate apprehension that it would be carried out. In recent criminal law cases, *R* v *Ireland*, and *R* v *Burstow*, silent telephone calls have been held to amount to actual bodily harm. So there is possibly some room for development on this point.

Nevertheless, it is generally taken that, whatever constitutes the assault, it must cause the claimant fear of impending violence of some kind.

SMITH V SUPERINTENDENT OF WOKING (1983)

It was accepted as a criminal assault when Smith entered the grounds of a private house and appeared at the bedroom window of a bed-sit, seriously frightening the occupant.

8.1.3 BATTERY

Battery in some ways should be the most straightforward form of the tort of trespass to the person since in its purest form it is the unlawful application of force. However, this is not always a satisfactory definition since it ignores those areas where no force as such is applied, notably in medicine.

Winfield traditionally argued that technically the 'ordinary collisions of life …' also amount to batteries. This would create impossible difficulties in a busy, modern, urban environment. For instance, a brief journey on the London Tube in the rush hour would result in countless batteries. Public policy and recent case law suggests that we need to show more than the 'ordinary collisions' to bring an action for battery.

A better definition, again from Baker on *Tort*, may be

'Where the defendant, intending the result, does an act which directly and physically affects the person of the claimant.'

Intention

Intention is in some ways a fairly recent development.

FOWLER V LANNING (1953)

The defendant had shot the claimant. The claimant, possibly acting under the mistaken belief that battery had traditionally operated as a tort of strict liability, merely referred in his claim to the fact that he had been shot. The appeal judge confirmed that no cause of action had been revealed in the statement of claim, since the claimant was obliged also to demonstrate either intention or negligence on the part of the defendant.

Direct

A modern development of the principle has been to replace the traditional distinction between direct and indirect interference with a distinction instead between intentional application of force and negligent application.

LETANG V COOPER (1965)

A woman was sunbathing in the grounds of a hotel near to where cars were parked. The defendant reversed over her legs injuring her. While there was no intention to hurt her, there was direct harm caused by the defendant's negligent act. The woman's claim in fact failed because it fell outside the limitation period for negligence. Lord Denning felt that there was no overlap between trespass and negligence, but Lord Diplock felt that there could be.

At times the courts have taken a fairly liberal view of what is and is not direct.

SCOTT V SHEPHERD (1773)

Shepherd was found liable for battery when he had thrown a lighted firework into a market. The firework had then been picked up and thrown by two further people before it exploded near to Scott, injuring him.

There are also instances of battery where the application of force can be said to be indirect rather than direct.

GIBBONS V PEPPER (1695)

A horse was whipped so that it bolted. It then ran down the claimant. The defendant who had whipped the horse was found liable for the claimant's injuries in battery.

But where the battery is not direct it can be shown to be negligent.

NASH V SHEEN (1953)

A woman went to the hairdresser's having asked for a 'permanent wave'. Instead she was given a 'tone rinse'. This caused her hair to change colour quite unpleasantly and it also caused a painful rash all over her body. The hairdresser was liable for battery.

In this way it is generally thought that only positive actions can amount to a battery and an omission would not presumably lead to liability.

Hostility

Hostility is another fairly recent requirement of the tort although it does have some foundation in tradition in Chief Justice Holt's judgment in *Cole* v *Turner*: 'The least touching of another in anger is a battery'.

The issue of hostility has been a recent focus because of some of the difficult circumstances in which a judge may be required to determine whether or not there is a battery.

WILSON V PRINGLE (1987)

The claimant, a 13-year-old boy, suffered injuries to his hip when a school friend played a practical joke on him. The court, referring to *Cole* v *Turner* (1704), held that hostility was a necessary element of an actionable battery.

Nevertheless, this position seems to be out of step with the previous presumed position that, subject to the everyday brushes of life, any intentional unwanted contact could amount to a battery. It also seems at odds with certain established practices in specific circumstances.

COLLINS V WILCOCK (1984)

A police officer was liable for a battery when he took hold of a suspect's arm but did not arrest her. Lord Goff here felt that the appropriate test was whether or not the contact was acceptable within the conduct of ordinary daily life.

Medical treatment and battery

Medical treatment with few exceptions is dependent on the consent of the patient. Medical treatment that exceeds the consent given by the patient then has always been seen as technically at least a battery.

IN RE F (MENTAL PATIENT: STERILISATION) (1990)

A woman in a mental institution, with a mental age of 4 or 5, had become sexually active with another inmate. Since other forms of contraception were considered unacceptable in the circumstances, the doctors applied to the court for a compulsory sterilisation, in the interests of the patient. The treatment was allowed because it was in the patient's best interests. However, Lord Goff confirmed the principle in the last case.

Consent will be invalid and treatment may amount to a battery where the patient is not broadly aware of the type of treatment that is to be given.

CHATTERTON V GERSON (1981)

Here, in an operation for a hernia, the patient's leg was rendered numb following an injection for a trapped nerve. She claimed that she suffered a battery because she had not been informed of the potential consequences of the injection. She failed because that court accepted that she had been informed in broad terms of the purpose of the injection.

Where the patient has been informed of the existence of the risks of treatment without full briefing on the full extent of the possible risk this will not be a battery either.

SIDAWAY V GOVERNORS OF BETHLEM ROYAL & MAUDSLEY HOSPITALS (1985)

Here where Mrs Sidaway was rendered paralysed following the operation there was no viable claim that she had not consented, having not been fully informed of the potential consequences of the risk. The court accepted that there was no doctrine of informed consent.

Generally, in any case, a patient complaining about medical treatment is more likely to bring an action in negligence according to the principles in *Bolam* v *Friern Hospital Management Committee* (1957).

Defences to assault and battery

There are a number of possible defences.

Volenti non fit injuria – consent

As we have just seen, a doctor will always try to avoid liability by means of consent to treatment.

Consent is also commonly available as a defence to sporting injuries, but only where the injury occurs within the proper bounds of the sporting activity.

SIMMS V LEIGH RUGBY FOOTBALL CLUB (1969)

A broken leg resulted from a tackle during a rugby game. Rugby is a quite dangerous contact sport and it was accepted that, as a professional rugby player, the claimant had accepted the normal risks of the activity.

Of course, by definition this means that injuries arising from foul and therefore unlawful play are not consented to and are actionable.

CONDON V BASI (1985)

In an amateur game an unlawful challenge did give rise to an action.

Necessity

Providing that the trespass is for the prevention of a greater harm then there will be a defence to any action.

LEIGH V GLADSTONE (1909)

Suffragettes in prison were force-fed while on hunger strike. This was allowable because it was to prevent their deaths.

Self defence

A person is entitled by law to protect himself or herself, another person or even property. However, the defence will only succeed where the force used is reasonable in all the circumstances.

LANE V HOLLOWAY (1968)

Neighbours enjoyed a fairly poor relationship. When one came home drunk and rowdy one night he was told to be quiet by the woman next door. He replied 'Shut up, you monkey faced tart', which led to an altercation between him and the woman's husband. He made a friendly and ineffectual shove at the husband who then beat him in the face so that he required 18 stitches. This attack was out of proportion to the gestures of the drunken man.

This principle may apply even where a person is dealing with a trespasser to his or her land.

REVILL V NEWBURY (1996)

It was not reasonable force where a person, through a hole in his shed, shot a trespasser to his allotment.

Parental chastisement

This, if done reasonably, has traditionally been a good defence. However, it may not have survived the Children Act 1989.

Inevitable accident

If the alleged battery is beyond the control of the defendant then there will be no liability in trespass.

> ### STANLEY V POWELL (1891)
>
> A beater was shot during a grouse shoot. It was inevitable accident because it was shown that the man was not shot directly. The bullet ricocheted off a tree before it hit him.

Lawful ejectment of a trespasser and lawful arrest

These are both possible defences.

Touching to gain atention

In general the ordinary touches of life give no rise to an action so that touching to gain attention is another possible defence.

8.1.4 FALSE IMPRISONMENT

The tort is committed where the defendant intentionally imposes a total restraint on the liberty and free movement of the claimant. The term 'false' is a bit misleading since in this context it means wrongful or unlawful.

In modern circumstances it is most usually associated with wrongful arrests and detention by the police or by people such as store detectives and security guards.

There is no requirement for actual imprisonment either. However, there must be total bodily restraint of whatever type.

> ### BIRD V JONES (1845)
>
> Bird wished to cross Hammersmith Bridge. The footpath was closed and cordoned off for people to watch a regatta and he was invited to return the way he had come. Since there was a way of him getting away there was no unlawful restraint and no actionable trespass.

In this way an action will fail wherever there is a reasonable means of escape which is open to the claimant to use.

> ### WRIGHT V WILSON (1699)
>
> Here escape from the alleged tortfeaser was available though it meant trespassing on someone else's land. It was held that that was sufficient to prevent liability.

The restraint must be direct. Nevertheless, if it is not an action in negligence may still be available.

> ### SAYERS V HARLOW URBAN DISTRICT COUNCIL (1958)
>
> Mrs Sayers became locked in the lavatory because the lock on the door jammed. This was negligence on the council's part rather than false imprisonment.

It has been suggested *in obiter* in *Murray* v *Minister of Defence* (1988) that there may be a false imprisonment even though the claimant is unconscious at the time. It is certainly the case that a false imprisonment can occur without the claimant being aware of it.

> ### MEERING V GRAHAM WHITE AVIATION (1919)
>
> The claimant was being questioned in relation to thefts from his employer. Unknown to him two men were posted at the door to prevent him from leaving. This was a false imprisonment.

It is not a false imprisonment merely because in the circumstances the claimant is obliged to pay for his release, providing there has already been a voluntary agreement to that effect.

> ### ROBINSON V BALMAIN NEW FERRY (1910)
>
> The claimant had entered an enclosed wharf from which the ferry sailed. He was obliged to pay a penny to enter and a penny to exit at the other side. When he had missed the ferry he changed his mind and wished to exit. The gate manager would not allow him to without paying a penny which he refused to do. This was not a false imprisonment.

In a similar way, there is no false imprisonment where an employer has a legitimate expectation that his employee will stay till the end of a shift and will not provide the worker with the means of leaving earlier.

HERD V WEARDALE STEEL, COAL AND COKE CO. (1915)

Miners already down a mine, but towards the start of their shift, decided that what they were being asked to do was too dangerous and asked to be returned in the cages to the surface. There was no false imprisonment when the employer refused since the men had already contracted to stay down the mine for a specific time and the employer was not obliged to use the lift until that time came.

It will be a false imprisonment to detain a person wrongly who has committed only a civil offence.

SUNBOLF V ALFORD (1838)

It was false imprisonment where a landlord wrongly detained his lodger for not paying the rent.

It will also be a false imprisonment to detain a prisoner past the proper date for his release – *Cowell* v *Corrective Services Commissioner* (1989).

Defences
Consent
This is again available. It may apply, for instance, where a lawyer is locked in the cell with his client for confidential consultation.

Mistaken arrest
This is only available as a defence to the police. It can also only apply where the officer has acted reasonably in the circumstances.

Lawful arrest
Powers of arrest differ between the police and the public generally, the latter being known as 'citizens' arrest'. This is important to store detectives who have no special powers of arrest. The police can generally arrest on suspicion, where the public can only arrest where they are sure that an arrestable offence has been or is being committed.

The arrest in any case must be effected with reasonable force.

TREADAWAY V CHIEF CONSTABLE OF WEST MIDLANDS (1994)

Medical evidence supported the claimant's allegation that while police were interviewing him they placed a bag over his head and threatened to suffocate him.

HSU V COMMISSIONER OF POLICE OF THE METROPOLIS (1996)

A hairdresser refused to allow police with a warrant to enter his house. He was grabbed, punched, kicked, and verbally abused and found to have blood in his urine. This would not be reasonable force.

The person being detained must also be informed of the reason for their arrest – *Christie* v *Leachinsky* (1947).

In a citizen's arrest the person detained must be transported to the police or the police fetched in a reasonable time.

TIMS V JOHN LEWIS & CO. LTD (1951)

Here an employee of a store locked up suspected shoplifters for an unreasonable time.

What is an unreasonable period of detention can be a very short time.

WHITE V W. P. BROWN (1983)

There was a false imprisonment when a lady was locked in a cubicle for 15 minutes by a store detective who suspected her of shoplifting.

8.1.5 INTENTIONAL INDIRECT HARM

In some past cases it was necessary to establish a novel cause of liability where trespass was apparently unavailable. Now these cases would probably be covered by negligence.

Negligence was used in giving limited protection

to trespassers, who were traditionally beyond protection.

BIRD V HOLBRECK (1828)

A trespasser succeeded in an action against an occupier of land who had set a spring-gun which caused him injury.

It also provided a means of action before nervous shock was accepted in negligence.

WILKINSON V DOWNTON (1897)

The claimant suffered shock when the defendant told her as a joke that her husband had been seriously injured in an accident. There was no direct interference to allow the action in trespass, but there was indirect but intentional harm.

JANVIER V SWEENEY (1919)

Here the claimant was able to recover damages for the shock caused to her when the defendant told her a false story that she was wanted by police for corresponding with a German spy.

8.2 DEFAMATION

8.2.1 THE CATEGORIES OF DEFAMATION

Defamation is a tort specifically having as its purpose the protection of a person's reputation. Traditionally it could be made in one of two ways, although the distinctions are now perhaps less important than in previous times.

The two specific types are slander, originally said to be the spoken word, and libel, originally recognised as written words. Modern technology has made this distinction somewhat outdated and most other jurisdictions have now abolished it. This was indeed recommended by the Faulkes Committee, though not taken up in the Defamation Act 1996.

The important modern distinction would probably be simply between a transitory and a

activity

SELF ASSESSMENT QUESTIONS

1 What does it mean that trespass to the person is actionable per se?

2 What are the major differences between assault and battery?

3 What generally are the effects of words where an assault is claimed?

4 What sort of behaviour is required for an assault?

5 To what extent is hostility a necessary ingredient of a battery?

6 To what must a claimant have consented to give rise to a successful defence in assault or battery?

7 How is consent measured in relation to medical treatment?

8 What exactly are the ordinary everyday brushes of life?

9 Of what must store detectives and security guards beware in relation to accusations of trespass to the person?

10 What exactly amounts to a lawful arrest?

11 What degree of restraint is necessary for a false imprisonment?

12 What does the 'false' in false imprisonment mean?

activity

MULTIPLE CHOICE QUESTIONS

1 Say which of the following situations raises a possible claim of assault:

A Nigel points a gun at his friend Nawab which Nawab knows is not loaded.

B Nigel argues with Claire and tells her that he hates her.

C Nigel waves his fist at Gustav and says that if he was not so easy-going he would thump Gustav in the face.

D Nigel is badly tackled in a football match by Kevin. He runs towards Kevin, fists raised but is stopped by the referee.

2 Say which of the following situations raises a possible claim of false imprisonment:

A Sukvinder wishes to go down the High Street but is stopped by police from going down it because there is a demonstration coming the other way.

B Sukvinder is arrested, for stealing goods, by store detectives after leaving a store, informed of the arrest and taken straight to the police station.

C Nigel holds Sukvinder tightly around the waist and will not let her go till she gives him a kiss.

D Nigel locks Sukvinder in his ground-floor front room. There are no locks on the windows.

---

permanent form of making the defamatory statement. Even so the difference is not always easy to see, though there are some accepted categories relating to one or the other:

● A written defamation for instance has long been accepted as libel.

● Film has also been accepted as libel and does seem to represent a permanent form.

YOUSSOUPOFF V MGM PICTURES LTD (1934)

The suggestion in a picture about the Tsars was that Rasputin had seduced the Princess Youssoupoff. She sued successfully for libel.

● Defamatory statements made on radio or TV will be libel as a result of the Defamation Act 1952 and the Broadcasting Act 1990.

● Defamation made in a live play may be libel as a result of the Theatres Act 1968.

● An effigy made in wax or other substance can be a libel.

MONSON V TUSSAUDS LTD (1894)

A man accused of murder had been released on a 'not proven' verdict. A wax effigy of him at the entrance to the Chamber of Horrors was held to be a libel.

● Spoken words and even gestures are very easily distinguishable as slander because of their transitory nature.

● Areas that present more difficulties are things like tape recordings of live performances.

Traditionally there were two reasons why it was important to distinguish libel from slander.

KEY FACTS

- Trespass involves a direct interference with the claimant's person
- It is actionable per se so there is no need to show damage
- There are three types: assault, battery and false imprisonment
- An assault occurs where a person intentionally and directly causes another to fear that he or she is to be the victim of physical violence – *Smith* v *Superintendent of Woking* (1983)
- No actual contact is required but there must be actions, words on their own are insufficient – *Read* v *Coker* (1853)
- And there must be active behaviour – *Innes* v *Wylie* (1844)
- A prevented battery may be an assault – *Stephens* v *Myers* (1830)
- Consent, self-defence and necessity are all possible defences
- A battery is the unlawful application of force to a person
- Intention is a fairly recent requirement – *Fowler* v *Lanning* (1953)
- The force must be directly applied – compare *Nash* v *Sheen* (1953) with *Scott* v *Shepherd* (1773)
- It can also occur through negligence – *Letang* v *Cooper* (1965)
- There is conflict over whether or not hostility is a requirement – compare *Wilson* v *Pringle* (1987) with *Collins* v *Wilcock* (1984)
- Battery is important in medical treatment – medical treatment in the absence of consent is generally a battery except where there is some justification for not obtaining consent – *Re F (Mental Patient: Sterilisation)* (1990)
- Defences include: consent, provided the actual risk is consented to – *Simms* v *Leigh RFC* (1960); necessity e.g. to protect life – *Leigh* v *Gladstone* (1909); self-defence, but only where reasonable force is used – *Lane* v *Holloway* (1968)
- False imprisonment involves total restriction of movement – *Bird* v *Jones* (1845)
- It can occur even where the claimant is unaware of the restraint – *Meering* v *Graham White Aviation* (1919)
- But it is possible that the claimant is required to pay for his freedom – *Robinson* v *New Balmain Ferry Co.* (1910)
- Or that the claimant can be legitimately restrained e.g. by his employer – *Herd* v *Weardale Steel, Coal & Coke Co.* (1915)
- Defences include: consent; mistaken arrest (in the case of police officers); and lawful arrest, where the proper requirements of arrest are adhered to
- Originally it was also possible to bring some actions for indirect but intentional harm where an action in trespass would have thus proved impossible – *Wilkinson* v *Downton* (1897) and *Janvier* v *Sweeney* (1919)

FIGURE 8.2 *Key fact chart for trespass to the person*

Libel could be a crime as well as a tort

R v LEMON AND GAY NEWS (1979)

This case involved a successful prosecution for blasphemous libel for a poem likely to shock Christians.

Libel is actionable per se

That is, actual damage need not be proved, whereas in slander damage must be shown except in four situations:

- Where a criminal offence is alleged to have been committed by the person slandered.

- Where the person slandered is accused of having a contagious or socially undesirable disease.

- Where a woman is accused of being 'unchaste'. This comes from the Slander of Women Act 1891, and was clearly important in times when such an accusation might damage a woman's marriage prospects.

- Where the accusation is that a person is unfit for any office, trade, profession or calling, or indeed any employment where the claimant could be harmed as the result of the slander.

8.2.2 THE NECESSARY INGREDIENTS OF DEFAMATION

The definition of defamation

Winfield has described defamation as the 'publishing of a defamatory statement which refers to the claimant and which is made without lawful justification'. Each of these elements will need to be proved in any successful claim:

- a publication

- of a defamatory statement

- referring to the claimant.

Finally, the inclusion of lawful justification is a reference to defences, so a final qualification is the absence of an appropriate defence.

Each element of the definition can then be considered in turn.

Publication

Publication involves repeating the defamatory statement to at least one person. This will inevitably not include the person defamed since damage can only be done to his or her reputation if someone else hears the statement. In this way a letter written to the claimant containing the defamation will not be a publication where the claimant then shows it to other people.

It may well be a publication, however, where the defamation is made in a postcard because we can assume that people other than the claimant might read it. A letter addressed wrongly and then opened could be a publication.

It could also be a publication where the defendant knows that a person other than the claimant will open the letter.

> **PULLMAN V HILL (1891)**
> Here it was a publication where the defendant was aware that the secretary would open the mail.

Such a person might obviously include a spouse.

> **THEAKER V RICHARDSON (1962)**
> A member of a local council wrote to another member calling her a 'lying, low down brothel keeping whore and thief'. When the claimant's husband opened and read it there was a publication. It was reasonable to assume he might open it thinking it was an election address.

Nevertheless, it will not be a publication when a third party not authorised to do so opens a sealed letter, addressed to the claimant.

> **HUTH V HUTH (1915)**
> Here the butler opened the letter and there was no publication.

Graffiti can amount to a publication and the owners of premises liable if they fail to remove it.

> **BYRNE V DEANE (1937)**
> Police had removed an illegal gambling machine from a golf club. A poem had then appeared on a notice board that remarked 'he who gave the game away may he byrne in hell'. The claimant was clearly concerned that because of the spelling the poem was an accusation that he was the one who reported the illegal machine. There was a publication here even though for other reasons there could be no liability.

It is important to remember that each separate repeat of the defamatory statement could be a separate publication. In this way a publisher could be liable under many different actions or indeed there could be many different defendants including for instance authors, printers, publishers, and those who repeat the defamation in another context such as reviewers and their publishers, and even booksellers and distributors.

VIZETELLY V MUDIE'S SELECT LIBRARY LTD (1900)

A mobile library was liable for defamation for failing to prevent circulation of a defamatory book after receiving a warning about its content. The court accepted, however, that there could be a defence available of innocent dissemination in such circumstances if the defendants could show:

● they were unaware that the book contained defamatory material at the time they distributed it;
● there was nothing suspicious to alert them to the presence of the defamatory material;
● there was no negligence on their part.

It has, however, been held possible for a party to be liable for repetition of a defamatory statement that is reasonably foreseeable.

SLIPPER V BBC (1991)

The defendants were liable here not just for their original statements but for repeats of the defamatory statement made in reviews of the film in which they were made, and which was seen as a foreseeable consequence.

Repetitions of defamatory comments through processes such as internal mail represent a less certain possibility, and in any case may be protected by privilege.

The defamatory statement

Defamatory statement is another term requiring exact definition. This has been supplied and explained, by Lord Atkin in *Sim* v *Stretch* (1936), as meaning

'a statement which tends to lower the claimant in the minds of right-thinking members of society generally, and in particular to cause him to be regarded with feelings of hatred, contempt, ridicule, fear and disesteem...'

What amounts to a defamatory remark then depends entirely on the context in which the words appear but can inevitably include vulgar and unjustified abuse.

CORNWELL V *DAILY MAIL* (1989)

The newspaper unfairly accused an actress of 'having a big bum ... and the kind of stage presence that blocks lavatories'. This was defamatory.

It might also include derogatory remarks of any kind.

ROACH V NEWS GROUP NEWSPAPERS (1992)

An actor was accused of being as boring as the character he portrayed in *Coronation Street*. This was defamatory.

It can also include references to a person's moral character.

CHARLESTON V NEWS GROUP NEWSPAPERS (1995)

The heads of two of the stars of an Australian soap were superimposed on the near naked bodies of a couple engaged in a sexual act with the caption 'Strewth! What's Harold up to with our Madge?' The picture was potentially defamatory. However, the action did not succeed because an article about the picture being reproduced from a computer game where it was used without the stars' knowledge or consent accompanied the picture.

It will not, of course, be defamatory where the accusation is one implying decency or honesty, even if it is untrue.

BYRNE V DEAN (1937)

Here Byrne's action could not succeed because the inference in the poem was that he had done his duty as a law-abiding citizen.

Neither will a statement be defamatory where, however untrue, it only produces feelings of sympathy rather than feelings of scorn or ridicule.

GRAPPELLI V DEREK BLOCK HOLDINGS LTD (1981)

Here an article suggested that a famous jazz violinist was ill and unlikely to tour again. It was not defamatory because it would not harm his reputation.

Statements may not be defamatory on their own but become so because of their juxtaposition to other things.

MONSON V TUSSAUDS LTD (1894)

The effigy on its own did not amount to defamation but indicating its connection with other tableaux in the Chamber of Horrors did.

Innuendo

Where the statement contains a hidden or implied meaning then this may also be defamatory.

CASSIDY V DAILY MIRROR NEWSPAPERS LTD (1929)

Mrs Cassidy sued successfully when a picture was taken of her husband at the races accompanied by a young woman described in the caption as his fiancée. The implication was that Mr and Mrs Cassidy were not married which was a slur on her character and defamatory.

This is otherwise known as defamation by innuendo and it may operate even though no positive statement is made.

TOLLEY V FRY & SONS LTD (1931)

A caricature of a famous amateur golfer of the time appeared in an advertising poster for Fry's chocolate bars with a bar of chocolate sticking out of his back pocket. He was disturbed that his amateur status was compromised as a result, since by implication people would think that he had been paid.

However, such cases may require the introduction of further evidence to show how exactly the statement is defamatory.

ALLSOP V CHURCH OF ENGLAND NEWS-PAPER LTD (1972)

A broadcaster was referred to as having a 'preoccupation with the bent'. Since the word 'bent' had a number of different slang meanings as well as its normal meanings it was ambiguous in the context. The claimant was therefore required to show which meaning was being applied.

Referring to the claimant

A claimant must be able to show that the defamatory statement referred to him or her. This proves simple enough when the claimant is actually named in the statement. This is not vital, however, providing people will know that the statement is referring to the claimant.

It could be proved for instance even where fictitious names are used.

HULTON & CO. V JONES (1910)

A humorous article about the London to Dieppe motor rally suggested that the rally was really all about chasing French girls. A central character in the article was called Artemus Jones, a churchwarden from Peckham. An Artemus Jones, a barrister from Wales, sued successfully. Even though any defamation was unintentional, his friends might easily believe that the article referred to him.

A claim is even possible then when there are two people with the same name, and people may think the one not in fact referred to is referred to.

NEWSTEAD V LONDON EXPRESS NEWS-PAPERS LTD (1940)

Two men were both named Harold Newstead, were both aged 30, and both lived in Camberwell. When the conviction of the one for bigamy was reported, the other was able to claim defamation because there was nothing to say which of them the report referred to.

A visual image such as a cartoon or caricature can also refer to the claimant.

TOLLEY V FRY & SONS (1931)

The caricature of the golfer was still identifiable as him so was defamatory.

Defamation of a class

Generally, a vague reference to people in general or to a class which is too large for the claimant to be recognised will not be actionable. For instance, the assertion that all law lecturers are boring could not be defamatory.

> **KNUPFFER V LONDON EXPRESS NEWS-PAPERS LTD (1944)**
>
> An article about the Young Russian Party described them as unpatriotic. Knupffer was head of the British branch of the party. It had only 24 members. His claim failed, however, because the party was international so an individual could not easily be identified.

A claim in respect of defamation of a class is possible, however, provided that an individual claimant can still show that (s)he is individually identifiable.

> **LE FANU V MALCOLMSON (1848)**
>
> Articles were published about cruelty to the work-force in Irish factories. The claimant's factory was described perfectly in the article so it was possible to say that the article referred to him.

8.2.3 DEFENCES

There are four basic common law defences to defamation:

- justification
- fair comment
- absolute privilege
- qualified privilege

but these have been added to over the years by different statutes. The defences are generally quite complex and often only apply to specific situations, but they are an important part of the law of defamation.

Justification

Justification basically refers to the fact that the statement is true. The basic principle is that the truth can never be defamatory, no matter how hurtful.

However, the defence is not straightforward since the burden of proof is on the defendant to show that the allegation was true.

> **JEFFREY ARCHER V *THE STAR* (1987)**
>
> The allegation was that the politician had visited a prostitute. She gave much of the evidence and she was treated by the court as an incredible witness. She was also compared to the politician's wife, who was described as of high social standing and elegant, so the allegations lacked credibility.

Proof of the truth of the allegation can also prove difficult where the claims are of a general rather than a specific nature.

> **BOOKBINDER V TEBBITT (1989)**
>
> The defendant, during an election campaign, referred to the policies of a local council as 'a damn fool idea'. The policy in question was over-printing stationery with 'Support Nuclear Free Zone'. The court would not allow the defendant to introduce evidence of the council's overspending, so the words in context were incapable of supporting the allegation made by the defendant.

By s.5 Defamation Act 1952 where there are many allegations the action should not fail 'by reason only that the truth of every charge is not proved'.

Justification can also sometimes be used in respect of spent convictions provided that there is no malice shown in revealing them.

Fair Comment

Fair comment is sometimes known as the 'critic's defence' because it is designed to protect the rights of the press in particular to state valid opinions. On this basis, of course, the defence can only succeed where to do so is a matter of public concern.

LONDON ARTISTS LTD V LITTLER (1969)

When actors resigned the director wrote to each of them accusing them of plotting against him and sent a copy to the press. The case was a matter of public concern because of the general interest in art and entertainment.

For the opinion to be fair comment of course it must be based on an appraisal of true facts.

KEMSLEY V FOOT (1952)

A former leader of the Labour Party while a junior MP wrote in response to an article attacking it as 'one of the foulest pieces of journalism perpetuated in this country for many a long year'. The defendant's article appeared under the headline 'Lower than Kemsley'. This was reference to another newspaper, it concerned their conduct, and so the defence could apply.

What is 'fair' comment is measured according to an objective test, so that there is no particular need for the author of the comment to prove an honest belief in it.

TELNIKOFF V MATUSEVITCH (1992)

The claimant wrote an article in the *Daily Telegraph* criticising the BBC Russian Service for over-recruiting employees from ethnic minority groups. The defendant then replied accusing the claimant of racism. HL felt that the defendant had to show that he was commenting since many people might not have seen the original article and would not necessarily know to what he was referring.

The defence can always be defeated where there is shown to be malice.

THOMAS V BRADBURY, AGNEW & CO. LTD (1906)

A review in *Punch* was critical not only of the claimant's book but made many personal slurs against the claimant also. The fact that there was malice was also then demonstrated by the defendant's conduct in court.

Absolute privilege

Defamation, as we have seen, has to be concerned with balancing the right to protect repu-

tation with the right to freedom of speech and expression. In certain circumstances the law recognises that the freedom to speak out without any fear of repercussions is vital to maintaining a free society. In many of these circumstances a defence of privilege has been applied. In some circumstances privilege will be absolute so that there is no right to challenge the making of the statement at all. These situations include:

- Statements made on the floor of either House of Parliament – this right is guaranteed by the Bill of Rights 1688, though it is now possible to waive the right under the Defamation Act 1996 s.13.

- Official reports of parliamentary proceedings (Hansard) – this is by virtue of the Parliamentary Papers Act 1840.

- Judicial proceedings – the right here covers judge, jury, counsel, solicitors, parties and witnesses, but not the public.

- 'Fair, accurate and contemporaneous' reports of judicial proceedings – this is by Law of Libel Amendment Act 1888 and the Defamation Act 1952.

- Communications between lawyer and client.

- Communications between officers of state.

Qualified privilege

There are also a number of situations where the communication rather than the occasion itself may be covered by privilege. In this case the privilege is qualified so that the defence can be lost by showing malice.

ANGEL V BUSHEL LTD (1968)

The defendant engaged in a business venture with the claimant who had been introduced to him by a mutual friend. When the venture failed the defendant wrote to the friend in a fit of anger saying that the claimant was 'not conversant with normal business ethics'. This was malice.

But there must be shown actual malice.

HORROCKS V LOWE (1974)

Both parties were members of a local council. The defendant called the claimant's actions into question calling them 'brinkmanship, megalomania or childish petulance'. He then tried to claim qualified privilege when the claimant sued. The claimant tried to defeat this defence by arguing malice but failed because the court accepted that the defendant believed the statements.

The defence can be claimed in a number of situations including:

- Comments made in the course of exercising a duty e.g. a reference.

- Comments made in the protection of an interest e.g. memos in business.

- Fair and accurate reporting of parliamentary proceedings.

REYNOLDS V TIMES NEWSPAPERS (1998)

The claimant had been leader of the Irish Parliament and had done much to promote the Northern Ireland peace process. A political crisis arose at which point he resigned his position and withdrew his party from the governing coalition. The *Sunday Times* then published an article which the claimant believed indicated that he had misled the Irish Parliament and had withheld information on the crisis from them. He brought his action when the newspaper failed to print an apology. The newspaper sought to rely on qualified privilege. CA held that qualified privilege can be argued by the press when (i) the paper has a moral, social or legal duty to inform the public of the matter in question; (ii) and the public has a corresponding interest in receiving the information; (iii) and the nature, status and source of the material and the circumstances of the publication are such as to warrant the protection of privilege.

- Fair and accurate reporting of judicial proceedings – which since the Defamation Act 1996 would include all court and other proceedings in e.g. Commonwealth or other courts.

- A complex list of situations identified in s.7

Defamation Act 1952: those privileged without explanation and identified in Part 1 (these might include public proceedings in Commonwealth parliaments); those privileged subject to an explanation and identified in Part 2 (which might include fair and accurate reports of trade associations or sporting associations).

Unintentional defamation and innocent dissemination

The general rule has always been that a person can be liable for a defamation even if unaware of the defamation, and every publication is a defamation. This is plainly unfair on many parties and the law has long had exceptions to this basic rule where the defamation has been made innocently:

Innocent publication under the common law

The leading case is *Vizetelly* v *Mudie's Select Library Ltd* (1900) which provided that there would be a defence of innocent publication if the defendant could show that: (i) publication was done innocent of the defamation; (ii) there was nothing suspicious to alert the defendant to the defamation; (iii) the publication was made without any negligence.

Innocent publication under the Defamation Act 1996

- The defence in *Vizetelly* has probably now been subsumed in s.1 Defamation Act 1996 which is similar but wider than the common law test.

- Under s.1(1) a defendant has a defence if he or she can show that he or she was not the 'author, editor or publisher' of the matter complained of; took reasonable care in relation to its publication; and had no reason to believe that his or her actions had contributed to the defamation.

Unintentional defamation

- This defence was originally available under s.4

Defamation Act 1952 and was available where the defendant was unaware of the defamatory nature of the remarks made.

- Provisions here were clearly designed to prevent situations such as those in *Hulton* v *Jones* (1910) and in *Cassidy* v *Daily Mirror Newspapers* (1929).

- The basics of the defence were that: (i) the statement must have been innocently made; (ii) the defendant could avoid an action by offering amends and a suitable apology, and a payment into court; (iii) if this was not accepted then a defence was still available if the publication was innocent, the offer of amends had been made promptly, and there was no malice.

- This defence was criticised by the Faulkes Committee and now a rebuttable presumption of innocent publication and an offer of amends is available under ss.2–4 Defamation Act 1996.

Consent

A claimant's apparent consent to publication may defeat a claim of defamation. This may be because the claimant has actually passed the material to the defendant. It may also occur where it can be shown that the claimant in effect invited publication.

NEWS OF THE WORLD V MOORE (1972)

The newspaper actually failed in their use of this defence here when they reproduced a private account of Dorothy Squires' private life with Roger Moore. She believed that she was being interviewed about her comeback and was not prepared for personal details such as were published. Otherwise the defence may have been available.

8.2.4 REMEDIES

There are two basic remedies available in defamation actions.

Injunctions

Interim injunctions are often awarded in advance of any action in order to prevent publication or broadcast of the alleged defamation. However, these are criticised and accused of being 'gagging orders'.

Damages

In defamation actions damages are of three types:

- Nominal cases – where the case is proven but there is little if any damage suffered.

- Contemptuous damages – where though the claimant wins it is felt that there is no real justification for the action having been brought as in *Dering* v *Uris* (1964) where damages of only $\frac{1}{2}$d were granted.

- Exemplary damages – used to punish the defendant and express disapproval, so damages are often high.

There are constant criticisms in defamation actions both of the fact that it is the jury that awards damages and that their awards are too high and are out of proportion with, for instance, personal injury awards. Lord Aldington received £1.5 million, and Jason Donovan came close to putting the magazine *Face* out of business when awarded £100,000. Nowadays it is possible for excessive sums to be reduced by CA, as when damages of £650,000 awarded to Sonia Sutcliffe, the Yorkshire Ripper's wife, against *Private Eye* were reduced to a more acceptable £60,000.

POINTS FOR DISCUSSION

PROTECTION OF REPUTATION AND FREEDOM OF SPEECH

Defamation is the main area of law used to protect reputation. It is clearly an important right that all people, particularly those in the public eye, should be able to use the law to protect their reputation from unwarranted attack. However, as with many other areas of tort, nuisance being an obvious example, this is an area of the law where a balance needs to be struck between this right and the right of others, particularly the press, to enjoy freedom of speech, and to be able to comment freely on issues of public importance, however damaging to another person.

Obviously one of the key issues here is that the comments complained of, in order that the right to make them can be protected, should be the truth, or at least a fair statement of opinion. It is important that the truth, however damaging, should never be suppressed in a free society. The common criticism of English defamation law is that it often does just that. In the recent defamation action by McDonald's (popularised as the 'McLibel case') against two environmental campaigners, many of their allegations against the fast food chain were accepted by the court as having foundation in fact, including that the company paid low wages to its employees in England, reared some of its animals in cruel conditions, and exploited children in its target advertising. Nevertheless, the case demonstrated how easy it is for a wealthy party or corporate body to 'protect reputation', possibly at the expense of the public's right to know matters of concern.

The current law is out of line with both US law, in the form of the First Amendment to the constitution, and with the European Convention of Human Rights, which at Article 10 states: 'Everyone has the right to freedom of expression.

This right shall include freedom to hold opinions and to receive information and ideas without interference by public authority and regardless of frontiers'. It is likely that the McLibel case will be tested in the European Court of Human Rights on a possible breach of Article 10. The passing of the Human Rights Act 1998 which comes into force in 2000 will not significantly alter the position on freedom of speech since the Act does not fully incorporate the provisions of the Convention. What it does do is to provide that all primary and secondary legislation must be interpreted, as far as possible, in line with the Articles of the Convention. It also provides that no public authority shall act in any way that is incompatible with the basic rights identified in the Convention.

On this basis, though the Act will certainly change the law of torts, actions before the European Court of Human Rights are still a possibility, particularly in this area. Significantly the courts had already previously accepted Article 10 in *Rantzen* v *Mirror Group Newspapers* (1996), in which HL said that the right of freedom of speech in Article 10 must underlie common law principles.

The danger of the libel laws in the UK as they currently stand is said to be that they discourage people from making comment on matters of public concern and 'may prevent the publication of matters which it is very desirable to make public'.

CRITICISMS OF THE ADMINISTRATION OF DEFAMATION LAW

One of the first and most obvious criticisms of defamation law is that it is really only available to the rich or to corporate or public bodies.

There is no legal aid available. As a result most defamation actions seem to be between famous personalities and the press. Apart from the obvious cynical view that 'any publicity is good publicity' and therefore that a defamation action may be as useful in publicity terms to a public figure as advertising, it is also evident that there are many people who suffer slurs on their character but are prevented from clearing their reputation because of the cost and restrictions on finance.

Certainly bringing defamation actions is expensive and costs are prohibitive. This was shown in *Taylforth* v *Metropolitan Police Commissioner and the Sun Newspaper* (1994) where a 'soap' actress's unsuccessful action left her with costs of half a million pounds.

Juries are commonly used in defamation actions. This is obviously justifiable since they are being asked to consider whether the defamatory remark would lower the estimation of the claimant in the minds of right-thinking people. Nevertheless, juries have come under attack, most commonly for their inconsistencies and more significantly for the level of damages they are prone to award.

The award of £1.5 million granted by the jury in *Lord Aldington* v *Tolstoy and Watts* (1989) was undoubtedly excessive and was criticised by the European Court of Human Rights for being 'not necessary in a free society'. Since the award of damages in personal injury cases is so carefully restrained it seems illogical that the award of damages in respect of protection of reputation should be left in the hands of an amateur body such as the jury.

There is of course now provision under s.8 Courts and Legal Services Act 1990 for CA to reduce excessive awards of damages made by the jury, and this has been used.

A different type of problem in relation to defamation actions is the number and complexity of defences available. This can make matters very difficult for particular types of claimant. In the case of employees suffering a damaging and inaccurate reference, traditionally any attempt to seek redress would be defeated by a claim of qualified privilege unless they were able to show malice. The development of a claim in negligence under the principle in *Spring* v *Guardian Assurance plc* (1995) has gone some way to modify this position.

One final criticism is that a significant class of people are denied the protection of the defamation laws, and these are the dead. It is possible to make any comment once a person is dead, which seems unfair since they are not then capable of defending their reputation.

REFORM OF DEFAMATION LAW

Defamation law has been criticised over many years. The Faulkes Committee in 1975 looked into possible reforms of the system and made many recommendations. Included in these were:

- Ending the unnecessary and cumbersome distinction between libel and slander.

- Altering the defence of justification to a simple defence of truth.

- Improving the defence of fair comment so that it will only fail if the comment does not represent a truly held opinion.

- Altering the defence of qualified privilege so that it will fail when the maker of the statement merely takes advantage of their privileged position as well as when malice is present.

- Simplifying the procedural requirements for unintentional defamation.

- Prohibiting punitive awards of damages.

- Reforming the law on defaming the dead.

- Reducing the limitation period.

- Making legal aid available.

- Making judges responsible for awarding damages.

Recommendations for generally much more

simplified procedures have subsequently been added to these recommendations. In fact, there has been reform through the Defamation Act 1996. However, this is partial rather than sweeping reform, making fairly minor changes.

The Act has created a new 'fast track' system for claims of under £10,000 in order to dispose of less significant cases more quickly. It has also created a new 'offer of amends' defence for newspapers to plead in the case of unintentional defamation. In certain cases judges will be able to hear a case without a jury, and the limitation period has been reduced.

activity

SELF ASSESSMENT QUESTIONS

1 Why is it necessary to have a law protecting reputation?

2 How does such a law affect basic principles such as freedom of speech?

3 What are the differences between libel and slander?

4 What must be proved to show defamation?

5 What is a 'publication' and what is not?

6 What exactly is meant by 'innuendo'?

7 When can a class of people be defamed?

8 How does the defence of 'justification' differ from that of 'fair comment'?

9 What are the differences between 'absolute privilege' and 'qualified privilege'?

10 To what extent has the Defamation Act 1996 altered the law on defamation and met criticisms of the law?

11 What are the roles of judge and jury in defamation actions?

12 Why did *Byrne* fail in his action against *Deane* (1937)?

13 Which is actually the more effective remedy in a defamation action, an injunction or damages?

- Defamation is a tort protecting a person's reputation from false allegations

- It is of two types: libel (a permanent form) and slander (a transitory form)

- Libel can be a crime as well as a tort – *R* v *Lemon and Gay News* (1979)

- Libel is actionable per se (without proof of damage), but slander is not except where contagious disease, commission of a criminal offence, unchastity in women, or professional unfitness is alleged

- Defamation is defined as a publication of a falsely made defamatory statement referring to the claimant and with no lawful justification

- Publication must be to a third party, so it will not be a publication where only the claimant is addressed, or where the defamation is contained in a sealed letter – *Huth* v *Huth* (1915)

- A defamatory remark is one that lowers the estimation of the claimant in the minds of right-thinking people or would cause them to shun or avoid him or her – *Sim* v *Stretch* (1936)

- Implying decency or honesty cannot be defamatory – *Byrne* v *Dean* (1937)

- Defamation can be by innuendo – *Tolley* v *Fry* (1931)

- The claimant must show that the statement referred to him or her personally, which could occur where two people have the same name – *Newstead* v *London Express Newspapers* (1940), or even where a fictional name is used – *Hulton & Co.* v *Jones* (1910)

- But a class defamation can only result in action where the claimant can show that (s)he is identifiable as a member of the class – *Le Fanu* v *Malcolmson* (1848)

- There are many defences available including:

  – justification: which is basically where the allegation is true – *Bookbinder* v *Tebbitt* (1989)

  – fair comment: where the press is entitled to express honest opinions on matters of public interest – *London Artists* v *Littler* (1969)

  – absolute privilege: for instance in respect of proceedings in parliament or in the courts

  – qualified privilege: which concerns confidential communications generally between privileged parties

  – unintentional defamation and innocent dissemination: where the party accused of publishing the defamation has done so in all innocence, ignorant of the fact of the defamation

- Remedies include both damages and injunctions

- There are numerous criticisms of defamation law including:

  – it is out of step with freedom of speech

  – it is basically for the rich i.e. lack of legal aid

  – juries award excessive damages

FIGURE 8.3 *Key fact chart for defamation*

CHAPTER 9

VICARIOUS LIABILITY

9.1 INTRODUCTION: ORIGINS AND PURPOSES OF VICARIOUS LIABILITY

Vicarious liability is not an individual tort in the same way as other torts we have looked at such as negligence or nuisance. It is a means of imposing liability for a tort onto a party other than the tortfeasor, the party causing the tort.

It was in fact originally based on the 'fiction' that an employer has control over his or her employees, and therefore should be liable for torts committed by the employee. This was possibly less of a fiction when the 'master and servant' laws still reflected the true imbalance in the employment relationship. In a less sophisticated society with less diverse types of work control was indeed possible. In domestic service for instance the master could dictate exactly the method of the work done by the servant.

Modern forms of employment make control less evident. For instance the actual work done by a surgeon can hardly be said to be under the control of a hospital administrator with no medical expertise. Nevertheless, the origins of the liability are important because it is rare that vicarious liability will exist outside of the employment relationship.

The rule has been criticised for being harsh and 'rough justice' since an apparently innocent party

is being fixed with liability for something which (s)he has not done. On this level, imposing liability by this method is a direct contradiction of the principle requiring fault to be proved to establish liability.

There are a number of justifications for the practice, many of which have to do with ensuring that the victim of a wrong has the means of gaining compensation for the damage or injury suffered.

- Traditionally, as we have seen, an employer may have had a greater degree of control over the activities of employees. Indeed it may well be that an employee has carried out the tort on the employer's behalf, in which case it is only fair that the employer should bear the cost.

- The employer, in any case, is responsible for hiring and firing and disciplining staff. The employer may have been careless in selecting staff, and, if employees are either careless or prone to causing harm and the employer is aware of this, then (s)he has the means of doing something about it. The internal disciplinary systems allow the employer to ensure that lapses are not repeated, ultimately to the extent of dismissing staff. The employer is also responsible for ensuring that all employees are effectively trained so that work is done safely.

- The major concern of an injured party is

where compensation is likely to come from. In this respect the employer will usually be better able to stand the loss than will the employee. In any case the employer is obliged to take out public liability insurance and can also pass on loss in prices.

- This is itself a justification for vicarious liability since it is also a means of deterring tortious activities.

- In certain instances imposing vicarious liability makes the conduct of the case easier for the injured party in terms of identifying specific negligence. This is particularly so in the case of medical negligence.

9.2 PROVING VICARIOUS LIABILITY

Proving vicarious liability first depends on satisfying a number of other basic tests:

- Was the person alleged to have committed the tort an employee? There is only very limited liability for the torts of independent contractors.

- Did that party commit the alleged tort 'during the course of his or her employment'? An employer is generally not liable for torts that occur away from work or while the employee is 'on a frolic on his own'.

- Was the act or omission complained of a tort? Again an employer will not generally incur liability for other wrongs such as crimes carried out by the employee.

9.3 WAS THE TORTFEASOR AN EMPLOYEE?

9.3.1 TESTING EMPLOYEE STATUS

It is not always possible to determine at first sight whether in fact a person is employed under a contract of service or not. It will often be in the interest of an 'employer' to deny that the relationship is one of employment. Definitions such as that contained in the Employment Rights Act 1996 that the employee is a person employed under a contract of employment are no real help in determining a person's employment status. It has been suggested in *WHPT Housing Association Ltd* v *Secretary of State for Social Services* (1981) that the distinction lies in the fact that the employee provides himself or herself to serve while the self-employed person only offers his or her services. This is no greater help in determining whether or not a person is employed.

There is in any case inconsistency in the methods of testing employee status according to who it is that is doing the testing. For instance, the only concern of the tax authorities in testing employee status is in determining a liability for payment of tax, not for any other purpose. So the fact that a person is paying Schedule D tax is not necessarily definitive of their status as self-employed. Again, industrial safety inspectors may have less concern with the status of an injured party and more with the regulations that have been breached.

Besides this a number of different types of working relationship defy easy definition. 'Lump' labour was common in the past. Casual and temporary employment is possibly even more prevalent in recent times.

Over the years the courts have devised a number of methods of testing employee status. They all have shortcomings. Some are less useful in a modern society than others.

The control test

The oldest of these is the 'control test'. This test did derive from the days of the 'master and servant' laws as we have already seen. In *Yewens* v *Noakes* (1880) the test was whether the master had the right to control what was done and the way in which it was done. According to McArdie J in *Performing Rights Society* v *Mitchell and*

Booker (1924) the test concerns 'the nature and degree of detailed control'.

Lord Thankerton in *Short* v *J. W. Henderson Ltd* (1946) identified a number of key features that would show that the master had control over the servant. These included the power to select the servant, the right to control the method of working, the right to suspend and dismiss, and the payment of wages.

Such a test is virtually impossible to apply accurately in modern circumstances. Nevertheless, there are circumstances in which a test of control is still useful, in the case of borrowed workers.

MERSEY DOCKS & HARBOUR BOARD V COGGINS AND GRIFFITHS (LIVERPOOL) LTD (1947)

Here the test was applied when a crane driver negligently damaged goods in the course of his work. The Harbour Board hired him out to stevedores to act as their servant. The Harbour Board was still liable for his negligence, however, since he would not accept control from the stevedores.

The integration or organisation test

Lord Denning in *Stevenson Jordan and Harrison Ltd* v *McDonald and Evans* (1969) established this test. The basis of the test is that someone will be an employee whose work is fully integrated into the business, whereas if a person's work is only accessory to the business than that person is not an employee.

According to this test the master of a ship, a chauffeur and a reporter on the staff of a newspaper are all employees, where the pilot bringing a ship into port, a taxi driver and a freelance writer are not.

The test can work well in some circumstances but there are still defects. Part-time examiners may be classed as employed for the purposes of deducting tax, but it is unlikely that the exam board would be happy to pay redundancy when their services were no longer needed.

The economic reality or multiple test

The courts in recent times have at last recognised that a single test of employment is not satisfactory and may produce confusing results. The answer under this test is to consider whatever factors may be indicative of employment or self-employment. In particular, three conditions should be met before an employment relationship is identified:

- The employee agrees to provide work or skill in return for a wage.

- The employee expressly or impliedly accepts that the work will be subject to the control of the employer.

- All other considerations in the contract are consistent with there being a contract of employment rather than any other relationship between the parties.

READY MIXED CONCRETE (SOUTH EAST) LTD V MINISTER OF PENSIONS AND NATIONAL INSURANCE (1968)

The case involved who was liable for National Insurance contributions, the company or one of its drivers. Drivers drove vehicles in the company colours and logo that they bought on hire purchase agreements from the company. They were also obliged to maintain the vehicles according to set standards in the contract. They were only allowed to use the lorries on company business. Their hours, however, were flexible and their pay was subject to an annual minimum rate according to the concrete hauled. They were also allowed to hire drivers in their place. McKenna J developed the above test in determining their lack of employment status.

The test has subsequently been modified so that all factors in the relationship should be considered and weighed according to their significance. Such factors might include:

- The ownership of tools, plant or equipment – clearly an employee is less likely to own the plant and equipment with which he works.

- The method of payment – again a self-employed person is likely to take a price for a whole job where an employee will usually receive regular payments for a defined pay period.

- Tax and National Insurance contributions – an employee usually has tax deducted out of wages under the PAYE scheme under Schedule E and Class 1 National Insurance contributions also deducted by the employer. A self-employed person will usually pay tax annually under Schedule D and will make National Insurance contributions by buying Class 2 stamps.

- Self-description – a person may describe himself as one or the other and this will usually, but not always, be an accurate description.

- Level of independence – probably one of the acid tests of status as self-employed is the extra degree of independence in being able to take work from whatever source and turn work down.

All of these are useful in identifying the status of the worker but none are an absolute test or are definitive on their own.

9.3.2 IRREGULAR SITUATIONS

Certain types of work have proved more likely to cause problems in the past than have others. Not every working relationship is clear-cut and judges have been called on to make decisions, sometimes based on the factors we have already considered. Often their answer will depend on the purpose of the case, so that the court might seek to bring a person within industrial safety law although they appear to be self-employed.

Casual workers

Such workers have traditionally been viewed as independent contractors rather than as employed. This may be of particular significance since modern employment practices tend towards less secure, less permanent work.

O'KELLY V TRUST HOUSE FORTE PLC (1983)

Here it was important for wine butlers, employed casually at the Grosvenor House Hotel, to show that they were employees in order that they could claim for dismissal. They had no other source of income and there were a number of factors consistent with employment. However, the tribunal took the view that, since the employer had no obligation to provide work and since they could if they wished work elsewhere then there was no mutuality of obligations and they were not employed.

Agency staff

Many large companies now hire staff through employment agencies. On past cases they have not always been seen as employees of the agency.

WICKENS V CHAMPION EMPLOYMENT (1984)

Here it was held that the agency workers were not employees since the agency was under no obligation to find them work and there was no continuity and care in the contractual relationship consistent with employment.

Workers' co-operatives

Again it is uncertain whether such workers would be employees or not. Usually we would expect them to be so. However, there are instances where such workers have been classed as self-employed.

ADDISON V LONDON PHILHARMONIC ORCHESTRA LTD (1981)

The orchestra operated as a co-operative. The musicians could do other work on their own account. It was held that they were subjecting themselves to discipline rather than control as employees.

Outworkers

People who work from home, usually women with young children, are a very disadvantaged sector of the workforce. They tend to work for little pay and have few rights. There is obviously little control over the hours that they work.

Nevertheless, working in areas such as the garment industry, they normally fall into a general framework of organisation. They were in the past always considered to be independent contractors. Some recent cases have suggested otherwise.

NETHERMERE (ST NEOTS) LTD V TAVERNA AND GARDINER (1984)

Here workers in the garment industry were held to be employees because it was felt that they were doing the same work as employees in the factory only at home.

Trainees

Apprenticeships were traditionally subject to their own rules but there are few of these now. In the case of trainees the major purpose in their relationship with the 'employer' is to learn the trade rather than to actually provide work. Therefore they have usually not been classed as employees.

WILTSHIRE POLICE AUTHORITY V WYNN (1980)

A female cadet tried to claim unfair dismissal, which required proving first that she was an employee. While she had been placed on various attachments, was paid a wage, could do no other work, and had set hours, she was only undergoing training with a view to becoming a police officer and was not yet employed.

Labour only sub-contractors (the lump)

Such workers are common in the construction industry where they will do work for a lump sum. There are advantages to both sides in not making tax and National Insurance contributions. These workers are classed as self-employed.

Crown servants

People working for the Crown were traditionally viewed as not being under a contract of employment. This meant that they had very restricted rights. The trend in modern times has been to move away from this position.

Office holders

An office is basically a position that exists independently of the person who currently holds it. So the general category might include ministers of the church and justices of the peace. The picture on these is confused but it has been held, for instance, that there is no vicarious liability on the part of the church.

Directors

A director may or may not also be an employee of the company.

Hospital workers

Obviously vicarious liability for the work of people in health care can be critical. Nevertheless, the traditional view in *Hillyer* v *Governor of St Bartholomew's Hospital* (1909) was that a hospital should not be vicariously liable for the work of doctors. This was justified on the grounds that hospitals generally lacked adequate finance before the creation of the National Health Service. The more recent view, expressed in *Cassidy* v *Ministry of Health* (1951) is that hospitals and health services should be responsible for the work done in them.

9.4 WAS THE ACT COMPLAINED OF IN THE COURSE OF EMPLOYMENT?

9.4.1 INTRODUCTION

We have already discussed whether or not it is fair to impose liability on an employer for torts committed by his or her employee. Since it is a potentially unjust situation it is strictly limited and the employer will only be liable for those torts committed while the employee is 'in the course of the employment'.

What is and is not in the course of employment is a question of fact for the court to determine in each case. It is often difficult to see any consistency in the judgments. It seems inevitable that judges will decide cases on policy grounds and this may explain some of the apparent inconsistency.

Regardless of the reasoning applied in them, there are two lines of cases:

- Those where there is vicarious liability because the employee is said to be acting in the course of the employment.

- Those where there is no vicarious liability because the employee is said not to be in the course of employment.

9.4.2 TORTS COMMITTED IN THE COURSE OF EMPLOYMENT

It is very hard to find a general test for what is in the course of employment. However, courts have appeared to favour a test suggested by *Salmond On Torts* that the employer will be liable in two instances:

- For a wrongful act that has been authorised by the employer.

- For an act that, although authorised, has been carried out in an unauthorised way.

Authorised acts

An employer then will inevitably be liable for acts that he or she has expressly authorised, and, since an employee is only obliged to obey all reasonable and lawful acts, he or she would be perfectly entitled to refuse to carry out tortious acts that the employer instructed him or her to.

The more difficult aspect of this rule is whether the employer can be said to have authorised a tortious act by implication and should therefore be liable. At least one case has suggested that this is possible.

POLAND V PARR (1927)

The employee assaulted a boy who was stealing from his employer's lorry. The employer was held to be vicariously liable since the employee was only protecting the employer's property.

Authorised acts carried out in an unauthorised manner

An employer can be liable for such acts in a variety of ways:

Where something has been expressly prohibited by the employer

LIMPUS V LONDON GENERAL OMNIBUS COMPANY (1862)

Bus drivers had been specifically instructed not to race. When they did and the claimant was injured the employer was vicariously liable. The drivers were authorised to drive the buses but not in the manner they did.

Where the employee is doing the work negligently

CENTURY INSURANCE CO. LTD V NORTHERN IRELAND TRANSPORT BOARD (1942)

A driver of a petrol tanker was delivering to a petrol station. He carelessly threw down a lighted match causing an explosion. The employer was still liable since the driver was in the course of employment, and merely doing his work negligently.

Where the employee gives unauthorised lifts contrary to instructions

ROSE V PLENTY (1976)

Here a milkman continued to use a child helper despite express instructions not to allow people to ride on the milk floats. When the boy was injured partly through the milkman's negligence his employers were liable. The milkman was carrying out his work in an unauthorised manner. Lord Denning suggested that the employers were liable because they were benefiting from the work undertaken by the boy.

Exceeding the proper boundaries of the job

BAYLEY V MANCHESTER, SHEFFIELD AND LINCOLNSHIRE RAILWAY CO. (1873)

Part of a porter's work was to ensure that passengers got on to the correct train. Here the porter pulled the claimant from the train in order to do so and the employers were vicariously liable for the assault.

9.4.3 TORTS COMMITTED NOT IN THE COURSE OF EMPLOYMENT

The area is confusing because many cases where the employer has been found not to be liable appear to cover the same areas as those that do fall within the course of employment. Usually there is some extra element but it is still confusing. In general though an employer will not be liable when the employee's tortious act fell outside of the course of employment or where the employee was 'on a frolic on his own'.

Expressly prohibited acts

BEARD V LONDON GENERAL OMNIBUS CO. (1900)

Here a bus conductor drove the bus despite express orders to the contrary and injured the claimant. The employers were not vicariously liable. The conductor was not carrying out his own work but doing something outside of the scope of his own employment.

Where the employee is 'on a frolic of his own'

An employer will not be responsible for acts that occur outside of the normal working day such as travelling into work. The same will apply where the employee does something outside of the scope of the work.

HILTON V THOMAS BURTON (RHODES) LTD (1961)

Workmen took an unauthorised break and left their place of work. On returning one employee, who was driving the works van, crashed the van and killed somebody. The employer was not liable since the workmen were 'on a frolic'.

Giving unauthorised lifts

TWINE V BEANS EXPRESS (1946)

A hitchhiker was injured through the negligence of a driver who had been forbidden to give lifts. The employers were not liable. This contrasts with the same situation in *Rose v Plenty* because here the employer was gaining no benefit from the prohibited lift.

Acts exceeding the proper boundaries of the work

MAKANJUOLA V METROPOLITAN POLICE COMMISSIONER (1992)

The claimant was persuaded into allowing a police officer to have sex with her in return for not reporting her to immigration authorities. There was no liability on the employer. The officer was not doing anything that could be described as falling within his work.

Travelling to and from work

Some situations still defy easy analysis. As we have seen an employer will generally not be responsible for the employee while the employee is travelling to and from work. In some situations, however, this may not be the case. This for instance might include where the employee works from home and travelling is part of the work.

SMITH V STAGES (1989)

The employer was liable here because the employees were paid both travelling expenses and travelling time.

9.5 LIABILITY FOR THE CRIMES OF THE EMPLOYEE

An employer will not usually be liable for the crimes of an employee that also amount to torts so that there can be civil liability.

WARREN V HENLEYS (1948)

Here a petrol pump attendant assaulted a customer who he believed was intending not to pay. The court was not prepared to hold that the assault took place in the course of employment.

The courts are more prepared to consider that the dishonesty of an employee falls within the course of employment and therefore to impose liability on the employer. This might apply in the case of fraud.

> **LLOYD V GRACE SMITH & CO. (1912)**
>
> Solicitors were liable when their conveyancing clerk fraudulently induced a client to convey the property to him.

It can also apply in the case of theft.

> **MORRIS V MARTIN & SONS (1966)**
>
> The employer was liable when the employee working in his dry-cleaning business stole a customer's fur coat.

9.6 LIABILITY FOR THE ACTS OF INDEPENDENT CONTRACTORS

An employer will not usually be liable for the tortious acts of independent contractors whom he has hired. The reason is the lack of control that the employer is able to exercise.

Nevertheless, there are some very limited circumstances in which an employer has been shown to be liable for the acts of independent contractors.

● If the contractor has been hired for the purpose of carrying out the tort then the employer may be liable, as he would be for his employees.

> **ELLIS V SHEFFIELD GAS CONSUMERS CO. (1853)**
>
> The defendants without authority hired contractors to dig a hole. When the contractors failed to replace the hole properly and the claimant was injured the defendants were vicariously liable.

● Where the employers are under a non-delegable duty of care imposed by statute. This might for instance apply where there is an obligation not only to provide but also to ensure that industrial safety equipment is used.

● Where a similar non-delegable duty of care is owed in common law.

> **HONEYWILL & STEIN V LARKIN BROS. LTD (1934)**
>
> Employers were liable for a breach of the implied duty to provide competent staff and a safe system of work when a freelance photographer set fire to a cinema when using magnesium flares for lighting.

9.7 THE EMPLOYERS' INDEMNITY

Where the employer is vicariously liable then both (s)he and the employee are joint tortfeasors. The consequence of this is that the claimant could actually sue either. One further consequence is that the employer who is sued may then sue the employee for an indemnity.

> **LISTER V ROMFORD ICE & COLD STORAGE LTD (1957)**
>
> A lorry driver knocked over his father who at the time was his driver's mate. The father then claimed compensation from the employers. The employer's insurers on paying out then exercised their rights of subrogation under the insurance contract and sued the driver. HL accepted that this was possible.

The case has been strongly criticised, not least because it destroys the purpose of imposing vicarious liability. As a result insurers do not generally exercise their rights under the principle.

9.8 VICARIOUS LIABILITY FOR LOANED CARS

Another area that creates problems apart from travelling to and from work is the practice of lending vehicles. The case law again seems confusing. The defining difference appears to be whether or not the vehicle is being used for a purpose in which the owner has an interest.

> **BRITT V GALMOYE (1928)**
>
> Here there was no liability on an employer when the car was lent to the employee for the employee's own personal use.

The result will be different where the owner has requested that the other party should borrow the car to carry out the purposes of the owner.

ORMROD V CROSVILLE MOTOR SERVICES LTD (1953)

The owner asked the other party to take the car to Monte Carlo where the owner would later join him, so the owner was liable.

However, in some instances it appears that the logic of the decision is merely that the judges wished there to be liability.

MORGANS V LAUNCHBURY (1973)

A wife allowed her husband to use her car to go out drinking on the promise that he would not drive while drunk. In the event he allowed another drunk and uninsured driver to drive him home. When there was an accident vicarious liability was imposed on the wife in order that a claim could be made against her insurance.

activity

SELF ASSESSMENT QUESTIONS

1 What justifications are there for making an employer liable for the torts of his or her employee?

2 What will a claimant need to show in order to establish liability on the part of the employer?

3 To what extent is it easy to demonstrate that a person is an employee?

4 How does the 'economic reality' test operate?

5 Is an employer liable for acts done in protection of his property?

6 Explain what is meant by an authorised act done in an unauthorised manner.

7 What exactly is a 'frolic of his own'?

8 Why were *Limpus* v *London General* (1862) and *Beard* v *London General* (1900) decided differently?

9 In what circumstances is an employer liable for the crimes of his/her employee?

10 Why is the principle in *Lister* v *Romford* (1957) criticised?

KEY
FACTS

- Vicarious liability is where one person is held liable for the torts of another

- This is usually where an employer is liable for the tortious acts of an employee

- For the employer to be liable: (i) the tortfeaser must be an employee; (ii) the tort must take place during the course of employment

- Various tests have been developed to determine whether or not someone is an employee rather than an independent contractor (self-employed) – these include the 'control' test, the 'organisation' (or integration) test and the economic reality or multiple test

- The most modern test is the 'economic reality' test from *Ready Mixed Concrete* v *Minister of Pensions and National Insurance* (1968) – all factors should be considered and their importance weighed

- A number of types of work defy easy description

- Course of employment can include:

  – authorised acts – *Poland* v *Parr* (1927)

  – acts done in an unauthorised manner – *Limpus* v *General London Omnibus Co.* (1862)

  – negligently carried out work – *Century Insurance* v *Northern Ireland Transport Board* (1942)

  – exceeding the proper bounds of the work – *Bayley* v *Manchester, Sheffield & Lincolnshire Railway* (1873)

- But there is no liability for:

  – being on a 'frolic on his own' – *Hilton* v *Thomas Burton* (1961)

  – things outside of the scope of employment – *Twine* v *Beans Express* (1946)

- An employer is not usually liable for an employee's crimes – *Warren* v *Henleys* (1948)

- Nor usually for torts of independent contractors – *Ellis* v *Sheffield Gas Consumers* (1853)

- It is rare but possible to recover the loss from the employee *Lister* v *Romford Ice* (1957)

- In some cases it is possible for owners to be liable for torts committed in cars that they have lent to the tortfeaser – *Morgans* v *Launchbury* (1973)

FIGURE 9.1 *Key fact chart for vicarious liability*

CHAPTER 10

GENERAL DEFENCES

10.1 INTRODUCTION

Defences in tort can be both general and specific. We have already seen a number of specific defences that apply only in the case of specific torts. This would include defences such as absolute privilege in defamation, and prescription in nuisance.

Other defences can be applied in numerous situations and are therefore known as general defences. Again we have already considered a number of these defences such as *volenti*, which is particularly appropriate in trespass to the person, and *novus actus interveniens*, which is particularly appropriate in negligence. This chapter includes a number of defences, some that have already appeared earlier in the book and some that have not.

Most of these provide a complete defence, in which case the defendant is relieved of liability. Some, however, will produce only partial relief and may for instance act to reduce the damages payable.

10.2 VOLENTI NON FIT INJURIA

Volenti as a defence concerns the consent of the claimant to the harm caused. Simply translated it means that no injury is done to one who consents.

The rule will not apply merely because the claimant has knowledge of the existence of the risk. On the contrary, the claimant must have a full understanding of the nature of the actual risk for the defence to succeed.

STERMER V LAWSON (1977)

Consent was argued when the claimant had borrowed the defendant's motorbike. The defence failed because the claimant had not been properly shown how to use the motorbike, and did not therefore appreciate the risks.

Neither will the defence work where the claimant is given no choice but to accept the risk. An assumption of risk must be freely taken.

SMITH V BAKER (1891)

A worker was injured when a crane moved rocks over his head and some fell on him. The defence of consent failed. The workman had already done all that he could in complaining about the risks involved in the work taking place above his head. He had no choice but to continue work and did not give his consent to the danger.

Clearly though consent is a defence that can naturally arise in certain types of employment because of the character of the work.

GLEDHILL V LIVERPOOL ABATTOIR (1957)

A worker in an abattoir was injured when a pig fell on him. This was accepted as a well-known risk of the work.

Consent is also a defence that is commonly applied in a sporting context, particularly in the case of contact sports. It will succeed where the injuries sustained fall within the normal activities of the sport.

> ### SIMMS V LEIGH RUGBY FOOTBALL CLUB (1969)
>
> A rugby player was injured when he was tackled and thrown against a wall. Because the tackle was within the rules of the sport there was consent.

But consent cannot be used as a defence where the injuries are a result of conduct that falls outside of what can be legitimately expected in the sport.

> ### CONDON V BASI (1985)
>
> A footballer in an amateur match was held liable for breaking another player's leg in a foul tackle. The injured player had not consented to foul play.

We have already seen also that the defence of consent is of critical importance to medical treatment.

> ### SIDAWAY V GOVERNORS OF BETHLEM ROYAL & MAUDSLEY HOSPITALS (1985)
>
> Here the doctor in question was required to seek the claimant's consent to an operation. However, HL was not prepared to accept the existence of a doctrine of 'informed consent' in English law. As a result there was no liability when the doctor had warned of the likelihood of the risk but not the possible consequences.

10.3 INEVITABLE ACCIDENT

One strange defence available in tort is inevitable accident. The basic proposition is that there will be no liability for a loss or injury arising from a pure accident. In negligence, for instance, this will indicate that the defendant has not fallen below the appropriate standard of care.

The appropriate test for the defendant to estab-

lish the defence is that the event leading to the loss or injury was beyond his or her control.

> ### STANLEY V POWELL (1891)
>
> The defendant 'accidentally' shot a beater while shooting pheasants. He was able to claim inevitable accident successfully because he showed that the injury was as a result of the pellet ricocheting off trees at unusual angles.

10.4 ACT OF GOD

This defence in reality refers to extreme and unusual weather conditions. As a result of this the events leading to the loss or damage are said to be beyond the defendant's control.

For the defence to succeed therefore the weather must be unforeseeable.

> ### NICHOLLS V MARSLAND (1876)
>
> Here exceptionally heavy rainfall caused artificial lakes to burst their banks flooding neighbouring land.

10.5 SELF DEFENCE

The basic principle here is that everybody is entitled to defend themselves in law. However, the defence can only then be claimed where reasonable force has been used.

> ### REVILL V NEWBURY (1996)
>
> An allotment holder fed up with trespasses on his allotment lay in wait in his shed and then fired through a hole in the door at a trespasser. This was out of proportion in the circumstances and the defence was unavailable.

10.6 STATUTORY AUTHORITY

Many torts in modern circumstances arise from activities that are authorised by Parliament. Indeed very often actions under various Acts can be more appropriate than an action in tort.

Where the activity is authorised by statute this can then provide a defence.

> **VAUGHAN V TAFF VALE RAILWAY CO. (1860)**
>
> Injunctive relief was denied to claimants when sparks from railway engines ignited embankments. The railway was authorised by statute.

10.7 ILLEGALITY (*EX TURPI CAUSA NON ORITUR ACTIO*)

A defendant will generally not be liable where the claimant sustains injury or loss while taking part in an illegal activity. The defence will operate, then, when both claimant and defendant are jointly involved in an illegal activity and the activity has a causal link to the damage.

> **ASHTON V TURNER (1981)**
>
> Here both parties were in a car escaping from a crime. When the car crashed and the claimant was injured the defence prevented him from suing the driver for negligence. His injury was a result of participating in the crime.

However, the defence was unsuccessfully raised in *Revill* v *Newbury*, because it is accepted that trespassers have limited rights of protection. The case did cause some controversy.

10.8 NECESSITY

This defence operates because the defendant's actions are said to be justified in that they were aimed at trying to avoid a greater harm than the one caused.

> **WATT V HERTFORDSHIRE COUNTY COUNCIL (1954)**
>
> The employers were not liable for the injury sustained by the fireman. The failure to properly secure the jack was because of the importance of reaching the scene of the accident and releasing the trapped woman.

Traditionally, acting to save the claimant's life would have naturally fallen within the scope of the defence.

> **LEIGH V GLADSTONE (1909)**
>
> Force-feeding of suffragettes on hunger strike while in prison was not a trespass to the person. It was necessary to save their lives.

This simple rule may have become more complex now that the courts are prepared to take a different view on a patient's right to accept or refuse treatment.

> **F V WEST BERKSHIRE HEALTH AUTHORITY (1989)**
>
> The case involved the sterilisation of a mental patient who was becoming sexually active and was incapable of consenting to the treatment. The court determined that in emergency situations a doctor might plead necessity if the treatment is in the best interests of the patient. If the patient is in a position to give consent, however, then the consent must be gained.

10.9 CONTRIBUTORY NEGLIGENCE

Contributory negligence was originally a complete defence and if successfully claimed the result would be that no damages at all were payable. This inevitably caused problems for many claimants, particularly in the nineteenth century for those claiming for injuries sustained while at work.

The Law Reform (Contributory Negligence) Act 1945 now governs the area. The effect of the Act is that a claimant can make a successful claim despite having contributed to the loss or injury suffered. Damages will then be reduced proportionately according to the degree that the claimant contributed to his or her own harm.

SAYERS V HARLOW URBAN DISTRICT COUNCIL (1958)

The council's negligent maintenance of the premises caused the claimant to become locked in a public lavatory. Her damages were then reduced by 25 per cent when she tried to climb out and stood on the toilet roll holder which collapsed.

On this basis 100 per cent reduction in damages has even been held to be possible, although this possibility has also caused some controversy.

JAYES V IMI (KYNOCH) LTD (1985)

The claimant lost a finger at work while cleaning a machine with the guard off. The employers were liable under statutory provisions for a failure to ensure that the guard was in place. 100 per cent contributory negligence was held on the part of the claimant who admitted his fault in taking the guard off.

The defence is now commonplace in some everyday situations.

STINTON V STINTON (1993)

Damages were reduced by one third for accepting a lift from a drunk driver.

O'CONNELL V JACKSON (1972)

Damages were reduced for a motorcyclist involved in a crash who had not worn a crash helmet and who sustained worse injuries as a result.

activity

SELF ASSESSMENT QUESTIONS

1 What specifically must the injured party have consented to for the defence of *volenti non fit injuria* to apply?

2 What are the most common contexts in which the defence of consent operates?

3 What is the difference between an 'inevitable accident' and an 'act of God'?

4 What is the key feature of a successful claim of self-defence?

5 Why is statutory authority a defence in tort?

6 How does the defence of 'necessity' interfere with civil liberties?

7 How does a successful defence of contributory negligence affect the claim?

8 How is it possible to have 100 per cent reduction in damages for contributory negligence?

FROOM V BUTCHER (1976)

Damages were reduced for a claimant injured in a car crash who had not been wearing a seat belt and had thus suffered greater injuries than he might.

The defence does not require that the claimant owed duty of care, merely that (s)he failed to take the appropriate care in the circumstances. It is, of course, always necessary to show causation, that is that the claimant's acts or omissions helped to cause the loss or injuries that (s)he sustained despite the defendant's liability.

WOODS V DAVIDSON (1930)

The defendant negligently ran over the claimant who was drunk at the time. The claim of contributory negligence failed since it was shown that the fact that the claimant was drunk was irrelevant in the circumstances and the claimant would have been run over even if sober.

activity

QUICK QUIZ

Suggest what defence may be argued in each of the following situations and explain whether or not it is likely to succeed.

1 Darren is being sued for negligence when his car collided with another vehicle. Darren claims that hurricane-force winds caused him to lose control of the vehicle.

2 Jed is being sued for breaking Raj's collarbone during a kick boxing contest.

3 A young boy is stealing apples from a tree in my garden. I throw a stone at the boy, hitting him in the eye and blinding him.

4 Marvin was playing darts in the pub. One of his darts hit the wire on the dartboard, bounced out onto the floor, and then bounced off the floor, hitting a table leg before embedding itself in Sarah's leg.

5 Manjit accepts a lift from Steven, who already has a car full of passengers. Manjit sits in the open boot of the car, and is injured when another car fails to stop when the traffic lights change and hits Steven's car from behind.

KEY
FACTS

- There are many defences that are available only to specific torts, but there are defences also that are generally available

- Consent is otherwise known as *volenti non fit injuria*

- The actual risk must be consented to not just risk in general – *Smith* v *Baker* (1891)

- Consent is particularly appropriate to sport where the incident falls within the rules of the game – *Simms* v *Leigh RFC* (1960)

- And in medicine where doctors generally require consent before engaging in intrusive medicine – *Sidaway* v *Bethlem Royal & Maudsley Hospitals* (1985)

- Inevitable accident can be claimed where the 'accident' and the damage suffered was beyond the control of the defendant – *Stanley* v *Powell* (1891)

- Act of God can be claimed only where the damage arises from weather conditions which are so extreme as to be unforeseeable – *Nicholls* v *Marsland* (1876)

- Self defence can be claimed where reasonable force is used – *Revill* v *Newbury* (1996)

- A statutory authority to commit the tort may cause an action to fail – *Vaughan* v *Taff Vale Railway* (1860)

- A claimant might lose a claim because the damage resulted from his or her own illegal act – *Ashton* v *Turner* (1981)

- Necessity can be a successful defence where the defendant has caused the damage in acting to prevent greater harm – *Watt* v *Hertfordshire CC* (1954)

- Following the Law Reform (Contributory Negligence) Act 1945 damages may be reduced where the claimant has helped cause his or her own damage – *Sayers* v *Harlow UDC* (1958)

- It is possible for damages to be reduced by 100 per cent – *Jayes* v *IMI (Kynoch)* (1985)

FIGURE 10.1 *Key fact chart for general defences*

PART 3 REMEDIES IN CONTRACT AND TORT

CHAPTER 11

REMEDIES IN CONTRACT AND TORT

11.1 LIMITATION PERIODS IN CONTRACT AND TORT

11.1.1 THE PURPOSE OF LIMITATION

All actions in contract law and tort are subject to limitation periods out of which an action cannot be brought. There are a variety of reasons why a claimant should be limited in the time that (s)he can wait before bringing an action for the damage suffered. Even in equity we can see the maxim 'delay defeats equity' operating so that a claimant who delays too long in bringing a claim will be prevented from succeeding.

Firstly, if there is a valid case to be fought then the claimant is to be encouraged to bring the action as soon as possible. If the evidence for the claim can be gathered there is no purpose in delaying.

Secondly, there is the difficulty of actually preserving evidence intact if a claim is delayed for too long. Certainly the scene will be disturbed over time, forensic evidence may deteriorate, but also the memory of witnesses can only fade.

Finally it is only fair on a defendant to bring the claim as early as possible if it is indeed action-able. Although many claims are settled out of insurance, a defendant may be damaged by the uncertainty of his or her budget when contemplating the possible costs of a successful action against him or her. This may in turn prevent the potential defendant from planning effectively for the future.

11.1.2 BASIC LIMITATION PERIODS

The majority of contract and tort actions are subject to the same basic limitation period of six years from the date on which the action accrues. In the case of tort this is contained in s.2 Limitation Act 1980 – 'An action founded on tort shall not be brought after the expiration of six years from the date on which the action accrued'. In the case of contract the period is identified in s.5 – 'An action founded on simple contract shall not be brought after the expiration of six years from the date on which the action accrued'.

There are also a number of different periods applying in more particular instances, for instance in the case of libel and slander, and speciality contracts, in respect of defective products under the Consumer Protection Act 1987, and in respect of latent damage to property under the Latent Damage Act 1986.

11.1.3 LIMITATION PERIODS FOR DEATH AND PERSONAL INJURY

Perhaps the most significant variation to the basic period is in claims for personal injury and death. This is not only because the period itself is different, but also because the method of calculating it is different too. Furthermore there is a means for disapplying the limitation period.

The period for personal injuries is identified in s.11(4) of the Limitation Act as – 'three years from – (a) the date on which the action accrued; or (b) the date of knowledge (if later) of the person injured'. In the case of death, which is identified in s.12, the same period applies. Where the death occurs within three years of the accrual of the action then the personal representatives have a fresh limitation period which runs from the date of death or the date of their knowledge.

The date of knowledge is a significant factor in personal injury claims. It is defined in s.14 and refers to the date on which the claimant first knew that the injury was significant, knew that it was attributable in whole or in part to the defendant's act or omission, knew the identity of the defendant, knew of facts supporting a claim of vicarious liability. A 'significant injury' is one where the claimant considers it sufficiently serious to justify beginning proceedings against a defendant not disputing the claim and who could pay the compensation. Knowledge refers to fact rather than law, and knowledge that the claimant might discover on his or her own or with the help of experts.

The power of the court to disapply the limitation period under s.33 is another important feature of personal injury claims. The court will only exercise this discretion where 'it would be equitable' to do so. In doing so it will consider a number of factors:

- the length of the delay and the claimant's reason for delaying

- the effect of delay on the cogency of the evidence

- the defendant's actions after the cause of action arose, including any response to reasonable requests for information by the claimant

- the duration of any disability of the claimant arising after the accrual of the action

- the extent to which the claimant acted promptly once aware of the possibility of bringing the action

- any steps taken by the claimant to obtain expert advice and the nature of any advice given

11.2 THE PURPOSE OF DAMAGES IN TORT AND CONTRACT COMPARED

Damages is a sum of money paid by the defendant to the claimant once liability is established in compensation for the harm suffered by the claimant.

11.2.1 CONTRACT DAMAGES

In the case of damages awarded for a breach of contract the purpose of the award is to compensate the claimant for the losses suffered as a result of the breach. As Baron Parke put it in *Robinson v Harman* (1848)

'the purpose is to put the victim of the breach, so far as is possible and so far as the law allows, into the same position he would have been in if the contract had not been broken but had been performed in the manner and at the time intended by the parties'

In this way damages in contract law are aimed to put the victim in the position (s)he would have enjoyed if the contract had been properly completed and performed by the defendant.

11.2.2 TORT DAMAGES

The purpose of awarding damages in tort, however, is altogether different, since in the case of damage to property, or personal injury, or indeed damage to reputation, a sum of compensation is an entirely artificial remedy. The purpose of damages in tort then is, as far as is possible to do so, to put the claimant in the position (s)he would have been in had the tort never occurred. Inevitably there is a large measure of speculation involved in awarding damages in tort since it involves predicting what would have happened if the tort had not occurred. It is a false remedy because a sum of money will not always repair the harm done to the claimant, and there is always the danger of overcompensating or undercompensating the victim of the tort.

11.3 THE PROBLEM OF REMOTENESS OF DAMAGE IN CONTRACT CLAIMS

There are in effect two tests used in assessing an award for an unliquidated sum of damages in contract. The first test concerns the loss in respect of which the claimant can recover. The second concerns the quantity of damages available.

The first of these two questions actually concerns causation. There must be a causal link between the defendant's breach of the contract and the damage suffered by the claimant. Moreover there is a general principle that damages will never be awarded in respect of a loss that it is too remote a consequence of the defendant's breach.

11.3.1 CAUSATION IN FACT

Causation is a question of fact in each case. The court will decide whether or not the breach is the predominant reason for the loss suffered by the claimant.

> **LONDON JOINT STOCK BANK v MACMILLAN (1918)**
>
> A customer of a bank owes a contractual obligation not to draw cheques so that they are easily alterable. Here the client who did so was liable when a third party fraudulently altered the cheque causing a loss to the bank.

If the loss arises partly from the breach and partly as the result of intervening events the party in breach may still be liable provided that the chain of causation is not broken.

> **STANSBIE v TROMAN (1948)**
>
> A decorator was entrusted with keys to the premises in which he was contracted to work. When he left the premises unlocked a thief entered and stole property. The decorator was liable for the loss which was the result of his failure to comply with his contractual duty to properly secure the premises on leaving.

11.3.2 REMOTENESS OF DAMAGE

The test of remoteness was originally derived by Baron Alderson in the case of *Hadley* v *Baxendale*:

'Where the parties have made a contract which one of them has broken the damages which the other party ought to receive in respect of such breach of contract should be such as may fairly and reasonably be considered arising either naturally, i.e. according to the usual course of things, for such breach of contract itself, or such as may be reasonably supposed to have been in the contemplation of both parties at the time they made the contract as the probable result of the breach.'

> **HADLEY v BAXENDALE (1854)**
>
> In the case a mill owner contracted with a carrier to deliver a crankshaft for his mill. The mill was actually not operating at the time because the existing crankshaft was broken. The carrier did not know this at the time the contract was formed. The carrier was then late with delivery. The mill owner sued unsuccessfully because the carrier was unaware of the importance of prompt delivery.

So in essence the test is in two parts: one is measured objectively according to what loss is a natural consequence of the breach, the second is subjectively based on specific knowledge of potential losses in the minds of both parties at the time the contract is formed.

The test remains to this day, although it has been modified on occasions.

VICTORIA LAUNDRY LTD V NEWMAN INDUSTRIES LTD (1949)

Here the defendants had been contracted to deliver a boiler to the laundry company and failed to deliver until five months after the contract date. The laundry sued for loss of their usual profits of £16 per week from the date of the breach. They succeeded since this was a natural consequence loss. They also sued in respect of lost profits of £262 per week from a Government contract that they had been unable to take up without the boiler. They failed in this action since the Government contract was unknown to the defendants at the time the contract was formed. Asquith LJ made a number of vital points on the issue of remoteness:

● To give the claimant a complete indemnity for any loss suffered by the claimant no matter how remote is too harsh a test to apply.

● As a result recoverable loss should be measured against a test of reasonable foreseeability.

● Foreseeability of loss is itself dependent on knowledge at the time of formation.

● Knowledge can be of two types: common knowledge and actual knowledge enjoyed by the defendant – the two types identified in *Hadley v Baxendale.*

● But knowledge can also be implied on the basis of what a reasonable man may have (rather than must have) contemplated in the circumstances.

Nevertheless the test can cause confusion and be made unnecessarily complex.

KOUFOS V C. CZARNIKOW LTD (1969) (*THE HERON II*)

A vessel was chartered to carry sugar to Basrah, a known sugar market. Owing to the carrier's breach the vessel arrived nine days late, during which time the price of sugar had fallen considerably. The claimant had intended to resell the sugar on its arrival in port, a fact unknown to the defendant carrier. The claimant sued for his reduction in profits following the fall in the price of sugar. This was held to be too remote in CA. HL, however, held that the claimant could recover under the first head of *Hadley v Baxendale*, and suggested that in certain circumstances the reasonable man ought to contemplate that a particular loss was a natural consequence of a breach (although this actually seems more like implied knowledge). It was also suggested that foreseeability differed between contract and tort, although different judges gave different definitions: Lord Reid described it as 'not unlikely ... considerably less than an even chance but nevertheless not very unusual and easily foreseeable'; Lord Morris as 'not unlikely to occur ... liable to result'; Lord Hodson as 'liable to result'; and Lords Pearce and Upjohn as 'a real danger ... a serious possibility'.

However, Lord Scarman has subsequently held that the test of remoteness depends not on contemplation of the level of injury but merely on proof that the loss could have been anticipated.

H. PARSONS (LIVESTOCK) LTD V UTTLEY INGHAM (1978)

The contract was for the sale and installation of an animal feed hopper. The ventilation hatch was sealed during transit and the installers then forgot to open it. As a result the feed became mouldy, the pigs contracted an intestinal disease and 254 died. The judge at first instance considered the loss was too remote and not within the contemplation of the defendants but this was reversed by CA.

11.4 QUANTIFICATION OF DAMAGES IN CONTRACT CLAIMS

Once the tests of causation and remoteness have established that there is indeed liability for the loss claimed the court then has to determine how much the claimant can recover.

11.4.1 NOMINAL DAMAGES

If no loss is actually suffered but the breach has

been established then it is possible for the court to award 'nominal damages'. Proof of damage has never been an essential of contract law as it is in many areas of tort.

The likely motive of the claimant in suing is to ensure that there is a declaration by the court that the contract is at an end.

STANIFORTH V LYALL (1830)

Lyall was under a duty to load his cargo onto the claimant's boat by a certain date. He failed and the boat owner sued for breach. He had actually hired his boat out to another party immediately following the breach and for a greater profit than he would have made. He succeeded in having the contract declared terminated and, having suffered no loss, was awarded a nominal sum.

11.4.2 THE BASES OF ASSESSMENT

There are normally said to be three bases for assessing awards of damages in contract claims.

1. Loss of a bargain

The idea here is to place the claimant in the same financial position as if the contract had been properly performed. This may represent a number of positions:

The difference in value between the goods or services of the quality indicated in the contract and those actually delivered where they are of inferior value

This sum can be assessed according to the diminution in value or the cost of bringing them up to the contract quality.

BENCE GRAPHICS INTERNATIONAL LTD V FASSON UK LTD (1996)

The defendant supplied vinyl film on which the claimant printed decals to put on bulk containers. In the claimant's contract with the container company there was an implied term that the decals would survive in a readable form for five years. In fact they lasted only two. The claimant sued for the whole purchase price or an indemnity against its customer's claim. This was rejected at first instance, but CA held that the claimant could recover the actual loss.

The difference between the contract price and the price obtained in an 'available market'

This applies where there is either a failure to deliver the goods or services and an alternative supply has to be found, or where there is a failure to accept delivery and an alternative market has to be found.

If the claimant's ability to make a profit remains then there is no entitlement to damages.

CHARTER V SULLIVAN (1957)

Here the defendant contracted to buy a car then refused to take delivery. Because demand for the particular model at the time easily outstripped supply there was no interference in the seller's ability to sell the car. In consequence he recovered only nominal damages.

However, if there is no available market then the claimant can recover the full loss.

W. L. THOMPSON LTD V ROBINSON GUNMAKERS LTD (1955)

Similar facts to the last case, but here there was an excess in supply of the type of car ordered. As a result when the buyer breached the seller could recover full damages.

Loss of profit

A claimant may recover for the profit on contracts that (s)he would have been able to complete but for the breach of contract.

Loss of a chance

In rare circumstances the courts have allowed a claimant to recover a loss that is entirely speculative in the circumstances, although generally in contract law a speculative loss is not recoverable.

CHAPLIN V HICKS (1911)

An actress had a contractual right to attend an audition. At this audition 12 actresses would be chosen out of the 50 invited to attend. When she was wrongly prevented from attending the court awarded her £100 in compensation even though she only had a 50:12 chance of gaining work from the audition. The court stated that the mere fact that damages were difficult to calculate should not prevent her recovering.

2. Reliance loss

A claimant is entitled also to recover for expenses (s)he has been required to spend in advance of a contract that has been breached.

Such a claim will normally be made where any loss of profit is too speculative to be able to calculate effectively.

ANGLIA TELEVISION LTD V REED (1972)

Anglia paid out a large sum of money in preparing to make a film, including paying scriptwriters, hiring production and technical staff and other necessary expenses. The actor contracted to make the film then backed out in breach of his contract and the company was forced to abandon the project, since there was no appropriate substitute. Their reliance loss was much easier to account for in the circumstances than any loss of profit.

Generally it is not possible to claim for both loss of profit and reliance loss since it is said to be compensating twice for the same loss. However, it is possible where the claim for lost profit concerns only net rather than gross profit which would include the reliance loss.

WESTERN WEB OFFSET PRINTERS LTD V INDEPENDENT MEDIA LTD (1995)

The defendant wrongly repudiated a contract under which the claimant was to print 48 issues of a weekly newspaper. The claimant sued for £176,903 having deducted the costs of printing such as ink and paper from the contract price. The defendant argued that labour costs and other overheads amounting to £38,245 should also be deducted from the claim. CA held that since the claimant had no alternative work for the workforce the whole claim could be recovered.

3. Restitution

This is simply a repayment to the claimant of any money or other benefits passed to the defendant in advance of the contract that has been breached.

11.4.3 THE DUTY TO MITIGATE

There is a clear principle of English law that the party injured by a breach of contract must take reasonable steps to minimise the effects of the breach, known as the duty to mitigate. The principle is as appropriate to tort as it is to contract law, and a failure to mitigate may be taken into account in awarding damages.

BRITISH WESTINGHOUSE ELECTRIC AND MANUFACTURING CO. LTD V UNDERGROUND ELECTRIC RAILWAYS CO. OF LONDON LTD (1912)

In a contract for the supply of turbines the goods delivered did not match the specifications in the contract. As a result the buyers had to replace them with turbines bought from another supplier. In the event these turbines were so efficient that they soon paid for the difference in price. As a result this could not be claimed for but losses sustained before the originals were replaced were recoverable. Lord Haldane LC said that a claimant has 'the duty of taking all reasonable steps to mitigate the loss consequent on the breach [which] debars him from claiming in respect of any part of the damage which is due to his neglect to take such steps'.

However, a claimant is not bound to go to extraordinary lengths to mitigate the loss, only to do what is reasonable in the circumstances.

PILKINGTON V WOOD (1953)

As the result of a solicitor's negligence the claimant bought a house with defective title, and was thus unable to take up residence for some time, and incurred the extra costs of hotel bills and travelling to and from his old house. The solicitor's argument that the claimant could instead have brought his action against the vendor and thus mitigated the loss in his action against the solicitor was rejected.

Similarly, in the case of an anticipatory breach, the claimant is not bound to sue immediately (s)he knows of the possibility of the breach.

WHITE AND CARTER V MCGREGOR (1962)

A firm had contracted to buy advertising space on litter bins to be fitted by the claimants to lamp posts. When they backed out in breach of their agreement the claimants continued to produce the bins. The argument that the claimants might have mitigated the loss by not continuing to fit the bins failed.

11.5 OTHER COMMON LAW REMEDIES IN CONTRACT LAW

11.5.1 LIQUIDATED DAMAGES

A sum of liquidated damages may be available where the parties have fixed the amount in the contract that will be available in the event of a breach. However, the courts will only accept this sum and deny the victim of the breach a claim for an unliquidated sum where the sum identified in the contract represents an accurate and proper assessment of loss. If it is not then this is seen as a 'penalty' and will be unenforceable.

Any clause providing for a greater sum than the actual loss is prima facie void.

> **BRIDGE V CAMPBELL DISCOUNT CO. (1962)**
>
> A depreciation clause in a hire purchase agreement for a car bore no relation to actual depreciation in value. The clause was declared void as a penalty.

The courts have developed rules for determining the difference between genuine liquidated damages and a penalty.

> **DUNLOP PNEUMATIC TYRE CO. V NEW GARAGE AND MOTOR CO. (1914)**
>
> Under their contract with Dunlop the garage was bound to pay £5 in respect of breaches such as selling under the recommended price. In this case HL accepted that the sum represented a genuine assessment so was not a penalty. Lord Dunedin's test included a number of points:
>
> * An extravagant sum will always be a penalty.
> * Payment of a large sum for a failure to settle a small debt is probably a penalty.
> * A single sum operating in respect of a variety of different breaches is likely to be a penalty.
> * The wording used by the parties is not necessarily conclusive.
> * It is no bar to recovering a liquidated sum that actual assessment of the loss was impossible before the contract.

11.5.2 *QUANTUM MERUIT*

This is merely recovery of an unqualified sum in respect of services already rendered, and we have seen its operation in relation to part performance.

There are three common circumstances in which such an award is made:

* Where there is a contract for services that is silent on the issue of remuneration.

> **UPTON RDC V POWELL (1942)**
>
> Where a retained fireman provided services with no fixed agreement as to wages the court awarded a reasonable sum in the circumstances.

* Where the circumstances of the case show that a fresh agreement can be implied in place of the original one.

> **STEVEN V BROMLEY (1919)**
>
> Steven had agreed to carry steel at a specified rate. The steel when delivered to Steven contained extra goods and thus Steven was able to claim extra for carrying them.

* Where a party has elected to consider the contract discharged by the other's breach, or where a party has been prevented from performing by the other party, in either case they might claim for work they have already done.

> **DE BARNADY V HARDING (1853)**
>
> A principal wrongly revoked his agent's authority to act on his behalf. The agent was then entitled to claim for the work he had already done and for expenses incurred.

11.6 THE EFFECT OF SPECULATION IN BOTH CONTRACT AND TORT

As has already been said, the purpose of awarding damages in contract and tort varies. Where in contract the compensation is to financially recreate the situation that would have been but for the breach of contract, in tort damages are to put the claimant in the position (s)he would have been in had the tort not occurred. On this basis in tort damages are frequently of a speculative nature, in other words an attempt to assess what the claimant's position would have been if (s)he had not been wronged by the defendant. This is known as general damages, and a major feature of tort claims, for instance in personal injury, is in calculating future losses.

In contract law, on the other hand, we have already seen that the courts have been careful to avoid granting damages of a speculative nature since damages in contract are awarded in respect of a specific loss. Of course there have been rare exceptions such as that in *Chaplin* v *Hicks* (1911) where damages were awarded for the loss of a chance in an audition.

The courts have always been careful to separate contract and tort. We have already seen this in the reluctance of judges to allow a remedy for a pure economic loss in negligence, which they see as being more appropriate to principles of contract law. They have been equally careful in traditionally avoiding allowing recovery in contract law for a claim seen as being more appropriate to principles in tort.

ADDIS V THE GRAMOPHONE COMPANY (1909)

The claimant was wrongly dismissed from his post as manager and replaced even before he left. HL refused his claim for damages for injury to his reputation and the mental distress caused by the humiliating manner of his dismissal, the proper place for this according to Lord Atkin being the tort of defamation. He recovered only for the loss of salary and commission owed.

However, an exceptional group of cases has developed a principle in contract law in recent times allowing damages of a highly speculative nature in relation to mental distress. The cases are generally known as the 'holiday cases'.

The principle was first accepted in relation to a spoiled holiday.

JARVIS V SWAN TOURS LTD (1973)

The claimant contracted for a Tyrolean holiday, advertised as a 'house party'. In fact he was on his own for the second week, and the holiday was inferior to most aspects advertised in the brochure. The judge at first instance awarded him £31.72 for the difference between the quality of the holiday as described and the actual holiday. However, CA upheld his claim for disappointment and mental distress and awarded him damages of £125.

The courts had actually previously created an exception to the rule in *Addis*.

COOK V SPANISH HOLIDAYS (1960)

Travel agents failed in their contractual duty when a honeymoon couple were left without a room on their wedding night and they were awarded damages for loss of enjoyment.

The principle has been extended, effectively as an exception to the doctrine of privity where the claimant has recovered not only for his own mental distress but that of his family also in *Jackson* v *Horizon Holidays* (1975).

The reason for allowing the claims is that in holiday contracts 'the provision of comfort, pleasure and "peace of mind" was a central feature of the contract'.

The principle also appears to have been extended to include certain problems caused by solicitors.

HEYWOOD V WELLERS (1976)

The claimant was awarded damages for mental distress where her solicitors, in breach of their contractual obligations, failed to obtain an injunction to prevent her former boyfriend from molesting her.

More recently damages for 'loss of amenity' have been allowed where the sole purpose of the contract was for 'the provision of a pleasurable amenity'.

**RUXLEY ELECTRONICS AND CONSTRUC-
TION LTD V FORSYTH; LADDINGFORD
ENCLOSURES LTD V FORSYTH (1995)**

A swimming pool was built six inches shallower than stated in the contract. Since this might prevent the purchaser from safely enjoying the pleasure of diving into the pool damages were awarded.

Nevertheless, the courts are still reluctant to allow the principle to develop too far or to extend into purely commercial territory. In *Hayes v James and Charles Dodd* (1990) Lord Justice Staughten stated that recovery for mental distress should not include 'any case where the object of the contract was not pleasure or comfort or the relief of discomfort, but simply carrying on a commercial contract with a view to profit'. Similarly, the court in *Woodar Investment Development Ltd v Wimpey Construction (UK) Ltd* (1980) suggested that the principle should be restricted to the holiday cases.

11.7 SPECIAL DAMAGES AND GENERAL DAMAGES IN TORT – CALCULATING FUTURE LOSS

As we have already seen, damages in tort are to place the victim of the wrong as far as possible as (s)he would have been in had that person not been wronged. In this way there are generally two types of damages: special damages, which account for losses already incurred up to the date of the claim, and future damages or general damages which concern how the claimant's future would have been but for the tort.

In the case of economic losses and property damage these can easily be compensated for as special damages and quantified before trial of the action. There is usually little problem in calculating such loss.

Damages in respect of property damage or loss are calculated according to:

- loss of the property and its value at the time of the tort

- any costs of transporting replacements if appropriate

- loss of reasonably foreseeable consequential losses associated with or caused by the damage to property

- loss of use until the property is replaced

- reduction in value if the property is to be retained and any costs of repair.

11.7.1 NON-COMPENSATORY DAMAGES

In some cases in tort damages are awarded even though there is no quantifiable loss. These could be in the form of nominal damages where the tort has been proved but there is no actual loss. An obvious example could be in a trespass to land action.

Although rare in England and Wales, exemplary damages are also possible. Certainly large awards of damages by juries in defamation actions would be seen as a punishment rather than representing any loss. Exemplary damages are common in other jurisdictions such as the USA.

In England and Wales the leading case on the issue is *Rookes v Barnard* (1964), which involved a dismissal for a refusal to be a member of a trade union in a 'closed shop' situation. Such damages are only awarded where:

- Government employees have acted in an oppressive, arbitrary or unconstitutional manner; or

- the defendant's conduct was calculated to profit from the tort, as in some defamation actions; or

- where statute has expressly allowed for such a provision as in the Copyright Act 1965.

11.7.2 DAMAGES IN PERSONAL INJURY CLAIMS

Damages in the case of personal injuries are divided into two types:

Special damages

These account for any quantifiable loss up to the date of trial. Such loss might include damage to any property, cost of medical care, any special equipment or similar requirements, for instance this might include the necessity to modify an existing residence to allow for effective wheel chair use, laundry, loss of earnings and all other pre-trial losses.

The principle of mitigation, of course, still applies and thus the court will only allow recovery for losses that it considers are reasonable in the circumstances, on which basis it is possible that private medical care may not be allowed.

General or future damages

These obviously include pecuniary or purely financial losses such as loss of future earnings, and of course any future medical costs or the cost of special care or other facilities.

They also include non-pecuniary losses that will be assessed as pain, suffering and loss of amenities. Such damages are clearly very difficult to quantify, but judges are guided by set sums for each type of injury. Clearly such calculations are entirely arbitrary. They can also show up various anomalies. For instance a claimant who has been in a coma will not get an award for pain or suffering though a claim for loss of amenities is still possible.

Future earnings are calculated by multiplying what is known as a 'multiplicand' (this is what the court decides is the claimant's actual net loss after taking account of factors such as payment of benefits) by a 'multiplier' (this is a number of years based on the claimant's age – but since judgment comes as a lump sum which can be invested and accrue interest the maximum multiplier is actually set quite low in real terms).

Deductions from the multiplicand are possible to take account of things like private insurance payments, disability pensions and other payments made to the claimant. Deductions can also be made from the multiplier where, for instance, a known illness would in any case have caused an early retirement.

In cases where it is hard to assess the full extent of the injury caused it is possible to seek a split trial with an award of interim damage. Alternatively where the claimant's condition is likely to deteriorate over time it is possible to seek provisional damages, allowing the claimant to establish liability but to return to court as the need for a greater level of damages arises with the deteriorating condition.

One final point, as is the case with all damages, interest is payable.

11.8 THE EFFECT OF DEATH IN TORT CLAIMS

A distinct possibility in a tort claim is that the claimant will have died as a result of the defendant's wrongful act or omission. Traditionally a person's tort action died with him or her which was clearly a very unfair situation. Now it is the case that a person's action against the defendant survives his or her death.

There are two possible actions where there is a death.

Firstly, an action is possible under the Law Reform (Miscellaneous Provisions) Act 1934. This is an action brought by the personal representatives of the deceased in the deceased's name. So any damages awarded will go into the estate of the deceased to be distributed to any beneficiaries along with his or her other assets. The action shares many of the characteristics with the action for personal injury from which it has developed.

The second action is on behalf of the dependants of the deceased. This is under the Fatal Accidents Act 1976. It is available to only a very small class of close relatives. As well as losses which have followed death it also includes an arbitrarily set fixed sum for bereavement.

11.9 EQUITABLE REMEDIES IN CONTRACT AND IN TORT

Equitable remedies are available in both contract and tort, although equity is much more closely associated with contract law. The whole purpose of equitable remedies is that they should operate where an award of damages is an inadequate remedy and justice is not served.

On that basis there are a number of different remedies available to the court, particularly in contract law, which more adequately reflect the need of the claimant. Equitable remedies are at the discretion of the court, unlike an award of damages which is an automatic consequence of liability being established. Because the remedies are discretionary they are awarded subject to compliance with the various 'maxims of equity' such as 'he who comes to equity must come with clean hands'.

11.9.1 INJUNCTIONS IN TORT

Probably the most common remedy in tort after damages is an injunction. An injunction will clearly be sought in order to try to put a stop to the tort. In this way it may be an appropriate remedy in torts such as private nuisance where a householder wants to end the indirect interference, or in the economic torts, where for instance an employer is seeking to end disruption in an industrial dispute.

The most common form of injunction granted is a prohibitory injunction, where the defendant is ordered to cease doing whatever amounts to the tortious action. Mandatory injunctions, those ordering the defendant to carry out a particular act, are granted less frequently because of the difficulty of courts overseeing them.

On occasions a court may grant a *quia timet* injunction. This has the effect of restraining conduct that is likely to cause severe damage to the party seeking the injunction, but before any damage has actually occurred. In this way in torts that are not actionable per se such an injunction would be available in effect before any cause of action has arisen so that the likelihood of substantial damage without the injunction being granted must be demonstrated to the court's satisfaction.

Injunctions can also be: final – that is where all of the relief required is contained in the order itself; or interlocutory – where the injunction is an interim measure sought in advance of the actual trial of the issue in question, so for instance this could be to prevent continued publication of an alleged libel pending trial for damages.

11.9.2 INJUNCTIONS IN CONTRACT LAW

Again in contract law injunctions are rarely mandatory and are usually then negative restrictions on the defendant. Again injunctions may be either final or interlocutory.

There are three common instances where an injunction is claimed in respect of contracts:

To enforce a contract in restraint of trade

Such contractual clauses are prima facie void, and so an injunction will only be granted if the restraint is reasonable as between the parties and in the public interest, and only if they protect a legitimate interest.

FITCH V DEWES (1921)

Here a lifelong restraint on a solicitor's clerk from taking up the same employment in a seven-mile radius of Tamworth Town Hall was held to be reasonable.

FELLOWES V FISHER (1976)

Here a five-year restraint on a conveyancing clerk from taking similar employment in Walthamstow was held to be unreasonable by Lord Denning since the clerk was relatively unknown in a densely populated area.

To enforce a provision protecting legitimate trade secrets or specialist information

FACCENDA CHICKEN V FOWLER (1986)

The injunction was sought to prevent competition by a former employee who had devised a sales system of fresh chickens from refrigerated vans. The action was unsuccessful because the termination was reasonable and there was no express provision in the contract.

To encourage compliance with a contract of personal service

Since this appears similar to a mandatory injunction it will only be awarded where there is an express negative restriction in the contract and will not be awarded where it amounts in effect to a mandatory award.

PAGE ONE RECORDS V BRITTON (1968)

'The Troggs', a sixties' pop group, were tied by contract, indefinitely, to their manager under extremely unfavourable conditions. When they became disillusioned and found a new manager the old manager tried to enforce the contract but failed.

Similarly it will be unavailable where the clause is unreasonably wide and would prevent the other party from earning a living.

LUMLEY V WAGNER (1852)

An opera singer had a contract with an express stipulation that during its three-months' currency she would not take up work with any other theatre. When she did so she was successfully restrained. Bearing in mind the duration of the contract it in no way interfered with her general ability to earn a living.

11.9.3 RESCISSION IN CONTRACT

This is particularly common in both misrepresentation and mistake and is an order of the court returning the parties to their original pre-contract position. As a result it is only available where to do that is actually possible.

Restitutio in integrum must apply for a successful claim for rescission of a contract. That is, it must be possible to return to the actual pre-contract position without the subject matter of the contract having been substantially altered in any way.

CLARKE V DICKSON (1858)

Clarke was persuaded to buy shares in a partnership as a result of misrepresentations made to him. Later the partnership became a limited company. When it failed Clarke then discovered the misrepresentation. He was unable to rescind because the nature of the shares had changed from partnership shares to company shares. The judge gave the example of a butcher who buys live cattle, slaughters them and then wishes to rescind. It would be impossible.

Other important requirements for rescission include that the party seeking rescission must not have already affirmed the contract.

LONG V LLOYD (1958)

A lorry was bought which proved defective. The purchaser lost the right to rescind after allowing the seller twice to make repairs to the lorry. He had thus affirmed the contract.

Also that (s)he has not delayed too long in seeking the remedy, as was the case in *Leaf* v *International Galleries* (1950) where the remedy was lost because the claimant waited five years.

Finally, that no third parties have subsequently gained rights over the subject matter, as occurred in *Oakes* v *Turquand* (1867).

11.9.4 SPECIFIC PERFORMANCE IN CONTRACT

This is an order of the court for the party in

default to carry out his or her obligations under the contract. It is rarely granted because of the difficulty of overseeing it.

RYAN V MUTUAL TONTINE WESTMINSTER CHAMBERS ASSOCIATION (1893)

Under a tenancy agreement the landlord was obliged to provide a hall porter to take care of the common areas. The person employed failed to do the work properly. An order for specific performance was refused because the court could not supervise the work.

This contrasts with *Posner* v *Scott-Lewis* (1987) which again involves an obligation to provide a hall porter. The court could award the remedy here where the landlord had merely failed to employ one.

Such an order is only usually granted, then, in the case of transfers of land or where the subject matter of the contract is unique in some way so that it could not be replaced in an 'available market' and an award of damages is thus inadequate. An example would be a valuable work of art as in *Falcke* v *Gray* (1859). So it will never be available for instance in a contract of service – *De Francesco* v *Barnum* (1890) where it was denied in the case of a breach of a contract of apprenticeship.

Since the remedy is discretionary under equity it will not be awarded where the claimant's actions in seeking the order are unconscionable, as would be the case with all equitable remedies.

WEBSTER V CECIL (1861)

The claimant was trying to enforce a written document for the sale and purchase of land that he knew contained an inaccurate statement of price. Since there was evidence to show what the actual price should be his action failed and the document of sale was rectified to accurately reflect the price actually agreed.

INDEX